Praise for *The Occidental Arts & Ecology Center Cookbook*

"I am wildly excited about *The Occidental Arts & Ecology Center Cookbook*! This handsome book shows how you can eat and live when you take gardening and community seriously. It's not about a restaurant, but about living and working with others, about being surrounded with gardens and the beautiful, nourishing meals made from the plants that grow in them. I found this to be a deeply inspiring and wise chronicle."

—**DEBORAH MADISON**, author of *Vegetable Literacy* and *The New Vegetarian Cooking for Everyone*

"The gardens and kitchen of the Occidental Arts and Ecology Center are magical places that have been nourishing and inspiring visitors there (myself included) for decades. This compilation of recipes from their kitchen opens this magic to a broader audience of people looking to cultivate values like sustainability, seasonality, and wholesome goodness into their kitchens. This broad-ranging and skill-building book has lots of great ideas for using acorns, garden weeds, less-common vegetables and fruits, and parts of garden plants at different stages of development, rather than just the usual vegetables."

—**SANDOR ELLIX KATZ**, author of *The Art of Fermentation*

"The Occidental Arts and Ecology Center is one of the most successful and established permaculture sites in the world. This cookbook introduces readers to their work and their irresistible cuisine. Want to learn how to cook gorgeous, healthy, delicious food from your permaculture garden? This book is for you."

—**ERIC TOENSMEIER**, author of *Paradise Lot* and *Perennial Vegetables*

"Cookbooks inspire us in creative ways for feeding family and friends, but this one goes further. The recipes are uninhibited, rich, and earthy, derived from a deep communal relationship with soil and sun and air and water. Some of them even show us how to live with each other more considerately on this earth. We all talk about community and sustainability, but talk is cheap. The folks at the OAEC are walking it, they've dedicated their lives to it, and now with this book they are sharing their experience in all of its complex, imperfect, delicious, and nutritious ways."

—**MICHAEL ABLEMAN**, author of *Fields of Plenty*

"If feeding a hungry crowd a healthy, delicious, non-hippie stir-fry is your quandary, *The Occidental Arts & Ecology Center Cookbook* offers many a charming solution. These inventive, scrumptious recipes show you how to weave a rich tapestry of varietals and flavors in your garden—and onto your table—with playful presentation techniques that crack open a new paradigm for eating and building community."

—**NOVELLA CARPENTER**, author of *Farm City: The Education of an Urban Farmer*

"Throughout human history, food has been intimately tied to community. At the Occidental Arts and Ecology Center, this vital connection is renewed. Reading this book and cooking these recipes will transport you to a magical place, where deep and important work is being done, beautiful and delicious food is being cooked, and the earth is being healed in a thousand ways each and every day."

—**JESSICA PRENTICE**, author of *Full Moon Feast* and cofounder of Three Stone Hearth Community Supported Kitchen

THE
Occidental Arts & Ecology Center
COOKBOOK

Fresh-from-the-Garden Recipes for Gatherings Large and Small

THE OAEC COLLECTIVE WITH OLIVIA RATHBONE

FOREWORD BY ALICE WATERS

CHELSEA GREEN PUBLISHING
WHITE RIVER JUNCTION, VERMONT

The OAEC property is not open to the public for drop-in visitors.
Please see our website www.oaec.org for ways to get involved,
such as tours, plant sales, events, and courses.

Project Manager: Patricia Stone
Developmental Editor: Makenna Goodman
Copy Editor: Laura Jorstad
Proofreader: Brianne Bardusch
Indexer: Peggy Holloway
Designer: Melissa Jacobson

Printed in the United States of America.
First printing March, 2015.
10 9 8 7 6 5 4 3 2 1   15 16 17 18

Our Commitment to Green Publishing
Chelsea Green sees publishing as a tool for cultural change and ecological stewardship. We strive to align our book manufacturing practices with our editorial mission and to reduce the impact of our business enterprise in the environment. We print our books and catalogs on chlorine-free recycled paper, using vegetable-based inks whenever possible. This book may cost slightly more because it was printed on paper that contains recycled fiber, and we hope you'll agree that it's worth it. Chelsea Green is a member of the Green Press Initiative (www.greenpressinitiative.org), a nonprofit coalition of publishers, manufacturers, and authors working to protect the world's endangered forests and conserve natural resources. *The Occidental Arts & Ecology Center Cookbook* was printed on paper supplied by QuadGraphics that contains at least 10% postconsumer recycled fiber.

Library of Congress Cataloging-in-Publication Data
Rathbone, Olivia.
  The Occidental Arts & Ecology Center cookbook : fresh-from-the-garden recipes for gatherings large and small / The OAEC Collective with Olivia Rathbone ; foreword by Alice Waters.
     pages cm
  Includes bibliographical references and index.
  ISBN 978-1-60358-513-2 (pbk.) — ISBN 978-1-60358-514-9 (ebook)
  1. Cooking (Natural foods) 2. Kitchen gardens. I. Occidental Arts and Ecology Center. II. Title.

TX741.R37 2015
641.3'02—dc23
                    2014043698

Chelsea Green Publishing
85 North Main Street, Suite 120
White River Junction, VT 05001
(802) 295-6300
www.chelseagreen.com

PAINTING BY ADAM WOLPERT.

This book is dedicated to the North Garden Oak, 1908–2008.

Contents

Foreword

I have visited the Occidental Arts and Ecology Center many times over the years since its founding, but every time I sit down to share a meal there, I am astonished anew by the beauty of their salads. Each one is dazzling: filled with an incredible variety of fresh organic greens plucked from the earth moments before, starred with edible flowers like borage, chervil, or forget-me-nots, and simply dressed so that the textures and flavors of the ingredients are allowed to shine. No two salads are alike, but each of them is a work of art, capturing the essence of the particular season and place, and celebrating the bounty of the garden and the aliveness of the food.

I have always been a believer in feeding people ideas; when you engage all your senses, as you do when you grow, harvest, and prepare your own food, you absorb the lessons of the land effortlessly. It is a testament to the remarkable biodiversity of the Occidental Arts and Ecology Center that something as ostensibly simple as a green salad can be such a revelation. But a revelation it is: Whether it is someone's first encounter with purslane or Andean oca leaves, mache rosettes or mizuna, there is always something new and surprising and delicious for the eater to discover. The OAEC has been at the forefront of seed saving, heritage food crop

preservation, and stewardship since long before those terms developed the sort of cachet they have today—and you can see the ethos of the place in every dish in this book.

These dishes represent the sort of hearty, nourishing, unpretentious fare that brings family and friends together at the table; I love that the recipes are scaled so that you can feed 4 people—or 30, should you so choose! But more than just being a collection of delicious recipes, these pages capture a way of life for a whole community, whose values of ecological research, sustainable farming, and environmental advocacy are so vitally important. Happily, the OAEC has made a powerful commitment to education, and through their many workshops, plant sales, and outreach programs, countless people have been taught about gardening and living in a way that is connected to the land. This book is a beautiful extension of that education, empowering the reader to draw inspiration from the garden and cook with intention, and showing how the love, warmth, and generosity of the land inform the generosity of the community.

ALICE WATERS
2015

PART ONE

PHOTO BY TALI AIONA.

Welcome to the Occidental Arts & Ecology Center

Everybody needs beauty as well as bread—places to play and pray in, where nature may heal and give strength to a body and soul.
—JOHN MUIR[1]

As stewards of this 80-acre piece of land nestled in the hills of western Sonoma County, California, the Occidental Arts and Ecology Center is pleased to commemorate two decades of restorative farming, community building, ecological research, training, and advocacy in presenting *The Occidental Arts & Ecology Center Cookbook*. This project came out of years of collective dreaming as well as nudging from visitors, students, and friends who have raved about the vibrant, nourishing meals and imaginative style of cooking birthed from this land. In addition to recipes, we delight in the opportunity to share personal reflections from our 20 years living and working together for strategic social change. And yet this book is not meant as a comprehensive retrospective of OAEC history; the memories of successes and failures through the years are endless, and it would be impossible to include or thank the thousands of people who have had a hand in making OAEC what it is today or what it will become in the next 20 years. Rather, these pages are but a fleeting snapshot in the long, historic arc of people in ever-evolving relationship to this landscape.

In an age where the word *sustainability* is used lightly, OAEC's long haul has earned us the right to use the term quite literally. The Mother Garden, as we call our farm, has been on the forefront of the organic agriculture movement and has served as a renowned demonstration farm, nonprofit educational retreat center, intentional community, and eco-think tank since the early 1970s, first as the Farallons Institute, next as the Center for Seven Generations, and now in its current incarnation as the Occidental Arts and Ecology Center and Sowing Circle Community. The Mother Garden was one of the first farms to be certified organic in California and in 1994 forged one of the first organic

Janell Lundgren, kitchen manager 2007–11, ringing the dinner bell, inciting a Pavlovian response as it resounds to all corners of the 80-acre piece of land. With two bells to announce the 15-minute warning and three bells to beckon, "Come and get it!" we estimate that since it went up 36 years ago, this dinner bell has rung more than 70,000 times! PHOTO BY JIM COLEMAN.

agriculture easements in the United States, preserving the land's status as an organic garden into perpetuity. The legacy lives on today as the Mother Garden continues to feed and inspire activists, biologists, educators, and artists seeking innovative and practical approaches to the pressing environmental, cultural, and economic crises of our day—all while having fun and eating well!

Delicious Biodiversity

Since the beginning of the 20th century, much of the genetic diversity of our food crops has been lost and continues to be threatened by industrialized agribusiness. It is one of the main goals of the Mother Garden to educate visitors about sustainable food production and the array of plant species, particularly food crops, thankfully still available to us. OAEC's Biodiversity Program focuses on curating and propagating a plant and seed collection of over 3,000 varieties of heirloom, open-pollinated annuals and over 1,000 varieties of habitat-friendly edible, medicinal, and ornamental perennials. Our collection, developed over the past 40 years through biointensive horticulture at the OAEC site, emphasizes food crops of special genetic, cultural, and historic importance. Over time, the garden has become something of a cradle of diversity for plant and animal life. We have collected and evaluated thousands of varieties, chosen our favorites, planted them again and again, and shared them with others. Sometime in the late 1980s, we started calling our gardens "the Mother Garden," referring, even at its relatively young age, to the fact that the garden was providing a wealth of seeds, plant material, and wisdom to other gardens and gardeners and figuratively giving birth to daughter gardens.

The happy by-product of this endeavor, of course, is that the Mother Garden and orchard provide organic fruit, vegetables, herbs, and flowers for thousands of meals prepared on-site each year. Food is an expression of the land that we steward, and truly vibrant food is proof that the more closely we can understand and emulate nature, the more abundant our lives become.

Heritage Harvest. The extinction of traditional food crop varieties since the turn of the 20th century is occurring at an unprecedented rate. Ironically, never have more heirloom varieties been available for home gardeners to grow and appreciate than today. PHOTO BY DOUG GOSLING.

We are the direct beneficiaries of the ecological services that a living, breathing ecosystem such as the Mother Garden provides. When we learn from and continuously reinvest our energy into Nature's infinite cycles and systems, She gives back generously and unconditionally.

Good food is also a manifestation of the creative sensibilities that we at OAEC seek to awaken and foster in ourselves and in others. We weave a thread of artistic awareness into all that we do here, from planting a garden bed with 25 varieties of bearded irises to attending a county board of supervisors meeting dressed in a salmon costume to testify on behalf of local salmon. However, nowhere is the intersection of arts and ecology more apparent on a daily basis than in the kitchen. A cook here once said that working in the OAEC kitchen and

garden is like being a painter and walking into a giant warehouse full art supplies. The vast palette of colors and flavors expressed in the Mother Garden is an endless source of inspiration. She is our muse.

To an outsider, some of the vegetables, fruits, and herbs in these recipes may seem like exotic luxury items—and while, yes, many of them are certainly unusual and hard to come by in many parts of the United States and the world, these are plants that we have found to grow well in our microclimate with minimal inputs. These plants range from California native plants, to hardy heirloom varieties, to unusual food crops from other parts of the world whose climate parallels ours. But our commitment to biodiversity and mission to preserve food crop heritage isn't about keeping ahead of the latest food trends. We are not seeking out rare and endangered

Sprouting like a potato when it is ready to grow, an oca tuber is planted in early May. Domesticated by the Incas thousands of years ago, oca, *Oxalis tuberosa*, is a staple root crop for the people of the high Andes. At OAEC, we grow and promote oca as a threatened species that has enormous cultural and historical value. It is productive, beautiful, and, not least important, delectable. PHOTO BY DOUG GOSLING.

agricultural practices require that we move away from conventional monocrop agribusiness and toward a resilience-based model of farming. The relentless advice that we get from nature toward this end is "diversify, diversify, diversify."

Not only is biodiversity the very backbone of ecological resilience, it is also the antidote for malnourishment, both of body and of soul. Humans cannot live on bread, or broccoli for that matter, alone. Variety in the diet both broadens our sources for macro- and trace nutrients and gives us the spice of life. A Japanese saying posits that every time you try a new food, you add a year to your life. This speaks not only to physical health, but also to a youthful flexibility that grows out of curiosity and open-mindedness. While this book is not expressly focused on nutrition, our hope is that it will nudge the boundaries of the "Standard American Diet" (which is rather SAD really) toward a more diverse palate of possibilities.

food crops of the world in order to "discover" and profit from the next exotic ingredient to be marketed and consumed by the industrial food system. In fact, it is quite the opposite. Through trial-and-error research, we are taking full advantage of our regional growing conditions to find out what works, and we encourage *you* to do the same kind of experimentation in your own backyard. While we employ age-old, tried-and-true methods, as modern farmers we also have the information and resources to not only preserve endangered food crops but also select for new varieties that can endure unstable weather patterns, water insecurity, poor soil conditions, pest pressures, shrinking open space . . . in short, peak-oil, peak-water, peak-population, peak-everything. Our changing climate and ever more ecologically and economically challenging

Why Vegetarian?

The OAEC kitchen is mostly vegetarian, and we chose mostly vegetarian recipes to include in this book. We are plant people. Covering up our world-class produce with assertively flavored meat or heavy sauces and spices would be a distraction. However, we don't follow any specific dogma about vegetarianism, and in fact most of us at OAEC eat meat and enjoy it with gusto—that is, in moderation and mostly on special occasions and celebrations. On a day-to-day basis, we prefer to eat lower on the food chain. When people think of a vegetarian kitchen, many conjure up the image of scarcity and asceticism, but our guests are so dazzled by the colors and smells of freshly and lovingly prepared food from the garden that most don't even think to ask, "Hey, where's the meat?" Meals at OAEC are conceptually interesting, nutrient-dense, and served within a context of community conviviality; hence, people feel satisfied on a physical, intellectual, and emotional level after eating their first few bites. While bumping shoulders with the cheerfully bustling cooks who prepared it, chowing down with the hungry, sun-kissed gardeners who raised and harvested it, and chatting it up with the instructors and visionaries who facilitate the container for the whole system to thrive in, guests and residents are able to connect to one another and thus to the food in ways that really are often life changing.

The Mother Garden has a spirit that makes our food incredibly alive. People come here and something powerful happens—this garden reconnects them with the origins of food and how it nourishes them. When they get the chance to plant and harvest food themselves, it tastes like nothing they've ever had before. —Michelle Vesser, garden manager and intern coordinator, showing garden intern Tali Aiona how to harvest salad. PHOTO BY JIM COLEMAN.

Garden interns harvesting in the South Garden. PHOTO BY JIM COLEMAN.

Celebrating Interdependence

In our workshops, the lessons taught in the classroom and out in the garden all come together right there on the plate. Food becomes both a centerpiece for meaningful conversation and an unspoken, cellular avenue for learning. So much of our mission and work is tied into the promotion of eco-literacy through gardening, and our guests get to experience on a gut level, "Oh, *this* is what sustainability *tastes* like! Food grown in healthy soil from locally adapted seed in a biodiverse ecosystem prepared by happy people tastes great!" Class dismissed.

A common misperception about the OAEC kitchen garden is that it is "self-sufficient." There are many accomplished homesteads out there with the goal of self-sufficiency, but ours is "interdependence" rather than "independence." OAEC is a hub of cross-pollination. Bioregional solidarity and support are necessary building blocks of community-scale resilience, and therefore we support local farms and micro-regional food distributors with our communally shared food dollars.

As an intentional community, OAEC and Sowing Circle venture to model the kind of cooperation that offsets the high cost of healthy food. We are pooling our resources to make healthy food a financial reality in the face of agricultural policies that subsidize industrialized junk food instead of incentivizing fresh produce raised on local, ecologically appropriate small-scale farms. Sharing food costs and cooking responsibilities means that we can afford to buy high-quality, whole, unprocessed ingredients in bulk because we ourselves are doing the processing. Pooling of resources makes sense in terms of equipment, too. Each of us doesn't need our own personal Vitamix or set of cookbooks (or table saw, tractor, or copy machine, either). Common ownership allows us a level of infrastructure and a quality of life that most of us couldn't afford on our own.

Of course, sharing comes with a level of compromise that most people have not been raised to accept in a culture that emphasizes individualism over cooperation. We all have different food preferences, likes and dislikes, diets and food philosophies, but have come to accept that living in community and committing to consensus-based self-governance means that when we do what is best for us as a whole, in the long run, we do what is best for us as individuals. Consensus decisions are often made at a snail's pace, and take longer than a quick vote, but are completely in line with our move away from a culture of instant gratification. In our commitment to self-governance through practicing the democratic arts, everyone can have a seat at the table.

Redefining Sustainability

Many of us in the eco-ag movement champion the "food theory of everything" with a belief that fixing the food system can be a solutions generator for a host of our nation's ecological, economic, health, and psychospiritual problems. At OAEC, we are attempting to redefine sustainability. We don't want to sustain our current system, which is obviously deeply flawed, but rather are working on the ground to move toward food systems and models of community that heal environmental and cultural degradation.

More than anything, food brings us together. The eco-crisis or the "crisis of home" can and must be addressed at *home*, and what better place to start than around the dinner table? In the regular practice of breaking bread together, we cultivate a deep sense of commitment to the land and to one another.

Because so many food cultures and traditions have been gobbled up by colonization and capitalism only to be regurgitated and sold back to us in a processed, packaged form, Americans are ravenous for authentic food and authentic food culture. And so in the spirit of Carlo Petrini's slow-food "protest of pleasure," we resist the industrialized food system not only through voicing our resistance to pesticide use, factory farming, and other unsustainable food practices, but by living out the solution pathway and cocreating the kind of restorative, celebratory, land-based culture we want

This is a thrivalist movement, not a survivalist movement. Participating in activities that are regenerative to the cycles of life—watershed cycles, soil cycles, food cycles—can also be simultaneously regenerative to the human spirit and to human connectivity. Contributing to the health and vitality and betterment of the planet can and should also be invigorating for us. As David Orr would say, "Hope is a verb with its sleeves rolled up." And so let's do this, but let's have fun while we're doing it. Let's find pleasure in the pursuit.

—BROCK DOLMAN, *Sowing Circle member, OAEC senior biologist*

to see thrive. As Sowing Circle member and OAEC executive director Dave Henson puts it: "Without art and celebration, the revolution is no fun!"

Stewards of the Land Through Time

As we look back on over two decades of OAEC's history, we owe a great debt of gratitude to the people who carefully tended this land prior to our arrival. We are heirs to a rich legacy of stewardship, from the first Southern Pomo and Coast Miwok who tended the oak savanna of the OAEC backcountry, to the Italian and Portuguese homesteaders in the 1800s who planted heirloom grapes and fruit trees that we continue to enjoy to this day. In more recent history beginning in 1974, the Farallons Institute, a nonprofit sustainability training center with a mission very similar to ours, became an outpost for forward environmental thinkers and laid both the physical and cultural groundwork for what is now the Occidental Arts and Ecology Center and Sowing Circle Community.

Left, Barn-raising party 1978. Much of the infrastructure that exists on the OAEC land was originally constructed as part of the Farallons Institute's living research in appropriate technology. The barn was constructed out of recycled beams from a defunct pier in the San Francisco Bay. *Top right,* Farallons residents erect a windmill-powered water pump, March 28, 1979. Ironically, the day the windmill was first powered up was the day of the Three Mile Island nuclear tragedy. *Bottom middle,* The interior of the Farallons kitchen featuring a handmade stained-glass window, 1976. *Bottom right,* The North Garden in 1979. There has been a continuous unbroken thread of people who have cared for the Mother Garden for 40 years. Much of what thrives here—the mature fruit trees, the signature vegetable varieties, the aliveness of the soil—is thanks to that active relationship and continuous loving care. PHOTOS COURTESY OF ALISON DYKSTRA.

A SENSE OF ARTISTRY

by James Pelican, OAEC site manager

I'm a child of the 1970s, when there was a big emphasis on crafts—the idea that you don't have to be a trained artist to have an aesthetic vision. Just do it—take the materials that you have and make something beautiful. As a woodworker and builder, my palette is this semi-wild place; we've carved out a little piece of it, but the blackberries and the forest are always trying to take it back over. When I repair one of these old buildings that we inherited from Farallons, there is a liberty to play with and add to what already existed. And while first and foremost it has to be functional, if I can give some sense of whimsy, of character, of energy to it, then I will. Wood is my medium, yet I get inspiration from the garden, I get inspiration from the crazy food being cooked up in the kitchen—ultimately, we all feed off one another's creativity. Our name is the Occidental Arts and Ecology Center, and even as our programmatic work in the arts has narrowed in recent years, we all still try to live up to our name and bring a sense of artistry to whatever we do.

Above, 10 x 10-foot Sunburst wood siding detail by James Pelican that decorated the front of the kitchen for over a decade. PHOTO BY TALI AIONA.

Cultivating an Old-Growth Community

by Adam Wolpert, Sowing Circle member and OAEC Executive Staff Council chair

In the warm dry season, in the glow of the setting sun, you will find people together enjoying their evening meal, scattered comfortably about on kitchen steps and homemade benches or sitting at the large long table fashioned out of a huge slab of repurposed redwood. In the rain and cold of winter, they are snug inside the large dining room by a roaring fire. Whether the group has come to OAEC for a workshop or it is the community of residents or a mixture of the two, the act of gathering around the hearth to break bread brings us together in the most primal expression of Home.

A group of seven friends established residency here in 1994, forming a limited liability company (LLC) called Sowing Circle. Soon after, the OAEC was formed by the same group, a nonprofit 501(c)3 organization that would reside in the same place. These two entities formed a lasting mutually beneficial relationship, one enriching the other in a symbiotic reciprocity that continues to this day.

What Does It Mean to Act Like We Are Going to Be Here for Another 10,000 Years?

As in the study of permaculture, a design philosophy that bases human design on the study of nature, we at OAEC have learned a great deal from the study of land-based communities that came before or continue in modern times to organize culture around natural processes. Until relatively recently, the majority of human settlement has functioned much like an old-growth forest. Humans, acting as keystone species, have long had the skills and knowledge to actually *increase* the biological carrying capacity of the land rather than deplete it, to render the concept of "waste" obsolete, and to cycle and amplify rich physical and cultural resources through the generations. Unfortunately, like old-growth forests, there are very few intact traditional societies left unspoiled by the modern slash-and-burn economy. Catastrophic loss of cultural and linguistic diversity worldwide has paralleled a loss in biodiversity and, with it, precious links to clues about how to live in harmony with the land through language, food, story, and tradition. Yet some core characteristics of what we could call "old-growth" sustainable communities can serve as a foundation for a relatively new community like ours and help define the philosophical roots of the OAEC/Sowing Circle experiment.

Globalized capitalism, a system that incentivizes "cashing out" and moving on in the downward speculative spiral of real estate and resource extraction, consumption and disposability, is inherently nonsustainable. One of the first things that was done in the founding of the Sowing Circle community was to agree that it would take agreement by all partners to decide to sell the land and that each owner's "share" in the LLC that owns the land will not be linked to the land's market value. This bold and simple move took the land off the market and affirmed that relationship, the good of the whole, and kinship with the land are all more important than the conventional rights associated with ownership of property. This group of people

PHOTO BY JIM COLEMAN.

intends to stay and create real abundance in place over time, not only for themselves but for the many people who will come after them. This long-term orientation leads naturally to resource conservation and an interest in restoration not exploitation.

Like many traditional land-based cultures, in this community, most of the land and facilities are in the hands of the commons. Community members self-govern using consensus process, a cooperative and collaborative decision-making tool that brings together the best ideas and concerns of all group members to forge solutions that are in the best interest of the whole. Like the diversity of food grown in the garden, community members embrace a diversity of views. Group process can indeed slow things down, but this slowing is in keeping with the core values of reducing consumption and considering all points of view. Gradual development and change based on local knowledge of land, water, microclimates, and the creatures living on the land leads to more sustainable and durable outcomes.

"Instead of focusing on conflict resolution (which is necessary as a backup), we are putting energy toward strategies that are hopefully

Dave Henson counts the rings of a tree with his son Kelsey. PHOTO BY JIM COLEMAN.

conflict *preventing*. It's like investing in preventive medicine—if we put holistic decision making first, then we don't have to go into allopathic conflict resolution. By design, we are trying to figure out how to front-load communication and decision-making structures that support healthy, resilient relationships," says Brock Dolman.

Land-based peoples know that a long-term orientation that cultivates an evolved knowledge of place passed down through the generations leads to a feeling of continuity, groundedness, purpose, and, ultimately, right action. In traditional cultures, the worst shame and punishment one can receive is banishment; in modern mainstream Western society, there is often a construct of shame associated with having to live at home with one's parents. The modern discontent and disconnect between young and old, past and future, civilization and nature, work and play, speaks to a less sophisticated relationship to place.

The Concept of *Home*

The word or prefix *eco* comes from the Greek word *oikos*, which means "home." Ecology is knowledge of home, an ability to read and understand the relationships of home. *Nomy* in Greek is "management." Hence, *economy* is not the management of money, as capitalism leads us to believe, but the management of home—the organization and orientation of our relationships to place. Money is one way to measure economy, but why can't our management of home be measured by other standards? What about health? Happiness? Well-being? When there is no knowledge of home, modern humans wander uprooted, homeless, eco-illiterate, alienated from the landscape and from one another. Mismanagement of home is the direct result, as is painfully evident in our current ecological and economic crises.

It is precisely this concept of Home that is at the core of the OAEC experience. Amid all of the strategic work that happens here, from watershed restoration to social justice organizing, those of us who live and work here agree that the most fundamentally radical aspect of the OAEC model is Sowing Circle, the consensus-based intentional community of long-term residents on this land. When visitors come here, they are not showing up to a hotel or conference center; they come as honored guests in our home. With that comes a genuine sense of hospitality that is grounded and real. OAEC is not a headquarters for ecological stewardship in abstract terms, but our actual, physical home, complete with children's toys scattered about, morning meetings over tea amid remnants of last night's dinner party, and all the sometimes messy, authentic details of a rich home life. OAEC models an awareness, an aesthetic, and an ethic of "ecos" because our work *is* knowing and caring for the home place and those in it.

In this community, life and work are often inseparable. As in many traditional land-based societies, busy times of planting and harvest are times of relationship and connection; people work hard together and are bonded by the effort and the time spent sharing challenges and triumphs. Whether it is a plant sale, a wedding, or a theatrical production, the OAEC/Sowing Circle community often has this "all hands on deck" experience. We see the best and worst of one another and learn that we will be supported and accepted even under stress and strain.

The original group of 7 residents has now swelled to 22 and has spent the last 20 years experimenting, exploring, and working hard together. Many things have been learned and tried. Yet, after 20 years, there is no sign of burning out or giving up but rather a seasoned maturity is emerging.

"We've struck a good balance between standing for something, but not taking ourselves too seriously. There is a cultural taboo here against becoming too doctrinaire. Humor and perspective are key," says Sowing Circle member Susan McGovern.

Community is both a process and a practice, a dynamic experiment that constantly defines and refines the concept as we live it. By making our process transparent through workshops and consultation, we hope to serve others undertaking the same endeavor. Our aim is to create a resilient and restorative version of the best of what our ancestors enjoyed while also pioneering something contemporary, unique, and capable of addressing the challenges of today's world.

"Solar Suburbia," the cluster of low-square-footage houses where most Sowing Circle residents live, was originally built during the Farallons era as an experiment in passive solar design. Individual homes for each resident family positioned close together in one section of the land allow for both privacy and togetherness, while at the same time preserving space in the overall footprint of the land dedicated to gardens and wild nature. PHOTO BY JIM COLEMAN.

We channel the land we live on. The water, the earth, the air, the birds, the bees, everything that lives with the oregano that I harvested for the evening meal, becomes me. I enjoy the sheer pleasure of looking at what is growing well in that moment and let the garden decide who I am going to become.

—*KAMI MCBRIDE, garden intern 1991,*
author of The Herbal Kitchen

The Seasons

To interpret the meaning of seasonal cooking, we look to the roots of the word *season*. Season refers to a time of year, an epoch, a rhythm. In Latin, *serere* is "to sow"—to intentionally bring to life—a concept deeply rooted in agriculture and the yearly planting and harvesting calendar. To season, in the culinary sense, is to add flavor, spice, and subtlety to food. To season is also to ripen or develop in depth, maturity, and strength, as in a seasoned craftsman or a seasoned cast-iron pan. The multiple meanings from this common root word can be distilled into the idea that to season is to bring to life the fleeting experience of taste within the larger context of cyclical time or to develop, with intentionality, the full potential of the ripe moment.

Rooted in earth-based folk traditions, we base our garden planting calendar on the observation of the solstices, equinoxes, cross quarter days, full and new moons. To someone outside California, the character of the seasons in our temperate coastal climate may be barely noticeable, but the subtle changes in day length, tidal influence, precipitation, and temperature have a profound effect on the arc of our annual cycle. As the earth makes its circle around the sun, the seasons of work and of rest coincide with hot and dry transitioning to cool and wet. Ultimately, the seasons influence not only the daily activities of our workshops and programmatic work, but our moods, appetites, and artistic inspirations.

SPRING
February 2 to May 1

Spring is a time to appreciate the renewed profusion of life in the garden as wet and warm conditions give rise to an explosion of diversity. Fully hydrated soil means that microorganisms multiply, roots deepen, seeds sprout, and flowers bloom, bringing on the birds and the bees. The explosion of color in the moist spring garden is a reminder that water is the very foundation of life.

In March, we open the start of the OAEC guest season by bringing in the first of three "crops" of students for our Permaculture Design Course. Eager students witness the principles of ecological design in action, such as the vernal stream flowing at the bottom of the North Garden pumping water through our tiny "micro-hydro" plant that supplements power from the solar panels on overcast days.

The nursery is a flurry of activity in preparation for the annual Spring Plant Sales. Inside the greenhouse and out of the pouring rain, nursery staff and volunteers dance to African music tracks while potting up cold-weather spring crops, including salad greens, peas, scallions, and an array of biodiverse brassicas for the April sale. Frost-tender summer crops, including over 100 varieties of tomatoes and 25 varieties of peppers, size up in the greenhouse for the May Mother's Day sale.

In March, the one-hundred-year-old Epargne pear tree next to the kitchen erupts with popcorn-like blossoms. PHOTO BY JIM COLEMAN.

The new, bright-eyed interns in mud-laden boots follow Michelle, our intern coordinator, around the North Garden like baby ducklings as they harvest asparagus, garlic scapes, arugula, radishes, lettuces, cardoon, artichoke, and rhubarb. Cover crops planted last fall—Austrian field peas and fava beans—have enriched the soil over winter and are now ready to be cut and composted, giving us the added bonus of pea tendrils, fava leaves, and fresh fava beans for the kitchen. At this time of year, the famous Mother Garden Biodiversity Salad Mix tops out at a whopping 97 ingredients and includes things like tatsoi and shungiku, tender miner's lettuce, and baby brassicas. Tonic herbs and "weeds" like nettles, chickweed, fennel, and dandelion pop up in garden borders and go into sauces and pestos that cleanse the sluggish body from a long winter. Our diet shifts from heavy winter foods to lighter, brighter fare inspired by the fresh burst of green vegetables and herbs.

May is divine. The rains have died down to an occasional, lucky spring shower—the last of the season—giving way to balmy, sunny days. With the plant sales over and the threat of frost past, the tomatoes and peppers are planted out and carefully labeled to distinguish the dizzying number of varieties. Successions of salad beds are seeded in whimsical patterns and carefully timed to coincide their projected harvest dates with major groups of visitors scheduled in the months to come. The lush green grass growing in the garden paths is mowed, bringing some order to the chaos of "volunteers" sprouting with abandon in the warm, moist soil of the Mother Garden. Sweet orange and white loquats, the first fruits to ripen in the orchard, drip from the trees along the main driveway to greet and delight the students, activists, movers, and shakers now visiting the center in full swing.

Spring Equinox Biodiversity Salad Mix

We are known at OAEC for our famous Biodiversity Salad Mix (which we'll talk about in more detail on page 36). Salad mix is often referred to as Spring Mix for good reason—the garden sprouts forth with its biggest burst of new baby greens in fertile spring. In the Mother Garden, that means close to 100 potential ingredients to work with! Mild weather means mild flavor: Arugula is sweet rather than spicy, and normally bitter dandelion greens are mellow enough to be eaten raw at this time of year. Kales, mustards, lettuces, and buttery mache are at their most tender. Wild miner's lettuce springs up around the garden edges, and cover crops such as fava bean leaves and pea tendrils make their way into the harvest bin as well. Edible flowers in cheerful pastels decorate the spring mix—rare red fava flowers, bachelor's buttons, and delicate rose petals.

This nuanced salad demands a simple, light dressing—herb-infused vinegar with a nice olive oil (page 269).

PHOTO BY DOUG GOSLING.

SPRING SALAD MIX

Baby heirloom lettuces: Akcel,
Forellenschluss, Merlot, Red
Speckle, Pablo, Little Gem
Baby beet leaves:
Chioggia and Golden
Cress: Wrinkly Crinkly Curly
and Upland
Green mustard leaves: Golden
Streaks, Golden Frills, and
Old-Fashioned Ragged Edge
Kale leaves and flowers: Redbor,
Winterbor, Dinosaur, Russian
Red, Russian White
Sprouting broccoli leaves:
Purple, Spiagariello
Baby Swiss chard leaves: Rainbow,
Golden, Rhubarb, Flamingo
Pink, Oriole Orange
Arugula leaves
Sylvetta arugula leaves
Japanese red mustards: Osaka
Purple, Giant Red, Garnet, Red
Feather, Ruby Streaks
Mache rosettes and flowers:
Verte de Cambrai, Coquille
des Louviers
Baby amaranth leaves
Baby spinach leaves
Fava bean leaves and flowers
Pea shoots, tendrils, and flowers
French sorrel leaves
Sheep sorrel leaves

Plantain leaves: Buckhorn, Wild
Dandelion leaves
Mallow leaves
Miner's lettuce leaves and flowers
Chickweed leaves and flowers
Red-veined dock leaves
Salad Burnet leaves
Shungiku leaves and flower petals
Nasturtium leaves, buds,
and flowers
Chive leaves and flowers
Wild radish flowers and young pods
Yellow mustard and tatsoi flowers
Society garlic leaves and flowers:
Variegated and Green
Chervil flowers
Bronze fennel fronds
Fenugreek leaves
Dill leaves
Garlic chive leaves
Parsley leaflets
Mint tips: Spearmint, Peppermint,
Lemon Balm
Sweet violet leaves and flowers
Runner bean flowers
Forget-me-not flowers
Johnny jump-up flowers
Cecil Bruner rose petals
Abutilon flowers
Calendula petals
Anchusa flowers
Tulip petals

PHOTO BY KEVIN PAUL

ONE

The Mother Garden: Biodiversity on the Land and in the Kitchen

The Mother Garden serves a variety of roles in our nonprofit organization and residential community—a horticultural research experiment, an outdoor classroom, a food production farm, and above all a home. While her priorities and functions may vary from day to day, the Mother Garden provides a living foundation for OAEC's philosophical, intellectual, and cultural work.

Oak and coniferous forests border the Mother Garden where cultivated vegetables and medicinal herbs are intertwined with native plants. The deliberate presence of weeds and volunteer plants gives the Mother Garden an aesthetic that is unlike most food production farms or gardens—neither manicured nor unkempt, a balance of wildness and intentionality. Such edges where the wild meets the domestic are the most dynamic and interesting places for us to garden.

We have two main gardens, each with unique character. The larger North Garden is nestled on a north-facing slope in the bowl of a hugging forest. It is the more temperate garden over which cool salty ocean breezes tickle even in the warm afternoons of June and July. Here we have always planted crops that prefer more moderate temperatures, such as lettuces and salad greens, all the brassicas, beets and chard, basil and cut flowers.

One of the most sublime design features of the North Garden is its main pathway, which dates to the time of Italian homesteaders on the land over 100 years ago. Cattle ambling out to pasture in the Back Forty imprinted a pathway, a most elegant meander on perfect contour across the slope of the North

Garden, and the first Farallons gardeners had the wisdom to preserve its line. Inspired by the designs of bio-intensive gardening guru Alan Chadwick, this main pathway became the perennial backbone off which the annual "rib" beds are held. On either side, perennial flowering plants attract beneficial insects in the cool pastels of lavender, pinks, blues, and white.

The other main garden, the South Garden, sits in relationship to human settlement amid homes and useful buildings. Like the adjacent solar panels on the rooftop of the meeting room, the South Garden is situated on a south-facing slope and is oriented toward the sun to maximize the sunlight. It is the warmer of the two gardens, where we always plant the tropical crops that thrive in higher temperatures: tomatoes, sweet peppers, cucumbers, yacon, summer and winter squash. Frost-tender perennials have a better chance of survival through the winter here. The flower borders are planted in the

PHOTO BY JIM COLEMAN.

fiery brilliant colors of magenta, purples, oranges, and yellows.

We have many sites in which to garden, and at any given point, we have many microclimates to consider. We dance between the North and the South Gardens as to what we plant when and where throughout the year; we plant our salad greens, for example, in the South Garden in the wintertime, trying to avoid the heavy frosts, and then, as the year progresses into warmth, sow them in the milder North Garden for the rest of the summer months.

PHOTO BY JIM COLEMAN.

The South Garden. PHOTO BY DOUG GOSLING.

FROM THE MOTHER GARDEN:
A PERSONAL REFLECTION ON PLACE

by Doug Gosling, Mother Garden Biodiversity Program director since 1983

I did not know when I came to what was then the Farallons Institute as a summer garden intern in 1982 that I would end up spending the rest of my life here. For more than 30 years, I have walked the same soft path from my home to the garden gate for a full day of work nearly every day. Slowly, I fell in love with this garden, and it has remained my best friend, primary life partner, and most important teacher.

Over time, I've watched the Mother Garden change and age, deepen in character and complexity, settle more and more into its place, and develop into an identity with a layered story and rich history. I've watched the live oaks and California bay grow up alongside her. I've met the many creatures, domestic and wild, who are born of the generosity and abundance of the garden—lacewings, monarch butterflies, Pacific Coast tree frogs, California quail. They come, sometimes from across great, dry divides, shimmering into appearance seemingly out of thin air. I've gotten to know all of the garden's nooks and crannies, public and hiding places, the subtle differences of their soils and microclimates—its secrets.

The garden has engaged an essential maternal instinct in me to midwife babies into the world, nurturing them along their way, defending and protecting them against the worries of life, and trying to provide the best possible home so that they might grow to their fullest selves. By studying the endless diversity of plants here over and over again through the cycles of the years, I've come to know and love their forms—the miracle of their architecture, their colors and textures, the poetry of their gesture as they trace their way in the world. I've watched their motions in the wind, their dropping of petals and swelling with seed and ripening to fullness, their straining under heavy fruit or the weight of rain, their bending and breaking in the wind, their instant death in a sudden frost.

We birth, nurture, and appreciate food crops into their fullness knowing that we will eat their leaves, stems, roots, seeds, or fruit, or their entirety. The way to study plants most deliberately, quietly, and intimately is to harvest them and to finally eat them, bringing them into our bodies and absorbing their essential messages of nutrition. They understand this, too; we have been doing this together for millennia. Billions of macro- and microorganisms will savor, consume, and be enlivened by us one day as well.

I've come to know and love the soil and find comfort and familiarity in its black, cakey humus and the crumb of perfect tilth. I've savored the sweet taste of complete and well-made compost and have seen the thrill on the faces of thousands of volunteers and students who have reached into a garden bed with their bare hands to experience its rich luxurious body, the nuances of its texture and smell. To accept the infinite unknowable mystery and wisdom of soil and to trust and believe in the ancient cycle of decomposition is to embrace the inevitability and poetry of death.

The Mother Garden has provided an opportunity for me to be in body relationship with the skin and black flesh of earth. Learning to be at home on the ground, comfortable on my knees and haunches and the foundation of my feet, I do not feel a fear of darkness. Walking on soft green pathways and learning how to be barefoot on earth and stones, I've learned the importance of yielding in life.

There is a comfort in knowing the rightness of life's cycles and in being at peace with the earth from which we rise and fall. Learning to trust in the future by planting seeds and witnessing their enduring germination, we are given the hope we need to live through these perilous times.

Gardening and cooking from the garden are precious opportunities to develop a relationship to place, to feel connected to a coherent meaning of home, to reveal the possibility of being in right relationship with self, and ultimately to feel at home in self. To be involved with work that is generative, productive, meaningful, and cocreative, and involves bringing life into being, is to learn the rightness of being human and having a sure sense of place and purpose on earth. We can feel glad in realizing the beauty of our place in the garden.

One of the deep satisfactions of gardening is holding a handful of freshly sifted, sweet-smelling finished compost. PHOTO BY DOUG GOSLING.

BASIC RECIPE FOR COMPOST

Layer 1 part nitrogen (food scraps and fresh green material) to 25 parts carbon (brown stuff like dried leaves or grass) in a round pile. Allow the mixture to heat up to 180° and let it cook for about six weeks. Turn with a garden fork and let it rest. Repeat as necessary until the pile reduces in volume by two-thirds, about four to six months. Sift out any remaining woody parts and feed to your hungry soil!

Mmmmm, rich, moist compost cake! PHOTO BY TALI AIONA.

A lesson on nutrient cycling using round, nest-shaped compost piles. PHOTO BY JIM COLEMAN.

A Legacy of Soil

First and foremost, at OAEC we grow soil. From healthy soil, we grow healthy food. From healthy food, we grow healthy people. We are, and will always be, what we eat. At OAEC, we return about 6 tons of food scraps from our kitchen back to the soil via fodder for chickens, goats, worms, and compost piles every year. With more microorganisms in a few tablespoons of humus than there are humans living on earth, every shovelful of compost is an incomprehensible infusion of diversity and life force into a garden bed. Unquestionably, the longest-lasting durable legacy that the Mother Garden will bestow upon future generations is this black gold.

Seed Saving and the Beauty of Bolting

When most people see a lettuce plant that has gone to seed, they rarely recognize it as a lettuce plant. In fact, the very cultural expression *gone to seed* reinforces our construct of distaste for an aging life-form rather than reverence for its power and wisdom. Modern gardeners have been trained to loathe "bolting" and often pull out annuals or cut back perennials that have begun to flower. Yet lettuce would cease to

Seeds have co-evolved with humans, and it can be said that our stories live in them and theirs in us. PHOTO BY JIM COLEMAN.

A chickadee feasts on mullein seeds that are left on the stalk to dry in late fall. There is no better bird feeder than a seed saving garden! PHOTO BY JIM COLEMAN.

grace our salad plates if farmers and gardeners did not allow their favorite varieties to go to seed.

In a seed saving garden, plants are celebrated in all phases of their life cycle. Flowering—a necessary step in pollination and seed formation—provides forage for bees, hummingbirds, and other beneficial insects and adds color, fragrance, and splendor to the garden. As we observe this long arch of phases—a tall stem emerging from a rosette of leaves, its leaves becoming more toothed and spiky, and its flowerets forming white feathery tufts—we can track the garden's rhythms that in turn give us an opportunity to reflect on the changes in our own lives. Even as the life force in the plant has waned and dried down to a brown stalk, there is still so much grace in its architecture and its generosity— thousands of seeds spill out into the garden beds as bountiful food for humans, birds, and animals, as well as future generations of plantings.

Not only does seed saving give the Mother Garden a unique aesthetic and enhance its biodiversity, but the beauty of bolting also informs our cooking style. A bolting kale plant, for example, is every bit as edible

as the more familiar leaf form that we might see in the grocery store. Its sweet and tender side shoots are delicious sautéed like mini broccoli. Or we can pluck the small leaves off of the flowering stem and add them to the salad mix. If we wait a few weeks more, the vibrant yellow flowers open and can be used as piquant edible garnishes. Finally, after the plant has matured and dried up, we are rewarded for our patience with the gift of seed for the next generation. Obviously, we eat the seeds of many garden plants, too—scarlet runner beans and bread seed poppies are among our favorites. The recipes in this book will hopefully inspire you to discover the culinary value of plants throughout each phase of their life cycle.

Seed saving is also a deeply political act. At OAEC, we save, grow, promote, and teach people about open-pollinated seeds because, second only to cli-mate chaos, seed sovereignty and ownership is one of the most pressing agricultural issues of our time.

Why open pollination? Open-pollinated seeds are seeds collected from plants pollinated by insects, wind, or other natural mechanisms that grow true-to-type generation after generation.

The yellow flowers in the background are brassicas (plants from the cabbage family such as mustards, kale, and broccoli) that have been purpose-fully allowed to bolt for seed saving, pollinator forage, and food. PHOTO BY DAVE HENSON.

Isolation and selection of open-pollinated seeds are plant breeding methods that farmers worldwide have understood and practiced since the dawn of agriculture to continuously develop and improve crop varieties well suited to their region and culture. Due to naturally diverse crosses between parent plants, open-pollinated seeds carry with them wide genetic variations, and thus an ability to quickly evolve and adapt to local conditions such as soil type, pest pressure, and so on. New or accidental crosses can delight a home gardener with surprising beauty, flavor, or hardiness—traits that can be either encouraged or discouraged through the ongoing selection and growing out of seed stock. However, these crosses and off-types can also incite confusion in the untrained seed saver along

with a temptation to rely on hybrid or genetically modified seed, prized for uniformity and inherent lack of diversity.

At OAEC, we enjoy growing a small handful of organically grown seeds of hybrid F1 varieties, such as Nufar Basil, Sungold Cherry Tomatoes, and Cheddar Cauliflower. These varieties rank high on our list of favorites, so this is not to say that all F1 hybrids are categorically bad. But modern controlled pollination technologies are patented and owned by large agribusinesses that keep the parentage of these varieties proprietary. These businesses make their profit by rendering the offspring of hybridized or genetically modified plants sterile or vastly different from the parent plants. This forces the farmer/gardener to rely exclusively on seed

Renata Brillinger teaches seed saving in the School Garden Teacher Training course. PHOTO BY JIM COLEMAN.

companies for their seeds rather than saving seed from this year's crop to plant out next year.

In 2005, scientists miraculously sprouted a 2,000-year-old date palm seed excavated from the ancient Judean fortress of Mesada.[2] And yet, while many seeds have a remarkable capacity to remain viable under favorable storage conditions, the viability and germination rate under normal circumstances does depreciate over time. Seeds are not meant to be hoarded, but rather planted out, multiplied, and saved again in a cyclical living collaboration between farmer and seed.

The intentional, artisanal stewardship of open-pollinated seed keeps us—small-scale farmers and gardeners—in constant dialogue with nature as we interact with seeds over time, selecting for

Occasionally off-types or "sports" appear in a population of an otherwise uniform plant variety, as happened with "Shiny Diny"—a dark-green shiny-leaved dinosaur kale that Doug Gosling spotted among normal blue-green individuals and subsequently selected over several generations into a stable new variety. PHOTO BY TALI AIONA.

A tradition at Ecological Farming Association conferences under OAEC's leadership, seed swaps have gone viral across California and the country, empowering communities to engage in the collaborative act of preservation of seed and open-pollinated, publicly owned diversity. Clearly, while the revolution may not be televised, it will be planted!

—KEN DICKERSON, *executive director of the Ecological Farming Association, OAEC garden intern 1998*

varieties that enrich our lives. All heirloom seeds are open-pollinated, and the agricultural knowledge around how to successfully save seed from each of these varieties must also be passed down through the generations to keep these varieties current and viable. By empowering people with seeds and the knowledge of how to save them, we hold the resiliency of our food system in our own hands instead of the hands of corporations.

The relationship that we cultivate while saving seeds and learning the stories carried with them deeply connects us to the history of our food and our place in ways that have been virtually eradicated by our industrial food system. By sharing the stories of seeds' migration patterns and caring for generations of plant life seed to seed, we not only begin to appreciate where food comes from but, more broadly, become infused with a personal sense of continuity, purpose, and connection to the here and now. The maintenance of biodiverse seeds directly honors the cultures and the land from which they came and has the power to link us to our collective agricultural ancestry through a legacy of seedsmanship. Saving seeds, being part of an ancient life-giving and life-affirming act, reaches both into the past and into the future, connecting us to all who went before us and all who will come after us. For more information on the fine art of seed saving, we recommend *Seed to Seed: Seed Saving and Growing Techniques for the Vegetable Gardener* by Susan Ashworth.

Left, The OAEC seed vault houses the Mother Garden Biodiversity Program's vast collection of open-pollinated and heirloom seeds. *Right,* The EcoFarm Seed Exchange, among one of many regional seed exchanges that OAEC hosts every year. PHOTOS BY JIM COLEMAN.

In Defense of Weeds

Walking into the Mother Garden in spring is a like arriving at a party. One is immediately taken aback by the buzzing activity, abundance of food, outrageous beauty, and unruly wildness of some of the guests. It is a celebratory commingling of edible crops, culinary and medicinal herbs, perennial flowers, and, yes, weeds—those plants that "volunteer," appearing whenever and wherever they want.

So who *are* these plants that crashed the party?

Michelle Vesser, herbalist, teacher, and Mother Garden production manager since 2002, would respond by saying that many weeds in the Mother Garden are, if fact, honored welcome guests. In her classes, she teaches that if we are curious and take the time to meet these plants, we find that they didn't show up to the party empty-handed. As herbalists have known for millennia, many common garden weeds can be used as food and medicine. Contrary to the common misunderstanding that a weed is a plant that is in the wrong place at the wrong time, weeds often show up in our environment in meaningful ways—their timing and placement can actually be perfect for what we need, nutritionally or ecologically, in that particular place, climate, and season. For example, chlorophyll-rich lymphatic boosters such as chickweed and cleavers (see Herbal Pestos, page 255) pop up in early spring when our sluggish system is waking up from a long winter with little physical activity and few green vegetables. Juicy purslane, hydrating and emollient with omega-3 fatty acids, coincidentally appears in the garden right next to the cucumber in July (see Hydrating Lemon Cucumber Purslane Salad, page 125) to quench a parched summer palate.

As any gardener knows, weeds are stronger, more vital, and more vigorous than domesticated plants. They thrive in marginal conditions—even in infertile, polluted, and disturbed areas, they pop up through cracks in the cement and places where cultivated "prima donna" plants would never survive. Many have voracious roots that can penetrate deeply into the most inhospitable soil in search of water and nutrients. It is precisely this tenacity that makes many weeds nutritious food and potent medicine—they have the power to strengthen our immune systems, cleanse our body of toxins, and deeply nourish and tone our tissues with concentrated vitamins and minerals. Weeds have the strength needed to balance the disturbed and polluted landscape of both our land and our bodies.

Nasturtium "volunteering" amid a bed of Lolla Rosa lettuce. PHOTO BY DOUG GOSLING.

TAKING A STAND AGAINST GENETICALLY MODIFIED ORGANISMS

by Dave Henson, OAEC executive director, 1994–present

In educating and provisioning with seeds and starts many thousands of gardeners over the years, OAEC has been a leading advocate of the seed saving renaissance that we now see flourishing in communities all over the United States. So in the 1990s and 2000s, when the Monsanto, Syngenta, and Dow corporations (among others) began to aggressively patent and market their new genetically engineered crops (or "GE crops"), OAEC took particular offense.

Since their introduction in the mid-1990s, the chemical and biotech industries have told the world that we need GE crops to solve persistent nutrition and food security problems around the world. But these were always false promises. Over 95 percent of the GE crops planted around the world are still just four species (corn, soy, cotton, and canola), and they only express two GE traits (herbicide tolerance and plant-produced pesticide). None of these crops with either of these traits has increased nutrition for anyone, nor they have increased food security anywhere.

What the GE crop corporations have done very well is to sell the world a lot more herbicides. Washington State University published data in 2012[3] showing that between 1996 and 2011, the use of GE herbicide-resistant crops (like Monsanto's Roundup Ready crops, which farmers then spray with the herbicide glyphosate without killing the GE crop) has led to a 527-million-pound annual increase in herbicide use in the United States alone. That's half a billion more pounds of herbicide in our soil, water, farm communities, and food. This huge increase has in turn created an explosion of over 100 species of new "super weeds" on more than 60 million acres of US farmland. These super weeds have rapidly evolved to be immune to being sprayed by glyphosate, and now the GE/pesticide corporations are selling 2,4-D and other more toxic herbicides to kill the super weeds that they created, and selling farmers even more expensive "2,4-D ready crops." This circle of poison and profit is their business plan.

Maybe worse, by strategically focusing on patenting and owning the genes in the GE crops, these corporations have made it illegal for millions of farmers worldwide to save their own seed, and have forced tens of thousands of farmers—some of the poorest in the world—into bankruptcy, and their communities into great food insecurity.

In response, farmers and other citizens in communities all over the world have fought hard against the GE crop corporations, and for seed sovereignty, organic and other least-toxic farming methods, and regional food security. In the late 1990s, OAEC began

Signature gatherers celebrate putting the Sonoma County GE-free initiative on the ballot. PHOTO BY JIM COLEMAN.

working passionately on this issue. In 1999, we cofounded the national Genetic Engineering Action Network. In 2002, OAEC cofounded and became the fiscal sponsor of Californians for GE-Free Agriculture (Cal GE-Free)—a strong statewide coalition of farming, public health, environmental, and labor organizations. In 2004, the world's first commercial planting of a pharmaceutical crop—rice engineered with human genes—was stopped due to the efforts of Cal GE-Free. In 2004, we founded GE-Free Sonoma County and led a ballot initiative to ban the planting of GE crops in Sonoma County. We lost that vote, but our allies in four other counties have won—Mendocino, Marin, Trinity, and Santa Cruz. In 2008, Cal GE-Free won the passage of the first California state law to regulate GE crops. The law, AB 541, protects farmers from being sued by biotech companies when GE crops contaminate the non-GE crops in a farmer's field.

Since GE foods arrived on US supermarket shelves over 15 years ago, there still has been virtually no research into their short- or long-term health effects. A small percentage of GE corn, soy, or canola is now present in approximately 85 percent of all processed foods, and since these foods are not labeled anywhere in the United States, it is not possible to correlate any negative or positive effects to their consumption. We are part of the world's largest experiment on the subject . . . and no one is collecting the data.

Gene-splicing technologies are fascinating, and they may very well prove to be incredibly valuable in offering safe, ecologically sound solutions to persistent human and animal diseases. But decisions about releasing these novel organisms into our farms, food, bodies, and environment are being made by a few multinational chemical corporations with an astonishing lack of regulation or

Beautiful, shark-teeth-like seeds of teosinte, the plant thought to be the ancient Mexican predecessor of maize. An annual grass that arcs over Mother Garden pathways, teosinte produces many tiny husked ears. It presaged the development of modern corn, now the most widely produced grain crop in the world. The world's teosinte seed is at risk of contamination due to cross-pollination by genetically engineered corn developed by the global biotechnology industry. Out of gratitude for generations of seed saving ancestors before us, we have taken on the responsibility of stewarding this historically significant seed and its wild base genetics for future generations. PHOTO BY DOUG GOSLING.

accountability. OAEC supports mandatory labeling of all GE foods and products and a prohibition on raising any GE crops or animals anywhere— a prohibition that should only be lifted after comprehensive, independent, peer-reviewed, long-term assessments of the effects of such organisms on human and environment health. In any case, no person or corporation has the right to patent any life-form. To strengthen food security and seed sovereignty for every community, let's focus instead on the solutions that will serve the world for centuries to come: Let's celebrate small-scale farmers who use ecologically sustainable agriculture practices to mitigate climate change and empower them to remain the proud and lawful stewards of their own diverse, regionally adapted varieties of crops and animals.

Almost everything we find in a modern grocery store originally came from a wild plant. The spiky assertive weed that crops up in the understory of a garden bed, "wild lettuce" (*left*), is a reminder of this legacy. Ancient Egyptians long ago saw its hidden potential as a food crop, and since then, it has been selected and cultivated into the thousands of varieties of modern lettuce we now enjoy, including Red Speckles, an heirloom lettuce selected by German Mennonites (*right*). In the OAEC garden, abundant and diverse food crops are grown side by side with their wild ancestors. PHOTO (*LEFT*) BY TALI AIONA; PHOTO (*RIGHT*) BY JIM COLEMAN.

Uses of weeds include not only food and medicine, but also fiber, dyes, building materials, natural preservatives, beauty products and fragrances—the historical list goes on and on. But even weeds that do not have direct physical value can also be useful agriculturally and ecologically. In addition to cycling buried trace nutrients to upper layers of the topsoil, they can also be indicators of soil type, fertility, pH, or changing weather conditions. In the OAEC garden, the sprouting of volunteer amaranth greens throughout the garden in spring is the go-ahead signal that the soil is warm enough to transplant tomatoes and other cold-tender plants. An abundance of dock is a telltale sign of wet, acidic soil—perfect for growing berries. Weeds make natural companion plants, too—nasturtium grows happily among cucurbits (cucumber/squash/pumpkin family) and is known to repel cucumber beetles, squash bugs, and woolly aphids. In short, weeds can be messengers and allies in the garden—a boon to gardeners who are willing to work with rather than against them.

This is not to say that weeds should be permitted to completely dominate the garden, as Bermuda grass, the Mother Garden's nemesis, could easily do. Ecology is about balance. Agriculture is a co-evolution between plants and humans, and allowing a wild element into the garden is an essential part of this two-way relationship. As a society, we are increasingly becoming alienated from the natural world and from the ancient, life-sustaining wisdom of plants that only a few generations ago, was common knowledge. Radical as it seems, if we can put aside our agenda for just a moment and begin to listen to, work with, and at times even go so far as *tend to* the weeds, we open ourselves to receive the multitude of gifts that wild plants have to offer—an opportunity to connect to our environment, our heritage, and to our own wild nature.

On Art and Ecology

by Adam Wolpert, resident artist and Sowing Circle member

When I first moved to the OAEC, the relationship between art and ecology was unclear to me even though the two words appear together in the name of our organization. My formal university education had never connected the two disciplines. But over time, as my understanding of my own creative process grew alongside my deepening understanding of ecology, I came to see how much they share. Permaculture, like art, integrates qualities along with quantities, values, sensitive observation, participation, and collaboration, and sees the artist or the ecologist as a part of, not apart from, nature. Ultimately this relationship between art and ecology is rooted in their common source of inspiration, wisdom, and guidance—nature herself.

PHOTO BY JIM COLEMAN.

MOTHER GARDEN BIODIVERSITY SALAD MIX

from an interview with Doug Gosling, Mother Garden Biodiversity Program director

It has been a fascinating experience to watch the evolution of the specialty produce market and particularly salad mix as it has risen to the status of staple in California cuisine. Chef and author Alice Waters played a huge role in bringing French mesclun to California from France, though it is a very prescribed list of usually only about four things—arugula, chervil, lettuce, and endive. In the beginning, our mix was fairly standard, too, but over time, we started tossing in unusual things like orach and shungiku. We started adding edible flowers and the whole range of different mustards and chicories and baby everything, and then a lot of weeds, wild things, and herb tips. Before long, our mix had 60 or more ingredients in it! While we certainly didn't invent salad mix—there were many other early pioneers doing it on a larger scale—ours became a highly sought after favorite because of its extreme diversity.

During the early 1980s when the whole California cuisine movement was taking off, Michael Stusser, the garden manager during the Farallons era, was already growing many unusual food crops, so when I first arrived here, I was exposed to vegetables I had never seen or heard of, like radicchio, which, of course, is now commonplace. People were discovering so many things for the first time, and because we loved to experiment, we were usually ahead of the curve. For instance, I remember we were the first people in Sonoma County to grow chervil on a significant scale. We would grow large beds of it and sell it at top dollar. Then, of course, people would find out about chervil, so the next year there would be many other chervil growers. Farmers always had to keep one step ahead to survive and keep it interesting. Like it or not, the specialty produce market is still that way.

Besides the fact that it's fun, we grow diverse crops in the garden because healthy natural systems have intricate webs of relationship that make them more resilient when stressed. On the other hand, if you get a disease or pest problem in a farm or garden where there are just one or two crops, you can lose all of it in one fell swoop. Having a diverse garden ensures that you will always have food—in this case, ingredients throughout the year to add to the salad mix.

More than any other crop, salad mix is an expression of the character of the garden—a snapshot of the garden on any given day. You always discover something new that has either come to a point or gone past the point where it is harvestable, and so the salad you pick today will always be different from the salad you picked yesterday. You can also appreciate the unintentional things about a garden with its "volunteerism"—the amaranth or the chickweed or whatever pops up on its own allows you to take advantage of whatever is happening in the moment. I love picking and composing the salad as I go, and sometimes I like to work with a color palette. In fact, sometimes I have a hard time mixing hot colors with pastels—such as putting orange calendula petals in when I have picked pinks and lavenders! Another approach is doing the opposite, actually putting less in—having an amazing choice of things to work with but then narrowing it down to simple juxtapositions of color and taste. For example, as we speak, we have baby blond escarole leaves, and wouldn't that be lovely

Mother Garden Biodiversity Salad Mix. Heritage cultivars and wild species rotate seasonally in a flamboyant kaleidoscope of diversity. Dazzling to both the eye and the palate, components range from heirloom lettuce varieties to specialty kales bred on-site at OAEC to edible flowers to common garden weeds. The "100 Ingredient Salad Mix" is the crowning expression of the OAEC food philosophy. PHOTO BY DOUG GOSLING.

with pink rose petals, a light vinaigrette, and that's it—a simple paring of ingredients at the perfect moment for the season.

I have a few pet peeves when it comes to salad. I can't stand gloppy or heavy dressings. Once in a while, it is possible to make a substantial dressing work if you have a mix that can stand up to it, like a green goddess dressing with hearty kale leaves or romaine hearts. But when you are presenting a mix that has many nuanced ingredients, to overwhelm it with something like creamy tahini is an insult! The other thing that bothers me is when ingredients

A tradition that goes way back and continues to this day is that we always sow salad beds in a pattern or intentional design. We sow up to 20 varieties of cutting greens in contrast to set off the many different colors and textures. PHOTO BY JIM COLEMAN.

are chopped up, especially lettuce. When we harvest, we take the time to protect the integrity of each leaf by leaving it perfectly whole so that you can experience the character of each plant on the plate. When it gets chopped up, the plant loses its identity.

Besides the diversity, the OAEC salad mix is different from other mixes in that it is very sturdy. It comes from a garden that has well-balanced, healthy soil, not soil that has been pumped up with nitrogen. Our mix really lasts, sometimes for as long as two weeks, whereas most salad mixes spoil in three days or so. A lot of mixes are grown in greenhouses so they are tender, whereas ours is grown out in the elements. Our mix is toothsome and I think people appreciate its heartiness—not that fragile, homogeneous consistency that most mixes have. Sometimes we use our mix more as garnish or as a bed for a warm dish, like sautéed mushrooms (page 184) so that it wilts down just slightly with the sauce.

I almost always eat salad with my hands—it is such an elemental way of appreciating it, and I love it when other people do that, too. Another fabulous way to enjoy salad is to serve it in a big mound right on the countertop or present it in patterns or mandalas. I have served it on cake pedestals tiered like a wedding cake!

The salad mix makes an impression on people—it is our defining signature dish. It is also the crop that we have grown most consistently here through the years because it is such an appropriate crop for us. We are coastal and coolish for most of the year, here the salad mix is appropriate to place, our place. It is such a great symbol of OAEC and the food at OAEC—fresh, diverse, flavorful . . . medicine. Each plant has its own particular

profile of vitamins and minerals, and with 60 or more ingredients, what you are getting is a very potent infusion of plant medicine.

I think what I love most is sharing our salad with people. It's so gratifying when people taste the different leaves and say, "Wow what are all these things?" I love to tell them about each one as they discover it. They get the wonderful surprise of finding things in the salad that they might not expect or never knew were edible. The salad itself can be a journey of discovery of tastes, textures, colors, and ideas—a revelatory learning experience.

Staff enjoying salad for lunch in the North Garden. PHOTO BY TALI AIONA.

Why Do We Love Perennial Crops?

Mostly because it's less work. Perennials are low-maintenance compared with the labor that annuals require. Not that perennials can be completely neglected—they must be tended to periodically—but the process of cultivation and soil prep, planting and tenuous "babying" as the plant gets established happens only once. Perennials are often hardier and more drought-tolerant due their woodier stems and extensive root systems, which continue deepening in search of water and nutrients year after year. The hardy nature of many perennial food crops can also extend the growing season, widening our choices for year-round food. They need less fuss, less water, less fertilizer, less fossil fuel, and fewer trips to the chiropractor. We like that.

The perennial love fest doesn't stop there. Not only can perennial crops give us food, fiber, dye, medicine, building materials, and beauty, but they can also simultaneously provide an array of ecological services for the health of the garden system as a whole, which makes our work even easier. When non-invasive perennials are interplanted with annuals, the garden mimics the kinds of interdependent plant communities present in wild ecosystems. A diverse polyculture of annuals and perennials that flower at different times of the year attract an array of beneficial insects that pollinate crops. The bushy protective cover of perennial border plants provides habitat for birds and wildlife that prey upon pests and in turn fertilize the soil with their droppings. Shrubs and trees moderate the garden microclimate by providing shade in the summer and insulation and wind protection in the winter, not to mention improving carbon sequestration and oxygen production. Permanent root systems encourage the growth of soil microbes and prevent the kind of erosion and depletion that frequently tilled soil is vulnerable to between annual crops. The overall effect is a healthy, resilient garden with nature doing the work for us. What's not to love?

Sowing Circle member and permaculture instructor Kendall Dunnigan holds a giant basket of Hayward kiwis on the deck of our meeting room overlooking the South Garden, illustrating one of the key principles of good ecological design: stacking functions. The perennial kiwi vines that gracefully wind up this arbor serve a dual purpose beyond just providing delicious fruit. In the summer when the leaves are full, they shade the deck and cool the hot south-facing wall of our meeting room. When the leaves drop in the winter, sun is allowed to beam in to heat up the space. Air-conditioning never tasted so good. PHOTO BY TALI AIONA.

Ecological Design

OAEC is well known for being one of the leading permaculture design centers on the West Coast; students from all over the world come to see permaculture principles in action. And while this book isn't expressly about permaculture, its ecological design methodology pervades much of what we do here. So what exactly is permaculture, anyway?

Contrary to popular belief, permaculture itself is not a gardening technique. Nor is it

INVOCATION TO THE SEED

By Doug Gosling, read at the beginning of the 17th Annual OAEC Seed Exchange at the Ecological Farming Conference 2014 in Monterey, CA

We have not existed apart from you. We would
not exist without you. We cannot not survive
without you.

You are the germ! You are the grain!

You wait in the darkness of earth many, many times
longer than you might live above ground—
what are you doing down there? What are you
dreaming down there?

You are so many brilliant ideas waiting to happen,
wanting to happen, all the while holding the
memory of your old stories.

You have been beckoned by the Moon, invigorated
by showers, lit by the sun and sung by our Tribes
into being.

You've been split open into birth by scarification,
frozen in permafrost, sparked by the wildest
of fires.

You have survived the hostile acids of the gut and
the ferment of the moldering mother fruit.

You are the kernel of our food and medicine, dye
and fiber. You sprout, rise up and unfold into
our shade.

You are the germ of the blossoms gathered into our
most beautiful bouquets that hold the germs of
the blossoms of our most beautiful bouquets.

You float the lightest breeze and fly the Jetstreams.
You have stuck-tight to the nap of the backs of
the furriest ones and hitch-hiked on feathers.

You have floated from source to mouth of the great riv-
ers and fallen over seething waterfalls. You've been
held inside bladders rafting round whole oceans.

You have been released in clouds, parachuted and
helicoptered to safe landings, exploded from
splitting legumes, catapulted from capsules.

You have been shucked and threshed from your
mother's ovaries and been winnowed by
human breath.

You have been folded into cuffs, carried lovingly to
new lands. You've been smuggled across borders.

You have circulated as currency.

You have been grateful in our marriage with your
generosity and offered hope and given us Faith
even in these Dark Times.

You are embedded in our history and we are inseparable from yours.

We would not exist without you! And you would
not exist without us! We must honor you for
who you are.

Bless the seeds and bless us. Make them a part of
your story and may you be a part of theirs.

---

a solar food dehydrator or a gray water system. Rather, *permaculture* is a verb—it is a design method for creating regenerative human settlements based in natural patterns and processes. It is a set of principles—a checklist for critical whole-systems thinking—that asks us to consider both the needs of people and those of the planet when looking for the most efficient and elegant solution. We may apply the techniques of gardening, rainwater harvesting, or energy efficiency to achieve an integrated design, but the things themselves are not permaculture—only an expression of good design process and artisanship. Put simply, permaculture is the TIY, Think It Yourself, process that comes before the Do It Yourself, DIY.

SUMMER
May 2 to August 1

Early summer is perhaps the most confusing of all seasons here on the cool and foggy Northern California coast—the notorious "June gloom" is what led Mark Twain to say, "The coldest winter I ever spent was a summer in San Francisco." Thankfully, red and golden raspberries, an assortment of heirloom plums, shiso, summer squash, and amaranth greens volunteering in multicolored tapestries throughout the North Garden keep our mouths busy grazing and thwart most complaints about the fog. The outrageous collection of dozens of varieties of poppies and irises mesmerize garden visitors with bright summery color. As Phil Tymon, our wry administrative director, would say in his thick New York accent whenever anyone kvetches about the foggy weather, "Yep, another crappy day in paradise."

The first successions of fresh basils from all over the world—Iranian, Greek, Thai, and every shade of Italian—taunt us with the false promise of summer tomatoes. Neighbors 10 miles inland can enjoy a tomato by the Fourth of July, but alas, ours won't start to ripen in this chilly summer garden until September. The famous Sebastopol early Gravenstein apple eschews any preconceived notions of seasonality held by most of the country—the Gravs have come and gone long before anyone is in the mood for an apple pie. And forget melons or eggplants—it never gets hot enough to grow those here at all, so most years we don't even bother—instead we

No water = no food. During the summer dry cycle of our Mediterranean climate, many farms in the West rely on groundwater reserves for irrigation without taking measures to sink storm water back into the ground during the rainy season—an unsustainable practice that is teetering on catastrophic depletion. The water storage capacity of the OAEC pond, spring-fed and boosted by OAEC's groundwater recharge efforts such as swale digging, provides biologically active irrigation water for the Mother Garden throughout the summer dry season. PHOTO BY JIM COLEMAN.

happily buy them from neighboring farms that are just outside the fog belt.

The dry season sets in at the beginning of July as the fog tapers off and green grass fades to the golden hues of summer. Residents take advantage of the long daylight hours to head up to the pond after the workday is over for a cooling dip and a fruity cocktail while lounging in the hammock before dinner. Meals at this time of year focus on naturally juicy and hydrating raw fruits and vegetables—simply marinated cold salads such as the Rainbow Beet and Carrot Salad with Garden Herbs (page 129) or our quintessential Heirloom Tomato Platter (page 121) showcase garden diversity at its peak of abundance in the playful colors of summer. BBQ parties abound—quick grilled veggies with a side of fresh pesto always accompany the burgers. And no one wants to fire up the oven in this heat to make dessert; a light "fool" is all that is needed—fresh peaches and blackberries, ribbons of purple basil, a flop of whipped cream, a few calendula petals, and *voilà*!

Sunny late summer and early fall probably demands its own season altogether. In many cultures, such as in traditional Chinese medicine, there are in fact five distinct seasons, "Indian summer" being the time of abundance and nourishment, which is certainly the case here in our local food shed. This is the time of year when a true locavore can have it all—the summer crops are hitting their stride and the cool-weather crops start to come on as well. Cucumbers, peppers, tomatoes in every imaginable size, shape, and color, and surprisingly brassicas, chicories, and pumpkins all arrive in the very same harvest basket—conditions that give rise to creative combinations in the kitchen with nary a trip to the market.

It is during this time that both the garden and the OAEC staff give their last and biggest burst of output in a grand finale of the Fall Plant Sale, Chautauqua Revue, and the last of our courses and retreats for the year, before the busy season winds down.

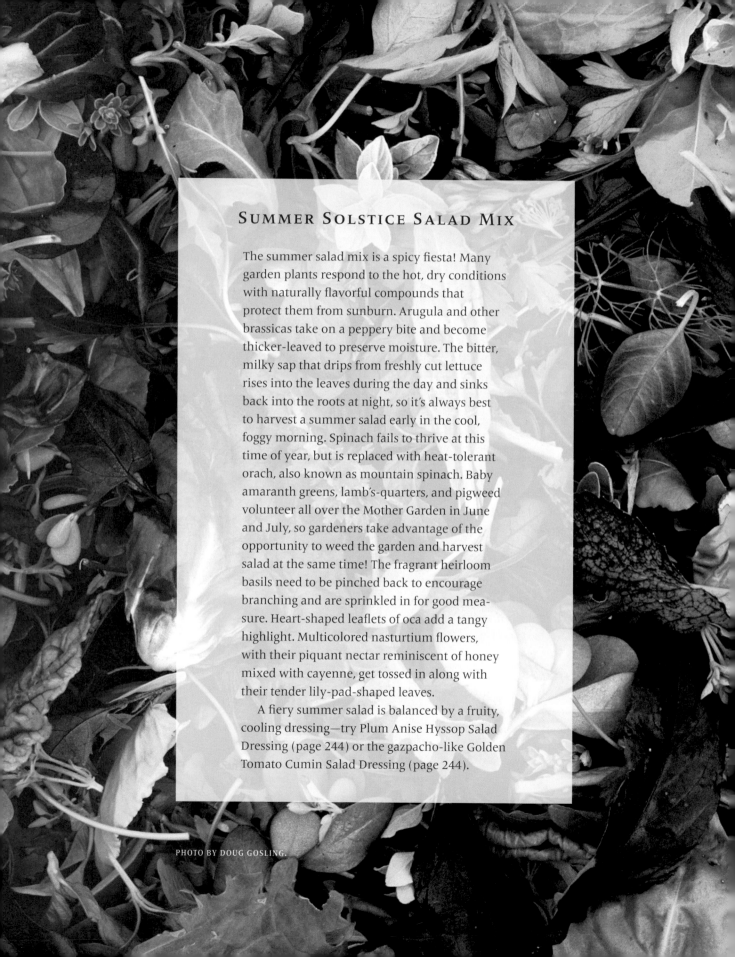

SUMMER SOLSTICE SALAD MIX

The summer salad mix is a spicy fiesta! Many garden plants respond to the hot, dry conditions with naturally flavorful compounds that protect them from sunburn. Arugula and other brassicas take on a peppery bite and become thicker-leaved to preserve moisture. The bitter, milky sap that drips from freshly cut lettuce rises into the leaves during the day and sinks back into the roots at night, so it's always best to harvest a summer salad early in the cool, foggy morning. Spinach fails to thrive at this time of year, but is replaced with heat-tolerant orach, also known as mountain spinach. Baby amaranth greens, lamb's-quarters, and pigweed volunteer all over the Mother Garden in June and July, so gardeners take advantage of the opportunity to weed the garden and harvest salad at the same time! The fragrant heirloom basils need to be pinched back to encourage branching and are sprinkled in for good measure. Heart-shaped leaflets of oca add a tangy highlight. Multicolored nasturtium flowers, with their piquant nectar reminiscent of honey mixed with cayenne, get tossed in along with their tender lily-pad-shaped leaves.

A fiery summer salad is balanced by a fruity, cooling dressing—try Plum Anise Hyssop Salad Dressing (page 244) or the gazpacho-like Golden Tomato Cumin Salad Dressing (page 244).

PHOTO BY DOUG GOSLING.

SUMMER GREENS MIX

Baby grain amaranth greens
Pigweed leaves
Magenta lamb's-quarters leaves
    and young shoots
Orach leaves:
    Purple and Golden
Quinoa leaves
Baby beet leaves: Bull's Blood,
    Macgregor's Favorite,
    Detroit Red
Mizuna leaves and flowers:
    Green and Purple
Agretti leaves
Oca leaves
Mashua leaves and tips
New Zealand spinach tips
Purslane tips
Perpetual spinach leaves
Salad burnet leaflets
Red-veined dock leaves
Wild plantain leaves
Basil leaves: Purple and Green
    Ruffles, Spicy Globe, Osmin,
    Purple Petra
Parsley leaflets: Curly and
    Italian Flatleaf
French sorrel leaves
Smallage leaflets
Tarragon tips

Anise hyssop tips, leaves,
    and flowers
Society garlic leaves and flowers
Cilantro flowers
Celery flowers
Dill leaves and flowers
Yellow mustard and wild
    radish flowers
Sylvetta arugula flowers
Bronze fennel flowers
Garlic chive flowers
Shungiku flowers
Nasturtium leaves, buds,
    and flowers
Upland cress flowers
Dahlia petals
Sunflower petals
Calendula petals
Pineapple sage flowers
Kennikura petals
Marigold petals
Daylily buds and petals
Stock flowers
White and blue borage flowers
Carnation petals
Bachelor's button petals
English daisy petals
Hollyhock petals
Rose petals

PHOTO BY JIM COLEMAN.

TWO

The Grandmother Garden:
Remembering Our Relationship
to the Landscape

*I would feel more optimistic about a bright future for
man if he spent less time proving that he can outwit
Nature and more time tasting her sweetness and
respecting her seniority.*
　　　　　　　　　　　　　—E. B. WHITE [4]

We affectionately refer to the backcountry, the wildlands beyond the deer fence surrounding our core
10-acre human settlement, as the Grandmother
Garden. She serves as our physical and mythical
link to the big picture, our umbilical cord to the
greater ecosystem, and our window into the past
and future of human relationship to this land. By
reading and interpreting the ancient story of the
Grandmother Garden, we can contextualize our
role in stewardship within the long arc of history.

Pacific tree frog on Wide-Leaved cress. Small catchment ponds in our North and South Gardens create breeding habitat—and amphitheaters for deafening amphibian choirs—for Pacific tree frogs, *Pseudacris regilla*. As these ponds dry up in warm weather, thousands of the tiny frogs venture out into the gardens to assist our integrated pest management program. PHOTO BY DOUG GOSLING.

Farming and Gardening with the Wild

In 2000, OAEC helped to cofound the Wild Farm Alliance, a coalition of conservationists and farmers who recognized that modern industrial agriculture is the primary cause of ecosystem devastation, pollution, and species loss. The coalition envisions a future where healthy, economically viable small-scale farms and ranches are ecologically managed and seamlessly integrated into landscapes and habitats in ways that benefit farmers and consumers and, at the same time, protect and preserve wild nature. Despite increasing phobia and segregation of wildlife from food crops in industrialized agriculture, in the Mother Garden and other Farming with the Wild coalition members, we not only allow but also encourage these symbiotic relationships.

Biologist and Sowing Circle member Carol Nieukirk leads her herd of milking goats through the OAEC backcountry. The California landscape evolved with its plant communities being browsed and grazed by free-ranging herds of animals. There is encouraging momentum in modern ranching toward managing livestock in ways mimicking native grazing patterns that actually rebuild rather than degrade critically endangered grasslands. At OAEC, we are using domestic goats . . . turning thickets of blackberry and poison oak into goat's milk and cheese is a tasty way to restore balanced ecosystems! PHOTO BY JIM COLEMAN.

Participants in the Tending the Wild course collect native perennial grass seed for propagation. PHOTO BY JIM COLEMAN.

Conservation Hydrology

*Do unto those downstream as you would have those
upstream do unto you.* —WENDELL BERRY[5]

Currently, 97 percent of the world's water is held in the salty oceans; another 2 percent is locked up in ice caps and glaciers. This leaves only 1 percent of the world's water supply available as mobile fresh water. With ongoing climate change presenting serious water-related challenges, especially in California, this remaining 1 percent needs more careful stewardship than ever. Without water, there is no food.

Typically, land development and modern industrial farming removes or dramatically modifies native vegetation to support human interests at the expense of watershed health, causing

NATIVE BIODIVERSITY

—A report from the Ecological Reserve at OAEC by Brock Dolman, senior biologist

The Sowing Circle and OAEC community reside on 80 acres in western Sonoma County. The land provides a bountiful home for a dynamic community of people and their richly diverse gardens, orchards, and ornamental landscapes. This land, well known as a preserve for a wide diversity of cultivated crops, is also an ecological preserve for a precious heritage of native biodiversity. As landowners, we take seriously our responsibilities to ensure the health and viability of the wildlands under our care. Ultimately an ethos guided by a vision thought of as Landscapes of Thanksgiving offers us an intergenerational challenge to work on this land in a manner that would make the ancestors proud and the grandchildren grateful. Gratitude for big trees, pure water, living soils, and robust communities of diverse life that express resiliency through time will be a future gift worth giving thanks for by all dwellers on this land.

The term *biodiversity* describes the exuberant expression of life in all forms and ecological relations. From individual species to populations of interconnected co-evolved symbiotic life-forms, biodiversity is the very tapestry upon which life depends for its own continuance. A study by Conservation International[6] designated 25 regions on the planet as "Biodiversity Hotspots." These biodiversity hotspots "cover only 1.4 percent of the earth, but are home to 44 percent of all vascular plant species and 35 percent of all vertebrate animal species." These areas have been designated hot spots not only because of their outstanding diversity, but also because of their extreme peril from human-caused habitat destruction. The study goes on to state that "these endangered areas have already lost 88 percent of their original vegetation.

The 10-acre "Core Area" including buildings and gardens is contained within an 8-foot-high fence that protects our landscaping and gardens from the threat of munching deer who have the remaining 70 acres to roam freely. Foxes, though usually too shy and skittish to venture into areas of high traffic, can easily move through holes in the fence if they so choose. Planning development in ways that cluster human activity into smaller impact zones while maximizing linked, permeable, and uninterrupted habitat corridors for foraging, access to water, mixing of genes, and seasonal migration is critical to supporting healthy populations of wildlife. PHOTO BY JIM COLEMAN.

Unless conservation efforts are increased, most of the rest will disappear in the foreseeable future."

Costal California is listed as one of the world's 25 biodiversity hot spots. Tragically, however, coastal California has lost to human development over 95 percent of its old-growth coniferous forests, fresh-water wetlands, saltwater estuaries, bunchgrass prairies, and riparian gallery forests. According to studies by The Nature Conservancy, the Bay Area, including Sonoma County, ranks nationally as one of the areas with the highest number of federally listed endangered species. This same area is leading the nation in "growth" and median home prices, and is over 95 percent privately owned. It is imperative that private landowners and residents take on active roles as stewards of biodiversity. As citizens, it is also our democratic responsibility to ensure that public land-use decisions are made that do not reduce the ecological carrying capacity of the land that supports biodiversity.

Since the founding of OAEC in 1994, staff biologists have been compiling a species list of wildlife sightings and native plants. As ecological preserve managers, a critical component of any strategy to enhance biodiversity is an accurate list of species utilizing the site. Any species that are of special concern or are listed as threatened or endangered can be highlighted to focus enhancement efforts on their behalf. A summary of the species-level biodiversity of native plants and vertebrate animals observed on site to date is as follows: Native plants are represented by at least 120 species. We have documented 162 native vertebrate species at OAEC's preserve represented by 7 species of amphibians, 12 species of retiles, 117 species of birds, and 26 species of mammals. These numbers will increase as additional plant and animal species are observed and the rodents, shrews, and bats are

Sowing Circle member Katy Mamen plants a coast redwood (*Sequoia sempervirens*) seedling as part of OAEC's reforestation efforts. PHOTO BY BROCK DOLMAN.

more accurately identified. In the future, we also aspire to more accurately understand and list our species diversity of fungi and invertebrates. We are deeply humbled by both the incredible diversity on this 80-acre parcel and the deep responsibility we thus share with this "intentional community" of nonhuman denizens.

The ecological mosaic of OAEC's preserve offers numerous niches for plant and animal diversity to

Brock Dolman leads bird-watchers through the OAEC backcountry. With a grant from the US Fish and Wildlife Service's Partners for Wildlife Program, OAEC resident wildlife biologists track neotropical songbird migration with the goal of maintaining and restoring the vegetation and habitat that support them. PHOTO BY JIM COLEMAN.

flourish. A short walk in the backcountry at OAEC takes us through a number of native plant associations from annual grasslands to soft chaparral slopes of coyote bush and poison oak. An old logging road meanders along the contour through evergreen hardwoods mixed with a canopy of second-growth Douglas fir. Descending the grassland slopes of Sunrise Meadow with its undulating ecotones and encroaching Douglas fir saplings, one is welcomed into the redwood/tan oak forest. Ascending an old logging skid trail, a subtle transition occurs onto the thin soils of rock outcroppings surrounded by deciduous black and white oaks and wildflowers. The footpath reenters another grove of mixed hardwood/conifer forest that shortly opens onto a perennial prairie fragment distinctively dominated by the presence of yampah. This well-trodden trail traverses a spillway to afford a

view of a startled great blue heron as it lifts off with a prehistoric squawk from the edge of the pond's reflected sunset glow.

In reading the landscape, one is challenged to interpret the many patterns of human presence here for thousands of years and—more dramatically—the land-use decisions of the last 150 years. The recognition that since the turn of the 20th century, all of the forests on the property have been clear-cut of mature trees is profound. Additional removal of native vegetation for grazing, vineyards, and human occupation is also clearly evident. However, some elements of the pre-European indigenous story can still be observed. Several on-site native bunchgrass prairies contain a preponderance of plant species that were wild-tended by the Pomo Indians for their roots and seeds. Extensive fields of cultivated edible wildflowers, such as yampah, harvest brodiaea, blue dicks, yellow mariposa lily, and soap root were often remarked upon by early European settlers speaking about the bucolic beauty of California's landscape. In this region, these apparent root crop/grain fields were reverentially maintained with the regular use of fire, digging sticks, and the active harvesting and replanting of bulbs. Surrounding the root/grain fields are oak woodlands that were managed with fire for the production of nutritious and sustaining acorns. The encroachment of Douglas fir that can be observed today was traditionally managed with the judicious use of fire as a primary land sculpting tool. Honoring indigenous ecological literacy provides us with caregiving concepts that can be utilized to foster the abundance of biodiversity characteristic of this place and embody this edible landscape.

OAEC has held a long-standing partnership with the Federated Indians of Graton Rancheria, the Coast Miwok/Southern Pomo tribe whose ancestral territory encompasses much of western

Sonoma County. Over the past decade, OAEC and FIGR have come together in a fascinating community process that blends tribal stories, traditions, and values with modern environmental study in stewardship of the land. Tribal chairman Greg Sarris says, "This is a collaboration of returning. Of coming home. In sharing the stories and seeds of traditional environmental knowledge, we are creating a home for all of us."

Our modern human communities have a choice to either view ourselves as *a part of or apart from* the fabric of biodiversity. As the current caregivers of this land, we are challenged to interact with this dynamic living process of evolution in a manner that enhances the presence of biodiversity. Through intelligent and heartfelt land-use decisions and ethno-ecologically proven practices, we are choosing to participate in the process of rebuilding soil, recharging groundwater, and re-creating wildlife habitat toward re-storying our relationship with the land as re-weavers of this tapestry of life.

Yampah (*Perideridia gairdneri*)—an edible wild root related to parsley—was an important food plant for the native people of the San Francisco Bay region. Over many years, OAEC has tended to our wild patch of yampah in an effort to bring this once plentiful food crop back into abundance. Someday, we will have enough yampah to create some recipes to share, but first things first. Recipe Step One: Carry out a decade-long restoration project! PHOTO BY BROCK DOLMAN.

In this photo, Federated Indians of Graton Rancheria tribal leaders dig for yampah during a workshop on gardening and nutrition in the OAEC upper meadow. Tasting traditional foods, like this mild carrot-flavored root, is a key sensory moment in the process of restoring connections to health and ancestry. PHOTO BY JIM COLEMAN.

Brock Dolman sits overlooking one of nine seasonal creeks that course through our 80 acres. OAEC believes in water *responsibilities* as much as water *rights* and works to ensure that storm water flowing from our headwater creeks doesn't compromise the downstream health of Dutch Bill Creek and the Russian River. PHOTO BY JIM COLEMAN.

biodiversity loss, species extinction, cultural genocide, habitat fragmentation, topsoil erosion, waterway sedimentation, increased flooding, and severe reductions in the quantity and quality of clean fresh water. But, as WATER Institute Associate Director Kate Lundquist asserts, not all farms and development need be harmful— some return more clean water to streams than they use, reduce erosion, and restore native species. As more people eat locally and seasonally, support organic agriculture, and request meat and fish raised using regenerative practices, our food production systems improve and watersheds can begin to recover.

As we're shopping, growing fresh herbs in the garden, and even doing the dishes, we can think about the ways that we use water, directly in our homes and indirectly through the farms and businesses we support, to promote Conservation Hydrology. In contrast with the pavement, pipes, and pollution we've become accustomed to, our ideal water- and land-use practices should slow water down; spread it out on the landscape; sink it into the ground; and return more water than we used, cleaner and colder.

BASINS OF RELATIONS

by Brock Dolman, 1998

This idea of place,
Let us locate ourselves on this watery planet
On this tectonic Turtle Island
Welcome to the eruptive Shasta Bioregion
Sinuous, crenellated Russian River Watershed
Undulatory Western Sonoma County
Here in the generous headwaters of Dutch Bill Creek
On this land, a simple east-facing coastal
    mountain ridge
Where forested slopes percolate the ephemeral
    bounty of falling water
Bestowing gifts of new quail coveys and western
    pond turtles basking on logs
Swallowtail butterflies and Aeolian turkey vultures
    riding thermals

Naming your watershed, filling it with stories and
    clear running creeks
Realizing that without exception, everyone lives in
    a watershed
Our inseparable watery bond we have with place
that so elegantly defines the ecological boundaries
of our enmeshed relations with landscape
Each home basin a flowing, whispering, respiring being
upon which we are all primarily dependent
and dedicate our lives in observant service

Take a moment, appreciative of the many wonders
which surround our lives and bear forth
    such inspiration
We give thanks for:
Pacific Steelhead and Coho Salmon
Tree frogs and immense Chain Ferns
Queen Boletes and Agaric Princes

Resident Pileated Woodpeckers and Neo-tropical
    Western Tanagers
Bay laurel nuts and Pacific Giant Salamanders
Old growth forests and old growth soils
Spotted Owls, Red Tree Voles and Gray Squirrels
these dancing arboreal makers of magic

Uplifted, folded mélange mountains with youthful soils,
lichen riddled blue schist rock outcrops
Valley heat derived coastal fog inhalation
Redwoods dendritic precipitation structures
Hardwood forests, perennial bunch grass prairies,
    soft chaparral
Wet, Wet winters and dry, dry summers
and poison oak and yellow jackets galore
Such teachers of patience and observation,
coyote spirits that remind us to slow down and take
    time to watch

Welcome to this land so accustomed to abundance
Acorn meal and deer hides; Calochortus bulbs and
    salmon flesh,
Hazel nuts and Yampah roots
Buoyant with interactive diversity
sculpted through intergenerational successionary
    caregiving
A land expectant of mutual respect

It is with intention that we live together
It is with gratitude and honor that we welcome you here
to celebrate with us
and hope you find joy and intrigue
and carry with you
blessings from this land and its family

FALL
August 2 to November 1

In many parts of the United States, folks welcome the first sunny day of spring after the cold, dark winter as a joyous day to be celebrated. Here in the West, the cycle is somewhat reversed. After sometimes as long as six dry months without a single drop of rain, we are parched, dusty, and anxious as water tables run low and wildfires rage high. Native vegetation goes largely dormant. As local West Sonoma County folk music legend Kate Wolf sings unromantically of California, "There's no gold, I thought I'd warn ya, and the hills turn brown in the summer time." When the first precious drops hit the ground, usually in October, we feel a spring-like renewal as the plants begin to sprout green again and our spirit is quenched.

Just before the rains arrive is the time for harvesting seed for the biodiversity collection. Brown stalks of dried seed heads—sunflower, mullein, brassicas, and amaranth—stand tall in the dry fall garden, every last drop of the plant's life force concentrated in the seed. Garden volunteers clip the dried seedpods into large paper bags for storage and cleaning later in the winter.

The last of the summer crops come into the kitchen before the rains in a flurry of tomatoes and hot pepper sauces for canning. Soon food preservation projects get under way on every available shelf and corner of the kitchen. A surplus of fall cabbage means that crocks of sauerkraut begin to bubble in the pantry. Perennial herbs are cut back for drying. Olives are cured in salt. Storage crops like onions and winter squash are squirreled away in the basement for winter—cooks try to resist roasting the first pumpkin as long as they possibly can, knowing that

The perennial Michaelmas daisy, *Aster novi-belgii*, is named after the feast of Saint Michael, which is associated with autumnal equinox and the shortening of days. It explodes into bloom just before the winter rains arrive just as the seed heads of the Golden Giant and Burgundy amaranth hurry to maturity. The furious activity and roaring buzz of the overwhelming diversity of beneficial insects drawn to this apical moment stop many human visitors to the North Garden in their tracks. PHOTO BY DOUG GOSLING.

these hardy orange beauties will still be around in January, long after this abundant harvesttime is over.

Harvesttime is when bakers roll out unique pies and tarts that celebrate the peak bounty of the heirloom fruit orchard such as the Epargne Pear Frangipane Tart (page 344). The orchard manager runs a marathon harvest of apples—dozens of varieties ripen in sequence and get juiced every Wednesday volunteer day for what seems like months. Interns invariably head up the hard cider brewing that, with any luck, will be done fermenting in time to taste before they leave. We bid farewell to our beloved, hardworking interns in an appreciation dinner to culminate the fall Thanksgiving season of gratitude.

The transition from hot and dry to cool and wet is an abundant time, not just in the garden and orchards, but in the backcountry as well. Fall rains bring wild mushrooms—chanterelles, oysters, and more exotic princes and candy caps. Many other wild foods, including acorns and bay nuts, also come into season during fall, inspiring foraging missions in the OAEC backcountry where

we gratefully fill our backpacks and baskets with whatever we can carry back to the kitchen.

Fall is the harvest season, both for food and for water, which is a big concern in California. As we reap the bounty of produce and seed, we must also lay the groundwork for next year's crops by recharging our groundwater wells, topping off our water tanks, and filling up the irrigation pond through diligent management of storm-water runoff. Throughout the OAEC grounds, a variety of simple rainwater harvesting techniques are employed at this time to ensure next year's abundance, including a favorite activity in the fall permaculture course—swale digging. A swale is an on-contour water infiltration device—aka a level ditch. Swales dug strategically around the land slow, spread, and sink hundreds of thousands of gallons of rainwater into the soil while simultaneously controlling erosion and protecting water quality downstream. Water stored in the soil is the cheapest form of water storage known. The subsurface water slowly moves downhill, charging springs, seeping into creeks, lengthening the time that surface water is available to plants and riparian critters.

FALL EQUINOX SALAD MIX

At the peak of the harvest season, the salad mix takes on the robust, earthy flavors of fall. Kales and other broccoli relatives, such as collards and mustards, sweeten and soften in the cool weather, providing the bulk of the fall mix. With the heat dying down, lettuces and spinach once again flourish in the North Garden. Mildly bitter chicories like Palla Rossa and Red Traviso provide a welcome digestive aid and a contrast to rich holiday harvest feasts. The fall mix is garnished with edible flowers in warm earth tones—yellow brassica flowers, calendula, and the very last of the sunflower petals.

A hearty fall mix can stand up to a more substantial dressing such as a creamy buttermilk ranch (salad dressing variation on page 277) or the Roasted Onion, Sesame Seed, and Tamari Salad Dressing (page 251).

FALL GREENS MIX

Baby collard leaves:
  Morris Heading, Variegated
Cress leaves: Wide-Leaved, Persian
Green mustard leaves:
  Southern Curled, Green Wave,
  Suehlihung, Pizzo
Japanese red mustards: Ruby
  Streaks, Scarlet Frills, Purple Wave
Kale leaves: Frizzy, Scotch Curled,
  Lacinato Rainbow
Sprouting broccoli leaves:
  Purple, Spiagariello
Mizuna leaves: Green and Purple
Ornamental kale leaves: Christmas
  Fringed Red and White
Tatsoi leaves
Pok Choi leaves: Yukina Savoy
Arugula leaves and flowers
Sylvetta arugula leaves
Heirloom lettuces: Merlot, Red
  Speckle, Pablo, Little Gem, Lolla
  Rosa, Tom Thumb
Baby beet leaves: Chioggia, Bull's
  Blood, Macgregor's Favorite,
  Golden, Crosby Egyptian

Baby Swiss chard leaves:
  Rainbow, Golden, Rhubarb,
  Flamingo Pink, Oriole Orange
Baby escarole
Baby frisée leaves: Green Curled
  Ruffec, Tres Fin Maraichere
Green chicory leaves:
  Puntarelle, Sugarloaf
Radicchio: Palla Rosa, Red Treviso,
  Variegata di Lusia
Buckhorn plantain leaves
Garlic chive leaves
Parsley flowers and leaflets:
  Curly and Italian Flatleaf
Pea shoots and flowers
Smallage leaves
Bronze fennel leaves
Calendula petals
Chervil leaves
Cilantro flowers
Society garlic leaves and flowers:
  Variegated and Green
Mashua flowers
White and blue borage flowers

PHOTO BY JIM COLEMAN.

The Daughter Gardens:
Cultivating Eco-Literacy
for Social Change

*The more clearly we can focus our attention on the
wonders and realities of the universe about us, the less
taste we shall have for destruction.*

—RACHEL CARSON[7]

While the OAEC site offers a model for the eco =
home ethos where ideas are put to the test, the ultimate goal of OAEC is to effect change on a larger
scale. The Mother Garden disseminates seeds, both
physical and inspirational, to daughter gardens
throughout California. Plant sales, seed exchanges,
School Garden Teacher Trainings, internships,
permaculture courses, and collaborations with
major food, farming, social, and ecological justice

organizations throughout the country are among the myriad ways that the Mother Garden shares her abundance.

The Nursery

The OAEC plant nursery is one of the few independently owned, California Certified Organic nurseries that grows all of its stock on-site. Plants for sale come directly from our vast seed bank and rooted cuttings from Mother Plants on display in the demonstration garden. From our collection, we've chosen the tastiest, most beautiful, most interesting or rare, and most regionally appropriate varieties to offer the public with these specific goals in mind: We're interested in promoting personal and regional food security by offering as many perennial food crops and culinary herbs as we can. These include food crops that have been important to peoples throughout the world and throughout history and have potential as valuable and nutritious foods for us to grow in our local Bay Area climate. We believe in the healing and health-promoting power of plants, so in addition to healthy food crops, we offer a wide array of medicinal herbs as well. We encourage the practice of permaculture by offering plants appropriate to its designs and applications, such as drought-tolerant landscaping plants, natives and habitat-friendly plants that attract beneficial insects for pollination and pest management.

As the little babies leave the nursery and proliferate into gardens throughout our area, there is immense satisfaction in sharing them with our neighbors. Whatever plants are not sold are either replanted in the Mother Garden or given away to schools and other community-based gardening projects. The OAEC Nursery gives away around $5,000 worth of plants every year.

Edible landscaping covers every square inch of land surrounding Food for Thought, the Sonoma County AIDS Food Bank, established in the late 1990s as one of the first "Daughter Gardens." With ongoing support from OAEC, the garden provides clients with organically grown vegetables, herbs, fruit, and fresh flowers and offers a gathering place for education, connection, and healing. PHOTO BY DOUG GOSLING.

Training Change Makers

We believe that showing people how to restore land begins with transformational experiences that allow them to "re-story" their connection to it. When humans rediscover our reciprocal relationship with the earth—that we are part of ecosystems, not separate—we become inspired to help create more regenerative systems. The center's educational opportunities promote this paradigm shift and the practical tools to translate it into action.

How do we decide whom to train? The local community? Whoever shows up? Only the most powerful? The most disenfranchised? Through an arch of experimentation and analysis, we think we've landed on the recipe for success: Bring together teams of individuals that represent their home communities, then connect them to larger networks into an effective "trans-local" web. This home team, supported by diverse webs of connection, sets the stage to make eco-literacy accessible to all and its expressions long lasting.

Empowering Whole Communities

In the face of a global ecological crisis, we see an opportunity for place-based communities to thrive and unite. Change happens fastest at the regional scale; that's why we form strategic partnerships with community leaders—from tribal citizens to teachers to urban activists—and empower them to integrate an ecological consciousness into their communities.

The Movement Generation Justice & Ecology Project, in collaboration with OAEC, brings together Bay Area racial, economic, and social justice organizers to address the impacts of global environmental problems on urban low-income communities and communities of color. The flagship program of Movement Generation is a series of transformative retreats held at OAEC with the goal of connecting urban communities back to the land and to the earth.

The Democratic Arts

Over the years, we have had the privilege to be part of a growing movement of people forming

Since 1998, OAEC's nationally recognized School Garden Teacher Training Program has trained and supported over 800 teachers, helping to establish gardens in more than 275 schools in Northern California and beyond. The program uses a team-based approach to mobilize teachers, parents, and administrators to infuse garden-based education into their school campuses and curricula. Over 75,000 students directly benefit from these programs annually. PHOTO BY JIM COLEMAN.

intentional communities or introducing consensus-based participatory democracy to their civic groups and organizations. As part of our efforts to support others on the same path, we founded the Intentional Communities Program and offered intensive workshops on group process and effective meeting facilitation. In these courses, we made our experiment transparent and crafted a curriculum that allowed others to learn from our mistakes as well as our successes. We have tried to articulate the many questions communitarians need to ask

All peoples, no matter where they are now, were once land-based peoples. As such, all of our cultural traditions carry kernels of wisdom rooted in this experience—one of deep linkage to place, land, and the stories and traditions that are born out of this experience. This exploration is critical, especially for city-based organizers, as it stands to challenge one of the dominant "control mythologies" of our industrial culture—that humans are separate from nature. . . . One of the most powerful instruments of oppression has been to tear people away from the land . . . The Movement Generation trainings are a space for people to reconnect to some of the basic resources we once knew how to use to provide for our own needs.

—MOVEMENT GENERATION COLLECTIVE, *Justice and Ecology Project*

Movement Generation hosts "Permaculture for the People" and a series of Earth Skills trainings to empower urban community organizers with practical tools to weather the impacts of the ecological crises. PHOTO BY JIM COLEMAN.

and answer and to explore deeply what is involved when a group of like-minded people collaborate deeply to turn a shared vision into reality. We have since welcomed over 500 participants to complete courses in the democratic arts.

Changing the Rules

Legalize sustainability! Our goal is to inject resilient systems thinking into governance and economy. The challenge is to shift our culture's paradigm of progress = profits to a new framework based on cooperation and on a reverence for all life in the hope that laws and infrastructure supporting biological and cultural diversity will follow. OAEC has worked to change the rules through projects and partnerships such as the Wild Farm Alliance, Cal-CAN, Bring Back the Beaver Campaign, among many others. The center's program trajectory is building increased advocacy work in the coming years.

Seasonality in the Age of Climate Change

The choice of crops you are able to grow at a given time in your garden is obviously based on where you live, but increasingly, seasonality is also changing as a function of larger trends in the earth's weather patterns. In the years leading up to the production of this book, we have observed changes in the Mother Garden's seasonal cycles that we had previously taken for granted as normal. A wealth of current scientific studies, such as the California EPA's 2013 update on the "Indicators of Climate Change in California,"[8] are documenting significant evidence of change afoot. Meanwhile, OAEC ecologists have been tracking rainfall and harvest records for 20 years and are seeing signs of some unexpected climate curveballs here in our own backyard.

This rain year in California has been one of the worst droughts in recorded California history. In the early years here, rain came down gently and steadily from October through May, yet in recent years, we've seen a trend toward the extremes—long dry spells followed by torrential downpours that tend to cause flash flooding and erosion rather than slowly sinking into the water table. While the installation of a storm-water swale system has mitigated some of the pressure, our well for potable water is taking longer than ever to recharge.

We've always enjoyed a short but pleasant burst of sunshine at the end of January, but each year, these midwinter heat waves have become longer and hotter, causing the fruit trees to bloom up to a month ahead of schedule. Last-frost dates have crept steadily earlier, reducing the number of "chill hours" required for many pome and stone fruit trees to remain productive. The Epargne pears were harvested two weeks early this year. To keep up with the changing times, our Spring Plant Sale event—historically held on Mother's Day in May—has now been moved up to April!

As any farmer will tell you, there have always been and always will be natural variations in weather from year to year to keep us on our toes in the garden and orchard. In geologic time, 20 years is but a blink of the earth's eye and cannot serve as a basis for serious scientific trend prediction. And yet, folk-based observations are what guided agricultural knowledge for millennia, so we can't help but take notice.

This is all to say that the seasonal references in this cookbook may not stand the test of time. Global "weirding" is already affecting the way we all farm and the way we eat. An optimist might say that if we continue to observe the trends as closely as our agrarian forbearers did, stay flexible and responsive to changes, and reduce our consumption by using our limited resources more wisely, we could hope to be growing avocados here in a few years! Yet while the gardens of OAEC—with its incredible biodiversity, relative water security, rich organic soils, and surrounding wildlife habitat (plus an embarrassing overabundance of optimism)—are resilient and adaptable to climate impacts, this is not true for much of California's agriculture system.

The stakes are high for farmers, and the impacts of climate change are already being felt in the form of reduced crop yields. Though California's farmers and ranchers are adept at dealing with variability in weather and access to natural resources, the speed and scale of the changes threaten to compound their challenges and put the state's $43 billion agricultural economy and the country's food security at risk.

In addition to needing to adapt to climate change, agriculture can also contribute climate solutions by lowering its greenhouse gas emissions and—uniquely—by removing carbon dioxide from the atmosphere and storing carbon in soil and woody plants. Some of the practices with the most promise for doing this include on-farm renewable energy production, improved water- and energy-use efficiency, use of cover crops and compost instead of synthetic nitrogen fertilizers, shifting to organic systems, grazing management practices, and more. The same practices that have climate benefits also often enhance the resilience of California farms and provide other environmental and health benefits such as clean air and water.

In 2009, OAEC cofounded a new coalition—the California Climate and Agriculture Network (CalCAN)—to advocate for policies that provide resources for farmers to transition to "climate-friendly" farming practices. CalCAN executive director (and former OAEC garden intern) Renata Brillinger says, "While it won't be easy, I see the climate crisis as an opportunity to transition to a truly resilient, ecologically based farming system that minimizes greenhouse gas emissions, sequesters carbon, contributes to cleaner air and water, provides wildlife habitat, and produces safe and healthy food."

By responding to the climate crisis with sustainable agricultural solutions, we have the opportunity to solve multiple environmental and health problems and safeguard the long-term viability of California's agricultural communities in the face of climate change to ensure food security in these unsure times.

For me, each painting is an adventure, a journey of discovery where images mysteriously emerge out of the process. My aim was not illustrative and I surprised myself with the imagery. In this time of upheaval and cataclysm we are all awed by what we see and hear about climate change. I think this crisis is the defining characteristic of our era and has had a profound impact on our individual and collective psyches. As this series took form, these paintings began to evoke visions of elemental upheaval and metamorphosis. As systems collapse and the incalculable powers latent within the natural world are unleashed, although we are engulfed by catastrophe, we are still surrounded by beauty.

—ADAM WOLPERT

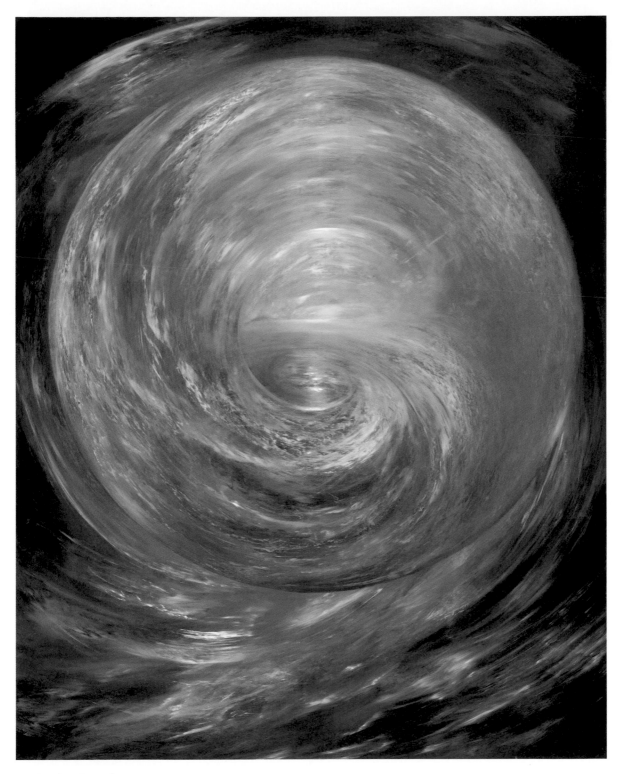

Singularity by Adam Wolpert.

WINTER
November 2 to February 1

In winter, the days shorten and the long-awaited slowdown begins. Workshops and visitor traffic tapers off. Residents celebrate the winter solstice with their immediate families, leaving the last two weeks of the year in the big communal kitchen as empty "Dark Nights." Ahhhh. Hibernation.

Winter is, in fact, a lush, verdant time in the Mother Garden. By the first of the year, the sun-baked hills of the previous harvest season have metamorphosed into a misty temperate rain forest as the grass, leaves, and moss wake up to take a drink. Once again, the landscape is saturated with every shade of brilliant green. Winter temperatures drop down to just below freezing about 8 or 10 nights per year, so while we do need to cover our citrus trees and other tender subtropical plants

with frost protection blankets, most garden plants bounce back quickly from occasional frost.

We stay grounded in winter with warming, nourishing foods. Our cozy old oven doubles as a heat source—cooks seize every opportunity to slow-roast or bake, chipping away at the basement full of winter squash and the glut of Andean root crops—mashua, oca, and yacon—coming out of the ground. Gophers and root maggots prevent us from growing large quantities of long-season root crops like celeriac, parsnips, rutabaga, and potatoes over the winter—but luckily, surrounding local farms are able to grow enough to tide us over until spring. Yet our winter diet is not always dominated by stereotypically starchy food and preserved goods from the larder—the mild climate blesses us with

Winter harvest. PHOTO BY JIM COLEMAN.

plenty of fresh food as well. Our winter salad plates are punctuated by fanciful compositions of chervil, mache, and violets. Cool wet weather means the sauté greens such as kale and our favorite tree collards are at the height of sweetness. We even have "tree tomatoes" and manzano peppers from our perennial Andean plants that set fruit in late fall and, with a little TLC, usually manage to hang on the bushes all winter.

Pears, apples, and kiwi from the South Garden are slowly pulled from storage in the walk-in cooler and enjoyed in solstice desserts. Both the medieval medlars and bright-orange Haichya persimmons dangle from frost-kissed trees like Christmas tree ornaments, bletting and softening to sweet, pudding-like consistencies. As on-site fruit production slows and homegrown stores are depleted, glorious citrus pours into the farmers' market from warmer farms around California—mandarins, Meyer lemons, and bright-pink cara-cara oranges.

A favorite winter ritual is to stay warm inside by the fire to clean seeds for the biodiversity collection. Garden volunteers unpack paper bags of dried seed-pods and crush them in their hands to release the seeds. The seeds and debris are sifted through fitted screens into large bowls or baskets and are then taken out on the porch for "winnowing"—blowing or fanning the chaff away from the seeds. Some are stashed away safely in the seed vault, and some are taken in January to the Ecological Farming Conference Seed Exchange to be given away and traded with other farmers throughout California.

As the rains come down, the Sowing Circle residents gather casually in the evenings around the kitchen hearth or in the wood-fired sauna in a time of sharing, resting, and planning for next year's cycle. Simultaneously, the OAEC staff delves deeply into a collective planning process, coming together in a series of self-governance meetings to make decisions as a group about the year to come. This downtime from the hustle and bustle is a critical moment in the yearly rhythm to focus on togetherness and collaborative visioning as the wheel of the calendar turns and starts all over again.

WINTER SOLSTICE
SALAD MIX

Winter salads at OAEC tend toward the succulent and perfumed. Crunchy butter lettuces and escaroles that manage to escape the frost provide structure to the winter mix. The leaves of cold-tolerant edible chrysanthemum, called shungiku, introduce a floral flavor note. With fewer ingredients to choose from, it's time to get creative—brussels sprouts are deconstructed, curly frisée is added to fluff up the volume, and the edge tips are removed from some fully grown leaves of red feather mustards. Variegated collards and Christmas Fringed Red ornamental kale add a neon streak of color to a sometimes gloomy time of year. Sweet violets and Johnny jump-ups garnish the finished mix with cool colors.

California winter salad begs for citrus—a mixed citrus dressing with cara-cara oranges, grapefruit, mandarin, and Meyer lemon (page 249) is just the thing to create a burst of freshness in midwinter.

PHOTO BY DOUG GOSLING.

WINTER GREENS MIX

Baby heirloom lettuces:
Akcel, Forellenschluss, Merlot,
Red Speckle, Pablo, Little Gem,
Lolla Rosa, Tom Thumb
Baby Escarole leaves
Green chicory leaves: Puntarelle,
Sugarloaf, Witloof
Frisée leaves: Green Curled Ruffec,
Tres Fin Maraichere
Radicchio: Palla Rosa, Red Treviso,
Variegata di Lusia
Brussels sprouts, deconstructed
Baby collard leaves: Morris
Heading, Variegated
Cress leaves: Wrinkly Crinkly
Curly, Wide-Leaved, Persian
Green mustard leaves:
Old-Fashioned Ragged Edge,
Golden Streaks, Golden Frills,
Southern Curled, Green Wave,
Suehlihung, Pizzo
Arugula leaves
Japanese red mustards: Osaka
Purple, Giant Red, Garnet, Red
Feather, Ruby Streaks, Scarlet
Frills, Purple Wave
Kale leaves: Redbor, Winterbor,
Dinosaur, Russian Red, Russian
White, Dinosaur, Frizzy, Scotch
Curled, Lacinato Rainbow
Sprouting broccoli leaves:
Purple, Spiagariello
Tatsoi leaves

Ornamental kale leaves: Christmas
Fringed Red and White
Pok Choi leaves: Yukina Savoy
Sylvetta arugula leaves
Mizuna leaves: Green and Purple
Baby Swiss chard leaves: Rainbow,
Golden, Rhubarb, Flamingo
Pink, Oriole Orange
Baby beet leaves: Chioggia, Bull's
Blood, Macgregor's Favorite,
Golden, Detroit Red
Mache rosettes: Verte de Cambrai,
Coquille des Louviers
Fava bean leaves and flowers
Pea shoots and flowers
Mallow leaves
Miner's lettuce leaves and flowers
Plantain leaves: Buckhorn, Wild
Red-veined dock leaves
Chickweed leaves and flowers
Shungiku leaves
French sorrel leaves
Smallage leaves
Parsley leaflets: Curly and
Italian Flatleaf
Chervil leaves
Cilantro leaves
Calendula petals
White and blue borage flowers
Wild radish flowers
Johnny jump-up flowers
Sweet violet leaves and flowers
Abutilon (flowering maple) flowers

PHOTO BY TALI AIONA.

FOUR

How to Use
This Cookbook

Most of the staff and resident cooks in the OAEC kitchen came to cooking through a combination of farming and communal living and have little to no formal culinary training. We take for granted our instinctual relationship to growing and cooking food, knowing from experience that *What grows together, goes together.* You could say we've acquired a high level of "vegetable literacy," as chef and author Deborah Madison calls it. Recipes are rarely used in the OAEC kitchen—not only is it extremely hard to find accurate recipes that are scaled up to feed a crowd, but we have mostly cooked by feel, improvising and teaching one another our tips and tricks, and collectively developing a style of treating vegetables rather than an actual body of hard-and-fast recipes. This is all to say that it was actually

Add to all of that our individual taste preferences and the quirks of the OAEC's big old oven and it becomes near impossible to say definitively how many minutes to cook things or how many teaspoons of salt, acid, sweetener, or fat to add. Hence, the measurements and cooking times in this book are mere suggestions somewhere in the middle of the spectrum. Start with a little, taste, and add more if you think it needs it. Or offer the tasting spoon up to the lips of a loved one and get a second opinion. Watch, smell, and nibble often and don't hesitate to go off script. Experimentation with curiosity, coupled with a willingness to fail occasionally, will inevitably lead to both confidence and satisfying culinary surprises.

Sound overwhelming? Don't worry. All you really need to remember is: salt, lemon, and olive oil. Seriously, that's it. With farm-fresh produce, *keep it simple* and you basically can't go wrong. Even if the wildness and unpredictability of nature jumps into your harvesting basket in the form of a moth-bitten apple or a stalk of bolted chard, fear not! Granted, it may take some creative knife skills to make gopher-nibbled carrots look good, but it's actually pretty easy to make them taste good. Through your experience cooking from the garden, you will develop a relationship to the plants and learn how their tastes, textures, and personalities change through the seasons.

quite a challenge to spell out in detail the types of decisions we make in the OAEC kitchen every day with out even thinking. But there are some tenets we do stand by in our kitchen, at least roughly.

Taste and Adjust

You will read these words so often in this book it will seem redundant, though this is part of the joy and art of seasonal cooking.

Fresh fruit, vegetables, and herbs vary drastically in strength and flavor depending on their varietal genetics, growing conditions, freshness, and the time of year. A sprig of woody marjoram foraged from a parched sunny slope in August will have a much spicier bite than the sweet green shoots snipped from a fertile garden bed in March. Kale grown in clay soil may need more salt than kale grown in sandy loam. A strawberry picked prematurely and shipped in a clamshell to sit refrigerated in a grocery store will need much more added sweetener than the one plucked warm from the sunny backyard container garden. A soup made with kabocha squash will need more emulsified oil than one made from naturally creamy red kuri. A thicker, older fennel bulb will take longer to roast than a young one. And so on.

Choose Quality Ingredients

In this book, you will find simple recipes that aim to showcase the inherent vitality and subtle character of fresh plant-based ingredients without losing them in a lot of hodgepodge. That said, the simplicity of these recipes means that they are

My daily cooking routine starts with a walk to the kitchen through the garden where I might encounter a luscious green patch of French sorrel that is screaming to be made into a sauce or stock flowers syrupy sweet in the air calling to be made into a salad dressing. This is where the magic is. This is what keeps me inspired to be a chef.

—GABRIEL TIRADANI, OAEC chef

only as good as their ingredients. Produce from the grocery store needs more dressing up than garden-fresh goods picked at the height of ripeness from your own backyard, local farmers' market, or CSA. If you don't have your own garden, buy (or trade for) the freshest, most ecologically and justly raised food you can afford, ideally from someone you know. We don't bother to mention "organic" before every ingredient, though we feel it is especially important to make sure your sugar, corn, and soy products are organic and thus GMO-free. See resources for more tips on avoiding pesticides and artificial food additives and for sourcing healthy ingredients that bring you closer to the land and to your neighbor.

Use Fresh Herbs

There are no two ways about it: Most of the recipes in this book rely on fresh herbs. Even if you do not have an extensive vegetable garden or orchard of your own, the most instantly gratifying entrée into growing your own food is to begin with a modest herb garden, whether it's the 2 x 2-foot patch of dirt by your front steps or even just a ceramic pot with a few basic herbs in the kitchen window of your apartment. Some grocery stores are even starting to sell pre-planted herb boxes—an encouraging trend! Most herbs like thyme, rosemary, mint, and even lemon verbena are rather indestructible—you don't need to have a particularly green thumb to keep them thriving. Having fresh herbs on hand is not only a convenient and nutritious way to liven up your cooking, but the two-way relationship that begins between you and your plants is part of the seasonal medicine.

Wash and Cut Produce with Intention and Care

In the recipe directions, we assume that you will wash your produce, and for the most part, we do not bother to mention this outright. In the OAEC kitchen, the gardening crew always gives the produce a good "field wash" at the outdoor sink to avoid dripping mud and unleashing nests of hiding earwigs into the kitchen. Then the cook washes the produce a second time, with the exception of delicate edible flowers and fragile berries, which don't get washed at all.

For some vegetables such as leeks and sauté greens, we tend to follow the chop-then-wash protocol since so much of the dirty part of vegetables gets cut off anyway—save water and put the dirt directly back into the compost rather than down the drain to clog your pipes. Wash the cut greens by submerging in a bin of water and lifting them out to drain—repeat with fresh water as necessary, giving the spent water to your patio herbs. Salad mix should also be washed this way and spun without overloading the spinner, which causes the leaves to bruise.

While we admit to using a commercial food processor for really big chopping jobs, if we have time, we prefer and recommend cutting produce by hand, even if it means getting more help from friends and making a party out of it. The most skilled cooks are the ones who know how to make the ingredients in a dish speak for themselves; chopping your vegetables by hand is a wonderful way get to know the character of the plant—it will let you know how it wants to be chopped.

Respect Ripeness

To know when something is ripe, you must pay attention and have patience. Just because you may be ready to eat that tomato or peach, it may not be ripe. Respecting ripeness is a practice that also applies to social change. Social, economic, and political conditions are often unripe for the change we so passionately desire today. Rather than act out of time, and harvest a sour or rotten fruit, we seek to prepare well and act when the moment is truly ripe.

This cookbook is organized by dish, but you'll see recipe listings at the beginning of each section separated by season, which of course reflects the placed-based reality of our coastal Northern California microclimate. We recognize that seasonality is completely relative—we consider fennel a spring crop, whereas in the Upper Midwest, fennel is only available in the late summer. The point here is not to import fennel from California to use in springtime, but to become curious and inspired by the unique varieties of produce that thrive in your own bioregion. We encourage you to take every liberty in substituting ingredients and switching around the seasons to fit your own growing conditions, above and beyond the suggestions given in this book.

Though some of the basic recipes may be housed in a particular season, many are adaptable to variations. Pesto, for example, is something that we eat almost every week all year round, not just in the summer when basil is coming in from the garden. While a purist may disagree, there are dozens of other herbs, wild and cultivated, that can be incorporated into a "pesto" and are fresh in spring, fall, and, for us, even winter.

We also recognize that seasonal cooking isn't just about the ingredients—the weather has a major influence on what we feel like eating and how we feel like cooking—we have an appetite for raw or simply steamed veggies in the summer and warmer, heartier renditions of some of those same ingredients in the winter.

As a general guideline, we will highlight our favorite version of a recipe that works especially well for us, give you a few ideas to get the creative juices flowing, and then invite you to run with the recipe and make it your own. It is our sincere hope that through this book, you will begin to use more and more of what you have available in your own bioregion because you can *taste* the difference. Follow the motto, *What grows together goes together*, and ultimately, you will hone your ability to coax the most flavor out of your ingredients at any given moment of the year.

Cooking from the garden means that we swing on a giant pendulum between glut and dearth. As the primary link between the kitchen and the garden, I try to inspire chefs and community cooks to stretch their creative muscles and enjoy the culinary challenge of using what the garden provides and to purchase as little as possible from elsewhere for the meals. Gophers unexpectedly chomped down the chard patch? No problem. We substitute New Zealand spinach or quinoa greens at the last minute. What? Another 200 pounds of zucchini? How do we make it taste good . . . again? Eating seasonally reminds us to enjoy the moment—to feel grateful for what we do have, rather than deprived about what we don't have. The spontaneity of incorporating what the garden gives us on any given day is often when the most deliciously imaginative creations happen.

—OLIVIA RATHBONE, *kitchen manager*

Even having worked as a chef at a "seasonal" restaurant, I had only seen vegetables delivered in boxes. In the OAEC garden, getting to know the structure and character of the plants before they are harvested, tasting different parts of the plants during various stages in their life cycle, and really understanding their place in the seasonal calendar gave me a whole new appreciation. I could see that, "Oh this beet is a root," and that then would inform how and when I would prepare it with so much more sensitivity and subtlety. I tend to cook a lot more simply now in order not to cover up this essential character of the vegetable. I also feel much more in touch with my own cycles, my own ups and downs, and I now know that eating is a central part of that. The way I'm responding to the weather each day and what I'm craving in the moment is all part of a cycle that is much bigger than me.

—RACHEL GARDNER, *Food for Thought Sonoma County AIDS Food Bank executive deputy director and client services manager, OAEC garden intern 1994, and Cooking from the Garden instructor*

How to Feed a Marching Band

It's volunteer day, there's a tour coming through, a resident's extended family is in town, and now what? The marching band is here to rehearse for the Chautauqua variety show?! While we always cook for a community, sometimes the numbers get really big. Thankfully, the loaves-and-fishes miracle seems to happen on a regular basis at OAEC, where we have become quite adept at making something out of nothing to feed the multitudes.

The key to not only feeding but actually impressing a crowd is to *create the illusion of abundance*, even if you don't actually have a lot of food. While there are some active people who can work up a real appetite, most of us—especially those of us with desk jobs—just need a taste to feel satiated. We are nourished more by the sensual experience of eating diverse, nutrient-dense, and lovingly prepared food than we are by stuffing ourselves with mass quantities. By creating a bountiful and celebratory atmosphere, people already begin to feel cared for, relaxed, and satisfied the minute they walk into the kitchen, rather than annoyed by having to wait in the buffet line.

Here are a few of tricks of the trade from professional caterers that can help home cooks not only satiate but also dazzle a crowd.

Create a Colorful and Lively Buffet Bar

We eat first with our eyes, so it cannot be understated that a visually appealing spread is our tactic sine qua non for wowing the masses. Even if the food itself is less than gorgeous, a carefully chosen tablecloth or serving bowl that contrasts the colors of the meal will work wonders. It goes without saying that fresh flowers are fabulous for painting a festive scene. We love to use our garden ingredients themselves as still-life decorations—for instance, that perfect mushroom that was just too beautiful to cut up or a bunch of herbs neatly arranged like flowers can pique the guests' interest in the delights that await them. Quirky party conversation starters can also add to the jovial ambience while people are waiting in line—mutant root vegetables with funny human-like arms and legs often show up perched on our buffet line, as do clever quotations and illustrations on the menu board.

Avoid Anything That Suggests "Institutional"

Cooking for a marching band does not mean that the hordes line up to feed at giant industrial troughs of gruel. Make eaters feel special; serve food on a platter, not right out of the hotel pan. Use pretty serving spoons instead of metal mixing spoons. Rather than mixing everything together in

Menu Planning

Here is the checklist of questions that we cooks at OAEC ask ourselves to guarantee a dynamite meal that covers all the bases:

- Is the meal colorful and beautiful?
- Are the flavor themes simple and fresh? Is the garden produce showcased?
- Is the meal nutritionally well balanced?
- Is the meal appropriate for the season and for the weather?
- Is the meal well suited to the group and the occasion?
- Have we had the same thing lately? Is there enough variety?
- Is the meal too complicated to pull off in terms of timing?
- Are costs being taken into consideration?
- Are dietary needs and allergies addressed?

A Balanced Meal

Every meal at OAEC includes a variety of dishes served buffet-style for communal eating, each of which offers a selection of lighter and heartier fare. They include:

- One or two garden vegetable dishes— usually a sauté green plus one more colorful veggie—the more colors, the more nutrition
- One protein dish—beans, nuts, seeds, eggs, dairy, occasional meat
- One carbohydrate—whole grain or root vegetable (note: Nutritionally speaking, root vegetables are starches, not "vegetables")
- Usually a side of pesto, spread, sauce, or kraut to bring the flavors together and add more trace nutrients
- OAEC salad with a light dressing
- Drinking water garnished with garden herbs or fruit
- Sometimes dessert, not more than twice a week

The menu board is a tradition at OAEC and usually includes a "from the garden" list. PHOTO BY TALI AIONA.

The significance of garnishing shouldn't be underestimated. It isn't about gratuitous ornamentation; it's an opportunity to amplify or complement the tastes of the dish—think lemon balm leaves on a citrus salad, pineapple sage with many other kinds of fruit, cucumber-like blue borage flowers on a summer green salad or gazpacho. A garnish also might "educate" about or comment on the ingredients of a dish, especially if they have been obscured by processing: fresh Opal or Genovese basil leaves on a pesto, whole chervil leaves on a cream of chervil soup, whole epazote leaves on a bean dish that contains it, or apple leaves (or even blossoms, if you can find them at the same time) on an apple tarte tatin.

I find that plants in the same family have complementary and related tastes. For example, rose petals are a beautiful and perfumy garnish for anything in the rose family: strawberries, loquats, blackberries, raspberries, peaches, or plums. Sometimes, the garden itself has suggested unexpected pairings that go well together. We have a particularly robust and happy lovage plant that volunteered in the middle of our raspberry patch, and often while harvesting berries, I nibble on the lovage at the same time—the combination of the two is a revelation! I've since minced a few lovage leaves on fresh raspberries to the delight of the eaters.

—Doug Gosling

one big pot, make separate smaller dishes that will eventually mix together on the plate. Now, there is a time and place for the single gigantic cauldron approach, which can be very effective at conserving dishes and filling up the bellies of truly hungry people in a pinch. But if you have time or can prep ahead, going the extra mile to make individualized servings where everyone gets a distinct little "something" like a hand-rolled dolma or empanada, a fritter that has been pre-topped with fixings, or even a simple whole baked potato, makes people feel like more than just another cow in the herd.

Garnish!

Whether you're cooking a large meal from scratch or reheating a pot of leftovers, the copious addition of garden-fresh herbs is the key to making food sparkle with vitality. Just about any dish can be livened up in visual appeal, taste, and digestibility by a liberal scattering of freshly chopped parsley or whatever you might have on hand. Edible flowers add another luxurious touch to otherwise boring bulk dishes. We can't recommend strongly enough planting your own herb garden or planter box—our plot of fresh

herbs and edible flowers is planted right outside the kitchen for quick and easy last-minute access.

Subliminally Manage Portion Control with Utensils and Plates

Without posting a physical person on the buffet line to dish out individual servings, you can still make it easy for people to self-regulate while stretching your food dollar at the same time. It's textbook reverse psychology—a small plate or spoon that is mounded high is somehow more gratifying than a big plate or spoon that is half empty. So, use generously large serving scoops for the plentiful dishes and tiny teaspoons or tongs for the more precious items. Worried that you don't have enough soup to go around? Put out mugs rather than bowls, or vice versa if you want people to fill up on soup. We have tiny ramekins that we sometimes put out for the self-serve dessert, rather than larger bowls begging to be filled to the brim.

Be Strategic with Layout and Signage

When eating buffet-style from the garden, there is really no such thing as a main dish, side dish, appetizer, and so on. Whatever we have the most of *is* the main dish!

People tend to fill up their plate with whatever they see first on the buffet line. So put the most abundant, cheapest, and/or most filling dish first, such as a bulk grain or perhaps the surplus zucchini dish that you really want to use up. Deemphasize your higher-end items or anything you are worried about running out of by putting it last on the bar. If you are really running low on something, as a last-ditch resort, post a sign that politely suggests, PLEASE TAKE JUST ONE TO START. COME BACK FOR SECONDS LATER.

Reinvent Leftovers

Again, having a garden full of perennial food plants close to the kitchen comes in handy, especially in a pinch when there is no time to run to the store—having a fresh supply of herbs and greens at our disposal allows for endless opportunities for revitalizing leftovers.

Food safety reminder: Be sure to reheat leftovers thoroughly (above 165°F) to ensure that any unwanted bacteria get zapped. Only reuse leftovers once—after a dish has been reheated or reincorporated into another dish, that's the last hoorah. Composting your kitchen scraps and spent leftovers helps to mitigate the guilt of throwing food away. Don't fret—the microbes, chickens, and worms will love to facilitate their next reincarnation.

On Bulk Measurements

We have attempted to standardize the format of these recipes to feed 4 to 6 people family-style as well as scaled up to feed a large gathering of 30 to 40. As anyone who has ever cooked for a crowd will tell you, large scale does not always mean that you simply do the math. Garlic, for example, does not typically need to be multiplied as many times as the other ingredients. Baking soda acts peculiarly when multiplied. That said, the *Taste and Adjust* rule still applies.

In most recipes, we will list the ingredient quantities for small and large batches separately or occasionally refer to the large-batch quantities in parenthesis. The methods will be combined, with special instructions for the large crowd noted where relevant.

This format works well for bulk savory dishes, but can become awkward, especially when baking. For example, some cakes and desserts do not set properly in the middle if scaled up to a large sheet pan size. Tart pans don't come in extra large, and besides, we don't own a giant industrial dough mixer, so instead we often make multiple smaller batches of some baked goods.

For ease of scaling up or down with drinks, it's often more useful for bartenders to know the proportions per drink versus per pitcher, rather than 4-to-6 people versus 30-to-40. Don't worry, we will coach you on how many pitchers to make for your party.

As for preserves and condiments that are meant to be stored, like Mother Garden Bitters (page 322), we include measurements that make sense for that number of people to use up in a year. For example, the Preserved Meyer Lemon recipe (page 293) makes 1 quart for the small batch—a year's supply for a small family of four to six. The large batch makes a gallon, a nice round number that's enough to last us a year here at the retreat center or—for the lucky owner of a backyard lemon tree—enough to give away as presents.

In conclusion, if we deviate from the standard 4-to-6 or 30-to-40 format, we will let you know how many multiples to make as well as any tips or tricks for serving the dish to a crowd. While they may not be completely uniform, our intention is to give measurements in the most handy and intuitive ratios that will give you the highest success rate.

Tools of the Trade

The food at OAEC would not be what it is without a few of our favorite essential tools that can make cooking for a crowd possible. Some may seem unfamiliar if you're used to a regular home-scale kitchen, but they can come in very handy when cooking for a big dinner party.

Large Pots and Pans

If you are a novice at large-scale cooking, the first and most important step toward getting comfortable with quantity is having the right-sized cooking vessels. In this book, we will indicate the precise size of pot, sheet pan, and so on whenever possible, though this may be confusing in the methods section where we describe both small- and large-scale versions simultaneously. When we say a "medium" pot, a medium pot on a home scale would be about 4 quarts. For a large scale, a medium pot is more like 10 quarts. A large stockpot for home use is 8 to 12 quarts, whereas a large commercial stockpot is 18 to 24 quarts. A home scale 18 x 13-inch sheet pan is considered just a half sheet pan in commercial terms. In the OAEC kitchen, we use mainly three-quarter sheet pans (21 x 16 inches) and full sheet pans (26 x 18 inches), which are too big to fit into most home ovens. Likewise, a home-scale baking pan is 2½ inches deep by 9 x 9 or 9 x 13, whereas a commercial-sized baking pan—often referred to as a hotel pan or an entrée pan—is 2½ x 21 x 13 inches. If you don't have access to large pots and pans, it is preferable to work in smaller, sequential batches.

Vitamix Blender

A must-have tool for us is the almighty Vitamix, an industrial-strength juice blender so powerful

OUR FAVORITE MENUS INCORPORATING LEFTOVERS

All the meals in this book can more or less feed a crowd, but here are a few of our favorite menus that do it cheaply and calmly under pressure with the versatile reincorporation of leftovers.

Baked Potato or Sweet Potato Bar with Chili and Greens

We almost always have some chili in the freezer. Otherwise we use spiced-up leftover beans, grated cheese or a quick cheese sauce, steamed garden brassica shoots or greens, sour cream, chopped parsley and scallions, and whatever pesto, herb butter, sauce, or fun condiments we have waiting in the wings of the fridge.

Shakshuka (page 231)

You can poach eggs in just about any type of sauce or stew imaginable. Serve this standby with an inexpensive bulk grain such as Millet with Toasted Cumin Seeds (page 232), garlic bread, or simple roasted potatoes.

Frittata (page 202)

Slip odds and ends from the fridge into a protein-rich, no-fuss frittata. Leftover roasted veggies or potatoes, sautéed greens, grated cheese, fresh herbs, tapenades, and pestos all feel at home in there.

Blended Soup or Puree

Run yesterday's roasted veggies through the blender with a little stock and *presto*! Heat up and top with fresh herbs or a dollop of pesto, sour cream, or herb butter and you're golden.

that it could pulverize wood into sawdust. Its never-fail motor and well-designed blades puree and emulsify just about anything—from chunks of frozen fruit to nuts to solid raw vegetables—into a silky texture like no home-scale blender can. It comes with a pounding baton that allows you to safely push the contents all the way down without touching the blade. You can use a home-scale

A Buying/Harvesting Guide for Planning a Gathering for 30 to 40 Guests

This list is a good starting point for eyeballing how many cases of produce and other ingredients to harvest or preorder from your farmer or local grocer. We've listed how many pounds you'll typically need for the main ingredient in any given dish, but cross-check with the recipe and menu for specifics. The crowd, the occasion, and the time of day can also move the toggles from this baseline. In the Mother Garden, we use standard-sized 20 × 15 × 7-inch restaurant supply bus tubs to measure harvesting volume.

Produce

Root vegetables, like carrots, beets, parsnips: Around 15–20 pounds loose roots, tops removed or 15–20 bunches with tops.

Juicy vegetables such as cucumbers, tomatoes, zucchini: 20 pounds. For the best flavor, store tomatoes unrefrigerated.

Green beans, peas, broccoli, cauliflower, eggplant, or peppers: 12–15 pounds or roughly three-quarters of a packed bus tub.

Salad mix: 3 pounds, and make sure it's nice and fluffy. It usually comes in a 3-pound standard case, equivalent to one full bus tub in volume. Salad mix lasts only a few days in the fridge, so wait to harvest or buy this until the last possible minute.

Sauté greens and cabbage: 6–10 pounds = 15–20 bunches of greens or 4–5 medium-sized heads of cabbage. Envision about two full-packed bus tubs of raw greens cooking down.

Onions and garlic: Check the recipe, but we like to keep approximately 3 pounds of onions and 2 heads of garlic on hand for each meal, just in case—they keep for a long time unrefrigerated, so better to stock up.

Fresh herbs: 1–3 large bunches per dish per meal, depending on the recipe.

Fruit: 20 pounds of pome/stone fruit, or melon, or 8–10 pints of berries.

Starches

Potatoes and yams: ⅓ pound per person = around 12–15 pounds.

Most whole grains: A little less than 2 ounces or ¼ cup dry grain per person = about 4–6 pounds or 8–12 cups. White rice, millet, and quinoa use a 1:1¼ cooking ratio of grain to water. Brown, red, and wild rices use a 1:2 ratio.

Polenta: 1 ounce dry polenta per person = about 3 pounds or 4 cups dry. Polenta is made with a 1:4 ratio of corn to water.

Bread: 1–2 slices per person = 3 or 4 large, artisanal loaves or 6 baguettes.

Pasta: 2 ounces per person = around 5 pounds.

Protein

Eggs: 2 per person = around 6 dozen.

Cheese: 2 tablespoons or 2 ounces per person = 3 pounds total when used for melting or adding to other dishes, more if served alone as part of a cheese plate.

Beans: Less than ¼ cup dry beans per person = about 4 pounds or 8 cups dry.

Seeds, nuts, and nut butters: 2 tablespoons or 2 ounces per person = about 3 pounds, depending on the recipe.

Tofu or tempeh: 3 ounces per serving = about 5–6 pounds.

Meat: 4 ounces per person = about 9 pounds lean and boneless, more for bone-in cuts, less if it will be cooked with other ingredients as part of a stew, casserole, or dish.

blender or a food processor where our recipes call for the high-powered blenders, but be prepared for disappointment—you will miss the velvety ultra-creaminess that only the Vitamix can deliver. Sorry to sound like a commercial here. We realize that this is an expensive item (a new one sells for around $400, though it will last forever) and debated about using it so ubiquitously throughout the book, but in order to represent our large-scale recipes accurately, we have to be honest—we can't live without this thing.

And/Or Immersion Blender

Actually, the most cost-effective substitute for the Vitamix is an immersion blender or immersion wand fitted inside a large glass jar or similar narrow, tall-walled container. While you won't get the same lush uniformity, you can still maneuver it and lean your weight into it so as to incorporate the stubborn bits that a regular blender would refuse to bite.

Quart-Sized Canning Jars and Gallon-Sized Storage Jars

Canning jars are often referred to interchangeably by their brand names: Ball jars or Mason jars. In addition to committing to sensory memory the quantity of your own hand for measuring, knowing the Ball jar in various sizes—but especially the

quart size—allows you to intuitively eyeball quantities and scale up and down. All-in-one measuring cup, blender pitcher, serving vessel, to-go mug, fermentation crock, sprouting jar, food storage container, flower vase . . . need we say more? The gallon-sized storage jars, while not appropriate for hot food, come in handy for many of the same reasons when scaled up to feed 30 to 40 people.

Cast-Iron Skillet or Griddle

We love cooking with cast iron. Over time, a well-cared-for cast-iron pan builds up a natural nonstick surface, adds trace amounts of iron to the diet, and—most important—imparts a soulful authenticity, as chef Gabriel Tiradani calls it, a "flavor ghost" to the food. Our flat-top cast-iron griddle allows us a large surface area on which to sauté or sear large quantities of greens, pancakes, or whatever in one go, though you can use a wide cast-iron skillet instead. To protect the seasoning, don't use soap or cook acidic foods such as tomato sauces in your cast-iron pan or allow it to remain wet for more than a few minutes—these will all cause your pan to rust. Gently clean it with a nonmetal scrubber to prevent gouging the seasoned surface. Rinse and dry on low heat on the stovetop. Wipe inside and out with a thin, even coating of saturated (solid at room temperature) fat after every use.

Spider

The spider is a woven-wire mesh ladle often used in Asian cooking that is particularly handy for blanching. You can substitute a wide-mesh strainer with a handle or a large slotted spoon.

Garlic Press

Most of us prefer to crush garlic cloves through a garlic press, pound in a mortar and pestle, or grate them finely with a microplaner (below) rather than mincing them with a knife, which lets all the juices soak into the cutting board instead of into the food. Also, minced garlic tends to burn into crispy chunks rather than infuse uniformly throughout a dish. When you see "garlic, crushed," this is what we mean.

Microplane Zester

This is a woodworking-tool-turned-indispensable-kitchen-gadget, a superfine grater for hard cheeses, garlic, ginger, and citrus zest. You can substitute the finest scales on a four-sided cheese grater.

Mandoline

This inexpensive tool cuts uniformly paper thin slices—great for gratins, slaws, and stir-fries. Careful of your fingers!

On Oils

Throughout the course of OAEC's lifetime, there has been a tide of debate about the health benefits and risks of various types of oils. Once upon a time, "fat-free" was all the rage. Next, saturated fats were bad and unsaturated fats were good. Now comes the predictable backlash. The latest theory is that cooking unsaturated fats denatures them, releasing free radicals, and so saturated fats are back in style. It's hard to keep up. Can we turn to traditional cultures for guidance? The Inuit practically survive on whale blubber alone. The Japanese eat very little fat at all. Italians have been cooking with olive oil for centuries. How do we distinguish a marketing trend from scientific fact from age-old food wisdom?

In an effort to avoid seeming dated once the next trend rolls around after this book is printed, we are taking a neutral stance on oil in most of our recipes—we may suggest a specific oil or simply state "cooking oil" and leave it up to you to decide which one feels right for you. We don't carry corn or canola oil in our kitchen mostly because even organic corn and canola oils tend to be of low quality and questionable purity. Sunflower, safflower, grape seed, avocado, and rice oils are unsaturated fats that are neutral in flavor, though they are highly refined, for better or worse, to withstand high heat. We carry both plain sesame oil for cooking and toasted sesame for raw drizzling. Cold expeller-pressed olive oil is the least refined of the unsaturated oils, but imparts a distinct grassy flavor that may or may not be desired and does scorch at medium-high heat—we usually reserve olive oil for raw applications, though many of us do not shy away from cooking with it once in a while. Some swear by good old-fashioned butter, though it does scorch at medium heat and should be avoided for those who are lactose-intolerant. Others are devoted to luxurious ghee, a nutty-flavored clarified butter that is exquisite for cooking, but prohibitively expensive. Then there is coconut oil, a saturated fat that doesn't scorch, but the assertive flavor can be overpowering—plus it's a tropical import that those who are moving toward a locally based diet tend to avoid. Of course, if you are a meat eater, feel free to substitute bacon grease or duck fat, as you see fit. Anyway, the list of pros and cons goes on and on ad nauseam. You do the research and decide for yourself.

Special Diets

We've had a string of diet requests a mile long made through the years—raw, paleo, diabetic, serious anaphylactic-shock-level allergies, dislikes masquerading as allergies, against-my-religion vegan, sugar-lactose-gluten-salt-nightshade-allium-soy-grain-free—you name it and we've tried our best to accommodate it. The most memorable was a "fruitarian" who would eat a whole 10-pound watermelon by himself in one sitting!

Even the vegetarianism practiced in our own kitchen has become largely passé with a conscientious new generation of farmers humanely and ecologically raising local meat. Whether the choice of diet is motivated by a health condition or a philosophical stance, our job as communitarians holding the sacred space of the hearth is to honor everyone's food choices magnanimously. We alienate no one yet set firm boundaries on what demands can reasonably be asked of the cook and of our infrastructure and budget. We empower people to self-regulate and have a sense of humor about our own idiosyncrasies and paradoxes. In a nutshell, we try to make most of the people happy most of the time. This is no small task.

We would like to think that there is a little something for everyone in this book. Some of the recipes happen to be *insert-your-pet-prohibition-free*, but we include them because they are good, not necessarily because they are in line with a certain dietary regime. Read the fine print—we won't advertise "soy-free," for example, even though the recipe very well may be. There are plenty of raw, vegan menus simply by virtue of the fact that we serve simply prepared, garden-fresh veggies with every meal, though we also recognize that most of the world's population doesn't have the appetite for (or—perhaps better stated—the luxury of) eating nearly as many fruits and vegetables as the quantities we've come to expect here in Northern California. There are sugar-free recipes appropriate for diabetics and those wishing to kick the sugar habit, such as the surprisingly healthy Stevia Lemon Curd (page 367). And for those who want fully decadent, artery-clogging, pancreas-corroding treats and cocktails—we've got a little something for you, too.

This is not a book on nutrition, but rather a book about putting the *culture* back into agriculture. Beyond reductionist theories about calories and food groups, stepping outside and developing a holistic relationship with the land and all the plants, animals, and microbes that feed us inevitably leads to a deeper sensation in the body of real nourishment, and is the most direct path to a healthy way of life.

FOOD BLESSING

Provided courtesy of the Federated Indians of Graton Rancheria, Southern Pomo-Coast Miwok

PHOTO BY TALI AIONA.

Tuun Wee'a Food Prayer

'Ow,

Ma molis nis weya,
We are grateful for this world,

Ma molis hii,
We are grateful for the sun,

Ma molis is liwaako,
We are grateful for the waters,

Ma molis nis tuu.
We are grateful for this food.

'Ow.

PART TWO
RECIPES

PHOTO BY TALI AIONA.

RECIPE LIST

Carrot Chamomile Soup

A strong chamomile tea is used here instead of stock as a complement to sweet fresh carrots. True comfort food. Don't serve this soup for lunch, however, unless you plan time for a nap! We recently served it at the midday meal during Michelle Vesser's Healing Through Food, Herbs and Gardening. In the middle of our afternoon work party while digging in the soil right near the bed of chamomile, a spell came over us—we all dropped our shovels and lay down in the garden paths, dazed (from the word *daisy*—chamomile is part of the daisy family) by the lazy sunshine of the afternoon. As if hypnotized by garden angels, one participant picked up her instrument and began serenading us into a blissful impromptu siesta!

Serves 4–6

5 cups water

1 cup dry chamomile flowers, 1½ cups fresh flowers, or 10 organic tea bags

3 cups peeled and roughly chopped carrots (about 6 large carrots)

⅓ cup olive oil

1 teaspoon honey or to taste (optional)

Pinch of salt to taste

Serves 30–40

8 quarts water

4 cups dry chamomile flowers, 6 cups fresh flowers, or 40 tea bags

5 quarts peeled and roughly chopped carrots (about 30 large carrots)

2 cups olive oil

⅓ cup honey or to taste (optional)

1 tablespoon salt or to taste

Boil the water in a medium-sized pot, turn off the heat, add the chamomile, and let steep 10 to 15 minutes. Do not boil the chamomile; it will become bitter. Meanwhile, prep the carrots—it's important to peel them, or the flavor gets muddy and the chamomile taste doesn't come through. Strain the tea into a large stockpot and discard the chamomile. Add the carrots to the pot and return the liquid to a simmer until the carrots are soft, about 10 minutes. Blend the carrots and tea together either with an immersion wand or in a blender. When the puree is very smooth, add the oil in a thin stream while continuing to blend. Taste for salt and sweetness and adjust accordingly. If the carrots are really fresh and sweet, you shouldn't need to add much honey, if any. Garnish with fresh chamomile flowers, calendula petals, or chopped herbs.

PHOTO BY TALI AIONA.

OAEC's Basic Veggie Stock

The key to making a vegetable stock that holds up to a meat stock in richness and *umami* is remembering to include a dash of that magical carrier of flavor missing in most vegetables—fat. Feel free to toss in whatever other veggie scraps you are trying to use up, but make sure not to add anything from the cabbage family (broccoli, cauliflower, kale, turnip . . .), as these will give the stock a sulfury smell and the stock will not last as long in the refrigerator. Likewise, avoid starchy vegetables such as potatoes, as they will make for a cloudy stock (they're okay, though, for a creamy soup). Everything else, including most herbs and whole (not ground) spices, are fair game for improvisation, depending on how the stock will be used. Start with this simple base recipe, a roasted stock (see the following recipe), and variations. They contain very little salt so they can be seasoned further when incorporated into a recipe.

This quick veggie stock is a versatile standby that requires minimal effort. Throw in the garlic cloves skins and all—we like to use the little ones at the center of the head that are too annoying to bother peeling. If you have room, keep a bin or bag in the freezer for collecting veggie scraps such as parsley stems or leek tops for making stock when you have more time.

Also: Save propane! Vegetable stocks do not benefit from hours of cooking like meat stocks—once the veggies have given their color, flavor, and life force over to the broth, there is nothing left to coax out of them. Boil the stock for 20 minutes, then cover it, turn off the heat, and let it steep for 20 more minutes.

Serves 4–6

MAKES 8 CUPS

4 cloves garlic, smashed

2 onions, quartered

2 tablespoons oil

¼ cup dry white wine

3 carrots, rough cut (about 1½ cups)

4 celery or 2 lovage stalks, rough cut,
    leaves and all

2 tablespoons whole black peppercorns

3 fresh or dry bay leaves

1–3 cups seasonal veggie scraps (see variations)

9 cups water

Serves 30–40

MAKES 13 QUARTS

1 head garlic, smashed

6 onions, quartered

1 cup oil

1 cup dry white wine

12–14 carrots, rough cut (about 8 cups)

1 head celery or 4 lovage stalks, rough cut,
    leaves and all

½ cup whole black peppercorns

12 fresh or dry bay leaves

2 quarts assorted seasonal veggie scraps
    (see variations)

12 quarts water

In a large stockpot, sauté the smashed garlic cloves and rough quartered onions in the oil on medium-high heat until they become translucent. Add the rest of the vegetables and spices and cook until the onions become somewhat caramelized. Deglaze the pan by adding the wine and stirring to loosen the browned bits from the bottom of the pan; allow the liquid to reduce a bit. Finally, add the water. Bring to a boil on high, reduce the heat, and simmer for 20 minutes. Cover the pot, turn off the heat, and let steep for 20 more minutes. Allow it to settle, then strain it through a fine sieve. Discard the spent veggies and any sludgy sediment at the bottom of the pot. This stock can be frozen or stored in the fridge for up to a week.

Roasted Vegetable Stock

A richer but more time-consuming stock, worth the extra effort!

Serves 4–6

MAKES 8 CUPS

1 medium onion, quartered

2 medium-sized carrots, rough cut

1½ cups seasonal vegetables
   (see variations)

1 tablespoon oil

¼ teaspoon salt

½ cup sherry or white wine

2 tablespoons dried mushrooms

9 cups water

Serves 30–40

MAKES 13 QUARTS

6 onions, quartered (about 4 cups)

14 carrots, rough cut (about 8 cups)

2½ quarts seasonal vegetables
   (see variations)

¼ cup oil

1¼ teaspoons salt

1½ cups sherry or white wine

½ cup dried mushrooms

12 quarts water

Preheat the oven to 400°F. Toss all the cut vegetables in the oil, sprinkle with salt, and roast in the oven for about 30 minutes. When the vegetables are soft and golden brown, deglaze the pan with the sherry and empty the contents of the pan into a stockpot along with the dried mushrooms. Cover with water, bring to a boil, and simmer for 30 minutes. Let cool slightly and strain through a very fine sieve.

VARIATIONS

Spring: Asparagus ends from when you trim the spears, leek tops, fennel tops (not too many), green garlic, parsley stems, shelling pea pods, nettles, or spinach.

Summer: Quartered red bell pepper, tomato shoulders, basil, marjoram, or cilantro stems, corncobs, green bean tops and tails.

Fall: Celery root tops and scrubbed peels, parsnip, salsify, thyme, or rosemary twigs, carrot peels.

Winter: Mushroom stems, parsnip and burdock root, small amounts of warming spices such as clove.

Spring Hot Pot Soup with Shungiku

This adaptation invokes the communal spirit of the Japanese *nakemono*, a large shared pot of broth and noodles where each person adds his or her own accompaniments from an array of artfully prepared seasonal raw and par-cooked vegetables. The act of adding fresh ingredients that cook down instantly when added to the hot broth in the bowl involves the eater in a magical step in the cooking process. In the moment of alchemy where the raw life force of the vegetable is transformed before our eyes, we are connected at once to the ephemeral nature of vitality and life itself. For more info on shungiku, see page 154.

Serves 4–6

1 cup raw shungiku leaves or other flavorful baby greens, such as mizuna or baby frilly mustards

1 cup carrot (about 1 carrot) shaved into long, thin ribbons with a mandoline or carrot peeler

1 cup 2-inch-diagonal-cut snow peas and/or asparagus spears

¼ cup chopped mitsuba or parsley

¼ cup thinly sliced scallions or chives

3 tablespoons toasted sesame seeds and/or Seaweed "Bacon Bits" (page 297)

6 ounces rice noodles

BROTH

6 cups OAEC Basic or Roasted Veggie Stock (pages 92 and 93)

¼ cup minced ginger

2 tablespoons minced garlic

3 tablespoons sesame oil

¼ cup miso

3 tablespoons mirin or dry white wine

1 tablespoon rice vinegar

Tamari to taste

Pluck the shungiku from the stems. Leave baby greens whole or chop any large leaves into thin strips. Prepare the raw vegetables, herbs, and seeds, and reserve them in separate, decorative serving bowls.

If you're making the broth from scratch, use any remaining scraps from chopping the vegetables and follow the instructions for stock on page 92. Strain. Rinse out the stockpot and return the stock to a low simmer. If you're using premade broth, bring it to a low simmer in a large stockpot.

In two rounds, blanch the asparagus and the snow peas separately in the hot stock for about 60 seconds each; remove with a mesh wire ladle. Reserve.

Meanwhile, in a separate pot, bring water to a boil and cook the rice noodles according to the package directions until they're done but slightly al dente. Drain. Toss with a splash of oil to avoid stick-togethers and transfer to a serving bowl with pasta tongs. Cover to keep warm.

In a small saucepan, fry the minced garlic and ginger in the sesame oil until they're just starting to get crispy and almost browned, but not burned. Add to the stock and bring up to a boil. Reduce the heat to a low simmer. Stir in the remaining broth ingredients, except the miso, and adjust the vinegar and tamari to your liking. Keep the broth at a low simmer until you're ready to serve. At the last minute, reduce the heat and add the miso (boiling miso kills the live probiotic organisms).

Serves 30–40

3 quarts raw shungiku leaves or other
    flavorful baby greens such as mizuna or
    baby frilly mustards
3 quarts carrots (about 2 pounds) shaved
    into long, thin ribbons with a mandoline
    or carrot peeler
3 quarts 2-inch-diagonal-cut snow peas
    and/or asparagus spears
1 cup thinly sliced scallions or chives
1 cup chopped mitsuba or parsley
⅔ cup toasted sesame seeds and/or
    Seaweed "Bacon Bits" (page 297)
40 ounces rice noodles

BROTH

12 quarts OAEC Basic or Roasted Veggie
    Stock (pages 92 and 93)
2 cups minced ginger
1 cup minced garlic (40 cloves)
1½ cups sesame oil
2½ cups miso
1¼ cups mirin or dry white wine
⅔ cup rice vinegar
Tamari to taste

OPTIONAL ADDITIONS

Poached eggs
Hot sauce, tamari, fish sauce
Cistocera Relish (page 284)
Naturally fermented sauerkrauts or kimchi,
    pickled ginger, etc.
Edible flowers

To serve larger crowds, set out the big pot of piping-hot broth on a burner, chafing dish, or Crock-Pot next to the mounded platter of noodles and all the smaller colorful bowls of veggies, herbs, condiments, and edible flowers. Preheat the soup bowls in the oven to take the chill off and ensure that there is enough heat to wilt the veggies. Demonstrate by putting the raw and par-cooked veggies in the bowl first, then the noodles, and pour the hot broth over everything. Finish with herbs, optional poached eggs, and condiments.

For smaller gatherings, the ingredients can be plated up with a little less fanfare directly into the soup bowls with the broth hot off the stove and served immediately.

VARIATIONS

For this soup, the seasonal variations are endless! Experiment and use whatever you have bursting forth from the garden. This meal should represent the utmost expression of the seasonal moment. Include roughly one-third raw greens, one-third raw paper-thin shaved root vegetables, and one-third larger chunks of parboiled seasonal vegetables to total 3 cups of veggies for the small batch or 12 quarts for the large batch.

Summer: Orach, lamb's-quarters, thinly sliced sweet red bell pepper, green beans, and corn. Top a summer soup with cooling fresh basil or cilantro instead of the parsley—or alfalfa and sunflower sprouts. You can use cellophane noodles instead of rice noodles.
Fall: Bok choi (sliced into thin strips), colorful watermelon radish or the standard carrot, small florets or side shoots of broccoli and cauliflower. Top with crispy fried shallots instead of or in addition to the sesame seeds. Try udon noodles instead of rice noodles.
Winter: Thinly sliced napa cabbage, burdock (thinly sliced on the diagonal), cubes of blanched winter squash tossed with oil. Add sautéed mushrooms and top with crushed toasted peanuts instead of the sesame seeds. For a warming winter broth that goes particularly well with winter squash, season the stock with a pinch of Chinese five-spice powder. Use soba noodles instead of rice noodles.

Roasted Fennel Soup

When we first started growing bulb fennel in the Mother Garden back in the 1980s, it was a little-known novelty crop. Now it can be found even in big chain supermarkets all over America. And for good reason—Italians have been using it for centuries to round out rich dishes and improve digestibility. Serving fennel as a first-course soup is a nice way to open up the appetite.

Serves 4–6

2–3 large fennel bulbs
1 small onion
2 stalks celery
2 cloves garlic
1 tablespoon oil
Pinch of salt
Pinch of red chili flakes
1 medium russet potato
1 quart veggie or fish stock
3 tablespoons white wine or sherry
Pinch of celery seeds
1 tablespoon fresh-chopped garden thyme,
    to taste
Salt and pepper to taste
Garnish: fresh-chopped parsley, crème
    fraîche, or plain yogurt

Serves 30–40

18 medium fennel bulbs
4 large onions
1 head celery
8 cloves garlic
¼ cup oil
1 teaspoon salt
1 teaspoon red chili flakes
12 medium russet potatoes
8 quarts veggie or fish stock
1½ cups white wine or sherry
2 teaspoons celery seeds
½ cup fresh-chopped garden thyme, to taste
Salt and pepper to taste
Garnish: fresh chopped parsley, crème
    fraîche, or plain yogurt

Roast the fennel, onions, celery, and garlic with the oil, salt, and chili flakes as described in Roasted Fennel recipe variation (page 148). Meanwhile, peel and cube the potatoes and boil them in the stock until soft. When the fennel is done, reserve a third of it whole and add the rest to the stock. Deglaze the roasting pan with the white wine, stirring off the brown bits with a wooden spoon, and dump the contents into the soup pot. Blend the soup with an immersion blender until creamy. Cut the remaining fennel bulbs on the bias, separating the half-moons into attractive bite-sized pieces; fold these into the blended soup. Stir in the celery seeds and thyme. Taste and add salt, pepper, or more thyme as needed. Dole out into serving bowls. Garnish with a dollop of crème fraîche or sour cream and a sprinkling of fresh herbs.

VARIATION

A squeeze of lemon and a sprinkling of bee pollen make an amazing garnish for this soup in place of the sour cream and herbs.

PHOTO BY TALI AIONA.

Crema de Calabacín

Kendra Johnson, one of our garden interns in 2003, learned how to make this light, nourishing summer squash soup from her host-mom Paquita Perez on the Mediterranean coast of Spain. Paquita taught her the joy of getting the simplest, freshest ingredients to speak for themselves, usually with a little help from salt, olive oil, and parsley. This is the simple version she used to make.

Serves 4–6

2 cups veggie stock (page 92)

2 leeks

2–3 medium- to large-sized summer
   squash, any variety (to equal 8 cups
   rough chopped)

¼ cup olive oil

Salt and pepper to taste

¼ cup finely grated Parmesan (plus any
   rinds you have for the stock) (optional)

3 tablespoons chopped parsley

1 tablespoon fresh lemon juice or lemon
   wedges, for serving

Serves 30–40

12 cups veggie stock (page 92)

12 medium leeks

20 pounds medium- to large-sized summer
   squash, any variety (to equal 15 quarts
   rough chopped)

2 cups olive oil

Salt and pepper to taste

2 cups finely grated Parmesan (plus any
   rinds you have for the stock) (optional)

1 bunch chopped fresh parsley

⅓ cup fresh lemon juice or lemon wedges,
   for serving

Make the stock as described on page 92. While the stock is boiling, rough chop the leeks and squash into chunks. No need to be perfect—these will be blended. Feel free to substitute onions and a little garlic if you don't have leeks. In a large stockpot with a lid, sauté the leeks with a generous pour of olive oil on medium heat, until soft, about 5 minutes, stirring occasionally. Add the chopped squash plus a little salt and pepper, and sauté 5 minutes more (a little longer for larger quantities). Then add broth to cover by about ½ inch—too little broth makes a thick, baby-food consistency, and too much becomes runny. Best to err on the side of too little, adding more as needed. If you have Parmesan rinds, you can add them here. Simmer on low for about 30 minutes, or until the zucchini is completely tender. Turn off the heat and add a generous amount of chopped parsley. Remove the Parmesan rinds if using, and puree the soup with an immersion blender. Stir in the optional grated Parmesan. Taste and adjust the salt and pepper to your liking.

Squeeze or stir in fresh lemon juice before serving, and serve with lemon wedges. The added tang makes a delicious difference!

VARIATION

Kendra's versatile soup base became an instant summer classic for many reasons. When the garden is producing more summer squash than we can keep up with, it's a great way to use them up, even those that got a little too big. Though it doesn't contain any dairy or potatoes, the soup is surprisingly creamy. It can be used as the base for other heartier summer soups, including the following recipe, Smoky Corn Chowder.

Smokey Corn Chowder with Fire-Roasted Poblano Peppers

Serves 4–6

4 cups Crema de Calabacín soup (page 97)

4 mildly spicy green peppers such as
  Poblano or Anaheim

¼ cup (½ stick) butter

A few sprigs fresh sage (10 large leaves)

2 ears corn

Salt and black pepper

1 clove garlic, crushed

Serves 30–40

8 quarts Crema de Calabacín soup (page 97)

4 pounds mildly spicy green peppers such as
  Poblano or Anaheim

1 cup (2 sticks) butter

1 bunch fresh sage

1 dozen ears corn

Salt and black pepper

5 cloves garlic, crushed

Make the basic Crema de Calabacín recipe (page 97), omitting the Parmesan. This is the creamy, chowder soup base to which you will add your fire-roasted veggies.

Fire roast the green peppers, then peel and cut into strips as described in the sidebar. Reserve. Melt the butter in a skillet and fry the sage leaves briefly until they crisp up. Remove with a slotted spoon and let cool. Crumble and reserve, but save some of the prettier ones whole for garnish.

Shuck the corn. Then place each whole cob on a hot flaming grill or directly on a gas stovetop burner until it just begins to char a little, turning frequently. Cut the corn off the cob and add to the buttered skillet with a little salt, a few generous grinds of fresh black pepper, and the crushed garlic. Sauté for a few minutes until some of the water from the corn evaporates and the garlic has mellowed.

Stir the corn, peppers, and crumbled sage into the blended Crema de Calabacín soup base. Stir in the lemon juice. Serve hot with a dollop of sour cream, reserved whole fried sage leaves, and a dash of your favorite hot sauce.

PHOTO BY TALI AIONA.

MAKING QUICK FIRE-ROASTED VEGGIES

Summer veggies such as peppers and eggplant can be quickly charred on a grill or gas stovetop for adding rich, fire-roasted flavor to any dish.

Place whole peppers or eggplant directly over an open flame, ideally on a grill above a blazing wood fire—this is a nice task to take advantage of the high flames licking up at the beginning stages of getting a bed of wood coals going for a barbecue. You can also place the vegetables directly on the gas burner of the stovetop. Take care and attend to them constantly, turning them with tongs to get an even char on the outside skin. When they are good and black all over, place them in a stockpot with a tight-fitting lid so that they continue to cook and sweat in the heat generated from charring. After 30 minutes or more in the enclosed pot, they should be cool and ready to be processed. Rub the skin off with your hands or with a towel to expose the flesh; discard charred skin and seeds. Slice into strips or use as directed in your recipe. Save the juice that remains in the bottom of the pot—you may want it for your recipe or for livening up a soup or salad dressing.

PHOTO BY TALI AIONA.

Roasted Eggplant Soup with Pasilla Pumpkin Seed Pesto

Serves 4–6

2 medium eggplant

1 tablespoon olive oil

1 yellow onion, diced

2 medium-sized potatoes, cubed

Salt to taste

2 cloves garlic

4 cups stock

1 teaspoon freshly toasted ground coriander

1 teaspoon apple cider vinegar

½ cup cream (optional)

Serves 30–40

10–12 eggplant

½ cup olive oil

4 yellow onions, diced

10 potatoes, rough chopped (about 10 cups)

2 tablespoons salt

5 cloves garlic

4–6 quarts stock

1 tablespoon plus 1 teaspoon freshly
    toasted ground coriander

1 tablespoon apple cider vinegar

2–3 cups cream (optional)

Roast the eggplant over an open flame on a gas burner to char the outside skin. Use caution and attend to them constantly. Turn them with tongs to get an even char. When they are good and black all over, place then into a stockpot with a tight-fitting lid so that they can cook in the heat generated from charring. It is important to cook them sufficiently in the open flame so they will soften in the enclosed chamber and retain the smoky flavor.

After about 30 minutes to an hour in the enclosed pot, they are ready to be processed. Skin the eggplant by rubbing off the burnt skin and cut off the stem top. Slice the eggplant lengthwise down the middle. If the seeds are on the tough side, scoop them out, though this is usually not necessary. Chop the flesh roughly. Strain any juice left behind from the steaming—this can be used in place of the stock or in addition to it.

In a medium stockpot, heat the olive oil. When the oil is hot, sauté the onion and potato with a pinch of salt for 3 to 5 minutes. Add the flesh of the eggplant with the garlic and stock. Cook until the potatoes are soft, about 30 minutes. Take the pot off the stove and blend with an immersion blender or in a blender. Add salt, coriander, and apple cider vinegar. Pour the mixture back into the stockpot and add the cream, stirring by hand.

Serve with Pasilla Pumpkin Seed Pesto (page 276) atop each bowl.

"Shady" Tomato Soup with Mint

Just for fun, we make this soup with Ailsa Craig tomatoes—a Scottish variety, named after an unpopulated, craggy island off the coast of Scotland, that actually manages to ripen in the shade! Along with a little mint, another shade-tolerant crop, comes a simple, cooling soup, perfect for summer. Of course, any sweet variety of heirloom tomato from your garden or farmers' market will be delicious here.

Serves 4–6

10–12 Ailsa Craig or other heirloom
    tomatoes (Ailsa Craigs are medium-sized
    tomatoes, like a Stupice or an Early Girl;
    if you're substituting a larger variety,
    use fewer)
¼ cup olive oil, divided
3 cloves garlic, crushed
3 sprigs mint, leaves removed
Red wine vinegar to taste
Salt to taste
Sweetener to taste (only if needed)

Serves 30–40

15–20 pounds Ailsa Craig or other
    heirloom tomatoes
2 cups olive oil, divided
8 cloves garlic, crushed
1 bunch mint, leaves removed
Red wine vinegar to taste
Salt to taste
Sweetener to taste (only if needed)

Quarter the tomatoes. Add the tomatoes and half of the olive oil into a large stockpot with a lid and cook, covered, on medium-low heat. Stir occasionally with a long spoon and simmer until the tomatoes have fallen apart and released their juices, about 15 minutes, or a little longer for the large batch. Add the garlic and continue cooking for another 5 minutes. Remove from the heat. Add the mint and the rest of the olive oil. With an immersion wand or blender, blend the soup until smooth and creamy. Taste. Add a small splash of vinegar and a pinch of salt and taste again. Add more vinegar and salt if needed. If you are using ripe heirloom tomatoes from the garden, you shouldn't need any sweetener, but feel free to add a few pinches of sugar or a little honey to sweeten it up, if desired.

Midsummer Fresh Runner Bean Soup

We've recently fallen in love with a huge white runner bean variety called Gigante or White Dutch Runner from seed shared by a fellow seed saving aficionado at the Ecological Farming Association seed swap. We prefer it for cooking fresh since it doesn't turn gray like the purple variety and is so big and meaty, it mysteriously tastes like it's been stewed with a ham hock! This version of fresh shelling beans in a bright-tasting, quick stovetop tomato sauce coupled with fresh corn custard is perfect for a hot August dinner. *Note:* Harvest fresh shelling beans when the pods become fully plump but are not yet dry.

Serves 4–6

2 cups fresh white runner beans, shelled
   from the pod, or other fresh shelling
   beans such as coco bianco
Olive oil
6 medium tomatoes, quartered
1 clove garlic
2 teaspoons minced fresh red-hot chiles,
   such as Thai dragon or Aji Cristal
2 tablespoons Preserved Meyer Lemons,
   minced (page 293)
2 tablespoons chopped fresh parsley

Serves 30–40

12 cups fresh white runner beans, shelled
   from the pod, or other fresh shelling
   beans such as coco bianco
Olive oil
36 medium tomatoes, quartered
6 cloves garlic
2–3 small red-hot chiles, minced, such as
   Thai dragon or Aji Cristal
½ cup Preserved Meyer Lemons, minced
   (page 293)
½ cup chopped fresh parsley

Shuck the fresh beans from the pods. Bring a pot of water to a boil and add the beans. Boil until the beans cook all the way through and are no longer starchy, about 20 minutes, then drain in a colander.

Meanwhile, in a shallow saucepan, put in a dash of olive oil and the quartered fresh tomatoes. Simmer covered on medium heat until tomatoes begin to fall apart, about 15 minutes. With a mesh ladle (aka spider), comb through the sauce and strain out the majority of the skins.

Put a dash of oil in a skillet on medium heat and add the garlic and red pepper. Then add the cooked, drained beans. Sauté for 2 minutes until the garlic cooks just a little.

Stir the bean mixture and preserved lemons into the tomato sauce. Stew covered on a low simmer for 15 minutes or so (a little longer for the large batch) until the beans absorb some of the liquid. Top with fresh parsley. Serve with your favorite pasta or atop Soft Polenta, Fresh Corn Variation (page 224).

RUNNER BEANS

A New World native plant, runner beans were originally cultivated in Central America, known in Nahautl as *ayoctl* or in Spanish *ayocote*. The perennial runner beans at OAEC have been in the ground for over 20 years and have literally produced hundreds of pounds of beans for the kitchen and for giving away at regional seed exchanges.

Runner beans are easy-to-grow, climbing perennial beans that will come back year after year in mild climates. They produce edible, hummingbird-attracting flowers and a bumper crop of beans that can be eaten in all stages of their development. Edible flowers and young tender snap beans appear in July, then fresh shelling beans in August; finally, as summer turns to fall, the dry pods yield fat, meaty dry beans for storage through the winter months. For the die-hard self-sufficient homesteader, this low-maintenance protein source is perfect post-peak-oil-collapse food.

Blackened Tomato and Scarlet Runner Bean Stew

The passage of just two months calls for completely different treatment of more or less the same ingredients—tomatoes, corn, and runner beans. In contrast with the previous recipe, the Blackened Tomato Stew here is perfect for the very end of September when the runner beans have fully dried down, the last of the tomatoes are coming into the kitchen for canning, and the cooling weather puts us in the mood to turn on the oven and cozy up to a slow-roasted stew with pumpkin polenta.

Despite their thick skins, dried runner beans do actually develop a deliciously creamy texture when cooked for a long time. This stew is a good one to make for a crowd ahead of time—the beans plump up even more in the juices overnight.

Serves 4–6

1 cup dry scarlet runner beans
4½ pounds fresh tomatoes: 2½ pounds for
    sauce, 2 pounds for blackening
2 tablespoons olive oil
Salt and pepper to taste
1 clove garlic, crushed
1 teaspoon minced fresh hot red pepper or
    a pinch of dried chili flakes
Apple cider vinegar to taste,
    about 2 teaspoons
Sunflower oil
1 tablespoon finely chopped thyme
2 tablespoons finely chopped parsley

Serves 30–40

8 cups dry scarlet runner beans
16 pounds fresh tomatoes: 9 pounds for
    sauce, 7 pounds for blackening
1 cup olive oil
Salt and pepper to taste
8 cloves garlic, crushed
¼ cup minced fresh hot red pepper or
    1 tablespoon dried chili flakes
Apple cider vinegar to taste,
    about 3 tablespoons
Sunflower oil
½ cup finely chopped thyme
1 cup finely chopped parsley

Follow the tips for cooking beans on page 218. Due to their large size and thick skins, anticipate long soaking and cooking times for runner beans. Soak them overnight in plenty of water for at least 12 hours. Rinse. In a large soup pot, add the beans and enough water to cover by several inches. Do *not* add salt—salt added to beans before they are fully cooked hardens the skins. Bring to a boil, then reduce the heat and simmer until completely cooked through. Depending on the freshness of your beans, this may take up to 2 hours. Drain and rinse.

While the beans are cooking: Cut the large sauce tomatoes in half. Drizzle the halves with the olive oil and salt. Roast on a baking tray for 30 to 40 minutes, until they're a little wrinkled and browned. Transfer to a large soup pot. Blend with an immersion blender. Put a dash of oil in a skillet on medium heat, add the garlic and red pepper, and sauté for 1 minute until the garlic mellows just a little. Add to the tomato puree.

Stir the cooked beans into the seasoned tomato sauce. Stew on a low simmer, uncovered, for 20 minutes or so (longer for the large quantity) until the beans absorb some of the liquid and the sauce thickens a bit. Taste and season with apple cider vinegar, salt, and pepper. (If you're making this stew base ahead of time, cool and refrigerate it overnight.)

When you're ready to serve, cut the blackening tomatoes in half. Heat up a cast-iron skillet or large flat-top griddle on high. When the pan is hot, add a shy drizzle of sunflower oil (too much prevents a good char from forming). Place the tomatoes cut-side down and resist the urge to move them or peek. Leave them to char until you literally smell them burning, at least a few minutes. With one swift movement, firmly pressing underneath them with a thin sharp spatula to preserve the crust, flip the tomatoes over and let them brown, skin-side down, for another few minutes.

To serve, top the stew with fresh thyme and parsley and individually place whole blackened tomatoes into each bowl. Serve with Soft Pumpkin Polenta (page 224).

Escarole White Bean Soup with Shaved Celery Root

The addition of crisp escarole and thin shavings of celery root at the last minute enlivens this clear brothy winter soup.

Serves 4–6

1 cup mushrooms, sliced

3 tablespoons oil

Pinch of salt

1 small onion, peeled and diced

1 stalk celery, diced

1 large carrot, peeled and small cubed

1 small celery root (or 2 small potatoes),
   peeled and small cubed

1 sprig thyme leaves

¼ cup white wine

6–8 cups rich veggie stock (page 92)

¾ cup white beans, precooked and rinsed
   (page 218)

2 teaspoons apple cider vinegar, to taste

Salt and pepper to taste

Tiny dash of hot sauce, to taste (optional)

1 large head escarole, chopped into ½-inch
   strips (about 4 cups chopped)

¼ cup chopped parsley (or 2
   tablespoons smallage)

½ cup peeled, thinly shaved raw celery root

Serves 30–40

6 cups mushrooms, sliced

1 cup oil

1 teaspoon salt

3 large yellow onions, diced

6 stalks celery, diced

6 carrots, peeled and small cubed

3 large celery roots (or 6 potatoes), peeled
   and small cubed

1 bunch thyme leaves

1 cup white wine

6–8 quarts rich veggie stock (page 92)

3 cups white beans, precooked and rinsed
   (page 218)

¼ cup apple cider vinegar, to taste

Salt and pepper to taste

Dash of hot sauce, to taste (optional)

5 large heads escarole, chopped into ½-inch
   strips (about 12 quarts chopped)

2 cups chopped parsley (or 1 cup smallage)

2 cups peeled, thinly shaved raw celery root

In a large, heavy-bottomed stockpot, sauté the mushrooms with the oil and salt until all the water has evaporated and they begin to caramelize. Add the onions, celery, and carrots—you can throw in the chopped parsley stems, too—and continue sautéing on medium heat until the onions are translucent. Add celery root or potato, thyme, and white wine and cover. Steam-sauté until al dente.

Pour in the stock and precooked beans, then raise the heat and bring to a boil. Reduce the heat immediately to a very low simmer or turn the heat completely off and let the soup sit covered until you are ready to serve. Do not overcook or the beans and roots will get mushy.

Season the liquid to your liking with vinegar, salt, pepper, and hot sauce. When you're ready to serve, add the escarole, parsley, and shaved celery root at the last minute. Serve with a Parmesan crouton.

Note: If you don't have stock already made, chop the veggies for the soup first so that you can use the scraps to make stock.

VARIATION

Substitute escarole with kale or other greens, sliced very thin.

PHOTO BY TALI AIONA.

Spiced Turnip Stew with Chickpeas and Turnip Green Yogurt Sauce

Chef Angela Ginsberg is beloved by our School Garden Teachers when they are in summer training at OAEC. She prides herself on preparing meals that educate her eaters. Here is her creative way of using both the turnip roots and tops in the same dish.

STEW

Serves 4–6

2 cups cooked chickpeas

1½ pounds small turnips with greens (reserve greens for yogurt sauce below)

3 carrots, chopped and peeled (reserve peels for stock)

4 leeks, chopped into rounds and washed (reserve green parts for stock)

4 cloves garlic

¼ cup oil

1 large onion, chopped

1 teaspoon finely grated gingerroot

½ teaspoon each cardamom, allspice, coriander, turmeric, paprika, and cinnamon

1 teaspoon pepper

½ teaspoon salt

6 cups water or stock

1 tablespoon apple cider vinegar

Serves 30–40

8 cups cooked chickpeas

6 pounds small turnips with greens (reserve greens for yogurt sauce below)

12–14 carrots, chopped and peeled (reserve peels for stock)

16 leeks, chopped into rounds and washed (reserve green parts for stock)

1 head garlic

1 cup oil

6 medium onions, chopped

2 tablespoons finely grated gingerroot

2 teaspoons each cardamom, allspice, coriander, turmeric, paprika, and cinnamon

2 teaspoons pepper

2 teaspoons salt

3½ quarts water or 3 quarts finished stock

¼ cup apple cider vinegar

If you're starting with dried chickpeas from scratch, soak and cook according to the recipe for OAEC Basic Beans on page 218. If you're using canned beans, rinse, drain, and reserve.

Trim off the tops and bottoms of the turnips, and if they're large, peel them and cut them into ½-inch cubes. Baby turnips can be used whole or halved, unpeeled. Set the peels aside for stock and the greens aside for the yogurt sauce. Peel and roughly chop the carrots in the same fashion, reserving the peels for stock. Cut the white part of the leeks into rounds and wash well. Peel and chop the onions.

If you're making your own stock, add the leek tops, onion skins, and root peels to 6 cups of water (3½ quarts for the large batch). Boil for 20 minutes, then steep for 30. Strain.

Bring the stock up to a boil. In a fitted colander or strainer, blanch the turnip greens for 30 seconds in the boiling stock, then remove and shock in an ice bath. Drain and toss the greens with a pinch of salt. Let them sit for 20 minutes in a colander while you prepare the rest of the soup.

Peel the garlic and simmer the whole cloves in a cast-iron skillet in the oil on very low heat until cloves are tender. Remove the cloves and reserve for the sauce.

Add the garlic-infused oil to a large stockpot on medium heat and add the onions. Sauté until golden. Add the gingerroot, spices, pepper, and salt; sauté for another minute. Add the chopped carrots, turnips, and stock. Cook, covered, until the turnips are tender, about 20 minutes. Add the cooked, drained chickpeas and the apple cider vinegar. To thicken the soup base, remove 1 cup (4 cups for the large batch) of the stew including a few chunks of veggies and beans, puree it in a blender until smooth, and return it to the pot.

Serve the stew with a dollop of turnip green yogurt sauce.

TURNIP GREEN YOGURT SAUCE

Serves 4–6

½ cup packed turnip greens

½ cup whole milk yogurt

Salt and pepper to taste

Roasted garlic cloves (above)

Serves 30–40

2 cups packed turnip greens

2 cups whole milk yogurt

Salt and pepper to taste

Roasted garlic cloves (above)

Put the greens, yogurt, and reserved garlic cloves in a blender and blend until smooth. Season well with salt and black pepper.

Borscht with Dollop and Swirl

A far cry from the chunky beef-based traditional soup, this blended, vegetarian variation of borscht still satisfies. Even teenagers who thought they hated beets love this bright purple bowl of goodness! Exercise your creativity with endless options for the dollop and swirl. Serve warm or chilled.

Serves 4–6

SOUP

4 medium-sized beets
3 cups vegetable stock (page 92)
2½ tablespoons balsamic vinegar
½ cup olive oil
Salt to taste

GARNISH

Savory or sweet edible flower
    (Johnny jump-ups, violet, borage,
    rose petals, society garlic)
Sprig of fresh herb (cilantro, chervil, parsley,
    fennel frond, or basil leaf)

DOLLOP

1 cup sour cream or Greek yogurt
One of the following: ½ teaspoon wasabi;
    1 teaspoon Thai green curry paste; 2
    teaspoons prepared horseradish; 2
    tablespoons chopped fresh herb such
    as cilantro, parsley, chervil, or basil; 2
    tablespoons herb pesto or pistou

SWIRL

1 bunch parsley or other light-tasting herb
    such as chervil, basil, cilantro
Juice of 1 lemon
1 small clove garlic, crushed
¼ cup olive oil
Salt to taste

To make the soup: Cut off the beet greens from the root, leaving a little bit of stubble from the stems on the top of the beet—this prevents "bleeding" color and flavor while cooking. Save the beet greens and use them for another dish. If the beets are radically different sizes, cut the big ones into smaller pieces for even cooking time. Cover with water in a stockpot and bring to a boil. Reduce the heat and simmer until the beets are soft when poked with a fork, about 20 to 30 minutes. Meanwhile, make the dollop and the swirl and refrigerate until ready to serve—see below. When the beets are done, drain and discard the water. Let beets chill in a container of cold water until they're cool enough to handle. With your hands, slip the skins and stubble off the beets and rinse again.

If you'll be serving the dish warm, add the beets to the veggie stock and heat up to temperature on the stovetop. If you'll be serving it chilled, use cold stock. Using a blender or immersion wand, blend the beets and most of the stock until smooth. Check the texture of the soup—if you like it thick, leave it as such; if you want it a little thinner, add more stock a little at a time until it reaches the desired texture. Add the balsamic vinegar and then pour in the olive oil in a thin stream until emulsified. Salt to taste—if you're serving it cold, you will probably need more salt. Return to the stovetop on low heat or chill in the fridge until you're ready to serve.

To make the dollop: Mix the yogurt and chosen seasoning until creamy.

To make the swirl: Rough chop the herbs and put them in a high-powered blender with the lemon juice and garlic. Blend until smooth. Blending the herb with lemon juice before adding the oil prevents it from turning brown. (If you don't have an accelerating tool for your blender, mash the herbs with a handheld immersion blender in a jar.) Cook's tip: Make the swirl while the soup is cooking and don't bother rinsing out the blender—blend the soup in the same pitcher and you'll get a little hint of the herb flavor in the soup. This recipe makes a little extra—save and use the excess as pesto sauce or a salad dressing.

Energy-saving tip for cooking large batches of beets and other root vegetables: If you have time, boil the beets for 10 minutes, cover, and let them sit in the hot water for an hour. The heat trapped in the large volume of water should be enough to cook the beets through.

Serves 30–40

SOUP

40 medium-sized beets (about 18 pounds)

8 quarts vegetable stock (page 92)

1½ cups balsamic vinegar

5 cups olive oil

Salt to taste

GARNISH

Savory or sweet edible flower
    (Johnny jump-ups, violet, borage,
    rose petals, society garlic)

Sprig of fresh herb (cilantro, chervil, parsley,
    fennel frond, or basil leaf)

DOLLOP

2 pints sour cream or Greek yogurt

One of the following: 1 tablespoon wasabi;
    ¼ cup Thai green curry paste; 6
    tablespoons prepared horseradish;
    ½ cup chopped fresh herb such as
    cilantro, parsley, chervil, or basil;
    ½ cup pesto or pistou

SWIRL

2 bunches parsley or other light-tasting herb
    such as chervil, basil, cilantro

Juice of 3 lemons

2 cloves garlic, crushed

1½ cups olive oil

Salt to taste

PHOTO BY TALI AIONA.

Creamy Parsnip Soup with Candy Cap Mushrooms

Candy cap mushrooms are found growing wild all over Sonoma County in the winter months and have a rare flavor somewhere between fenugreek and butterscotch. If you don't have access to candy caps, chanterelles are the best substitute, though this recipe is yummy with any type of wild or strongly flavored mushroom such as shiitake.

SOUP

Serves 4–6

MAKES ABOUT 8 CUPS

1 small onion, peeled and quartered

3 tablespoons ghee or 1 tablespoon butter
    plus 2 tablespoons cooking oil

1 clove garlic, crushed

3 cups parsnips, peeled and cut into chunks

1 small russet or other starchy potato,
    peeled and quartered*

4–6 cups strong veggie stock (page 92)

Pinch of white pepper

1 teaspoon dried thyme

Pinch of nutmeg

Salt and fresh-cracked pepper to taste

½ cup half-and-half or heavy cream (optional)

Serves 30–40

MAKES ABOUT 12 QUARTS

4 onions, peeled and quartered (about 4 cups)

1 cup ghee or ⅓ cup butter (¾ stick) plus ⅔
    cup cooking oil

3 cloves garlic, crushed

7 pounds parsnips, peeled and cut into
    chunks (about 5 quarts)

2–3 large russet or other starchy potatoes,
    peeled and quartered*

6–8 quarts strong veggie stock (page 92)

1 teaspoon white pepper

1–2 tablespoons dried thyme

½ teaspoon nutmeg

Salt and fresh-cracked black pepper to taste

2 pints half-and-half or heavy cream (optional)

In a large, heavy-bottomed stockpot, sauté the onions in the ghee or butter and oil with a light sprinkle of salt on medium heat until they start to become translucent. Add the crushed garlic and sauté for another minute. Then add the parsnips, potatoes, and enough stock to cover by 1 inch, and bring to a boil. Reserve any extra stock. Reduce the heat and cook covered until the roots are soft. With an immersion wand or blender, blend the hot soup until it's smooth and creamy. If the soup is too thick, add more hot stock or hot water. Stir in the white pepper, thyme, nutmeg, salt, and pepper. Stir in the optional cream to taste, though often the creaminess of the parsnips themselves is enough. Taste and add more seasonings, if desired.

To serve, dole out the soup into bowls and garnish each one with a twist of fresh cracked pepper and a little bouquet of perfect sautéed mushrooms. Contrast this rich soup with a salad of bitter winter greens.

MUSHROOM GARNISH

Serves 4–6

½ cup fresh candy cap mushrooms**
    (or any wild mushroom variety)

1½ cups white button or small, inexpen-
    sive, neutral-flavored mushrooms

2 teaspoons ghee or cooking oil

Sprinkle of salt

Serves 30–40

2 cups fresh candy cap mushrooms**
    (or any wild mushroom variety)

8 cups white button or small, inexpensive,
    neutral-flavored mushrooms

2 teaspoons ghee or cooking oil

Sprinkle of salt

For a dramatic presentation, choose mushrooms that are small and dainty enough to be sautéed whole, though if needed you can chop or tear them into bite-sized pieces. In a small sauté pan, heat the ghee on medium heat. Add the mushrooms and a sprinkle of salt and sauté gently until most of the water is pulled out and evaporates and the mushrooms become caramelized to a light golden brown.

* Do not use dense, waxy potato varieties such as fingerling or Yukon Gold; these become gluey when blended.

** Usually foragers dry their candy caps to preserve them—some might even argue that the aroma is concentrated and improved this way. If you're using dried mushrooms, combine them with button mushrooms to absorb and stretch out the wild mushroom flavor. Rehydrate 2 tablespoons (1 cup for the large batch) in a little hot water to cover, squeeze dry, and chop finely. Stir the mushroom water into the soup. Add the rehydrated candy caps to the cooking oil when you're sautéing the button mushrooms.

Rutabaga Soup with Lovage Butter

Rutabaga is an underappreciated vegetable that is easy to grow and store and deserves its due respect beyond the once-a-year appearance at Grandma's Thanksgiving table. Its pungency mellows and sweetens when cooked, even more so when blended with gentle carrot and fresh lovage—a low-maintenance perennial in the Mother Garden that we often substitute for parsley or celery leaf.

Serves 4–6

MAKES APPROXIMATELY 8 CUPS

1 small onion, peeled and quartered

1 tablespoon butter

2 tablespoons oil

1 clove garlic, crushed

1½ cups peeled and cubed rutabaga

1½ cups peeled and cubed carrots

1½ cups peeled and quartered russet or
	other starchy potatoes*

5–7 cups strong veggie stock (page 92)

¼ teaspoon white pepper

½ teaspoon dried thyme

Pinch of cayenne (optional)

Salt and fresh-cracked pepper to taste

Garnish: ½ cup lovage butter,** molded into a
	log and sliced into tablespoon-sized rounds

Serves 30–40

MAKES APPROXIMATELY 12 QUARTS

4 onions, peeled and quartered (about 4 cups)

⅓ cup (¾ stick) butter

⅔ cup oil

3 cloves garlic, crushed

4 pounds rutabaga, peeled and cut into
	chunks (about 2 quarts)

4 pounds carrots, peeled and cut into
	chunks (about 2 quarts)

3 large russet or other starchy potatoes,*
	peeled and quartered

5–7 quarts strong veggie stock (page 92)

1 teaspoon white pepper

2 teaspoons dried thyme

Pinch cayenne (optional)

Salt (about 2½ teaspoons) and fresh cracked
	pepper (about 1½ teaspoons) to taste

Garnish: 2 cups lovage butter,** molded into a
	log and sliced into tablespoon-sized rounds

In a large, heavy-bottomed stockpot, sauté the onions in the butter and oil and a light sprinkle of salt on medium heat until they start to become translucent. Add the crushed garlic and sauté for another minute. Then add the rutabaga, carrots, potatoes, and enough stock to cover by 1 inch; bring to a boil. Reserve any extra stock. Reduce the heat and cook, covered, until the roots are mostly soft. With an immersion wand or blender, blend the hot soup until it's smooth and creamy. If the soup is too thick, add more hot stock or hot water. Stir in the spices, salt, and pepper. Taste and add more seasonings, if desired.

Serve hot garnished with a generous round of herb butter that enriches the soup as it melts before the eyes.

* Do not use dense, waxy potato varieties such as fingerling or Yukon Gold; these become gluey when blended.

** Follow the directions for Basic Garden Herb Butter (page 271), using finely chopped lovage, parsley, or celery leaf.

PHOTO BY TALI AIONA.

COLD VEGETABLE
PLATES AND SALADS

RECIPE LIST

Spring

Delicate Wild Spring Greens with Mache, Violets, and Champagne
Blanched Asparagus and Garlic Scapes with Preserved Lemon Dip
Veggie Mandala
Fava Beans in Vinaigrette

Summer

Heirloom Tomato Platter
Summer Squash Ribbons with Purple Shiso
Summer Salad with Giant Yellow Mangel and Pickled Rainbow Chard Stems
Hydrating Lemon Cucumber Purslane Salad
School Garden Sprout Wraps

Fall

Rainbow Beet and Carrot Salad with Garden Herbs
Cumin-Marinated Runner Beans
Coriander Carrots with Black Olives and Orange Zest
Marinated Shaved Fennel
Raw Kale Salads—Three Variations

Winter

Zesty Purple Cabbage Slaw
Blanched Romanesco with Winter Pistou on a Bed of Ornamental Kale
Winter Frisée Salad with Crunchy Fried Mung Beans
Yacon and Radish Platter with Chili and Lemon
Papas a la Huancaina

PHOTO BY DOUG GOSLING.

Delicate Wild Spring Greens with Mache, Violets, and Champagne

Mache, or lamb's lettuce, is one of the first salad ingredients to appear in the Mother Garden in February and always happens at just the same time as the violets. One of the most memorable salad dressings ever was for a dinner we did during Organically Grown Week in Sonoma County, back when organics was really just starting. We served our salad mix at a fund-raiser where Alice Waters was the guest of honor. The chef tossed our salad mix with champagne right before serving it. It was as if it had been bathed in magic—the bubbles actually effervesced as you put the salad in your mouth.

Serves 4–6
¾ pound washed mixed greens, including
　　miner's lettuce, chickweed tips, crisp
　　butter lettuce, mache rosettes
2 tablespoons chervil tips
¼ cup bubbly champagne
Extra-virgin olive oil
Salt and pepper to taste
Garnish: 2 tablespoons violets or
　　small rose petals

Serves 30–40
3 pounds washed mixed greens, including
　　miner's lettuce, chickweed tips, crisp
　　butter lettuce, mache rosettes
1 cup chervil tips
1½ cups bubbly champagne
Extra-virgin olive oil
Salt and pepper to taste
Garnish: 1 cup violets or small rose petals

With great fanfare, open the bottle of bubbly over your big bowl of prewashed greens and chervil tips, letting it bubble over onto the salad. Toss gently and drizzle with fine olive oil, a sprinkle of salt, and a twist of fresh cracked pepper. Garnish lavishly with violet flowers or rose petals. Great fun for a dinner party.

MINER'S LETTUCE

Miner's lettuce, also known as winter purslane or Indian lettuce, grows abundantly in shady, moist places in Northern California and is easily identifiable by its parabolic leaves that look like mini satellite dishes orienting toward the sun. Native Californians ate it, as well as Gold Rush miners, as a source of vitamin C when they were suffering from scurvy.[9] The mild, succulent, and—best of all—*free* leaves aren't bitter or foreign tasting in the slightest and can serve as an approachable entrée into the world of wild foods.

PHOTO BY TALI AIONA.

Blanched Asparagus and Garlic Scapes with Preserved Lemon Dip

Pinching back garlic scapes and harvesting asparagus happens so naturally at the same time and with the same satisfying snap, the two beg to be served side by side. A classic example of *What grows together, goes together*. For more information on garlic scapes see the sidebar on page 151.

Serves 4–6

1 generous bunch asparagus

8 garlic scapes

Water, salt, and ice for blanching

⅔ cup Preserved Lemon Mayo (page 293)

Serves 30–40

8–10 bunches asparagus

2 bunches garlic scapes

Water, salt, and ice for blanching

2½ cups Preserved Lemon Mayo (page 293)

If you're using store-bought asparagus, snap off the tough ends and compost or save for stock. Cut the asparagus and garlic scapes in half to form dippable 3-inch spears, or—if they're naturally small and tender—leave whole. Blanch the scapes and asparagus separately according to blanching directions in the sidebar. Serve with Preserved Lemon Aioli as part of a crudités plate or a cold repast.

BLANCHING VEGGIES

One of the secrets to getting people to fall in love with vegetables, especially green ones, is blanching. By locking in the vivid color, fresh texture, flavor, and nutrients, veggies are elevated to center stage rather than being relegated to a forgettable side role. When cooking for a crowd, this is also a convenient way to prepare veggies ahead of time to be reheated or incorporated into a dish later.

Get a *big* pot of water (the higher the water-to-vegetable ratio, the better) to an aggressive boil on the stove. Add *lots* of salt, about ½ cup per gallon of water—this helps prevent the color from leaching out into the cooking water and perfectly preseasons the vegetables. Meanwhile, prepare an ice bath by filling a large bowl with ice and cold water. Slice and stage the raw veggies.

Note: Be sure to blanch each vegetable separately, as cooking times will vary.

Put your first round of raw-cut veggies into the basket and lower gently into the rapidly boiling salt water. For small veggies like peas, 30 seconds should do; with larger cuts or root veggies, like julienned carrots, you may need to cook them for 4 to 6 minutes. Keep a close eye on them because a few seconds can mean the difference between vibrant al dente and mushy gray. When the color brightens up and the texture is cooked but still retains a hint of firmness (stick a fork in or taste one), pull the colander basket out, draining out as much of the hot water as possible, and then submerge the colander in the ice bath to halt the cooking process. When the veggies have completely cooled, remove the colander and drain completely. Let the pot of water come up to boiling again before starting the next round and add more ice to the ice bath as needed.

Blanched vegetables can be frozen like this or stored in the fridge for a day.

To serve immediately as a simple side, return the vegetables to a clean pot on the stovetop and reheat on medium-high either covered with a dash of water or uncovered tossed with oil. Serve with simple olive oil and salt, a dash of tamari, or a tab of herb butter.

Veggie Mandala

An OAEC tradition for parties and celebrations is to create a giant colorful mandala out of diverse garden veggies served directly on the surface of the entire length of the table. An assortment of raw, blanched, and roasted elements adds to the diversity of flavors.

Serves 4–6

2½ pounds assorted brightly colored veggies: brassica florets, roots, and whatever other veggies are happening in the garden or at the farmers' market

1 bunch large edible garden leaves: Rainbow chard, variegated collards, fig or grape leaves, the large side leaves of cauliflower or broccoli—whatever looks big and healthy

Serves 30–40

15 pounds assorted brightly colored veggies: brassica florets, roots, and whatever other veggies are happening in the garden or at the farmers' market

5 bunches large edible garden leaves: Rainbow chard, variegated collards, fig or grape leaves, the large side leaves of cauliflower or broccoli—whatever looks big and healthy

Wash, peel, and chop the vegetables into attractive dippable spears and keep separate. Decide which vegetables make sense to blanch, roast, or leave raw, choosing a few for each category. For example, in the summertime, leave juicy vegetables like cherry tomatoes and cucumbers raw. In the winter, roast the fennel and winter squash. Parboil or roast the remaining roots or florets, depending on your mood.

Spread the vegetables to be roasted in a single layer on separate cookie sheets, drizzle with oil, sprinkle with salt, and bake in a 375°F oven for 20 minutes, flipping as needed. Meanwhile, blanch each type of vegetable separately according to directions in the blanching veggies sidebar (page 116). To serve, clean your serving table well with soap and water. Cover the surface with large edible leaves, and then thoughtfully arrange the assortment of veggies in a beautiful pattern with a bowl of Chervil Aioli (page 260) or an herb pistou for dipping. Circle around the food and meditate on the abundance!

Fava Beans in Vinaigrette

The humble fava is like the "Giving Tree" of the garden. It regenerates the soil over the fallow cold months with nitrogen-fixing roots and offers the added perk of delicious beans that can be eaten fresh or dried. Fava beans are one of the most widely cultivated food crops on earth and have been grown since the Stone Age.

Although time consuming to prepare, fresh fava beans are worth every ounce of effort. Prepping favas is a wonderful slow-food activity to do outside with kids or over a glass of wine and conversation. When buying or harvesting, choose the fattest of pods, and remember, 1 pound of whole pods will result in a scant cup of peeled beans.

This recipe is the essence of "primavera." Marinated favas add a quintessential burst of spring freshness to pasta, salads, and appetizers.

Serves 4–6

2 cups peeled fava beans (from about 8 pounds of whole pods)

Juice of 1 lemon

1 small clove garlic, crushed

1 tablespoon chopped fresh parsley, or other tender herb such as chervil, tarragon, or basil

1 teaspoon thyme or marjoram

3 tablespoons olive oil

Salt to taste

Serves 30–40

10 cups peeled fava beans (from about 40 pounds of whole pods)

Juice of 6 lemons

3 cloves garlic, crushed

1 cup chopped fresh parsley, or other tender herb such as chervil, tarragon, or basil

¼ cup thyme or marjoram

1 cup olive oil

Salt to taste

Start by shucking the beans from the thick, fibrous pods. Next, boil a pot of water and blanch the beans for about a minute, until they turn from pale to bright green. Strain and plunge into cold water until cool enough to handle. Nick the end of each fava bean with your thumbnail or a knife and squeeze until the inner bean pops out of its skin.

Mix all the ingredients together. Marinate in the refrigerator for at least an hour, up to a few days, in the refrigerator. Enjoy alone or add to your favorite springtime dish for seasonal flair.

VARIATION

Summer: Substitute parboiled fresh scarlet runner beans for the peeled favas.

COME TO THE TABLE

To celebrate the life force of our salad mix and the beauty of our salad beds themselves, Doug had an idea to create an event where people would get on their hands and knees and eat directly from a beautiful cut-and-come-again salad bed while the plants were actually still in the ground, before the spirit of the plants had gone.

"It was a magical night," he recalls, "and there was a light, misty rain, which made it all the more incredible. We lit torches made of mullein stalks painted with wax and processed through the garden. All the kids came and people really got into the festive atmosphere. We gathered around either side of the salad bed and I made some opening remarks and the instructions were that you were not allowed to use your hands. We provided kneeling pads, a spray-on vinaigrette, and croutons to sprinkle on. To my surprise, people loved it and got into it right from the outset—it was truly one of the most joyful and ecstatic eating events I have ever seen! And it was very sensual—people almost immediately started making sexual jokes about it. But at the same time, the kids were really into it—I remember one image of Dave holding his son Kelsey over the bed by the feet as he munched. People would pull plants out with their teeth, so there would be plants dangling out of people's mouths. It was just wonderful. In fact, some people even cried. One of the guests said it was a religious experience—she made some connection to living food in a way she never had before. It was so powerful. And with so much laughter—an absolute kick!"

A long salad bed with enough "place settings" for 30 people was sown a with a solid green "tablecloth" of mizuna and arugula with individual round "plates" of red and purple mustards. The gardeners covered the bed in shade cloth and were able to keep it a surprise until the night of the event—people walked right by it for a month without even noticing! Meanwhile, they sent out intriguing invitations to create a buzz. PHOTO BY JIM COLEMAN.

Heirloom Tomato Platter

A simple heirloom tomato plate is an altar to biodiversity and the sumptuousness of summer. Figure on about 1 medium-sized tomato per person, fewer for hefty heirlooms (2 pounds for 4 to 6 or 15 pounds for 30 to 40). Slice the tomatoes and arrange them artistically on a wide serving platter. Top with a demure spritz of sherry or balsamic vinegar (less is more), a drizzle of good-quality olive oil, and a sprinkle of coarse crunchy sea salt. Basil, of course, is the go-to garnish, but try another fresh summer herb like chervil, mint, or dill—we've even enjoyed the tiniest scatter of finely chiffonaded fresh epazote for a surprising variation on a theme.

PHOTO BY TALI AIONA.

Summer Squash Ribbons with Purple Shiso

Frilly purple or green shiso, also known as perilla, *Perilla frutescens*, is popular in Japanese cooking, particularly with sushi or as an accompaniment to rice or cucumbers. It has a minty, citrus flavor with a hint of clove and can be substituted wherever basil or mint is used. Try it in pesto, slivered in fruit salads, or added to pickles—it is the secret ingredient in *ume boshi* plums.

Longtime OAEC cook Holly Carter grew up eating shiso from her grandmother's Japanese cooking. She had forgotten about it until one day she saw it growing in the OAEC garden. We are always trying to find new ways to use summer squash, so she incorporated them both together in this dish to serve with or as a fresh alternative to rice noodles.

Serves 4–6
1 pound mixed summer squash
1 teaspoon salt
Juice of 1 lemon
A few sprigs fresh shiso, basil, or mint
2 tablespoons olive oil
Fresh cracked black pepper to taste

Serves 30–40
8 pounds mixed summer squash
2 tablespoons salt
Juice of 4 lemons
2 bunches fresh shiso, basil, or mint
½ cup olive oil
Fresh cracked black pepper to taste—
    about 1 teaspoon

Shave the squash into thin, wide ribbons with a carrot peeler or mandoline. Add the salt and lemon juice. Let marinate for 2 to 3 hours in the fridge, then drain in a colander for 15 minutes. Chiffonade the shiso leaves by stacking them one on top of the other, rolling them like a newspaper, and slicing them with a very sharp knife into tiny strips. Toss the shiso and remaining ingredients with the squash and serve.

Summer Salad with Giant Yellow Mangel and Pickled Rainbow Chard Stems

In front of the art studio, several beautiful Rainbow chards appeared spontaneously one summer nestling themselves nicely into the perennial edible landscaping. Doug had noticed one Golden chard in particular, which grew larger and more deeply golden than any other gold-colored chard he'd ever seen. Its stem grew noticeably wider and wider until he finally realized that it was in fact not a chard but a yellow mangel that somehow had found its way there. We have grown mangels before—they're a kind of sugar beet traditionally grown to feed animals, but they make great people food as well. A favorite, the Giant Yellow Mangel, is a variety we love for its bright-yellow outer layers and its pure-white core.

Doug boiled this 3-inch-diameter carrot-shaped root and found it to be the most succulently sweet and juicy beet he'd ever tasted! He decided to build a salad around it and was inspired to use its lemon-yellow color as both the motif for the color of the other ingredients and a suggestion of lemon as the dominant flavor. He contrasted all the yellows with some of the deep-burgundy salad greens he had also been so appreciating in the garden.

As written, this isn't a quick, throw-it-together type of salad, though some of the most interesting composed salads are spontaneously created. Feel free to simplify or take liberties in substituting other yellow or purple veggies or greens that you are already growing or pickling.

Serves 4–6

SALAD

1 Giant Yellow Mangel or 1 bunch
Golden beets

Stems of 1 small Golden and 1 small Ruby
chard, shoestringed into 1-inch pieces

Preserved Lemon Brine (page 293)

Hearts of 2 butter lettuce heads, separated
into leaves, washed, and spun

1 small head of Chioggia or Palla Rossa
radicchio, its inner brilliant leaves torn
into thin shreds

Several handfuls leaves of bite-sized feathery Ruby Streaks Mustard or some other
deep-burgundy Japanese red mustard

3 small lemon cucumbers, cut into wedges

12–15 yellow pear cherry tomatoes, halved

¼ cup toasted hazelnuts, skins rubbed off
and coarsely chopped

¼ cup shaved Parmesan

DRESSING

⅓ cup extra-virgin olive oil

1 preserved lemon wedge

Zest from 1 Meyer lemon

2 tablespoons white wine vinegar

2 teaspoons freshly squeezed lemon juice

1 clove garlic, minced

Boil the mangel or golden beets until soft when pierced with a fork. Slip off the skin. Cut into thick horizontal slices and then into large pie-shaped wedges—one large, meaty wedge per person.

While the mangel is boiling, make the salad dressing. Place all the dressing ingredients in a blender and blend until smooth. Marinate the mangel wedges in the salad dressing for several hours until ready to serve.

Fifteen minutes before serving, quick pickle the shoestringed chard stems in lemon brine. Submerge them in the brine for no more than 15 minutes or else they lose their crunch. Rinse with fresh water.

Toss the lettuce, radicchio, mustard leaves, and lemon cucumbers in the salad dressing just before serving. Put a small handful of each on chilled plates. Liberally garnish with pear tomatoes, hazelnuts, and Parmesan cheese. Place a marinated mangel wedge and pile of pickled chard stems near each other on the plate next to the salad. For a crowd, serve each element of the salad in concentric rings on a very large flat platter or mounded into discrete little piles. Serve with fresh cracked black pepper and a garlic crouton.

Serves 30–40

SALAD

6 Giant Yellow Mangels or 4–6 bunches
    Golden beets

Stems of 6–8 Golden and 6–8 Ruby chard,
    shoestringed into 1-inch pieces

Preserved Lemon Brine (page 293)

Hearts of 8 butter lettuce heads, separated
    into leaves, washed, and spun

3 heads Chioggia or Palla Rossa radicchio,
    its inner brilliant leaves torn into
    thin shreds

1 pound (about 12 quarts lightly packed)
    leaves of bite-sized feathery Ruby
    Streaks Mustard or some other
    deep-burgundy Japanese red mustard

14 lemon cucumbers, cut into wedges

3 pints yellow pear cherry tomatoes, halved

1 cup toasted hazelnuts, skins rubbed off
    and coarsely chopped

1 cup shaved Parmesan

DRESSING

1 cup extra-virgin olive oil

4 preserved lemon wedges

Zest from 4 Meyer lemons

½ cup white wine vinegar

3 tablespoons freshly squeezed lemon juice

3 cloves garlic, minced

"Five-color silver beet" or "rainbow chard" makes a stunning, edible bouquet. First selected in New Zealand, this collection of brilliant chard varieties was introduced into the American seed trade in the 1970s. PHOTO BY DOUG GOSLING.

Summer Biodiversity Tasting

A tradition that was held every summer for many years at OAEC was the Biodiversity Tasting. The event would attract several hundred people to the North Garden for a chance to sample the multitude of heirloom food crop varieties grown in our collection. Chefs demonstrated and prepared each of the varieties with identical simplicity, allowing discerning taste buds to compare and contrast the subtle nuances in color, texture, and taste. People nibbled, chatted, cleansed their palates with locally donated wines, and jotted down tasting notes. Meanwhile, featured speakers, such as Occidental's own heirloom garlic aficionado Chester Aaron or microbial ecologist Ignacio Chapella, inspired the crowd. By the end of the afternoon, guests would cast votes for their chosen favorites and the results would be announced and cheered.

SUMMER BIODIVERSITY TASTING MENU

*40 heirloom tomatoes,
sliced fresh for sampling with a toothpick*

*12 varieties of hard and softneck garlic,
roasted and piped onto slivers of cucumber*

*20 different sauté greens, simply sautéed
with olive oil, salt, and lemon*

*15 varieties of basil, made into pestos and
served on crustini*

*OAEC's 100-ingredient Summer Biodiversity
Salad Mix with a simple vinaigrette*

*A selection of rare heritage summer
stone fruits and berries*

*Cold infused garden herb water
with sweet edible flowers*

Andy's Polish Pink tomato shown here sliced with Purple de Milpa tomatillos. It can weigh up to 2 pounds and has incomparably sweet, creamy flesh. A friend introduced it to the Mother Garden 25 years ago when he gave us a handful of seeds from his father, a remarkable Old World seedsman, who had brought the seeds from his native Poland meticulously folded in a piece of tissue. It won our Tomato Tasting and, through our plant sales, has risen to the status of Bay Area legend! PHOTO BY DOUG GOSLING.

Hydrating Lemon Cucumber Purslane Salad

Purslane, or *verdogalas* as it is called in Spanish, is a common vegetable in Latin American cuisine as well as in the Middle East, North Africa, Europe, and Asia. Here in much of California, it volunteers as a heat-loving "weed" that we celebrate in the garden whenever it appears, though we also intentionally grow a fleshier, upright cultivar with golden leaves called Golden Purslane. It's a nutritional powerhouse, one of the few plant-based sources of omega-3 fatty acids, a welcome addition to our primarily vegetarian kitchen.

Cucumbers and purslane are a match made in heaven and always seem to appear together in the garden at the same time. *What grows together goes together* in this thirst-quenching summer side.

Serves 4–6

4–6 lemon cucumbers or 2 regular
    medium cucumbers
1 bunch purslane (about 1 cup plucked)
Juice of 1 lemon
¼ cup olive oil
4 sprigs parsley, finely chopped
Salt and pepper to taste

Serves 30–40

10 pounds lemon cucumbers or
    regular cucumbers
4–5 bunches purslane (about 5 cups plucked)
Juice of 6 lemons
1 cup olive oil
2 bunches parsley, finely chopped
Salt and pepper to taste

Slice the lemon cucumbers into half-moons and reserve in a mixing bowl. Pluck the leaves and small shoots from the tougher main stem of the purslane. Combine all ingredients in the bowl with the cukes. Adjust the salt, pepper, and lemon to your liking. Chill until ready to serve.

VARIATIONS

Summery Composed Salad: Substitute cilantro for the parsley, add a handful of lightly blanched and chilled green beans and cubes of avocado. Serve mounded over a bed of crisp romaine lettuce or as a side with summer tacos.

Chilled Cucumber Purslane Soup: For a luscious green gazpacho, blend chilled, leftover cucumber salad with equal parts Green Stripe or other ripe green variety tomatoes. Add a little more lemon and/or thin with a little water, if it needs it. Serve with a swirl of nice olive oil and a sprig of mint.

PHOTO BY TALI AIONA.

SCHOOL GARDEN TEA PARTY

A giant sunflower towers over curious residents Sabine and Lucy. PHOTO BY JIM COLEMAN.

*I see in the future the move-
ment for edible education, the
movement of school gardens,
being a major political force,
because when that child has
tasted a healthy tomato, and
more than that gone through
the miracle of having that
seed give them one hundred
tomatoes, that child can never
be brainwashed into the idea
of scarcity or dependence on
Monsanto. That child can never
ever be sterilized to think bad
food is good for you. They will
celebrate taste and quality and
nutrition and freedom. That is
going to be a very important set
of players.*
— VANDANA SHIVA

A sensory wander through
the garden brings learning
to life in ways that sitting in
a fluorescent classroom of
plastic furniture and recycled
air never could. Nibbling
on raspberries and mint
leaves, caressing lamb's ears,
listening to the hum of the
pollinators, smelling the
sweet perfume of a jasmine
flower . . . Although there
are unlimited academic
opportunities in gardens, the

most valuable concept for children to experience is that of wonder. The behavior patterns considered epidemic to our plugged-in generation of children, what Richard Louv has named "Nature Deficit Disorder," largely vanish when youth discover their own role in nature's web of connections. Narratives of scarcity, alienation, and boredom are replaced with discovery and awe.

The natural outcome of children's experience in the school garden is that they acquire a taste for seasonal healthy foods and become both informed food consumers and producers. Given what is currently available, how else could we expect them to know the difference? How could young people possibly develop a palate and craving for healthy food if they've never actually had access to it? The pleasure of being outside in the fresh air doing the physical activity it takes to sow and grow fruits and vegetables, coupled with the satisfaction of picking, preparing, and eating truly fresh, nutritious food, equips students with the sensory feedback they need to make healthy choices. When students are inspired through experiences in a school garden, integrated cafeterias, and other programs that support local seed-to-table food systems, their enthusiasm spreads and they become key promoters of health in their whole community.

Thanks to one of Sowing Circle's founding members, Susan McGovern, and her fourth-grade class in 1995 at local Harmony Elementary and Salmon Creek Middle School, OAEC supported the installation of a school garden just down the road. Profoundly influenced by David Sobel's book *Place-Based Education*, The Harmony Habitat Garden was born, a place-based experiential extension of the classroom. From these collaborative beginnings grew OAEC's nationally recognized School Garden Teacher Training and Support Program.

For nearly two decades, the program has developed into a unique offering that supports teams of teachers, administrators, parents, and garden coordinators to engage in a physical and pedagogical redesign of their campuses. Through a five-day intensive at OAEC followed by ongoing support back at school, teams experience garden-based whole-systems thinking and learn how to implement it. Each participant attends with the understanding of their commitment to being the bridge that brings this model back to their schools, curricula, and communities. Our Mother Garden grows excellent community organizers!

PHOTO BY TALI AIONA.

School Garden Sprout Wraps

It is a radical surprise—a revolutionary paradigm shift—for students to fully experience the answer to the question, "Where does my food come from?" A seed! Not a store!

Sprouting seeds with kids is a simple method that demonstrates a critical portion of a plant's life cycle and provides us nutrient-dense food in the process! Sprout farming can happen on your kitchen counter or your desk at school. All you need are some untreated organic seeds, clean water, a jar, cheesecloth, a ring lid or rubber band, and a few days. Mung beans and alfalfa seeds are easy to sprout and tasty to eat, though many different seeds will yield delicious sprouts ready to eat in less than a week.

For 4–6 kids

6–10 extra-large lettuce leaves or tender
  cabbage leaves
2 cups sprouts
1 cup optional additional vegetables such
  as shredded carrots or cabbage, thinly
  sliced peppers, greens like spinach or
  arugula, or anything else in season
⅔ cup Lemony Chickweed Pistou (page
  256) or OAEC Green Goddess Salad
  Dressing (page 241)
A pinch of edible flower petals for color:
  borage, calendula, sunflower, etc.

For a class or party of 30–40 kids

6 large heads of lettuce or 4 heads
  of cabbage
6–8 cups sprouts
6 cups additional vegetables such as shredded carrots or cabbage, thinly sliced
  peppers, greens like spinach or arugula,
  or anything else in season
4 cups Lemony Chickweed Pistou (page
  256) or OAEC Green Goddess Salad
  Dressing (page 241)
½ cup of edible flower petals for color:
  borage, calendula, sunflower, etc.

After rinsing and drying the large lettuce leaves, fill them with a small kid-sized handful of sprouts and garden vegetables (a scant ⅓ cup total). Try not to overfill them or they will be hard to close and messy to eat. Drizzle with dressing and roll up tight like a burrito. You can even try tying them closed with pea shoots, if you have them growing in your garden, or poke them with a "toothpick" improvised from a sprig of rosemary. Garnish with flower petals and *voilà*, an elegant snack for a garden tea party.

HOW TO MAKE SPROUTS

Place the seeds in a jar (less than a quarter full), and fill the jar with water. Seeds will expand significantly as they sprout, so be sure to leave plenty of room. Cover the jar with cheesecloth and use a fitted metal canning ring or a rubber band to hold it in place. Allow the seeds to soak overnight in order to break down the outer seed coat.

The next day, rinse the seeds with filtered water several times until the water runs clear. Making sure that your netting device is securely fastened, pour out all the water and invert the jar at an angle resting in a bowl so that there is sufficient drainage and airflow. Soggy seeds can rot! Store the inverted jar at room temperature. Less sunlight at the beginning encourages them to grow long as they reach for the sun. Moving them into sunlight after a few days allows the chlorophyll to turn green.

Rinse your sprouts twice a day with filtered water. When they are long, taste one!

Rainbow Beet and Carrot Salad with Garden Herbs

Beets come in a surprising variety of colors, shapes, and sizes—red, golden, white, and candy-striped, round and cylindrically shaped. Some of the varieties that we have trialed in the Mother Garden include Detroit Dark Red, Crosby Flat Egyptian, Bull's Blood, Chioggia, Burpee's Golden, Albino Vereduna, Formanova, and various types of mangels—the ancient predecessor of modern beets that was originally raised for livestock feed.

This salad is a simple way to highlight the diversity of heirloom beet and carrot varieties in the garden. Let the natural size, shape, and color pattern of the roots tell you how they would like to be cut—whole, quartered, diagonally sliced, or cubed. Make sure to keep all the vegetables separate until plating them up at the end, otherwise the red beets bleed all over everything and you will have a fuchsia salad instead of a rainbow salad.

Serves 4–6

ROOTS

1½ pounds mixed heirloom carrots and beets

DRESSING

4 sprigs fresh mitsuba, parsley, basil, or chervil
4 chives
Pinch of celery seeds
⅓ cup Summer Herb Flower vinegar (page 269), plain red wine vinegar, or apple cider vinegar
¼ cup olive oil
Salt to taste
Garnish: edible flowers, sprigs of herbs

Serves 30–40

ROOTS

10–12 pounds mixed heirloom carrots and beets

DRESSING

1 bunch fresh mitsuba, parsley, basil, or chervil
1 small bunch chives
2 teaspoons celery seeds
1½ cups Summer Herb Flower vinegar (page 269), plain red wine vinegar, or apple cider vinegar
1 cup olive oil
Salt to taste
Garnish: edible flowers, sprigs of herbs

If you're using baby beets, leave them whole. Cut large beets in half. Place the reds and Chioggias in one pot fitted with a steamer basket and the golden, yellow, and whites in another (or steam them one after another if you only have one basket). With a little water in the bottom, steam the beets for 15 minutes or so until soft when pierced with a fork. Drain and allow to cool. In a bowl of cold water, peel the skins with your hands and rinse, separating the varieties into individual bowls. Cut the beets into cubes, quarters, or slices, and reserve in separate bowls.

Boil a large pot of water and prepare an ice bath for blanching. Peel the carrots and cut into diagonal slices, cubes, or half-moons. Blanch each variety separately and shock in an ice bath. Reserve in separate bowls.

Whisk all the ingredients for the dressing together. Divide the dressing evenly among the bowls of roots and toss to coat. Allow to marinate for 20 minutes or longer for larger chunks of vegetables. Taste and adjust the salt and vinegar to your liking.

Mound the root varieties side by side in a pleasing pattern such as rings, a yin-yang swirl, asymmetric clusters, or of course a rainbow. You may serve this over a bed of raw greens such as miner's lettuce, frisée, romaine, baby mustards, or wild arugula. Garnish with sprigs of herbs or edible flowers.

PHOTO BY TALI AIONA.

PHOTO BY DOUG GOSLING.

Cumin-Marinated Runner Beans

We grow multiple varieties of runner beans in the same bed—big, fat brown ones, smaller pink polka-dotted ones, and the stunning and prolific purple speckled variety. Be sure to sort bean varieties and cook them separately as cooking times vary greatly.

Serve these plump beauties with toothpicks as part of a mezze plate along with your favorite olives and some spicy pan-fried almonds. Or use them to top a hearty salad.

Serves 4-6

1 cup dry runner beans, any color (will
    plump up to 2 cups cooked)
Juice of 2 lemons
¼ cup balsamic vinegar
1 clove garlic, crushed
1 teaspoon whole cumin or fennel seeds
1 small pinch red chili flakes
1 tablespoon finely chopped fresh marjoram
1¼ teaspoons salt, to taste
½ cup olive oil

Serves 30-40

5 cups dry runner beans, any color (will
    plump up to 10 cups cooked)
Juice of 10 lemons
1¼ cups balsamic vinegar
3 cloves garlic, crushed
1 tablespoon whole cumin or fennel seeds
1 teaspoon red chili flakes
¼ cup finely chopped fresh marjoram
2 tablespoons salt, to taste
2½ cups olive oil

Soak the dried runner beans overnight. Cook according to the directions on page 218 until completely soft and tender. Drain and rinse well. Mix with the remaining ingredients, except the olive oil, and salt to taste. Marinate overnight in an airtight container in the fridge. When you're ready to serve, stir in the olive oil.

Coriander Carrots with Black Olives and Orange Zest

Serves 4–6

2 pounds carrots, peeled

2 tablespoons olive oil

2 tablespoons sherry vinegar

1 clove garlic, crushed

1 teaspoon coriander seeds, dry toasted and crushed in a mortar and pestle

½ teaspoon cumin seeds, dry toasted

2 teaspoons fresh marjoram, chopped

1 teaspoon orange zest

¼ cup pitted oil-cured black olives

Serves 30–40

12 pounds carrots, peeled

¾ cup olive oil

¾ cup sherry vinegar

4 cloves garlic, crushed

2 tablespoons coriander seeds, dry toasted and crushed in a mortar and pestle

1 tablespoon cumin seeds, dry toasted

¼ cup fresh marjoram, chopped

1 tablespoon orange zest

2 cups pitted oil-cured black olives

Cut the carrots into 4-inch batons. Briefly blanch the carrots (directions for blanching on page 116), leaving them quite al dente, and shock in an ice bath. Combine with the rest of the ingredients and marinate in a shallow container for 20 minutes or more, stirring occasionally to distribute the marinade. Serve as a part of a mezze platter.

Marinated Shaved Fennel

Chunky marinades like this make nice salad dressings. Serve mounded on a generous bed of raw baby greens such as wild arugula, baby mustards, or miner's lettuce.

Serves 4–6

2 fennel bulbs, fronds removed

1 very small clove garlic, crushed

¼ cup nice white wine or sherry vinegar

½ cup olive oil

Pinch of red chili flakes

½ teaspoon lemon zest

Salt to taste

Serves 30–40

20 fennel bulbs, fronds removed

4 cloves garlic, crushed

¾ cup nice white wine or sherry vinegar

1½ cups olive oil

1 teaspoon red chili flakes

1 tablespoon lemon zest

Salt to taste

Shave the fennel on a mandoline or slice with a sharp knife into very thin half-moons. Stir all the ingredients together in a bowl. Allow to marinate for at least half an hour, as the intensity of the anise flavor mellows as it marinates.

VARIATION

Toss with ½ cup (2 cups) blanched, peeled fresh fava beans (for detailed directions, see page 118).

Raw Kale Salads—Three Variations

Yes, raw kale salad is a little retro at this point as far as food fads go, but somehow it never gets old for the true veggie-phile. Kale grows all year here and gets even sweeter in the cold fall and winter garden, so we like to perk up a meal of heavy cool season comfort food with this easy weeknight side.

Serves 4–6
1 generous bunch tender kale—any variety
Juice of 1–2 lemons
1 teaspoon salt
2 tablespoons olive oil
1 small clove garlic, crushed (optional)

Serves 30–40
6 generous bunches tender kale—
    any variety
Juice of 8–10 lemons
2 tablespoons salt
½ cup olive oil
4 cloves garlic, crushed (optional)

Strip the leaves off the kale stems. Feed the stems to the goats, compost, or reserve for another use, see page 155. Stack the leaves, roll like a newspaper, and chop into thin strips. Add the salt and lemon juice and massage with your hands until the greens begin to "cook" down. Let the kale sit for 10 minutes or so while you prepare the rest of the meal, then return and toss it again. When the greens have reduced down fully and released much of their moisture, add the olive oil and optional crushed garlic, and stir to incorporate.

VARIATIONS

Baby Ornamental Kale Leaves with Avocado and Cilantro: Choose either pink or green ornamental kale, as the colors of mixed varieties tend to run together. Complete the above directions for the basic recipe, then add 1 avocado (4 avocados) cubed and 2 tablespoons (½ cup) finely chopped fresh cilantro. Massage once more to gently break up and distribute the avocado, making a creamy dressing but leaving a few nice chunks.

Frizzy Kale with Agretti, Scallion, and Sesame: Substitute rice vinegar for the lemon juice and toasted sesame oil for the olive oil. Add 1 bunch (3 bunches) agretti, otherwise known as Italian salt wort, plucked from the stems, and 3 scallions (1 bunch scallions) sliced into thin rounds. When you're ready to serve, garnish with a sprinkle of 1 tablespoon (¼ cup) toasted brown or black sesame seeds.

Spigarello with Feta, Marjoram, and Toasted Sunflower Seeds: Tear the spigarello into bite-sized pieces rather than chiffonading them to preserve their deeply lobed leaves. Complete the above directions for the basic recipe. Then add ¼ cup (1 cup) crumbled feta and 1 teaspoon (1 tablespoon) finely chopped marjoram. When you're ready to serve, garnish with a sprinkle of 2 tablespoons (½ cup) toasted sunflower seeds. *Note:* The sunflower seeds get soggy if incorporated in the salad and left to sit, so reserve and garnish as needed.

Zesty Purple Cabbage Slaw

The locoto or manzano "aji" hot pepper is another Andean native that grows in our microclimate with the help of an occasional tucking-in with a frost protection blanket. Botanically unlike most common hot peppers, this shiny, black-seeded perennial variety brings us a taste of the tropics in January and February. Its distinctively fruity bite and lingering heat are sure to take the chill off!

We serve some variation of this mayo-free slaw all year round, but this one works great as part of a Winter Adapted Taco Bar (page 176).

Serves 4–6

1 small head red cabbage, shredded (about 6–8 cups)

½ teaspoon salt or more to taste

⅓ cup fresh lemon juice

1 teaspoon lemon zest

¼ cup chopped parsley or cilantro

2 tablespoons wild onions, society garlic, or scallions, cut into rounds

1 teaspoon finely minced fresh manzano or other hot pepper, or a dash of hot sauce

½ cup olive oil

Serves 30–40

5 heads red cabbage, shredded (about 12 quarts)

2 tablespoons salt or more to taste

1½ cups fresh lemon juice

2 tablespoons lemon zest

1 cup chopped parsley or cilantro

½ cup wild onions, society garlic, or scallions, cut into rounds

1 tablespoon finely minced fresh manzano or other hot pepper, or 2 teaspoons hot sauce

1 cup olive oil

For the best texture, slice the red cabbage by hand into very thin, long strips rather than shredding it with grater or a food processor. Combine the cabbage with the salt and lemon juice and massage for a minute with your hands to combine. Let the cabbage sit in this marinade for 15 minutes or so while you prep the remaining ingredients. Toss all the ingredients together, taste for salt and acid, and adjust accordingly. Serve with a rice meal—you'll want something to sop up the delicious purple juice!

VARIATION

Take it in an Asian direction by adding a teaspoon (2 tablespoons for the large batch) of freshly grated ginger—great with BBQ or as a side with a rice noodle dish.

PHOTO BY DOUG GOSLING.

Blanched Romanesco with Winter Pistou on a Bed of Ornamental Kale

Romanesco, an heirloom cauliflower from northern Italy, will continue to spin out its florets in Fibonacci spirals until it reaches a diameter of 24 inches! Its mild, sweet flavor is somewhere between broccoli and cauliflower.

While delicious sautéed and tossed with Parmesan or impressive roasted whole, we've found that the Day-Glo psychedelic florets of Romanesco are best showcased when simply blanched to lock in the chartreuse color and minimally disturb the form. Offset by outrageous pink ornamental kale, Romanesco is the centerpiece and inspiration for our famous Veggie Mandala (page 117).

Serves 4–6
1 large head Romanesco
Water, salt, and ice for blanching
½ pound pink ornamental kale leaves
1 cup marjoram pistou (page 286)

Serves 30–40
6 large heads Romanesco
Water, salt, and ice for blanching
2 pounds pink ornamental kale leaves
4–6 cups marjoram pistou (page 286)

Carefully cut the Romanesco into bite-sized florets. To avoid waste, you can also cut the core into batons (blanch them separately) or reserve it for a later use. Bring a pot of salted water to a boil. Blanch the florets for 2 minutes until they're cooked, but retain their bright green color. Plunge into an ice bath. Drain and reserve.

On a wide platter, thoughtfully arrange the florets on a bed of raw multicolored ornamental kale leaves. Serve with winter pistou and/or Preserved Lemon Mayo (page 293) for dipping.

Winter Frisée Salad with Crunchy Fried Mung Beans

Serves 4–6
1 grapefruit
1 cup Mixed Citrus Salad Dressing (page 292)
6 watermelon radishes, tops removed
1 cup mung beans soaked overnight and
    fried in coconut oil (Crispy Fried Beans
    variation page 298)
1 large head frisée
1 avocado

Serves 30–40
6 grapefruit
4 cups Mixed Citrus Salad Dressing (page 292)
4 bunches watermelon radishes, tops removed
3 cups mung beans soaked overnight and
    fried in coconut oil (Crispy Fried Beans
    variation page 298)
6 large heads frisée
6–8 avocados

Soak the mung beans overnight and drain. Cut the grapefruit into segments or supremes and reserve (for directions on how to cut supremes, see Mixed Winter Citrus Salsa with Yacon and Pineapple Sage on page 292). Squeeze and reserve any leftover juice from the grapefruit membranes for the dressing. Follow directions for the Mixed Citrus Salad Dressing.

Slice the watermelon radishes into thin half-moons. Pour half of the citrus dressing over the slices and let them marinate while you follow the recipe on page 298 to make deep-fried mung beans in coconut oil. Set the fried mung beans aside to drain on paper towels.

Wash and spin the frisée. In a large mixing bowl, drizzle the rest of the citrus dressing and swirl it around to coat all the way up the sides of the mixing bowl. Add the frisée and toss so that the leaves are evenly coated, but not soaked with dressing. Add a small handful of greens to each plate.

Cut the avocado into slivers and scoop out with a spoon. Top each mound of frisée with a few slivers of avocado and a few grapefruit segments. Arrange the slices of watermelon radish in a pretty pattern toward the edge of the plate. Top with a handful of fried mung beans and a sprig of parsley or mint. For a large crowd, arrange this salad on a single large platter rather than individually plated.

Yacon and Radish Platter with Chili and Lemon

Yacon is a crunchy white perennial sunflower relative that produces a tuber, similar to jicama, but juicier, sweeter, and in our opinion better, because it actually grows in our garden! Frost sweetens it as it sits in the ground over winter, so we keep it stored in situ until it's ready to dig up and be eaten. Another low-maintenance Andean perennial winter crop.

Serves 4–6

1 pound yacon, peeled

1 pound watermelon radishes

1 pound other radishes such as Spanish Black, Easter Egg, French Breakfast, or green meat daikon

1 teaspoon finely chopped manzano (also called rocoto or locoto) pepper, or small pinch of cayenne

¼ cup fresh lemon or lime juice

1 teaspoon lemon or lime zest

Salt to taste

Serves 30–40

8 pounds yacon, peeled

8 bunches watermelon radishes

8 bunches other radishes such as Spanish Black, Easter Egg, French Breakfast, or green meat daikon

1 tablespoon finely chopped manzano (also called rocoto or locoto) pepper, or 1 teaspoon cayenne

1 cup fresh lemon or lime juice

1 tablespoon lemon or lime zest

Salt to taste

Cut the raw yacon into batons and raw radishes into thin rounds or half-moons, keeping each variety in a separate bowl. Divide the pepper, lemon juice, zest, and salt equally among the bowls and toss. Arrange decoratively on a platter.

VARIATION

While fruitier than the radish platter recipe and best enjoyed as a snack, sweet pepino is also delicious prepared in the same manner, topped with lime juice, salt, and a sprinkle of cayenne. The name *pepino* was given by a Spanish conquistador in Peru who mistakenly called it a cucumber. While mildly sweet and melon-like in flavor, the plant is not related to melons or cucumbers. Botanically speaking, it isn't in the cucurbit family it all—this perennial (in frost-free areas) shrub, *Solanum muricatum*, is more closely related to peppers and tomatoes.

A Cautionary Tale, and
the Importance of Biodiversity

The diversity of potato varieties that have been developed in their native South American bioregion is staggering. In an OAEC exchange trip to Peru, we met a farmer growing over 200 varieties, all of which he could identify individually just by the foliage! PHOTO BY DOUG GOSLING.

In the 1840s, a fungus, *Phytopthera infestans*, also called late blight or potato blight, attacked the Irish potato crop, decimating entire harvests for many years and causing the death or emigration of over a million people. The famine was the result of only a single variety of potato, the Irish Lumper, being cultivated in Ireland. While the Lumper was well adapted to western Ireland's poor, soggy soil, the variety was not disease-resistant. In contrast, potato varieties in the Andes where the crop was first domesticated number in the thousands, intentionally diversified to survive a wide range of environmental stresses and avoid catastrophic crop failure. Thanks to strains bred for disease resistance found in the diverse Andean gene pool, potatoes worldwide have thankfully rebounded from this disastrous breakdown in the food supply.[10]

Papas a la Huancaina

Perhaps our version of this dish should actually be called "Papas a la Sonoma," as we like to incorporate our local Bodega Red potato into this classic Andean dish along with Rose Fir Apple Fingerlings and Peruvian Blues. This is an authentic way to showcase the glorious biodiversity of potatoes.

Salsa de Huancaina (recipe follows) is a spicy room-temperature cheese sauce that gets its kick from Aji Amarillo, *Capsicum baccatum*, one of our favorite Peruvian chiles that perennializes in our frost-free greenhouse. This bright-yellow beauty is long and tapered with a wonderful fruity flavor to balance the intense cayenne-like heat. If you can't grow fresh Aji Amarillos, you can substitute another fresh yellow, orange, or red hot pepper of your choice. Try yellow cayenne or Scotch bonnet, or look for jarred aji amarillo paste in Latin American markets.

Authentic salsa de huancaina almost always contains soda crackers, but we typically don't carry highly processed items like this in our kitchen. We've found that thickening the sauce with one of the potatoes and a few of the hard-boiled egg yolks does the trick.

SALAD

Serves 4–6

6 small new Bodega Red potatoes
6 small new Red Fir Apple Fingerling potatoes
6 small new Peruvian Blue potatoes
    or 2 pounds total small new potatoes,
    an assortment of any varieties
4–6 eggs
1 head crisp butter lettuce or romaine
½ cup Salsa de Huancaina
½ cup black olives
½ cup crumbled queso fresco, farmer's
    cheese, or feta
2 tablespoons finely chopped fresh parsley

Serves 30–40

4 pounds small new Bodega Red potatoes
4 pounds small new Red Fir Apple
    Fingerling potatoes
4 pounds small new Peruvian Blue potatoes
    or 12 pounds total small new potatoes,
    an assortment of any varieties
30–40 eggs, 1 per person
6 heads crisp butter lettuce or romaine
2 cups Salsa de Huancaina
2 cups black olives
2 cups crumbled queso fresco, farmer's
    cheese, or feta
¾ cup finely chopped fresh parsley

Boil the potatoes in water until they're just soft when poked with a fork. For best results, cook each variety of potato separately, as cooking times vary. Drain and allow to cool. Hard boil the eggs for 7 minutes, let them cool, peel them, and slice into halves. Arrange a bed of the lettuce with one or two of each variety of potato on top along with two hard-boiled egg halves. Cover with a few tablespoons of the huancaina sauce and top with black olives, queso fresco, and fresh parsley. Serve room temperature for a luncheon first course.

PHOTO BY TALI AIONA.

SALSA DE HUANCAINA

Serves 4–6

3 Aji Amarillo chiles, or 2 tablespoons
   aji amarillo paste

1 clove garlic

2 tablespoons sunflower oil, or other neutral
   oil for cooking

1 medium yellow onion, chopped

1 cup queso fresco, farmer's cheese, or feta

1 small, boiled potato (from the
   recipe above)

2 hard-boiled egg yolks (from the
   recipe above)

½–1 cup half-and-half

Salt to taste—will depend on the saltiness
   of the cheese

Serves 30–40

9 or so Aji Amarillo chiles, or ¾ cup
   aji amarillo paste

4 cloves garlic

⅓ cup sunflower oil, or other neutral oil
   for cooking

4 large yellow onions, chopped

4 cups queso fresco, farmer's cheese, or feta

4 small, boiled potatoes (from the
   recipe above)

8 hard-boiled egg yolks (from the
   recipe above)

2–4 cups half-and-half

Salt to taste—will depend on the saltiness
   of the cheese

Coarsely chop the chiles. Remove some of the seeds if you are concerned about the salsa being too spicy, or leave them in if you like it hot. Mince the garlic and reserve. Heat the oil in a small skillet and add the onions and chiles (or paste). Sauté until soft and translucent. Add the garlic and sauté a minute more. Remove from the heat and allow to cool slightly. Add the sautéed mixture, remaining ingredients, and some of the half-and-half to a blender and whiz to a smooth puree. Add more half-and-half (or oil) to thin, if desired. If you want a brighter-yellow sauce, add a pinch of turmeric.

VARIATIONS

Sauce: Instead of cheesy Salsa de Huancaina, use the lighter Aji de Huacatay sauce on page 275.

Elegant appetizer: During one of our "Honoring Crops of the Incas" dinners, Doug created an appetizer version by baking the baby potatoes instead of boiling them. He scooped out the innards and pureed them with the huancaina sauce, and then piped the mixture back into the potato skins with a star-tipped pastry bag. By sprinkling them with very finely cubed hard-boiled eggs and olives, he created a bite-sized appetizer for passing.

BODEGA RED POTATOES

Bodega Reds are one of only a handful of potato varieties introduced to the United States directly from the potato motherland: South America. Local legend claims that before the Gold Rush of the late 1840s, the Bodega Red potato jumped ship with a sailor from Chile in Bodega Bay in Sonoma County.

The Bodega Red prospered, and the area stretching from Bodega Bay to Petaluma became known as the Potato Capital of California. During this time, the Bodega Red was shipped on barges from Bodega Bay to San Francisco and was also taken to gold fields in the Sierras to feed the miners. Spud Point Marina in the Bodega Bay Harbor was given its name after a barge filled with Bodega Reds sank at that spot.

But in the 1970s, the Bodega Red disappeared. The Bodega Land Trust and Slow Food Sonoma County North educated the Bodega community about the potato and its historical significance, and it was listed by Slow Food International's Ark of Taste as a variety worth preserving. This resulted in an anonymous donation of a few tiny tubers, which, with the help of a plant lab in Washington and a team of devoted backyard garden enthusiasts, have now been grown out to a quantity where reintroduction to farmers and gardeners is possible. OAEC now offers them at our plant sales.

The Bodega Red potato is slightly flattened and oblong in shape with delicately thin pink-red skin and creamy flesh.

RECIPE LIST

Spring

Fresh Shelling Peas with
  Mitsuba Meyer Lemon Butter
Grilled Fava Pods
Garlicky Sautéed Fava Leaves
Roasted Fennel with Chili Flakes
Fennel Frond Fritters
Crispy Garlic Scapes
Sautéed Cabbage, Leeks, and Green Coriander
  with Roasted Garlic Scapes
Roasted Rainbow Carrots with
  Marinated Favas and Tarragon
Buttery Thumbelinas on a
  Bed of Braised Baby Amaranth Greens
Sautéed Shungiku Shoots with
  Sesame Seeds and Garlic
Simple Sautéed Chard with Onion

Summer

Early-Summer Flash-Braised Baby
  Amaranth Greens
Cumin-Roasted Summer Squash
Tromboncino Coins on a Bed of Their Own Greens
Pepita-Encrusted Squash Blossoms Stuffed with
  Goat Cheese and Mint
Young Runner Bean Pods with
  Marjoram Butter and Scarlet Flowers
Roasted Cherry Tomatoes with Lemon Verbena
Biodiversity Beans with Lemon Dill Butter
Orach Paneer—Spicy Creamed Mountain Spinach

Barbecued Eggplant Stacks with Coyote Mint
  Sauce and Chèvre

Fall

Griddle-Seared Brassica Shoots with
  Chili Flakes and Garlic
New Zealand Spinach Shoots with
  Parmesan and Almonds
Fall Garden "Stir-Fry" with Fresh Herbs
Wilted Arugula in a Whole Roasted Pumpkin
  with Candied Pepitas
Double-Roasted Beets with Balsamic Glaze

Winter

Grilled Nopalitos with Herbs and Cotija
Basic Winter Squash Puree
Brussels Sprouts with Alexanders, Leeks,
  and Dijon Beurre Blanc
Roasted Baby Turnips with Smallage, Lemon,
  and Capers
Perfect Sautéed Mushrooms
Slow-Roasted Sunchokes with Wild Mushrooms
Gently Boiled Variegated Collards with Lemon,
  Garlic, and Olive Oil
Wintry Oven-Crisped Tree Collard Ribbons
Dougo's Melted Leeks
Domino Potatoes with Society Garlic and Bay Leaves
Mashua Mashed Potatoes
Curried Mashua and Potatoes
Roasted Andean Tubers with Ocopa

Fresh Shelling Peas with Mitsuba Meyer Lemon Butter

Mitsuba, otherwise known as Japanese parsley, is not a true parsley, but an herb in its own right from a different genus. As a shade-tolerant and readily self-seeding perennial, it makes a graceful understory plant in an edible landscape—a great herb choice for planting on the shady side of the house. It is a favorite in the OAEC kitchen for its pleasant floral taste that pairs well with Meyer lemon.

Serves 4–6

3 cups fresh peas, shelled

½ cup Basic Garden Herb Butter
 (page 271); use mitsuba for the herb
 and Meyer lemon for the zest

Serves 30–40

10 cups fresh peas, shelled

2 cups Basic Garden Herb Butter
 (page 271); use mitsuba for the herb
 and Meyer lemon for the zest

Steam the peas in a pot fitted with a steamer basket and a little water in the bottom on high heat for a few minutes until they turn from pale to bright green. Serve while piping hot with a round of the mitsuba Meyer lemon compound butter.

The purple-podded pea is an extremely rare heirloom whose seed has been saved and grown for 28 years in the Mother Garden. Its flowers are edible, and the very young pods can be harvested as purple snow peas. Later in its life cycle, fresh shelling peas are wonderful steamed with a tab of garden herb butter. Finally, the dried seeds are stored for planting next year. PHOTO BY DOUG GOSLING

Grilled Fava Pods

Serve these whole as a grill-side appetizer while folks are waiting for the next course. Much like edamame, when people open up the pods with their hands, the salt and oil rubs off onto the beans. Don't forget the napkins!

Serves 4-6
3 pounds whole fava bean pods
Salt and olive oil

Serves 30-40
12–15 pounds whole fava bean pods
Salt and olive oil

Toss the whole fava pods with the oil, sprinkle with lots of salt, and grill them over medium coals. As the outsides get good and charred, the beans inside will steam to smoky perfection. Serve whole.

Garlicky Sautéed Fava Leaves

The extremely rare Red-Flowered Fava, pictured below, once on the verge of extinction, is grown out every spring in the Mother Garden. This variety is well worth saving because it adds yet another benefit to an already long list of fava attributes—in addition to enriching the soil and giving delicious beans and tender leaves, it adds a touch of beauty to an otherwise plain cover crop.

While waiting for the pregnant fava pods to fatten up in late spring, we get a little impatient and nibble on the tender leaves, too! Tender fava leaves make a wonderful sauté green with a nutty, beany flavor. Early in the season, the whole tender tips can be sautéed, but later on once the pods have set, it is best to pick off the large individual leaves from the stem as the stems become tough and stringy. These can be served alone as a side dish or as a bed for a mound of Green Garlic White Bean Primavera (page 197) or roasted baby carrots and turnips. For an added touch, garnish the finished dish with fava flowers.

Serves 4-6
1 pound fava leaves, any variety (3 quarts
    loosely packed)
2 tablespoons oil, for cooking
3 cloves garlic, minced
2 tablespoons dry sherry
Salt to taste

Serves 30-40
8–10 pounds fava leaves, any variety
    (21 quarts loosely packed)
1 cup oil, for cooking
10 cloves garlic, minced
1 cup dry sherry
Salt to taste

Wash the fava leaves and pick them from the stems, if tough. Warm the oil in a sauté pan on medium-high heat. For large quantities, cook in batches directly on a flat-top griddle. Add the crushed garlic, wait 5 seconds, then add the fava leaves and sherry and toss together in the pan. Sauté until the greens soften and cook down. Remove from the heat before the garlic turns brown. Salt to taste and serve.

PHOTO BY DOUG GOSLING.

Roasted Fennel with Chili Flakes

Fennel, garlic, and chili flakes in combination form the flavor base for many classic Italian dishes. Use this as the base ingredient for other recipes such as Roasted Fennel and Black Olive Salad Dressing (page 242) or Roasted Fennel Soup (page 96). You can also serve this as a stand-alone side dish with fish or pork, toss it with pasta, or use it to top a grilled pizza.

Serves 4–6
2–3 large fennel bulbs
2 cloves garlic, crushed
1 tablespoon olive oil
Pinch of salt
Pinch of red chili flakes

Serves 30–40
14–18 large fennel bulbs
5 cloves garlic, crushed
¼ cup olive oil
1 tablespoon salt
1 teaspoon red chili flakes

Preheat the oven to 375°F. Cut the fennel lengthwise into quarters, reserving the fronds for another use. Toss with the garlic and oil, sprinkle with salt and chili flakes, and spread on a cookie sheet, cast-iron pan or baking dish. Roast for 15 minutes, flip with a metal spatula for even cooking, and roast for another 10 minutes until soft and caramelized.

VARIATION

Add wedges of onion or ribs of celery cut into 2-inch diagonals.

Fennel Frond Fritters

Common wild fennel springs up like a weed everywhere in California, even in urban areas. While this wild variety doesn't make a bulb, chefs harvest the fronds, gather the seeds to flavor sauces and meat dishes, or use the pollen for dusting as a delicate garnish for soups and appetizers.

Here's the best way we've found for using up a proliferation of wild fennel that has sprung up in the garden or a big pile of fronds left over from a bulb binge. Blanching mellows out the licorice flavor for an elegant appetizer akin to a crab cake.

Serves 4–6

3 large bunches fennel fronds (1½ cups blanched and chopped)

2 eggs

1 bunch parsley, finely chopped

2 cloves garlic, minced

2 teaspoons lemon zest

½ teaspoon red pepper flakes

1 cup bread crumbs, total (⅔ cup in the mix, ⅓ cup for dredging)

Salt

Oil for the pan

Serves 30–40

12 large bunches fennel fronds (6–8 cups blanched and chopped)

15 eggs

4 bunches parsley, finely chopped

6 cloves garlic, minced

2 tablespoons lemon zest

2 teaspoons red pepper flakes

5 cups bread crumbs, total (3 cups in the mix, 2 cups for dredging)

Salt

Oil for the pan

Blanch the fennel fronds in boiling water for 15 to 30 seconds and shock in an ice bath. Squeeze out as much water as possible and pat dry. Chop the wispy parts of the fronds finely and discard the thicker stems. In a large mixing bowl, combine the fronds with the eggs, parsley, garlic, lemon zest, pepper flakes, and ⅔ cup (3 cups) of the bread crumbs. Form 2-inch patties with your hands and dredge them in the remaining bread crumbs to coat.

These fritters can be either baked or pan-fried. To pan-fry (easier for a small quantity), heat a tablespoon of oil for frying in a pan big enough to hold six patties or two rounds of three. When the oil is shimmering, lay the patties in the oil and fry for about 5 minutes on each side. Lift out of the oil with a slotted spatula and drain on paper towels. To bake (easier for a large quantity—the greens dull a bit in color, but are still delicious), preheat the oven to 400°F and generously coat a baking tray with oil. Lay the fritters out in a single layer and drizzle the tops with more oil. Bake for 15 minutes or so, flip with a spatula, and bake for another 10 minutes on the other side.

Serve immediately topped with a dollop of sour cream.

VARIATION

Replace a third of the fennel fronds with other oft-discarded tops of fennel cousins: celery leaf or carrot tops.

Crispy Garlic Scapes

Whole scapes crisp up when roasted to form an intriguing garlic wand with an addictive chip-like crunch. Serve bunched in a drinking glass or snifter for a cocktail snack or arrange atop a savory dish for a dramatic architectural garnish.

Serves 4–6
2 bunches garlic scapes—about 3 scapes
    per person
Salt and olive oil

Serves 30–40
6 plentiful bunches garlic scapes—about 3
    scapes per person
Salt and olive oil

Preheat the oven to 400°F. Spread the scapes out in a single layer on a baking sheet, drizzle with olive oil, and sprinkle with salt. Roast for 10 minutes until crispy. Watch them carefully, as they go from golden to burned in a heartbeat.

PHOTO BY TALI AIONA.

Sautéed Cabbage, Leeks, and Green Coriander with Roasted Garlic Scapes

Coriander is the seed of the cilantro plant. Harvest green coriander after the leafy cilantro has gone to seed, but before it dries down. At this halfway stage in its life, green coriander adds crunch and pungency to soups and sautéed dishes.

Serves 4–6

1 small head green and/or savoy cabbage

2–3 leeks

2 teaspoons green coriander seeds

2 tablespoons olive oil

Salt to taste

Crispy Garlic Scapes (page 150)

Serves 30–40

6 heads green and/or savoy cabbage

8 pounds leeks

2 tablespoons green coriander seeds

½ cup olive oil

Salt to taste

Crispy Garlic Scapes (page 150)

Remove the outer leaves of the cabbage and reserve for garnish. Slice the cabbage into thin strips and rinse. Do not grate. Chop the leeks into half-moons, using all of the white and most of the green parts. Submerge in water and toss with your fingers to remove all the grit—it's okay if the half-moons fall apart. Drain. Pluck the coriander seeds from the plant and crush slightly in a mortar and pestle or with the back of a knife against the cutting board. Reserve.

In a wide sauté pan (for large batch, use the flat-top griddle or a rondeau), sauté the leeks with the oil until lightly caramelized. Add the cabbage and coriander and a sprinkle of salt. Continue sautéing, tossing occasionally, until the cabbage is thoroughly wilted. Taste and add more salt, if desired.

On a platter, arrange the reserved whole cabbage leaves fanned out along the sides. Mound the sautéed cabbage into the middle. Top dramatically with a modern art exhibit of roasted garlic scapes.

GARLIC SCAPES

Garlic scapes, the curvaceous "flowering tops" of the garlic plant, must be clipped to redirect the energy of the plant downward and encourage the largest cloves to form. The delicate scapes are the culinary bonus of this springtime maintenance ritual, which comes at the perfect time—after the green garlic is too woody and before the fresh garlic is ready. Scapes are milder and sweeter than green garlic and have a tender texture akin to asparagus. Use garlic scapes chopped into rounds as you would green garlic, or better yet, showcase their appealing form and texture by serving them blanched, roasted, or sautéed whole as a vegetable rather than a mere seasoning.

Roasted Rainbow Carrots with Marinated Favas and Tarragon

Even the humble carrot expresses itself in a bouquet of colors and shapes with surprising nuances of texture and taste. Each variety represents an old story of relationship with people or culture, starting with its name: the round orange radish-shaped Parisian Rondo; the pearly Belgian White; the orange-cored Punjabi Purple; and the lemon-yellow Yellowstone from Holland.

Serves 4–6

1 bunch baby rainbow carrots

2 tablespoons olive oil

Sprinkle of salt

2 tablespoons sherry

1 tablespoon chopped tarragon

½ cup Fava Beans in Vinaigrette (page 118)

Serves 30–40

10 bunches baby rainbow carrots (about 12 pounds loose carrots)

1½ cups olive oil

Salt to taste

1½ cups sherry

½ cup chopped tarragon

4 cups Fava Beans in Vinaigrette (page 118)

Preheat the oven to 375°F. Remove the carrot tops and scrub the carrots clean with a natural-bristle veggie brush. Toss the carrots with olive oil, spread them out on a baking sheet, and sprinkle with a pinch or two of salt. Roast for 20 minutes or so until they soften and begin to turn golden around the edges. Turn and rearrange with a spatula for even cooking, and roast for another 10 minutes. Remove the carrots into a serving dish. Deglaze the pan with the sherry and add the juice to the carrots. Toss with the tarragon and marinated favas. Serve hot.

Buttery Thumbelinas on a Bed of Braised Baby Amaranth Greens

Late spring means thinning of carrots. Here's a little lunch dish that puts the original "baby carrot" to good use along with all those volunteer amaranth greens popping up in the same bed that need weeding. Round little Thumbelina carrots are lovely here as well.

Serves 4–6

2 bunches Thumbelina carrots or 1 bunch thinnings of other variety carrots

¼ cup (½ stick) butter

Pinch of salt

3 tablespoons water or stock

1 pound baby amaranth greens, braised according to page 156

Serves 30–40

12–14 bunches Thumbelina carrots or 7 bunches other variety carrots, total of 10 pounds

1 cup (2 sticks) butter

1 tablespoon salt

½ cup water or stock

5 pounds baby amaranth greens, braised according to page 156

Top, tail, and scrub the Thumbelinas or thinned carrots for use whole; if you're using a larger variety of carrots, chop them into rustic chunks. In a medium-sized pot with a tight-fitting lid, add the carrots, butter, salt, and water or stock. Cover and steam on medium-low heat, stirring occasionally, until the carrots soften, about 15 minutes.

Meanwhile, follow the directions for Early-Summer Flash-Braised Baby Amaranth Greens. Serve the carrots mounded in the middle of the platter with the amaranth greens arranged in a ring around the edge.

VARIATION

Summer: Instead of the baby carrots, substitute flat, meaty Romano beans cut into 1-inch diagonals. Butter steam them until bright green and just tender.

Sautéed Shungiku Shoots with Sesame Seeds and Garlic

Chrysanthemum coronarium, garland chrysanthemum, chop suey herb, or *shungiku* (in Japanese) is an edible chrysanthemum grown for its flowers and distinctively floral-tasting leafy greens. Grown as a cool-season crop in the mild coastal climate of Asia's Pacific Rim, shungiku is a common ingredient in Japanese and Korean soups, noodle dishes, and vegetable sides. It does incredibly well in our winter garden, and we have come to regard it as a staple here in the kitchen. We sauté the shoots with garlic or steam the tender stems like asparagus. The fragrant lobed leaves and flower petals perfume our winter and spring raw salads.

Gardener's tip: To encourage branching and a longer-lasting crop, harvest the shungiku side shoots by pinching them back before the buds appear.

Serves 4–6

1 tablespoon sesame seeds
1 tablespoon sesame oil
1 large bunch shungiku tips
1 clove minced garlic
Salt or tamari to taste

Serves 30–40

¼ cup sesame seeds
¼ cup sesame oil
3 pounds shungiku tips
4 cloves minced garlic
Salt or tamari to taste

Preheat a dry skillet or wok on medium-high heat. Add the sesame seeds and toast briefly, stirring frequently with a wooden spoon, until they begin to release a nutty aroma. Remove the sesame seeds from the heat and reserve. Return the skillet or wok to the heat, add sesame oil to coat, and then add the shungiku florets, garlic, and a light sprinkle of salt or tamari soy sauce. Sauté, tossing with tongs frequently, until completely wilted. Taste and adjust the salt; sprinkle with the reserved sesame seeds. Serve hot.

PHOTO BY TALI AIONA.

Simple Sautéed Chard with Onion

Chard is unique because of its beautiful, meaty stem. So often people discard the stems of leafy greens, but there is a lot of food there to be enjoyed—in fact, in some parts of the world, chard is grown for its stem instead of the green. Use this method with any sauté green whose stem might otherwise go to waste—mustard greens, collards, kale, or beet greens.

Serves 4–6

2 bunches chard or other greens with meaty
    stems, such as kale or collards
2 tablespoons oil, for cooking
1 small onion, small diced
Pinch of salt or dash of soy sauce to taste
Dash of vinegar, lemon juice, or white wine
    to taste

Serves 30–40

12–15 bunches chard or other greens with
    meaty stems such as kale or collards
½ cup oil, for cooking
4 large onions, small diced
Salt or soy sauce to taste, about 1
    tablespoon salt
Vinegar, lemon juice, or white wine to taste,
    about ⅓ cup

Cut the stem out of the chard leaf with a knife: Double the leaf over vertically through the middle and cut the stem out at an angle in a V-shape. In the case of brassicas such as kale and collards, the stalk is stiff and can be grasped in one hand while you strip the leaf off briskly with the other (page 187).

Reserve the stems and chop them into ¼-inch thin rounds or half-moons, roughly the same size as your chopped onions. Wash the stems and let them drain in a colander.

Chiffonade the leaves: Stack them four or five tall and roll them together like a newspaper. Slice the roll into thin ¼-inch strips. Separate the strands with your fingers so that they become thin ribbons.

Transfer into a large mixing bowl, tub, or container.

Fill your large bowl or container with plenty of water and swish the leaves around a bit. Then let them sit for a few minutes while you do something else, so that the dirt settles to the bottom of the bowl and any insects have a chance to swim up to the surface. Lift the leaves out of the water with your hands and transfer to a colander rather than pouring them in—that way the dirt stays at the bottom rather than getting redistributed onto the leaves. Check the water. Is it filthy? A few aphids left in your greens are not the end of the world—they will cook down (and add more protein), but you definitely want to avoid crunchy bits of sand. Repeat the process if needed.

Heat up a wide, thick-bottomed frying pan, skillet, or flat-top griddle (for large batches) on medium-high heat. Add the oil, chopped stems, and diced onion; sprinkle with salt. Sauté for 3 to 5 minutes until the stems and onions become soft and cooked through.

Add the leaf ribbons on top of the sautéed stems and toss with tongs to incorporate. Cover halfway with a lid to trap in some of the moisture. Sauté, tossing with tongs occasionally, until the leaves are just wilted. Taste and add a tiny dash of acid if you wish to brighten up the flavor—we think balsamic vinegar is delicious on chard in particular, but lemon juice, white wine, or even a splash of tomato juice will work. Salt to taste. Serve immediately.

IDEAS FOR USING STEMS FROM SAUTÉED GREENS

- Slice and add raw to slaws, marinades, or krauts, see Mother Garden Veggie Kraut (page 282), Zesty Purple Cabbage Slaw (page 135), or Summer Salad with Giant Yellow Mangel and Pickled Rainbow Chard Stems (page 122).
- Cut into tiny rounds and sauté in flavorful fat, and then add to stir fries, frittatas, or chunky soups.
- If you have a juicer, run them through with other vegetables in your morning green drink or carrot juice. Save the pulp/fiber to make the best veggie-burgers ever!

Early-Summer Flash-Braised Baby Amaranth Greens

Amaranth greens volunteer so prolifically in the early-summer garden that the baby sprouts, either raw or sautéed, are a staple at practically every June meal. Harvest the sprouts just before they start crowding out other plants in the bed when they reach around 4 or 5 inches tall. Baby greens deserve delicate treatment. In this uncomplicated steam-sauté method, no garlic or onions are used and the oil is added *after* cooking so as not to turn bitter or scorch—this allows for the subtle favor and texture of the greens to come through. Use this method with any tender young greens without tough stems or midribs.

Serves 4–6

1 pound baby amaranth greens, whole,
    or other baby greens such as spinach
    or arugula
1 tablespoon water
Salt to taste
Dash of lemon juice, about 1 tablespoon
3 tablespoons nice extra-virgin olive oil

Serves 30–40

5–6 pounds baby amaranth greens, whole,
    or other baby greens such as spinach
    or arugula
¼ cup water
Salt to taste, about 1 tablespoon
Dash of lemon juice, about ¼ cup
1 cup nice extra-virgin olive oil

Set a deep skillet or wok on the stovetop on high heat. When it's nice and hot, pile in the greens and pour in the water. Immediately cover to catch the steam that will billow up. After 30 seconds, open and toss with tongs. Re-cover and continue steaming until just wilted, about a minute (a few minutes for the large batch). Add salt and a dash of lemon juice to suit your taste. Toss in the oil. Serve as a stand-alone side or as a bed of greens for another dish, as in Buttery Thumbelinas on a Bed of Braised Baby Amaranth Greens (page 152).

PHOTO BY TALI AIONA.

Cumin-Roasted Summer Squash

After cooking literally hundreds of pounds of summer squash by midsummer, it's time to start thinking outside the box. Here's an easy way to mix it up that pairs well with a Mediterranean-themed meal such as Wine Country Grapeleaf Dolmas (page 206). This recipe also works great with eggplant in place of the summer squash.

Serves 4–6

2 medium summer squash
1 clove garlic, crushed
¼ cup cooking oil
1 tablespoon ground cumin
Salt and pepper to taste

Serves 30–40

20 medium summer squash
6 cloves garlic, crushed
1 cup cooking oil
¼ cup ground cumin
Salt and pepper to taste

Preheat the oven to 375°F. Cut the summer squash (or eggplant) into 3-inch lengths, then quarter them into ½-inch-thick spears. Toss with the remaining ingredients and spread on a cookie sheet, cut sides up to start. If you're using eggplant, you will probably need a little more oil, as eggplant tends to really soak it up. Bake for 20 to 30 minutes or until the veggies are crispy on the edges, tossing with a spatula once or twice during the cooking time for even browning.

Tromboncino Coins on a Bed of Their Own Greens

Tromboncino—the word is Italian for "trombone"—is one of our favorite varieties of summer squash because of its dense flesh that does not become mealy when the squash grows beyond the customary infanticidal harvesting stage. It can even be grown out for use as a winter squash. The seeds are concentrated in the bulbous end, rather than throughout—another plus in the texture department. Unlike sprawling zucchinis, it's a good climber, making it a great choice for trellising in small garden spaces.

Believe it or not, all members of the cucurbit family (pumpkins, summer squash, cucumbers, melons, gourds) have edible leaves that are delicious when sautéed—the vining-habit (not bush-habit) varieties of squash and gourds being the tastiest. When the squash vines are taking over the paths in your garden, trim them back and throw them in the pan!

Serves 4–6

2 Tromboncino squash, or any young, long-shaped summer squash such as zucchini, Costata Romanesco, Yellow Crookneck

¼ cup olive oil, divided

Sprinkle of salt

1 tablespoon finely chopped fresh oregano leaves, or 1 teaspoon dried

2–3 quarts tightly packed squash greens, stems removed

2 cloves garlic, crushed

Garnish: squeeze of lemon, black pepper to taste, grated Parmesan (optional)

Serves 30–40

10 pounds Tromboncino squash, or sub any young, long-shaped summer squash such as zucchini, Costata Romanesco, Yellow Crookneck

⅔ cup olive oil, divided

Sprinkle of salt

¼ cup fresh oregano leaves, finely chopped, or 2 tablespoons dried

3–4 pounds (30–40 quarts tightly packed) squash greens, stems removed

6 cloves garlic, crushed

Garnish: squeeze of lemon, black pepper to taste, grated Parmesan (optional)

Slice the tender long part of the Tromboncino into coins. Cut the rounded end in half, scoop out and discard the seeds, and slice the remaining part into half-moons. Heat up a large skillet with plenty of surface area on medium heat. You may need to sauté the squash in several rounds if your pan isn't wide enough. For the extra-large batch, use a flat-top griddle. Add half of the oil and then arrange the coins in as close to a single layer as possible. Sprinkle with salt. Allow the squash to sauté uncovered and undisturbed for about 4 minutes or so, until they just start to blister on one side. Sprinkle on the oregano, flip the squash with a metal spatula, and brown on the other side, about 2 or 3 more minutes. Remove the squash onto a serving platter. Hold for a few minutes in a warm oven while you sauté the greens.

Chiffonade the greens into thin ribbons. Drizzle the remaining oil to recoat the skillet or griddle. Add the crushed garlic and squash leaf ribbons directly on top. Sprinkle with salt. Cover with a lid and steam-sauté, tossing frequently with tongs, until just wilted. Squash leaves tend to be a little on the dry side—add a tiny splash of water, if needed, to get the steam going.

Plate up the dish by arranging the sautéed greens in a ring around the mound of Tromboncino coins. Top with a squeeze of lemon, a twist of fresh-cracked black pepper to taste, and an optional sprinkle of Parmesan. Garnish with a squash blossom, if you have one on hand.

PHOTO BY TALI AIONA.

Pepita-Encrusted Squash Blossoms Stuffed with Goat Cheese and Mint

With the bumper crop of summer squash, so comes the bumper crop of squash blossoms. Both male and female flowers can be used in this recipe, but more squash will grow if you only pick the male flowers. The males are large and showy on the end of long straight stems, as opposed to the females that are smaller, grow closer to the main stalk of the plant, and are often attached to a tiny squash beginning to bulb out.

This recipe works especially well for a crowd, as the blossoms are baked rather than fried. Serve piping hot with a lemon wedge as an appetizer.

Serves 4–6

⅔ cup chèvre
2 tablespoons finely chopped fresh mint
1 teaspoon lemon zest
1 egg
¼ cup toasted pumpkin seeds, crushed in a
    food processor
Salt and pepper to taste
8–12 male squash blossoms
1 tablespoon oil for cooking
Garnish: lemon wedges

Serves 30–40

3 cups chèvre (about 1¼ pounds)
⅔ cup finely chopped fresh mint
2 tablespoons lemon zest
7 eggs
3 cups toasted pumpkin seeds, crushed in a
    food processor
Salt to taste, about 1 tablespoon
Pepper to taste, about 2 teaspoons
60–80 male squash blossoms
¼ cup oil for cooking
Garnish: lemon wedges

Preheat the oven to 375°F. Let the goat cheese sit out at room temperature until it softens. In a bowl with a wooden spoon or electric mixer, whip the goat cheese until it gets smooth and fluffy in texture. Add the mint and lemon zest, stirring to combine. In another small bowl, whip the eggs. In yet another bowl, season the crushed pumpkin seeds with salt and pepper.

With a small spoon (a baby spoon works great for this—you want something skinnier than a teaspoon), gently stuff the flowers with about a teaspoon of herbed goat cheese, barely pressing the cheese down into the bottom of the flower and leaving the outer half of the flower relatively empty. Depending on the consistency of the cheese and the toughness of the flower, you may opt to shape tiny ovals of cheese by hand and ease them into the bottom of the flower so as not to force the delicate petals. Gather together the outer edges of the flower and smooth them around the goat cheese, massaging them together, and sealing it with a gentle twist. Dip the blossoms in eggs and then dredge in the seasoned crumbs. *Dredging tip:* Lay the egg-dipped blossom on a separate plate and sprinkle the crumbs on top—that way the crumbs in the main bowl stay dry and fluffy and do not turn into wet clumps that don't stick.

Lay the blossoms side by side on an oiled cookie sheet. Bake for 15 minutes or until golden on top. Remove from the pan and serve immediately with a lemon wedge.

Young Runner Bean Pods with Marjoram Butter and Scarlet Flowers

Harvest baby runner bean pods when they are still thin and tender, like romano beans. When the beans inside begin to plump up, it's too late, and the pod becomes inedibly fibrous. At this young phase, there are still plentiful flowers—pick a few to use as garnish.

Serves 4–6

1½ pounds very young runner bean pods

¼ cup (½ stick) butter, cut into cubes

2 tablespoons minced marjoram

Salt to taste

Garnish: a few scarlet runner bean flowers

Serves 30–40

12–15 pounds very young runner bean pods

1 cup (2 sticks) butter, cut into cubes

⅔ cup minced marjoram

Salt to taste

Garnish: ½ cup scarlet runner bean flowers

In a saucepot fitted with a steamer basket and an inch of water in the bottom, steam the beans on high heat until they're tender and bright green in color, about 8 to 10 minutes. Transfer to a serving bowl and toss with the butter, minced marjoram, and salt to taste. Top with edible flowers and serve immediately.

Roasted Cherry Tomatoes with Lemon Verbena

This is another of chef Gabriel Tiradani's brilliantly versatile garden-inspired sides. Spoon the tomatoes and the broth on top of white beans or pasta, use as a base for a soup such as minestrone or gazpacho, or add to Summer Risotto (page 210). Cooled to room temp, the sweet, tart juice makes a great salad dressing or even a mixer for a Bloody Mary!

Serves 4–6

**MAKES ONE 9 X 13-INCH BAKING
DISH; YIELDS 2 CUPS**

2 mounded pint baskets cherry tomatoes,
    mixed heirloom varieties preferred

1 large sprig fresh lemon verbena

½ cup dry sherry

¼ cup olive oil

Sprinkle of salt

Serves 30–40

**MAKES 1 FULL-SIZED ENTRÉE PAN;
YIELDS 6 CUPS**

12 pints cherry tomatoes, mixed heirloom
    varieties preferred

1 bunch fresh lemon verbena

2 cups dry sherry

1 cup olive oil

Generous sprinkle of salt

Preheat the oven to 375°F. Pop the stems off the tops of the cherry tomatoes and rinse them. In an entrée pan or shallow baking dish, spread the cherry tomatoes to cover the bottom of the pan, ideally in a single layer, although if they are crowded and overlap a bit, that's okay. Nestle the sprigs of lemon verbena among the tomatoes, drizzle on the sherry and the olive oil, and sprinkle with salt. Roast in the hot oven for about 20 minutes, until the liquid bubbles and the cherry tomatoes deflate a little.

Biodiversity Beans with Lemon Dill Butter

"Green beans" don't just come in green! Pictured on pages 162–163 are Provider, Roc d'Or, Royalty Purple Pod, Cranberry Bush, Rattlesnake, Yellow Anellino, and Dragon's Lingerie.

Serves 4–6

1 pound mixed beans

2 tablespoons butter

1 small clove garlic, crushed

2 teaspoons lemon juice

½ teaspoon lemon zest

1 large sprig dill, chopped finely

Salt to taste

Serves 30–40

10 pounds mixed beans

½ cup (1 stick) butter

3 small garlic cloves, crushed

3 tablespoons lemon juice

1 tablespoon lemon zest

1 bunch dill, chopped finely

Salt to taste

Top and tail the beans and cut them into 2-inch pieces. Scissors work well for this task. Bring a large pot of water to a boil. While the water is boiling, melt the butter in a very small pan and add the garlic. Cook ever so briefly, less than 30 seconds, just until the green smell is released from the garlic; do not let the butter or garlic scorch. Remove from the heat. Blanch the beans for 4 minutes or so, until they're just cooked but still bright in color. Drain and toss with the garlic butter while they're still hot. Toss in the lemon juice and zest, chopped dill, and a pinch of salt. Taste and adjust the lemon juice and salt to your liking.

VARIATION

Try substituting summer savory for the dill—beans and summer savory are a classic combo.

PHOTO BY TALI AIONA.

Orach Paneer—Spicy Creamed Mountain Spinach

Red and yellow orach, or mountain spinach, are widely cultivated as salad or sauté greens around the world and can be used as a spinach substitute during the hot, dry summer months when spinach is hard to grow. A riff on the classic Indian dish palak paneer, this is a great recipe if you are clearing a garden bed and have an overabundance of cosmetically challenged greens to use up, as they get finely chopped and reduce way down. Orach is delicious, but any combination of greens that you have in abundance such as spinach, chard, collards, kale, turnip or mustard greens, beet tops, amaranth, or even the outer leaves of cauliflower or broccoli will work.

Paneer is a type of farmer cheese, like a ricotta that has had the whey squeezed out to form a dense, sliceable cheese that seers and browns beautifully rather than melting when heated. For a lighter dairy-free version, omit the sour cream and paneer, though if you are working with mustard or turnip greens, which are on the punchy side, we recommend the full-fat dairy version—the cream mellows out the spiciness.

Serves 4–6

3 bunches orach, magenta lamb's-quarters,
    or any abundant sauté greens
1 cup paneer, Hallume, or other grilling
    cheese, cut into cubes (optional)
2 tablespoons oil or ghee, plus more
    for frying
Sprinkle of salt
1 tablespoon cumin seeds
1 onion, diced
1 hot green chile, minced, such as jalapeño,
    Serrano, or Thai dragon pepper
2 cloves garlic, minced
2 teaspoons ground or fresh-grated turmeric
1 teaspoon garam masala
2 tablespoons tomato paste

Cut or strip any large stems out of the orach or other greens. Chop the stems into a small dice and reserve. Wash, drain, and chop the greens relatively finely.

Meanwhile, brown the cubes of paneer, if using, in a nonstick skillet on medium-high heat with a little ghee or oil. Wait until the cubes are good and crispy on one side before attempting to turn them, lest you end up with a gooey mess. Drain on paper towels and immediately sprinkle with a little salt. Reserve.

Heat oil in a skillet on medium heat. Add the cumin seeds and toast briefly. Then add the chopped stems, diced onions, and minced green chiles and cook until the onions become translucent and the stems become totally soft. Add the garlic, turmeric, and garam masala and cook for a minute or two so that the garlic releases its green flavor and the herbs infuse the oil. Stir in the tomato paste. Add the greens and toss to coat. Reduce the heat and cook uncovered for 20 minutes or longer, tossing occasionally, until the greens cook way down.

1 cup or more sour cream, buttermilk, or
   heavy cream (optional)
1 tablespoon fenugreek leaves, if you have
   them (we grow them at OAEC)
2 tablespoons chopped fresh cilantro
Dash of lemon juice or vinegar to taste,
   if needed

Serves 30–40
10 pounds orach, magenta lamb's-quarters
   or any abundant sauté greens
6 cups paneer, Hallume, or other grilling
   cheese, cut into cubes (optional)
½ cup oil or ghee, plus more for frying
1 teaspoon salt
⅓ cup cumin seeds
4 onions, diced
3 hot green chiles, minced, such as jalapeño,
   Serrano, or Thai dragon peppers
10 cloves garlic, minced
¼ cup ground or fresh-grated turmeric
2 tablespoons garam masala
½ cup tomato paste (6-ounce jar)
2 cups sour cream, buttermilk, or heavy
   cream (optional)
¼ cup fenugreek leaves, if you have them
   (we grow them at OAEC)
1 cup chopped fresh cilantro
Dash of lemon juice or vinegar to taste,
   if needed

Stir in the sour cream and the fenugreek leaves and keep cooking for 3 or 4 more minutes until the mixture thickens. Taste and add more salt, if needed. You may want to add a splash of lemon juice or vinegar, depending on your chosen greens and whether or not you are using dairy. If a very smooth texture is desired, remove half of the mixture, puree in a food processor, and add back in. Gently fold in the paneer and serve.

Serve with Lemon Verbena Steamed Rice (page 212), along with your favorite curry.

PHOTO BY TALI AIONA.

Barbecued Eggplant Stacks with Coyote Mint Sauce and Chèvre

Coyote mint, *Monardella villosa,* is native to the California Coastal Range and the Sierra Nevada foothills and is a fabulous drought-hardy plant with purple pompom flowers and potent mint flavor. It is planted in our core-area dry garden and grows wild on the hilly coastal trails between OAEC and the ocean.

While some cooks insist on pre-salting and draining eggplants to draw out the bitter, with garden-fresh eggplant, this is unnecessary. Buy eggplants only in the summer season when they are fresh, not imported from far away.

Serves 4 to 6

1 tablespoon coriander seeds

1 tablespoon cumin seeds

2 cloves garlic

Salt and pepper to taste

½ cup coyote mint leaves, or ¼ cup
    spearmint and ¼ cup oregano

½ cup parsley

Juice of 1 lemon

½ cup olive oil, plus more for grilling

1 tablespoon finely chopped Serrano chile

3 large eggplants

1 cup soft chèvre

Garnish: thinly sliced roasted red peppers or
    halved cherry tomatoes

Serves 30–40

3 tablespoons coriander seeds

3 tablespoons cumin seeds

5 cloves garlic

Salt and pepper to taste

3 cups coyote mint leaves, or 1½ cups
    spearmint and 1½ cups oregano

3 cups parsley

Juice of 4 lemons

3 cups olive oil, plus more for grilling

¼ cup finely chopped Serrano chile

20 large eggplants

4 cups soft chèvre

Garnish: thinly sliced roasted red peppers or
    halved cherry tomatoes

Light the barbecue grill, and while the coals are heating up, make the sauce. In a small, dry cast-iron skillet, toast the cumin and coriander seeds until they begin to smell nutty. Using a mortar and pestle or herb grinder, crush the seeds, garlic, and a pinch of salt into a fine paste. Add the coyote mint, parsley leaves, and lemon juice and continue processing until a bright-green sauce is formed. Add the olive oil and stir in the chopped chile. Adjust the salt and pepper to taste. Reserve.

Slice the eggplant crosswise into large ½-inch-thick round steaks—you should get around six slices per large globe-style eggplant. Sprinkle with salt and drizzle with olive oil. When the flames have died down to a nice bed of medium-hot coals, grill the eggplant until they're soft and striped with crispy grill marks. Reserve.

For each portion, layer slices of eggplant with a scant tablespoon of chèvre and a tablespoon of sauce, three stories high. Top with a final, generous drizzle of sauce that runs down the sides, a dollop of chèvre, and garnish with something red for contrast—either a few thin slivers of roasted red pepper or a few halved cherry tomatoes mounded on top.

PHOTO BY TALI AIONA.

PHOTO BY TALI AIONA.

Griddle Seared Brassica Shoots with Chili Flakes and Garlic

Modern broccoli has been bred to create a single large head—facilitating industrial harvesting—but the plant's ancestral tendency is to make lots of smaller side shoots. Why grow a broccoli plant for months in the garden, taking up space, water, and nutrients, to produce just one single meal when it's time to off-with-its-head? Leave it in the ground after the main growth center is cut and it will continue producing side shoots, similar to rapini or broccoli rabe, for weeks. Simply snap off the delicate bite-sized florets, and that's it, a prep cook's dream! This season-extending trick can be practiced with many brassicas, including our plant sale bestseller, purple sprouting broccoli, pictured below and others such as kale, collards, and cauliflower.

Serves 4–6

¼ cup oil

2 large bunches (2 pounds) brassica shoots or rapini (aka broccoli rabe)

Salt to taste

2 cloves garlic, crushed

Small pinch chili flakes

Juice of 1 lemon or 1 tablespoon apple cider vinegar

Serves 30–40

1 cup oil

12 large bunches (12 pounds) brassica shoots or rapini (aka broccoli rabe)

Salt to taste

6 cloves garlic, crushed

½ teaspoon chili flakes

Juice of 6 lemons or ¼ cup apple cider vinegar

Heat up a large cast-iron griddle or skillet on medium-high heat. Decide if your skillet or griddle is big enough to hold all the veggies in a single layer—if not, you may have to work in smaller batches to avoid crowding. Coat the surface with oil and spread out the brassica shoots or rapini on the griddle. Sprinkle with salt. Sauté on one side until the rapini begins to blister, about 4 minutes. Add the crushed garlic and chili flakes and toss with tongs to distribute, turning the veggies to cook on the other side for another 3 minutes. Toss with lemon or vinegar. Taste and add more salt, if needed. Serve immediately.

PHOTO BY JIM COLEMAN.

New Zealand Spinach Shoots with Parmesan and Almonds

New Zealand spinach, despite its name, is possible (and easy!) to grow in most of the United States and is a perennial in our neck of the woods—a great choice for the late summer when regular spinach and other greens bolt or peter out in the heat. In fact, it can become quite invasive, so research your area before planting.

New Zealand spinach won our biodiversity taste test hands down. The texture of the whole shoot is outstanding—meaty but not fibrous—and the nooks and crannies absorb and hold on to flavor unlike any other sauté green. This sauté method capitalizes on its superior form and texture as a vehicle for lots of garlic, Parm, and crunchy almonds. Substitute any other shaggy green that is harvested in shoots such as broccoli rabe (also known as rapini), spigarello, or sprouting broccoli.

Serves 4–6

2 tablespoons oil, for cooking
2 cloves garlic, crushed in a garlic press
2 bunches New Zealand spinach, or about
    ¾ pound loose shoots, or other shoots
    such as broccoli rabe, spigarello,
    sprouting broccoli
Pinch of salt to taste
Dash of vinegar, lemon juice, or white wine
    to taste
¼ cup Parmesan cheese
2 tablespoons crushed toasted almonds or
    seasoned bread crumbs

Serves 30–40

½ cup oil, for cooking
5 cloves garlic, crushed in a garlic press
12–15 bunches New Zealand spinach, or
    about 4 pounds loose shoots, or other
    shoots such as broccoli rabe, spigarello,
    sprouting broccoli
Salt to taste, about 1 tablespoon
Dash of vinegar, lemon juice, or white wine
    to taste
2 cups Parmesan cheese
1¼ cups crushed toasted almonds or
    seasoned bread crumbs

Heat a wide skillet (or flat-top griddle for large batch) on medium-high heat. Coat the surface with oil and scatter the crushed garlic onto the oil. Immediately pile the greens directly on top and sprinkle with a little salt. Toss with tongs frequently until just wilted. If the greens seem to be drying out too quickly, reduce the heat and cover halfway with a lid to trap in some of the steam, though this shouldn't be necessary. When wilted down, taste one. Add a tiny dash of vinegar, lemon juice, or white wine. Taste again and adjust the salt and acid to your liking. Serve with topped with a sprinkling of Parmesan cheese, crushed toasted almonds, or bread crumbs.

Fall Garden "Stir-Fry" with Fresh Herbs

Ah, the veggie stir-fry—that stereotypical hippie staple—a big trough of gray, mushy vegetables drowning in garlic, soy sauce, and every spice in the rack. Don't get us started, but suffice it to say that this slapdash treatment of vegetables is what gives vegetables, not to mention vegetarians, a bad name.

Making stir-fry in the traditional way by flash-searing the vegetables in a flaming-hot wok only really works in very small batches to be served immediately, a method that is not practical for serving family-style or bringing to the proverbial potluck. While the one-pan method is tempting for the dishwashing-averse, the key to a great "stir-fry" for a crowd that doesn't overcook as it sits out on the table is to avoid the stir-fry method altogether. Instead, blanch the veggies individually first to lock in the fresh texture and the vivid colors. At that point, the flavors of the vegetables can practically stand on their own and don't need a complicated sauce to make them sing. The best thing to do for a crowd is to serve the veggies in a simple flavor base and allow folks to spice up their own portion as they choose.

While experienced stir-fryistas can pull it off, we tend to treat leafy greens such as kale, cabbage, and bok choi separately, as they give off a lot of water, fall apart, and tend to detract from the texture of the other vegetables if added prematurely. Follow directions for any of our featured sauté greens methods and serve as a separate dish alongside the mixed veggies. They will naturally combine together on the plate.

Obviously, garden stir-fry can be infinitely adapted to the season. This version is for early fall when peppers are still abundant and the cool-weather cauliflower, broccoli, and peas are just coming on—see other seasonal variations below.

VEGETABLES

Serves 4–6
2 carrots
½ head broccoli, or ½ pound shoots
½ head cauliflower, or ½ pound shoots
1 pound snow peas

Serves 30–40
12 carrots
3 heads broccoli, or 3 pounds side shoots
3 heads cauliflower, or 3 pounds side shoots
6 pounds snow peas

Slice root vegetables such as carrots into thin diagonal rounds or matchsticks. Cut the broccoli and cauliflower into florets. Top and tail beans or snap peas. Meanwhile, get a big pot of salt water boiling on the stove and prepare an ice-water bath. Blanch and shock the roots, broccolis, and legumes (not the peppers, onions, and garlic) separately (page 116). Drain and reserve.

FLAVOR BASE

Serves 4-6

2 red or yellow bell peppers

½ medium onion

2 cloves garlic

2 tablespoons grated fresh ginger

1 small fresh hot chile (or less to taste), or
    pinch of red chili flakes

2 tablespoons neutral oil such as safflower

Tamari to taste

Rice vinegar or lemon juice to taste

2 tablespoons fresh cilantro, parsley, and/
    or basil

Serves 30-40

10 red or yellow bell peppers

4–6 medium onions

4–6 cloves garlic

3 tablespoons grated fresh ginger

3 small fresh hot chiles (or less to taste), or
    2 teaspoons red chili flakes

1 cup neutral oil such as safflower

Tamari to taste

Rice vinegar or lemon juice to taste

1 cup fresh cilantro, parsley, and/or basil

Make the flavor base: Slice the bell peppers and onions into ¼-inch wedges. Peel and grate the garlic and ginger on a microplane or fine grater. Finely chop the fresh hot chiles.

Allow a dry wok or skillet to heat up over a medium-high flame for a minute. Add a splash of oil and the onions and let them cook down a bit. Then add the red peppers and cook until the peppers soften, stirring frequently. Finally, add the garlic, ginger, hot chiles (or flakes), and cook for a minute or two.

Toss the blanched veggies with the flavor base in the wok and continue gently tossing periodically until the vegetables warm up to temperature but don't actually cook much more. Add a conservative splash of tamari and rice vinegar to taste. Remove from the heat. Toss in the fresh parsley, cilantro, and/or basil (if the leaves are tender, toss them in whole) and dress with more oil if you wish. Taste and adjust again for salt and acid.

Serve with Lemon Verbena Steamed Rice (page 212) and an array of condiments like hot sauce and toasted sesame oil. Also, offer something a with bit of crunch in the form of candied almonds, toasted sesame seeds, crunchy fried garlic or shallots, or Crispy Fried Beans (page 298) in a bowl on the side.

VARIATIONS

Spring: Use green garlic, garlic scapes, or leek half-moons instead of the onions. Omit the fresh peppers and substitute a small amount of fennel. Add blanched asparagus or fiddleheads and lots of garden-fresh snow peas. Sprinkle in mitsuba, scallions, and shungiku with the fresh herbs. A little lemon zest is also nice in spring.

Summer: Substitute green beans for the snow peas. Instead of broccoli and cauliflower, lightly sauté (don't blanch) some thinly sliced summer squash in the flavor base with the bell peppers before tossing in the blanched veggies. The purple Thai basil variety is perfect as an herb choice, if you can find it.

Winter: Try more root veggies in addition to the carrots, like turnips or very thinly sliced burdock root. Winter is also mushroom time—sauté mushrooms separately as described in Perfect Sautéed Mushrooms (page 184) and toss in with the flavor base and parboiled veggies. Because of the heaviness of the roots and mushrooms, you may want to add a little more fresh parsley to brighten up the flavor.

PHOTO BY TALI AIONA.

Wilted Arugula in a Whole Roasted Pumpkin with Candied Pepitas

Choose squash varieties with thick rinds that will hold their shape when roasted, such as Queensland Blue, Marina Di Chioggia, or Winter Luxury Pie Pumpkin.

Serves 4–6

1 whole medium-sized (5-pound) red kuri squash, kabocha, or sugar pie pumpkin

1 pound baby arugula (about 2 quarts lightly packed leaves)

½ cup (4 ounces) goat cheese

Nice extra-virgin olive oil

Salt and pepper to taste

1 tablespoon fresh chopped parsley

Serves 30–40

1 whole large 15- to 20-pound Cinderella pumpkin or hubbard squash

4 pounds baby arugula (about 16 quarts lightly packed leaves)

2 cups (1 pound) goat cheese

Nice extra-virgin olive oil

Salt and pepper to taste

¼ cup fresh chopped parsley

Preheat the oven to 400°F. Remove all but one oven rack and move it to the lowest position—you will need enough height to fit the whole pumpkin in the oven. Cut the top third of the pumpkin, as if you were carving a jack-o'-lantern, with a slightly larger opening. Scoop out the seeds and stringy innards. Place the pumpkin on a baking tray cut-side down and place the lid alongside. The roasting time will vary greatly based on the size and variety of the squash. Keep a close eye on it. Roast for about 30 minutes, then flip the squash right-side up to catch the juices. Continue roasting for another 20 to 30 minutes or so until the flesh of the squash is just soft when pierced with a fork, but the rind holds its shape and does not become so soft that it slouches over.

When the squash is done and ready to be served, scrape all the flesh off the lid into the bowl of the pumpkin. Scrape most of the flesh away from the sides of the pumpkin shell in bite-sized spoonfuls. Fill the bowl with the arugula and soft goat cheese separated into tabs with a spoon and toss with the pumpkin flesh. Drizzle generously with olive oil, season with salt and pepper, and sprinkle on the parsley and candied pepitas. Serve family-style with two large beautiful salad spoons. Encourage guests to dismantle the pumpkin and take sections of the pumpkin shell to scrape and toss with the greens to wilt.

CANDIED PEPITAS

Serves 4–6

1¼ cups seeds from the squash or store-bought pumpkin seeds, if too tough

¾ teaspoon olive oil

½ teaspoon salt

1 teaspoon chipotle

¼ cup maple syrup

Serves 30–40

4 cups seeds from the squash or store-bought pumpkin seeds, if too tough

2 tablespoons olive oil

2 teaspoons salt

1 tablespoon chipotle

¾ cup maple syrup

While the squash is roasting, heat a cast-iron skillet with the olive oil and pepitas. Toast for a few minutes until the aroma and color come out, being careful not to burn. Add the salt and chipotle and stir to combine. All at once, add the maple syrup and stir constantly for another 1 to 2 minutes. The mixture will get very sticky. Immediately turn it out onto a piece of parchment paper, spread, and let cool to a hard candied exterior.

Double-Roasted Beets with Balsamic Glaze

Steaming or boiling beets before putting them in the oven saves time and renders the beets deeply roasted but not dry. Truth be told, the main reason we prefer this method is that the sensual task of peeling them by slipping the skins off in warm water is so much more appealing than hacking at raw beets with a carrot peeler.

Serves 4–6

4 medium-sized beets
2 tablespoons oil
1 tablespoon balsamic vinegar
2 sprigs thyme or 1 teaspoon dried thyme
Salt and pepper

Serves 30–40

35 medium-sized beets
1 cup oil
⅓ cup balsamic vinegar
1 bunch thyme or 2 tablespoons dried thyme
Salt and pepper

Cut off the beet greens from the root. Save and use the greens for another dish. If the beets are radically different sizes, cut the big ones into smaller pieces for even cooking time. Preheat the oven to 400°F.

For the small batch: Pile the beets in a pot fitted with a steamer basket with an inch of water in the bottom. Bring the water to a boil, reduce the heat, and steam. Watch to make sure the bottom doesn't boil dry and burn—add more water as needed. Steam until the beets are soft when poked with a fork, about 20 minutes. Drain.

For the large batch: In a large stockpot, cover the beets with water. Bring to a rolling boil for 15 minutes, then turn off the heat and let rest, covered, for 45 minutes to an hour—the large quantity of water should hold enough heat to cook the beets. Drain.

Let beets chill in a container of cold water until they're cool enough to handle. Using the water in the bowl to help rinse as you go, slip off the skins and stubble with your hands. (Most recipes tell you to do this step under running water, but this wastes water.)

Put the boiled beets in a baking pan and drizzle with oil and balsamic. Toss with a spatula to coat. Tuck sprigs of thyme under the beets and sprinkle with salt and pepper. Roast for 20 minutes or so until edges start to brown up and the dressing bubbles and reduces a little. Serve with Blue Cheese Dip or Horseradish Dip (page 246).

PHOTO BY TALI AIONA.

Teaching Ecological Design Principles Through Food

As the oldest continuously operating permaculture design course site in California, OAEC certified its 1,000th student in July 2013. Using the 80-acre site as a living laboratory, individuals learn the practical skills to manage natural elements such as water, soil, and energy in restorative ways. Graduates learn the critical problem-solving and collaborative decision-making techniques necessary to lead important sustainability initiatives as agents of rapid change in their home communities.

Winter-Adapted Taco Bar

Here's an inexpensive standby menu for a crowd that we use to feed the class of "permies" (permaculture students) when they come in hungry from digging swales, sheet mulching, and installing gray-water systems. This menu not only features many of the perennial multipurpose food crops that they've been learning about in class, such as nopal cactus and scarlet runner beans, but also includes a staggering number of items from our winter garden and allows students to taste the reality of utilizing on-site resources.

PHOTO BY TALI AIONA.

PHOTO BY JIM COLEMAN.

Grilled Nopalitos with Herbs and Cotija

Native to Mexico and prevalent throughout the Southwest and California, the prickly pear or nopal cactus, *Opuntia ficus-indica*, is a stunning drought-hearty landscaping plant, natural barbed-wire fence, and source of nutritious food—both pads and fruit are edible. Inside the prickly pads lies a cooling, mucilaginous flesh with flavor akin to green beans. In Mexico, "nopalitos" are often prepared grilled and served in tacos, boiled and marinated with garlic, herbs, and crumbly cheese, or scrambled with eggs.

Serves 4–6

2 cactus pads, de-spined and peeled

1 clove garlic, crushed

3 tablespoons chopped parsley or cilantro

1 tablespoon chopped fresh oregano

2 tablespoons fresh lemon juice or 1½ tablespoons lime juice

2 tablespoons olive oil

⅓ cup crumbled feta or cotija cheese (optional)

Serves 30–40

8 cactus pads, de-spined and peeled

3 cloves garlic, crushed

1½ cups chopped parsley or cilantro

¼ cup chopped fresh oregano

1 cup fresh lemon juice or ¼ cup lime juice

½ cup olive oil

⅓ cup crumbled feta or cotija cheese (optional)

Harvest cactus pads in the late winter or early spring after the rains have saturated deep into the soil and the cactus is fully hydrated and juicy. Choose the young, green tender pads from this year's growth, not the older callused ones. Handle cactus pads with thick leather gloves—they are armed with long stiff needles as well as inconspicuous little hairs that will insinuate themselves into your skin and clothing if you aren't careful.

For small, young tender pads, simply peel off the spines with a vegetable peeler. For larger ones, remove the spines using an old-fashioned potato peeler equipped with a sharp nose at the end for digging out the eyes. Dig out each of the follicles at the base of the spines all over the pad. Once the spines have been dug out, rinse the pad and use the peeler or a sharp knife if needed to remove some or all of the outer skin if it seems tough.

Slice the pad in five or so "fingers" that run down the length of the pad but remain intact at the end, resembling the giant slimy green hand of an alien. Brush lightly with olive oil and grill on medium-hot coals until cooked through and slightly charred. Remove from the heat, slice off the strips, and dice. Toss with garlic, herbs, lemon juice, and oil. Top with crumbly cheese such as feta or cotija. Serve in tacos or with scrambled eggs in a breakfast burrito.

Winter grilling on a sunny day between rain showers—grilled nopales along with parboiled slices of potatoes doused in melted butter. PHOTO BY TALI AIONA.

Basic Winter Squash Puree

First domesticated in the Americas, squash has spread all over the world to become an important food crop to many peoples. The warty Italian Marina di Chioggia, the rust-colored French Musquée de Provence, and the slate-gray trilobular Australian Triamble are all rare winter squash varieties, testaments to humankind's ability to breed unique and diverse food crops to suit regional needs and tastes.

With a creative garnish, winter squash puree can be served as an easy side dish to any type of cuisine. It is also the base for dishes such as Winter Squash Dip with Dukkah (page 288), Soft Pumpkin Polenta (page 224) and the Dark Roast Winter Squash Tart (page 359). The varieties shown in the photo (opposite) are all great choices for this recipe, though any creamy, dense-fleshed winter squash or pie pumpkin can be used. Our all-time favorite variety for puree is Winter Luxury Pie Pumpkin because of its smooth, creamy sweet flesh.

The exact proportion will vary according to variety, but when shopping for your recipe, figure that for every pound of whole squash or pumpkin, you will get 1 cup of finished puree, give or take.

Serves 4–6

MAKES ABOUT 2 CUPS

1 medium-sized, 2-pound pumpkin or
    winter squash

Serves 30–40

MAKES ABOUT 12 CUPS

1 large 12- to 14-pound pumpkin or
    winter squash

Begin by cutting the squash in half or in quarters and scooping out the seeds and stringy innards. (Rinse the seeds and toast them with salt and oil in a toaster oven for munching or serving on top.) Then roast or steam the squash, following one of two methods:

Slow-roast method: Preheat the oven to 375°F. Place the squash on an oiled baking tray, cut-side down. Bake until the rind browns and the flesh softens—baking time will vary by variety and size of squash, but about 45 minutes.

Quick-steam method: In a large pot fitted with a steamer basket and lid, add about an inch of water in the bottom of the pot and arrange squash pieces into the steamer basket. Cover, bring to a boil, and then reduce the heat, steaming the squash for about 10 to 15 minutes until soft, depending on the thickness of the squash. Keep a close eye so it doesn't boil dry.

Allow roasted or steamed squash to cool. With a large spoon, scoop out the soft flesh. Compost the rind. If the squash variety is watery or if an extra-thick puree is desired (recommended for pie), allow the excess moisture to drain from the flesh in a colander for about an hour. For a rustic mash, crush the squash with a fork or ricer. For a more refined puree, run it through a food mill or blend in a food processor.

If serving as a side dish, stir in a long drizzle of oil, and salt to taste.

VARIATIONS

The secret to this versatile side dish is the garnish. Use a sauce or herb to tie it together with the other flavor themes in your meal. Here are some ideas:

- Fry sage leaves or cumin seeds quickly in ghee or olive oil, then drizzle on the infused oil and top with the crispy leaves or seeds.
- Serve with a coin of Basic Garden Herb Butter (page 271) of your choice and let it melt in at the table. Cilantro butter is fabulous, as is fennel with orange zest.
- Serve with a drizzle of chili oil, your favorite hot sauce, or a sprinkle of paprika.
- Add a tab of plain butter and some maple syrup.
- For utter pumpkin simplicity, drizzle with high-quality toasted pumpkin seed oil.

PHOTO BY DOUG GOSLING.

Brussels Sprouts with Alexanders, Leeks, and Dijon Beurre Blanc

Named after Alexander the Great, alexanders, *Smyrnium olusatrum,* is an herb that was planted by the Romans during their conquests and now grows wild throughout much of Northern Europe, thriving in a variety of soil types and temperature zones. Blanching the leaves first tempers their bitterness and brings out a surprising sweetness that pairs especially well with brussels sprouts and other winter brassicas such as cabbage and turnips.

Serves 4–6

2 tablespoons butter

1 leek, thinly sliced into half-moons

Salt to taste

1 pound brussels sprouts, trimmed and cut in half lengthwise

2 cups loosely packed leaves of alexanders, lovage, or smallage, or substitute celery leaf

Serves 30–40

¾ cup (1½ sticks) butter

6 leeks, thinly sliced into half-moons

Salt to taste

6 pounds brussels sprouts, trimmed and cut in half lengthwise

4 quarts loosely packed leaves of alexanders, lovage, or smallage, or substitute celery leaf

In a shallow, wide saucepan with a lid, melt the butter on medium heat. Add the leeks, sprinkle with a pinch of salt, and sauté uncovered for a few minutes until they begin to melt down a little. While the leeks are still only just slightly cooked, toss in the brussels sprouts. Cover and cook until the brussels sprouts are fully cooked through.

Meanwhile, blanch the alexanders leaves. Drop into boiling water for 20 seconds, remove with a wire-mesh ladle, and shock in an ice bath. Squeeze out all of the water and chop finely. Reserve.

To serve, toss the blanched alexanders with the leeks and brussels sprouts. Serve the sauce in a gravy boat on the side for pouring.

VARIATION

Summer: Replace the alexanders or celery leaf with ½ cup (2 cups) fresh dill, not blanched. This sauce tastes great with steamed baby turnips, green beans, hard-boiled eggs, or fish.

DIJON BEURRE BLANC SAUCE

Serves 4–6

2 minced shallots or 3 tablespoons minced yellow onion

½ cup white wine

1 tablespoon white wine, vinegar, or lemon juice

6 tablespoons butter, cut into small pieces

1 tablespoon Dijon mustard

Salt to taste

Serves 30–40

8 minced shallots or 1 large minced yellow onion

2 cups white wine

¼ cup white wine, vinegar, or lemon juice

2 cups (4 sticks) butter, cut into small pieces

¼ cup Dijon mustard

Salt to taste

In a shallow saucepan, bring the wine, vinegar, or lemon juice and shallots to a low simmer and reduce the liquid by a third. Turn off the heat and whisk in the butter, one cube at a time. Whisk in the mustard and salt.

Roasted Baby Turnips with Smallage, Lemon, and Capers

Serves 4–6

3 bunches baby turnips

¼ cup oil, divided

Salt to taste

1 small clove garlic, crushed

3 tablespoons butter, cut into pats

2 tablespoons smallage, finely chopped, or use half celery leaf, half parsley

2 teaspoons lemon zest (Meyers are best, if you can find them)

2 tablespoons capers

Serves 30–40

18 generous bunches baby turnips

½ cup oil, divided

Salt to taste

2 cloves garlic, crushed

½ cup butter, cut into pats

½ cup smallage, finely chopped, or use half celery leaf, half parsley

2 tablespoons lemon zest (Meyers are best, if you can find them)

½ cup capers

Preheat the oven to 375°F. Cut the greens from the turnip roots and reserve. Scrub the roots. If the turnips are very small, leave them whole; otherwise, cut into quarter wedges. Spread on a cookie sheet, drizzle with half of the oil and a sprinkle of salt, and roast for 20 minutes until they are soft and the edges just begin to turn golden.

While the roots are roasting, prepare the greens. If they are young and tender, you may leave them whole for a pretty effect, but if they are the least bit fibrous, chop them into crosswise strips. Heat the remaining oil in a sauté pan, then add the greens and garlic with sprinkle of salt. Sauté uncovered for a few minutes until the greens wilt.

When the turnips come hot out of the oven, toss with pats of butter, finely chopped smallage, lemon zest, and capers. Arrange a bed of sautéed greens on the plate and nestle the roasted, dressed turnips on top.

LOVAGE, SMALLAGE, AND ALEXANDERS

Celery is difficult to grow in our garden microclimate, so we grow these lower-maintenance celery cousins instead. The darker-green leaves of these herbs are similar in flavor to celery leaf or parsley with a bit more punch that speaks to the plants' hardy nature. While not intended for raw munching as we are accustomed to with blanched (and bland) stalks of store-bought celery, these perennial or self-seeding potherbs are useful to have on hand year-round for seasoning broths, stews, and beans or for adding a handful to sauté greens for extra flavor.

Left to right—lovage, smallage, and alexanders. PHOTO BY TALI AIONA

Perfect Sautéed Mushrooms

The nooks and crannies of the OAEC backcountry hide secret caches of edible mushrooms—so secret, in fact, that we don't even tell each other where we've found them! Varieties include morels, chanterelles, king boletes, and the more exotic prince, a huge, amaretto-flavored mushroom. In a nutshell, the key to great mushrooms is to concentrate the flavor by drawing all the water out. Serve alone or add to other dishes.

Serves 4–6

MAKES 2 CUPS

2 pounds fresh mushrooms, any variety
    (about 8 cups chopped)

⅓ cup (¾ stick) butter

⅓ cup oil

Generous amount of salt, about
    1½ teaspoons

2 shallots or 1 clove garlic

⅓ cup white wine

Serves 30–40

MAKES 8 CUPS

8 pounds fresh mushrooms, any variety
    (about 12 cups chopped)

1 cup (2 sticks) butter

1 cup oil

Generous amount of salt, about
    2 tablespoons

8 shallots or 4 cloves garlic

1½ cups white wine

Use a mushroom brush or a dry cloth to brush any visible dirt off the mushrooms. Do not rinse them or they will take on water like a sponge and become soggy. Many believe that mushrooms should not be sliced, but rather torn, broken, or shredded by hand in order to preserve their natural texture. Hence, tear mushrooms to desired size. Leave smaller, more unusually shaped mushrooms whole.

In a sauté pan on medium heat, add the mushrooms and salt; dry sauté uncovered, stirring occasionally, for about 15 minutes. The mushrooms will release a lot of water—keep sautéing until *all* of this water evaporates. Then add the butter, oil, and shallots or garlic. Sauté about 5 minutes more until the butter melts and the shallots caramelize. Then add the wine and continue sautéing until it evaporates. Remove from the pan and serve. If desired, deglaze the pan with a splash more of wine and serve this concentrated "*jus*" along with your dish.

Stir into stir-fries, omelets, pasta, and more.

VARIATION

Mushroom Sauce: Follow directions for Perfect Sautéed Mushrooms above. Remove the mushrooms from the pan and reserve. Add another ½ cup (2 cups for the large batch) wine to deglaze the pan, loosening the brown bits with a wooden spatula, and let reduce by half. Then add 1 cup (4 cups) heavy cream, lower the heat, and reduce liquid by one third. While the gravy is reducing, finely chop half of the mushrooms and leave the other half in larger chunks for varied texture. Add all of the mushrooms back in to the sauce. Serve hot.

Slow-Roasted Sunchokes with Wild Mushrooms

Slow-roasting sunchokes not only improves digestibility, but also brings out their earthy-sweet flavor, which pairs well with wild mushrooms.

Serves 4–6

2 pounds sunchokes, well cleaned
    and scrubbed
5 tablespoons oil, divided
Salt and pepper
2 pounds wild mushrooms or shiitakes
1 clove garlic, crushed
Salt

Serves 30–40

8 pounds sunchokes, well cleaned
    and scrubbed
¼ cup plus 1⅓ cups oil, divided
Salt and pepper
8 pounds wild mushrooms or shiitakes
2 cloves garlic, crushed
Salt

Preheat the oven to 325°F. If the sunchokes are large, cut them into rough chunks or simply snap the tubers with your hands into smaller segments. Toss with 2 tablespoons (¼ cup for the large batch) of the oil and salt and spread on a cookie sheet. Bake for 1½ to 2 hours, tossing once or twice during cooking. Drizzle with more oil if they get too dry.

Meanwhile, sauté the mushrooms uncovered on medium heat with the remaining 3 tablespoons (1⅓ cups) oil and salt. When they have released their juices, the water has finally evaporated, and the mushrooms are beginning to caramelize, add the crushed garlic and sauté for another minute or two.

Toss the mushrooms with the roasted sunchokes. Serve with a dollop of sour cream. For over-the-top decadence, stir a few drops of truffle oil into the sour cream!

PHOTO BY TALI AIONA.

SUNCHOKE: THE JERUSALEM ARTICHOKE

Jerusalem artichoke is a misnomer. The vegetable is not from Jerusalem, nor does it look or taste remotely like an artichoke. A botanical relative of the sunflower and therefore sometimes called sunchoke, it is native to North America and is a low-maintenance, yellow-flowering, bee-friendly tuber that produces abundant winter food. The sunchoke contains a "prebiotic" fiber known as inulin rather than starch as its main form of carbohydrate, which means beneficial food for the intestinal flora and a low-glycemic option for those watching their blood sugar levels.

There has been many a rural legend here about these knobby little tubers—some unforgettable soups have gone down in history and fueled arguments to rename them Jerusalem Fartichokes. The gaseous side effects seem to severely affect certain individuals and most others not at all—about one in six according to a recent post-lunch poll. If you've never eaten them before or are unsure about where your system falls on the spectrum, heed these true cautionary tales—we don't recommend trying them on or before a first date, serving them at dinner for a group sleeping in a communal dorm, or eating them before giving a presentation in front of a large group of strangers.

Gently Boiled Variegated Collards with Lemon, Garlic, and Olive Oil

Variegated collards are one of our absolute favorite sauté greens. Okay, we've already said this about New Zealand spinach, baby amaranth, and tree collards, but our community of greens aficionados has voted variegated collards a top contender as well. Not only are they gorgeous, but they are also surprisingly sweet and tender, especially in the wintertime. Horticulturally speaking, variegated plants are, by nature, weak plants. That means a more succulent leaf than standard collards, which have a reputation for being a little tough and stringy. Gently blanched and rolled up with fresh shredded veggies and sprouts, they make a magnificent spring roll!

When most Americans think of boiled collard greens, we think of southern soul-food-style greens that have been boiled all day with chile pepper and ham—delicious, but often more about the ham than the collards themselves. This method produces a melt-in-your-mouth texture and flavor that is pure collard.

Serves 4–6

1½ tablespoons salt

2–3 bunches collards, de-stemmed and sliced into ¾-inch ribbons (about 4 quarts)

Juice of 1 lemon

1 small clove garlic, crushed

½ cup olive oil

Serves 30–40

5 tablespoons salt

12–16 bunches collards, de-stemmed and sliced into ¾-inch ribbons (about 17 quarts)

Juice of 4 lemons

3 cloves garlic, crushed

1½ cups olive oil

Fill a large stockpot about three-quarters of the way full with water (roughly 8 quarts for the small batch, 22 quarts for the large) and bring to a boil on high heat. When water boils, add the salt and stir to dissolve. Add the prepped collards and stir so that all the greens get covered in water. Place the lid on the pot and turn off the heat. Set a timer for 4 minutes. Strain into a colander after cooking for 4 minutes only. Toss the greens in a bowl with the lemon juice, garlic, and olive oil. Serve hot.

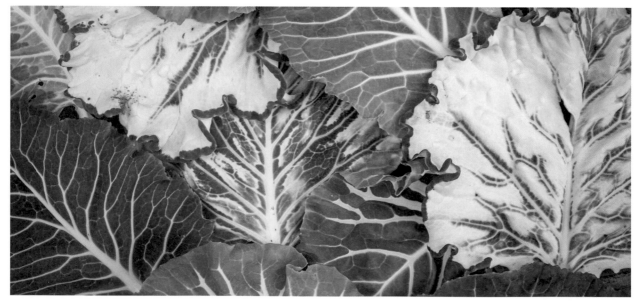

PHOTO BY TALI AIONA.

Wintry Oven-Crisped Tree Collard Ribbons

Tree collards are far and away the Mother Garden's most beloved and requested edible landscaping crop at our plant sales. They grace both our garden borders and dinner tables with stunning silvery-purple leaves. A distant relative of standard collards, tree collards are a tropical species believed to have come from Africa. They flower in response to equatorial sunlight (even daylight-to-darkness for prolonged periods), meaning that at our latitude, tree collards are perennial and never flower, but are propagated instead by cuttings passed along from gardener to gardener. A beautiful, hardy, and generous producer, tree collards keep us flush with greens, even in the dead of winter—you could say that they give us the year-round convenience we've come to expect from a modern supermarket!

The robust texture of tree collards is accentuated when they are roasted until slightly crispy in the oven, somewhere between sauté greens and kale chips. Tree collards have a semi-spicy bite—as if they already contained garlic and chili flakes—feel free to play this up by tossing in a little of each before roasting.

Serves 4–6

2 large bunches tree collards, or regular
    Vates- or Georgia-style collards
2 tablespoons olive oil
Pinch of salt to taste
1 small lemon, cut into wedges

Serves 30–40

12–15 bunches tree collards, or regular
    Vates- or Georgia-style collards
½ cup olive oil
Salt to taste, about 1 tablespoon
4 lemons, cut into small wedges

Preheat the oven or broiler to 400°F. Chiffonade the tree collards and reserve the stems for another use. Spread the collard ribbons out onto the biggest sheet tray you have and drizzle generously with oil. Toss with your hands to coat evenly and fluff up the ribbons as much as possible so that there is lots of surface area open for crisping. Sprinkle with salt. Roast on the top shelf for 5 to 10 minutes, keeping a close eye on them. Remove from the oven when the edges are slightly browned and the rest has steamed to a brilliant green. Serve hot with lemon wedges.

How to chiffonade greens: (1) strip or cut out the stem; (2) stack and roll; (3) slice into thin ribbons. PHOTOS BY TALI AIONA.

Dougo's Melted Leeks

Doug Gosling (affectionately referred to as Dougo) is famous for cooking with copious amounts of butter. Leeks, which are usually a secondary ingredient, are showcased in this lavish side dish—an OAEC classic.

Serves 4–6

MAKES ONE 9 X 13-INCH BAKING DISH

6 medium leeks or 4 cups prepped leeks

¼ cup oil

Salt to taste

½ cup (1 stick) butter

¾ cup sherry

Fresh-cracked black pepper to taste

Serves 30–40

MAKES 2 HOTEL PANS

6 pounds leeks or 12 quarts prepped leeks

1 cup oil

2 teaspoons salt, or to taste

1½ cups (3 sticks) butter

4 cups sherry

Fresh-cracked black pepper to taste

Preheat the oven to 375°F. Cut the root bottoms and most of the green parts off the leeks. Reserve for later use in stock. Cut the remaining white and light-green parts into 4-inch pieces and slice lengthwise into halves or quarters, depending on the width of the leek, to make evenly sized pieces. Wash the leeks thoroughly by soaking them in a large bowl of water and separating some of the leek layers to remove any dirt. Drain and rinse. Toss with the oil and salt and arrange in a casserole, baking dish, or entrée pan with a cover. Cut the butter into tabs and tuck them into the bed of leeks. Pour in the sherry. Cover. Bake for 45 minutes to an hour, stirring several times during baking, until the leeks are completely soft and falling apart. Season to taste with salt and pepper.

VARIATION

Leek Butter: Melted leeks can be instantly transformed into a decadent and creamy leek butter by pureeing them in a food processor or immersion blender while they're still warm. Allow to cool and pipe onto croutons or serve with seafood.

Domino Potatoes with Society Garlic and Bay Leaves

Society garlic, *Tulbaghia violacea*, is a drought-tolerant perennial landscaping plant from South Africa that produces delicate, garlic-flavored purple flowers and leaves. It is called society garlic because it was once believed not to cause bad breath. While we haven't found society garlic to be any less offensive in the halitosis department, it is a beautiful and low-maintenance edible flower and chive alternative that thrives all year round in our climate.

Serves 4–6

MAKES A 9 X 9-INCH BAKING DISH

⅓ cup olive oil

Salt

4 medium potatoes—a dense waxy variety like Yukon Gold, Carola, or German Butterball

3–4 culinary bay leaves (not California bay)

3–4 leaves of society garlic or garlic chives

Garnish: society garlic flowers

Serves 30–40

MAKES A 12 X 20-INCH HOTEL PAN

1½ cups olive oil

Salt

20 large potatoes

3–4 sprigs of culinary bay leaves (not California Bay)

1 small bunch society garlic, or substitute garlic chives

Garnish: society garlic flowers

Preheat the oven to 375°F. Coat the bottom of the baking pan with olive oil and sprinkle with salt. Scrub and slice the potatoes thinly to ⅛ inch on a mandoline, keeping them stacked together. Lay the stacks of slices in a pan on a slight diagonal so that they flay out like tumbling dominoes. Tuck a few bay leaves down between the rows. Drizzle the tops liberally back and forth with olive oil—the oil will absorb quickly down between the slices. Sprinkle with more salt. Bake on the bottom rack of the oven for about an hour. Sprinkle chopped society garlic over the top and return to the oven for another 30 minutes or so until the potatoes start to crisp on top. Remove one of the slices and taste—if the potatoes are still al dente, continue roasting until they soften. Serve garnished with fresh society garlic flowers.

HONORING ANDEAN FOOD CROPS

by Doug Gosling

Back in 1989, when garden intern Dean Dalton arrived from the Northwest, he brought with him a tuber of a plant from Peru called mashua, *Tropaeolum tuberosum*, that was being grown for market outside of Seattle on several small farms. We grew it successfully, surprised by its rambling beauty, the exotic floral taste of its cooked tubers, and the peppery earthiness of its fresh leaves and persimmon-orange flowers. We had been growing other indigenous crops from the Americas—quinoa, amaranth, Jerusalem artichokes, and Purple Peruvian potatoes—since 1982, but the arrival of mashua triggered an exploration and study that continues today of one of the great epicenters of food crop domestication and advanced agriculture on the planet, the high Andes regions of Peru, Ecuador, and Bolivia.

By the time OAEC arrived here on the land in 1994, we were growing oca, pepino, tamarillo, red manzano and Aji Amarillo peppers, and Cape gooseberries. We were further inspired by a trip that five of us OAEC staff made to Peru in 1999 on which we were hosted by ANDES, an organization of indigenous farmers keenly dedicated to preserving and protecting its traditional crops and agriculture. We witnessed many of these crops growing in fields in extremely remote villages at 9,000 to 12,000 feet in sophisticated agricultural systems, some of which exist almost intact since from before European contact.

We soon were growing Bolivian yacon, Peruvian Kiwicha, tarwi, and achira. By the time we had our first plant sale in 1996, we were propagating so many of these crops that the theme of the first plant sale had to be "Crops of the Incas," a festive

Andean tubers—mashua, yacon, and oca. PHOTO BY DOUG GOSLING.

Oca, a sorrel that produces a tuber, is the second most important root crop in the Andes, next to the potato. It comes in an astonishing number of shapes, colors, and sizes. PHOTO BY DOUG GOSLING.

event complete with the kitschy Incan decorations and paraphernalia from a faux-Andean market that we inherited from the San Francisco Orchid Show (which that year had featured the orchids of Peru). We are likely the only plant sale on earth that has had a petting zoo with a live llama!

In addition to figuring out how to successfully grow these crops in Northern California, over the years, we have made concerted efforts to bring them into our kitchen to learn how to cook and savor them and adapt them to our ways of cooking. We initiated a series of fund-raising dinners in 1999 that we produced for five years to celebrate these foods and educate others about their value to modern gardeners and chefs. We attempted to feature these crops and other appropriate vegetables and herbs common to Peruvian cuisine and used traditional recipes as jumping-off points to explore new ways of using them in contemporary cooking.

In recent years, we have discovered additional crops like naranjilla, achocha, maca, and ulluco, and have become particularly fond of the Peruvian marigold, huacatay, widely used as an herb to flavor a variety of Andean dishes.

HONORING ANDEAN FOOD CROPS MENU

Papas a la Huancaina

Locro de Zapallo stew served with Quinoa Confetti Salad

Simply roasted Andean tubers with ocopa, a traditional spicy peanut sauce

Yacon salsa with red manzano peppers

Toasted spiced seeds and nuts

OAEC Mother Garden salad with Tree Tomato Vinaigrette

Cape Gooseberry Frangipane Tart

Mashua Mashed Potatoes

Mashua, (*Tropaeolum tuberosum*) a relative of nasturtium that produces a tuber, is an important root crop in the Andes and is extremely prolific in the Mother Garden. Culinarily, it behaves much like a strong radish: Raw it is extremely spicy, but when cooked, the flavor mellows into a distinctive floral sweetness, further softened by potato and celeriac in this rustic mash.

Serves 4-6

½ pound mashua

½ pound russet potatoes

½ pound celeriac

Salt to taste

¼ cup butter

¾ cup milk

Pepper to taste (optional)

Serves 30-40

6 pounds mashua

6 pounds russet potatoes

6 pounds celeriac

Salt to taste

2 cups butter

6 cups milk

Pepper to taste (optional)

Chop the mashua, potatoes, and celeriac into chunks. Place in a pot with enough water to cover by at least 2 inches. Add 1 tablespoon salt per 8 cups water, and bring to a boil. Once the water is boiling, cook for about 15 minutes, or until the veggies are soft and easily pierced with a fork. Drain.

If you have a potato ricer, push the roots through it for extra-fluffy results. Otherwise, mash by hand with a masher. Add the butter and milk, and mix throughout. Do not use a blender or get overzealous with the mashing or else the potatoes will become gluey and paste-like. A few rustic lumps are okay. Season to taste with salt and pepper.

Curried Mashua and Potatoes

By the end of January, we are reaching deep into our creative pockets to come up with yet another way to cook prolific winter mashua (our next book should be called *101 Mashua Recipes* . . .). Here's an easy one that uses curry to bring out its spicy sweetness.

Serves 4-6

1 pound mashua

2 tablespoons olive oil, divided

¾ teaspoon salt, divided

1½ teaspoons curry powder

1 pound fingerling potatoes

1 small clove garlic

3 sprigs fresh cilantro, finely chopped

Serves 30-40

6 pounds mashua

1 cup olive oil, divided

4 teaspoons salt, divided

6 teaspoons curry powder

6 pounds fingerling potatoes

4 cloves garlic, crushed

1 bunch fresh cilantro, finely chopped

Preheat the oven to 400°F. Cut the mashua into thin ⅛-inch rounds and toss with half the oil, half the salt, and all of the curry powder; spread on a cookie sheet. Cut the potatoes into thicker ½-inch rounds, toss them with the rest of the oil and salt, and spread on another cookie sheet. Roast both trays of root veggies for 30 minutes or so (longer for the large batch), rotating halfway through cooking, until they're soft in the middle and slightly crispy on the edges. Toss everything together with cilantro and serve.

Roasted Andean Tubers with Ocopa

This dish features several of the perennial root crops that grow so well in the Mother Garden. Favorites at the center, oca and ulloco melt in your mouth when salted, painted with olive oil, and baked. They're served in this dish with ocopa, a traditional Andean spicy peanut sauce.

Serves 4–6

1 pound assorted tubers—ulloco, oca,
    and mashua, or more common root
    vegetables such as yams, carrots,
    and potatoes
Olive oil
Salt

OCOPA SPICY PEANUT SAUCE

MAKES 1½ CUPS

½ red manzano (rocoto) pepper, de-seeded
½ small sweet onion, peeled
Olive oil
1 cup toasted peanuts
½ pound queso fresco
1 clove garlic
3 tablespoons chopped fresh huacatay or
    cilantro (optional)
Milk

Serves 30–40

8–10 pounds assorted tubers—ulloco,
    oca, and mashua, or more common
    root vegetables such as yams, carrots,
    and potatoes
Olive oil
Salt

OCOPA SPICY PEANUT SAUCE

MAKES 4 CUPS

2 red manzano (rocoto) peppers, halved
    and de-seeded
1 large sweet onion, peeled and halved
Olive oil
3 cups toasted peanuts
2 pounds queso fresco
2–3 cloves garlic
1 small bunch fresh huacatay or cilantro,
    about ½ cup chopped (optional)
Milk

Preheat the oven to 450°F. Scrub the tubers. Cut up any really large ones, but most of the mashua, oca, and ulloco should be the size of fingerling potatoes and therefore small enough to leave whole. Toss all the root vegetables, each separately, in enough olive oil to lightly coat, then with salt. Roast until perfectly cooked. It is advised to bake each variety on separate cookie sheets and watch closely as they will cook in significantly different times.

To make the sauce: On one corner of a cookie sheet or on a separate small one, roast the manzano peppers and the sweet onion, also tossed with oil. Remove when soft and crispy. Put the roasted peppers, sweet onion, peanuts, cheese, garlic, and huacatay or cilantro in a food processor and puree until smooth. Add olive oil and milk, alternating them, until you achieve the consistency of a thick dressing.

Arrange the vegetables on a platter and place the sauce in a bowl in the middle for dipping the vegetables.

Ulluco (*Ullucus tuberosus*), one of the most striking foods seen in the markets of the high Andes, is among the rare crops being grown in the Mother Garden nursery. PHOTO BY DOUG GOSLING.

PHOTO BY TALI AIONA.

MAIN DISHES: USING GRAINS, BEANS, EGGS, AND CHEESE

RECIPE LIST

Spring

Green Garlic White Bean Primavera
Spring Risotto: Roasted Asparagus and Nettle with Pea Tendrils
Spring Carrot Soufflé with Sorrel Sauce
Lemon Thyme Duck Egg Soufflé
Garden Vegetable Frittata
Thai Omelet
Smoky Bitter Greens Over Griddled Potatoes and Scrambled Eggs

Summer

Stuffed Tomatoes with Borage, Nettles, and Ricotta
Wine Country Grape Leaf Dolmas
Quinoa Confetti Salad
Summer Risotto: Lemon Verbena and Roasted Cherry Tomato
Lemon Verbena Steamed Rice
Tepary Beans with Oregano and Seared Padrón Peppers
Nana's Chiles Rellenos

Fall

OAEC Basic Beans
Ali's Copper Kettle Beans
Hot-Pink Fall Risotto with Chèvre
Fig-Leaf-Infused Basmati Pilaf
Soft Pumpkin Polenta
Polenta Moons with Roasted Red Peppers, Collard Ribbons, and Feta
Savory Tan Oak Acorn Mush
Baked Eggs with Seasonal Vegetables
Shakshuka
Millet with Toasted Cumin Seeds

Winter

Yellow Split Pea Puree with Caramelized Onion and Black Olives
Bernie's Pierogi
Winter Wild Mushroom Barley Risotto

PHOTO BY TALI AIONA.

Green Garlic White Bean Primavera

Like other spring crops waiting to mature, green garlic is an ingredient born out of impatience. We just can't help but harvest a few stalks of garlic prematurely for a potent alternative to leeks.

Serves 4–6

1 cup white beans such as runner beans, baby limas, cannellini, or navy beans

¼ cup butter or oil, for cooking

2 green garlic stalks, chopped into ¼-inch half-moons, or leeks

1 small bunch asparagus, chopped into 1-inch pieces; leave the decorative tips whole

Juice and zest of 1 lemon

¼ cup extra-virgin olive oil

½ cup chopped parsley

Pinch of fresh-cracked black pepper

Salt to taste

1 cup Fava Beans in Vinaigrette (page 118)

Serves 30–40

8 cups white beans such as runner beans, baby limas, cannellini, or navy beans

1 cup butter or oil, for cooking

8 green garlic stalks, chopped into ¼-inch half-moons, or leeks

6 bunches asparagus, chopped into 1-inch pieces; leave the decorative tips whole

Juice and zest of 6 lemons

1 cup extra-virgin olive oil

1½ cups chopped parsley

1 tablespoon fresh-cracked black pepper

Salt to taste

5 cups Fava Beans in Vinaigrette (page 118)

Soak the beans overnight. When you're ready to cook, rinse the beans. In a medium pot, cover the beans with plenty of water. Bring to a boil, reduce the heat, and simmer until the beans are soft but not mushy, about 25 to 50 minutes depending on the bean. Drain and rinse the beans thoroughly.

In a large brazier, warm the oil or butter and sauté the green garlic until soft and translucent. Add the asparagus (and/or other spring veggies; see variations) and continue cooking until it turns bright green and mostly soft.

Add the cooked beans. Combine and heat through. Add the lemon juice, olive oil, chopped parsley, and salt and pepper to taste. Taste and adjust. Some varieties of white beans can be a little on the dry side, so don't be afraid to drizzle on a little more oil if you think it needs it. Toss in the marinated fava beans. Serve mounded on a bed of sautéed greens, like Garlicky Sautéed Fava Leaves (page 146) or raw baby spring greens such as arugula, frisée, cress, or miner's lettuce.

VARIATION

Along with or in place of the asparagus, sauté other spring vegetables such as snow or snap peas, or brassica shoots, spigarello, or broccoli raab cut into thin florets.

PHOTO BY TALI AIONA.

Spring Risotto: Roasted Asparagus and Nettle with Pea Tendrils

Serves 4–6

1 bunch asparagus

1 tablespoon olive oil

2 cloves garlic, minced

Salt and pepper to taste

7 cups vegetable stock (page 92)

¼ cup (½ stick) butter

2 shallots or ½ onion, finely minced

1½ cups arborio rice

¾ cup dry white wine

1 cup blanched nettle leaves, pureed (see
   sidebar), or ⅓ cup dried nettles

1 tablespoon lemon thyme, minced

Zest of 1 Meyer lemon

½ cup grated hard cheese, Parmesan
   or Romano

Salt and pepper to taste

2 tablespoons fresh-chopped parsley

Small handful of tender pea tendrils
   and shoots

Lemon juice and olive oil

Garnish: chopped parsley

Serves 30–40

6 bunches asparagus

⅔ cup olive oil

4 cloves garlic, minced

Salt and pepper to taste

7 quarts vegetable stock (page 92)

½ cup (1 stick) butter

6 shallots or 1 onion, finely minced

8 cups arborio rice

1 bottle dry white wine

4 cups blanched nettle leaves, pureed (see
   sidebar), or 1 cup dried nettles

1 bunch lemon thyme, minced

Zest of 4 Meyer lemons

2 cups grated hard cheese, Parmesan
   or Romano

About 1 tablespoon salt and
   1 teaspoon pepper

¼ cup fresh-chopped parsley

Large handful of tender pea tendrils
   and shoots

Lemon juice and olive oil

Garnish: chopped parsley

Preheat the oven to 400°F. If you're making stock from scratch, trim the ends of asparagus and reserve for stock. Slice the asparagus on 1-inch diagonals. Toss with the olive oil, garlic, and salt and pepper to taste. Arrange on sheet pan and roast for 15 minutes on the top rack of the oven until just barely roasted. Remove from the oven, let cool, and set aside.

While the asparagus roasts, make the vegetable stock.

To make the risotto base: Heat the stock in a large saucepan to a simmer and keep warm on the stove. Heat a Dutch oven or a heavy-bottomed saucepan with the butter on medium heat. Add the shallots and a pinch of salt. Sauté until the shallots are translucent, about 2 minutes. Add the arborio rice and stir to coat. Add the dry white wine and let everything deglaze in the pan for a few minutes. Add 1 cup of warm stock and stir with a wooden spoon. Turn the heat to medium-low so that it stays at a very low simmer, uncovered. When the cup of stock is almost all absorbed, then add another cup and repeat the process until all the stock is absorbed and the rice is a creamy fluid texture. This will take about 30 minutes.

At the last addition of stock, add in the reserved roasted asparagus, the nettles, lemon thyme, and zest. Let this mixture cook together for a few minutes. Turn off the heat. Mix in the grated hard cheese. Taste and adjust the seasoning with salt and pepper. Toss the pea tendrils in a separate bowl with a drizzle of olive oil, lemon juice, and salt. Serve the risotto with a sprinkling of parsley and garnish with the pea tendrils.

STINGING NETTLES

Preparing Nettles

Harvest: To avoid getting stung, you will need to work in long sleeves and thick leather work gloves. Snip the tender leaves from the stem with scissors and use the scissors as tongs to place them into a bowl or container (they will sting through a plastic or cloth bag.) Pull off any twigs or debris.

Blanch: Bring a large pot of water to a boil. Use long tongs to avoid touching the nettles. Submerge the nettles in boiling water for about 30 seconds or more, until they are completely limp. Strain and plunge into cold water to preserve the bright-green color and retain nutrients. Now the needles are deactivated and you can handle them just like any other green. We usually pull the leaves off of the fibrous main stem and chop them finely or puree them in a food processor at this point.

Spring Carrot Soufflé with Sorrel Sauce

When the hens start laying again after a much-deserved winter rest, there is no better way to celebrate the renewal of their cycle than with a soufflé.

While the idea of making soufflé can be intimidating at first, the process can be mastered relatively easily with a little patience and unhurried practice. Read through the complete recipe before beginning and plan for plenty of time—the hands-on preparation takes about 45 minutes, plus ½ hour for cooling the mixture, and up to an hour for baking, for a little over 2 hours from start to finish.

Fancy ramekins and soufflé dishes are not necessary—we use small teacups and regular casserole dishes instead.

Serves 4–6

MAKES SIX 4-OUNCE RAMEKINS OR A 1½-QUART SOUFFLÉ DISH

¼ cup (½ stick) unsalted butter, divided, plus more for ramekins
1 small shallot or small onion, thinly sliced (about 2 tablespoons)
1 pound carrots, peeled and cut into ½-inch pieces (about 2 cups)
1 bay leaf
½ teaspoon salt
3 tablespoons all-purpose flour
1¼ cups whole milk
½ cup heavy cream
⅛ teaspoon freshly grated nutmeg
⅛ teaspoon ground ginger
Freshly ground pepper
3 large egg yolks
2 large egg whites

Serves 30–40

MAKES THIRTY-SIX 4-OUNCE RAMEKINS OR FOUR 2-QUART SOUFFLÉ DISHES

1½ cups (3 sticks) butter, divided, plus more for ramekins
3 shallots or onions, thinly sliced (about ¾ cup)
6 pounds carrots, peeled and cut into ½-inch pieces (about 3½ quarts)
3 bay leaves
1 tablespoon salt
1 cup plus 2 tablespoons all-purpose flour
7½ cups whole milk
3 cups heavy cream
½ teaspoon freshly grated nutmeg
½ teaspoon ground ginger
Freshly ground pepper
18 egg yolks
12 egg whites

Melt a tablespoon (¼ cup) of the butter in a medium saucepan over medium heat. Add the shallots, chopped carrots, bay leaves, and a pinch of the salt. Cook covered, stirring occasionally, until the carrots are tender, about 20 minutes. Reduce the heat to medium-low after 15 minutes if needed to prevent the carrots or butter from browning.

While the carrots are cooking, make the roux. Melt the remaining butter in a medium saucepan over medium heat. Stir in the flour with a wooden spoon; cook, stirring constantly, 3 minutes. With a whisk, pour in the milk gradually and whisk to combine. Use the wooden spoon to scrape the bottom and corners of the pan. Reduce the heat to low. Cook, stirring often to prevent lumps from forming, 15 minutes. Remove from the heat.

When the carrots are cooked through, remove from the heat and add the cream. Discard the bay leaves. Using an immersion blender or a food processor, puree the mixture (use caution when pureeing hot liquids in a food processor). Set aside.

Whisk the roux into the carrot puree. Stir in nutmeg, ginger, and season with salt and pepper to taste. Let cool completely, about 30 minutes. *Tip for easy entertaining:* Make this soufflé base (the roux-and-carrot mixture, without eggs) ahead of time and refrigerate up to 24 hours until ready to use.

While the soufflé base is cooling, preheat the oven to 400°F. Nest the soufflé dishes or ramekins inside a larger baking tray, roasting pan, or hotel pan. Boil a teakettle of water for the hot-water bath. Separate the eggs.

Add the yolks, one at a time, to the carrot mixture, whisking well after each addition. In an electric mixer, beat the egg whites until soft peaks form. Overbeating the whites will make for a texture that's chunky and stiff instead of lush and billowy. When the whisk is lifted out of the bowl, a point will form between the whisk and the bowl. Mix a third of the whites into the carrot-yolk mixture to lighten, then gently fold in the rest of the whites.

Ladle the mixture into buttered ramekins or soufflé dishes, filling three-quarters of the way up to the rims. Nest the ramekins inside the larger roasting pan and transfer to the oven. Pour enough boiling water into the pan to come about three-quarters of the way up the sides of the ramekins. Bake in the hot-water bath until the soufflés are puffed and set, and their tops begin to brown, about 35 minutes for small ramekins (50 to 60 minutes for the larger 2-quart casseroles.) Using tongs, carefully transfer the soufflés to a wire rack. Serve immediately before the soufflé falls, with French Sorrel Sauce (page 286).

Lemon Thyme Duck Egg Soufflé

This is chef Gabriel Tiradani's ode to spring—the delicate brightness of lemon thyme with duck eggs is utter poetry.

Serves 4–6

**MAKES SIX 4-OUNCE RAMEKINS OR
A 1½-QUART SOUFFLÉ DISH**

Soft butter for the dishes

¼ cup dry bread crumbs

2 tablespoons plus 1 teaspoon butter

2 tablespoons plus 1 teaspoon
   all-purpose flour

¾ cup whole milk

3 duck egg yolks

Pinch of salt

2½ teaspoons fresh lemon thyme, finely
   chopped, or 2 teaspoons regular thyme
   plus 1 teaspoon lemon zest

Pinch of fresh-ground nutmeg

4 ounces grated Gruyère or Parmesan
   (about 1⅓ cups)

Fresh-ground black pepper

4 duck egg whites

Serves 30-40

**MAKES FORTY 4-OUNCE RAMEKINS
OR TWO 2-QUART SOUFFLÉ DISHES**

Soft butter for the dishes

1½ cups dry bread crumbs

1 cup plus 2 tablespoons (2¼ sticks) butter

¾ cup all-purpose flour

6 cups whole milk

16 duck egg yolks

1½ teaspoons salt

6 tablespoons fresh lemon thyme, finely
   chopped, or 6 tablespoons regular
   thyme plus 1 tablespoon lemon zest

1 teaspoon fresh-ground nutmeg

24 ounces grated Gruyère or Parmesan
   (about 7 cups)

Fresh-ground black pepper

20 duck egg whites

Preheat the oven to 375°F. Generously coat the ramekins or soufflé dishes with butter. Dust with the bread crumbs. Set up for the hot-water bath by nesting the soufflé dishes inside a larger baking pan—a 9 x 13-inch baking dish for the small batch or two standard-sized hotel pans for the large.

Separate the egg yolks from the whites. Grate the cheese and chop the lemon thyme. Boil water in a teakettle.

Make the soufflé base: Melt the butter in a medium saucepan on medium heat. Add the flour to the melted butter and whisk continuously until it lightens in color and the aroma is nutty, about 1 minute. Pour in the milk all at once and whisk until the mixture heats completely; the mixture will slowly thicken. Keep stirring for about 2 to 3 minutes, or a little longer for the large batch.

Take the pot off the heat and mix in the yolks and salt, then return to the heat and continue to whisk constantly until the mixture comes to a boil. Take it off the heat and whisk in the lemon thyme, grated nutmeg, grated cheese, and fresh black pepper. Transfer to a large mixing bowl and let sit while you whip up the egg whites. This soufflé base can be refrigerated up to 2 days in an airtight container.

Beat the egg whites with an eggbeater or stand mixer until they form soft, smooth peaks but are not dry—overwhipping the whites makes for a grainy texture that doesn't rise as well. The whites will more than triple in size when they are whipped, so for the large serving, you will need to divide the whites into two batches in order to fit them into the bowl of an 8-quart stand mixer. Fold a third of the egg whites into the soufflé base to lighten the mixture. Fold in the rest of the egg whites, but don't overmix.

Pour the mixture into your prepared soufflé dishes, leaving ¼ inch at the top. Place the soufflés in a large baking dish in the oven. Pour boiling water into the baking dish until it comes about halfway up the soufflé sides, being careful not to splash water into the soufflé mixture. Bake 20 to 25 minutes for individual ramekins or 30 to 40 minutes for larger dishes, until the tops are brown and they have risen above the rims.

Transfer from the hot-water bath, using tongs for the small ramekins. Serve immediately.

VARIATIONS

Flour-free version: Omit the bread crumbs. Substitute 1 tablespoon (¼ cup) each of rice flour, amaranth flour, and tapioca starch for the flour in the roux.

Chicken-egg version: Use 4 yolks and 6 whites for the small batch or 20 yolks and 36 whites for the large batch.

Garden Vegetable Frittata

Frittata is an easy and inexpensive standby that we eat some variation of at least once a week for either breakfast, lunch, or dinner. This chard, marjoram, and Swiss cheese frittata is perfectly delicious without any dairy, so feel free to omit the cheese if you prefer.

Serves 4–6

MAKES ONE 10-INCH SKILLET

1 tablespoon butter or oil, for the pan

10–12 eggs

1 teaspoon salt

½ teaspoon black pepper

2–3 cups Simple Sautéed Chard with Onion (page 155) or any precooked garden vegetable (see variations)

2–3 teaspoons finely chopped fresh marjoram (or whatever garden herb is freshest)

⅔ cup shredded Swiss cheese

Serves 30–40

MAKES 2 EXTRA-LARGE 16-INCH SKILLETS

¼ cup butter or oil, for the pans

70 eggs

1 tablespoon salt

2 teaspoons black pepper

10–12 cups Simple Sautéed Chard with Onion (page 155) or any precooked garden vegetable (see variations)

¼–⅓ cup finely chopped fresh marjoram (or whatever garden herb is freshest)

4 cups shredded Swiss cheese

Coat a cast-iron skillet generously with oil or butter, making sure to grease all the way up the sides. Follow directions for Sautéed Chard, making sure that most of the liquid released from the vegetables has evaporated. (If you're substituting leftovers, simply reheat them in the pan.) Reduce the heat to the lowest setting possible.

Crack the eggs into a bowl and whisk thoroughly. Stir in the salt and pepper. Arrange the precooked chard or other vegetables evenly around the bottom of the slightly warm skillet. Pour in the egg mixture, sprinkle the chopped herbs, and top with the cheese.

Turn the broiler on. Cook the frittata in the skillet on the stovetop on *very low* heat without stirring until the egg sets on the bottom and begins to bubble up around the sides. For the large-sized skillet, rotate the pan around the burner periodically so that the edges get cooked as evenly as the middle. Pop the pan under the broiler for 5 minutes to set the top. Serve warm or at room temperature.

VARIATIONS

Spring: Sautéed asparagus and garlic scapes (cut into equal-sized 1-inch spears) with fresh chervil and parsley. Instead of the shredded hard cheese, add small dollops of chèvre or homemade ricotta.

Summer: Leftover BBQ veggies from the grill—zucchini, eggplant, peppers, onions, etc.—fresh sage and dry Jack.

Fall: Pre-roasted cauliflower and red peppers. Instead of the salt, stir in 2 teaspoons (3 tablespoons) minced preserved lemon or preserved lemon brine. Add a pinch of red chili flakes.

Winter: Substitute kale for the chard and add slices of oca or potato that have been pre-roasted with rosemary. Instead of cheese, scatter with black olives.

Thai Omelet

Anna, who has been working in the OAEC kitchen since she was 17, brought this recipe back from a recent trip to Thailand. We've adopted it as an instant classic because it's the perfect lunchtime accompaniment to stir-fried veggies from the garden. And not a moment too soon—the gardeners have just figured out how to grow fresh turmeric in the greenhouse!

Serves 4–6

**MAKES 3 LARGE OMELETS,
CUT INTO STRIPS**

6 eggs

1 tablespoon tamari

½ teaspoon ground turmeric, or grated fresh if you have it

1 clove garlic

1 teaspoon coriander seeds

½ teaspoon peppercorns

4 scallions, thinly sliced

1 tablespoon chopped fresh marjoram

1 teaspoon chili flakes

3 tablespoons coconut oil

Serves 30–40

**MAKES 18 LARGE OMELETS,
CUT INTO STRIPS**

40 eggs

¼ cup tamari

3 teaspoons ground turmeric, or fresh grated, if you have it

6–8 cloves garlic

2 tablespoons coriander seeds

3 teaspoons peppercorns

3 bunches scallions, thinly sliced

⅓ cup chopped fresh marjoram

2 tablespoons chili flakes

1 cup coconut oil

Whisk the eggs, tamari, and turmeric together until lightly beaten. Using a mortar and pestle, smash the garlic. Add the coriander seeds and peppercorns and crush together until the seeds are well ground. (This can also be done in a food processor or spice grinder.) Stir in the sliced scallions, marjoram, and chili flakes.

Heat a wok or cast-iron pan on medium-high heat. Add a tablespoon of the oil and a tablespoon (3 tablespoons) of the spice mixture. Cook until the spices are fragrant. Add ½ cup (1½ cups) of egg and let sit a minute. Push the cooked egg to the center, allowing raw egg to pour over onto the pan. This isn't like a French omelet, so don't worry about the form too much—it just needs to be cooked into a pancake, more or less. Let sit another minute, then flip and cook a minute on the second side. Work in batches like this until all the eggs and spice mixture are used up.

Cut the cooked omelet into 1-inch strips. Serve over steamed rice with stir-fried seasonal vegetables.

Smoky Bitter Greens Over Griddled Potatoes and Scrambled Eggs

In the absence of bacon, this is the next best way to serve dandelion greens. This hardy assemblage is served with a side of fluffy scrambled eggs for breakfast.

Serves 4–6

3 tablespoons ghee, fat, or cooking oil, divided

2 large German Butterballs or other yellow
    waxy potatoes such as Yukon Gold

Salt and pepper to taste

6 eggs

¼ cup whole milk

1 yellow onion, diced

1 clove garlic, crushed

½ teaspoon smoked paprika

1 large bunch dandelion greens, chopped,
    or other wild bitter greens such as sow
    thistle or nipplewort

Squeeze of lemon or dash of vinegar, to taste

½ cup sour cream

Serves 30–40

1¼ cups ghee, fat, or cooking oil, divided

12 large German Butterballs or other yellow
    waxy potatoes such as Yukon Gold

Salt and pepper to taste

40 eggs

1 cup whole milk

6 large yellow onions, diced

4 cloves garlic, crushed

1 tablespoon smoked paprika

6–8 large bunches dandelion greens,
    chopped, or other wild bitter greens
    such as sow thistle or nipplewort

Lemon juice or vinegar to taste, about ¼ cup

4 cups sour cream

Slice the potatoes on the bias lengthwise into oblong ¼-inch-thick "steaks." In a large cast-iron pan or on the flat-top griddle, melt 2 tablespoons (1 cup) of the ghee or cooking oil over medium heat and lay out the potato slices in a single layer side by side. Fry the potatoes on one side until they are golden brown, flip with a spatula, and fry on the other side. Sprinkle with a little salt. Remove and place in a warm oven to hold while you cook the greens and scramble the eggs.

Crack the eggs into a bowl and whisk together with the milk. Season with a sprinkle of salt and pepper. Melt a tab of the remaining ghee, fat, or oil in another skillet (don't use the cast iron for this—your eggs will turn gray) and turn the heat down to *very* low. Gently pour in the eggs and wait. The key to big, fluffy curds is to let them cook as slowly as possible and resist the temptation to stir them constantly. Once the eggs have set up around the edges, use just two or three gentle folding motions to slide the spatula through the middle and then around the edges. Turn off the heat so that they don't dry out. As they sit, the remaining heat will cook them through.

Meanwhile, heat another drizzle of cooking fat or ghee in the cast-iron pan you used to cook the potatoes and add the onions. Sauté until translucent. Add the garlic and smoked paprika and stir to combine. Sauté for a quick moment until the garlic releases its green flavor, but doesn't brown. Add the dandelion greens and let them wilt down, tossing occasionally with tongs. Take off the heat and season to taste with salt, pepper, and a squeeze of lemon or vinegar.

Serve the eggs and greens spooned over the slices of potato and top with a generous dollop of sour cream. Serve with your favorite hot sauce.

Nipplewort—another wild bitter sauté green found growing in the Mother Garden. PHOTO BY TALI AIONA.

Stuffed Tomatoes with Borage, Nettles, and Ricotta

Both the blue-flowered and rare white-flowered borage volunteer prolifically in the Mother Garden, providing nectar for bees throughout most of the year. The flowers are a neutral-flavored edible garnish, suitable for both sweet and savory applications, and the nutritious leaves are a mild cucumber-flavored sauté green commonly eaten in the northern Italian region of Liguria. Raw, the leaves are hairy and unappetizing, akin to chewing on a strip of Velcro, but finely chopped and cooked, borage has a subtle, summery charm.

Serves 4–6

MAKES ONE 9 x 9-INCH
SQUARE BAKING PAN

Dash of olive oil

8 medium-sized tomatoes

½ teaspoon salt

1 bunch borage, about 12–16 medium-sized
    leaves, or lamb's-quarters, amaranth
    greens, spinach, or other tender mild greens

1 small bunch nettles, 4–5 sprigs, or 3
    tablespoons dried nettles

4 sprigs fresh basil, about ⅓ cup finely chopped
    leaves, or 2 tablespoons dried basil

1 clove garlic, crushed

1 teaspoon lemon zest

1 cup ricotta cheese, or cottage cheese
    whizzed through the food processor

Salt and pepper to taste

1 egg

1 cup shredded Parmesan or Romano
    cheese, divided

Serves 30–40

MAKES TWO 13 x 23-INCH HOTEL PANS

Dash of olive oil

60 medium-sized tomatoes

1 tablespoon salt

4 large bunches borage, about 2 pounds
    of leaves, or lamb's-quarters, amaranth
    greens, spinach, or other tender mild greens

2 bunches nettles, or ⅔ cup dried nettles

2 bunches fresh basil, finely chopped, or ⅔
    cup dried basil

7 cloves garlic, crushed

Zest of 4 lemons

7 cups ricotta cheese, or cottage cheese
    whizzed through the food processor

Salt and pepper to taste

7 eggs

7 cups shredded Parmesan or Romano
    cheese, divided

Preheat the oven to 375°F. Coat a baking dish (two hotel pans) with a dash of olive oil. With a small paring knife angled toward the center stem, cut the tops off the tomatoes. Scoop out all the seeds and juice with a spoon or melon baller (reserve for another use—gazpacho anyone?) to form a little cup with the outside shell of the tomato. Dab the insides of the tomato cup with a napkin to remove any excess moisture. Line up the empty tomato shells in the baking tray, packing them in tightly so they don't slump over and spill during baking—for the large batch about 30 medium-sized tomatoes should fit snugly in a standard-sized hotel pan. Sprinkle with the salt. Let sit while you prepare the filling.

Blanch the borage and nettles (or other greens) in boiling water for 15 seconds. Remove and shock in an ice bath; let drain in a colander. For special directions on handling nettles, see page 198. Squeeze all the water out, cut off the stems, and either finely chop by hand or puree in a food processor.

Prepare the filling: Mix the greens, chopped or dried basil, crushed garlic, lemon zest, ricotta, salt, and pepper. Taste and adjust the seasonings. Then mix in the eggs and half of the shredded cheese.

Again, dab the insides of the tomato cups one more time to remove any moisture that has been drawn out by the salt. Stuff the tomatoes with about 2 heaping tablespoons of filling, or a little more depending on the size of the tomato, and top with the remaining shredded cheese. Bake for 35 to 45 minutes, until the filling has set and the cheese on top is melted and crusty.

PHOTO BY JIM COLEMAN.

Wine Country Grape Leaf Dolmas

The ritual of folding dolmas is one of the great joys of living in a grape growing region of the world—the way the perfect lobes of the leaf come together around the rice just feels so right in the human hand. (If you don't live in wine country, rolling dolmas with canned grape leaves is just as satisfying.) Chef Coby Leibman adds lemon thyme for extra tang in this version.

Serves 4-6

**MAKES 15 DOLMAS IN
ONE 9 X 13-INCH BAKING PAN**

15 large fresh grape leaves
1 small onion, diced
1½ tablespoons salt, divided
1½ teaspoons cumin
1 cup olive oil, divided
1½ teaspoons honey
2 cups long-grain white rice
6 cups salted vegetable broth, divided
1 cup lemon juice, divided
½ cup pine nuts
A few sprigs of lemon thyme
A few sprigs of parsley

Serves 30-40

**MAKES 60 DOLMAS IN
2 FULL-SIZED HOTEL PANS**

60 large fresh grape leaves
2 large onions, diced
3 tablespoons salt, divided
2 tablespoons cumin
4 cups olive oil, divided
2 tablespoons honey
8 cups long-grain white rice
24 cups salted vegetable broth, divided
4 cups lemon juice, divided
2 cups pine nuts
2 bunches lemon thyme
1 bunch parsley

If you're using freshly harvested grape leaves, pick them with the whole stem on from an unsprayed vineyard. (You can also forage them from elsewhere.) They should be young, large leaves, light green in color—early summer is the best time, but you can usually find a few tender ones hidden underneath later in the season. Unfortunately, wild grape varieties, which usually have a tan film layer on the back distinguishing them from domestic grapes, are too thick and bitter to make dolmas. If you don't have access to fresh, store-bought canned grape leaves are perfectly fine to use.

Blanch the fresh leaves in boiling water—this makes them more pliable and easy to work with. To do this, fill a medium-sized pot with water and add 2 tablespoons salt. Bring to a boil and remove from the heat. If the stems are still on the leaves, hold the stem and dip the leaves one by one into the pot, submerging for about 2 seconds each, keeping the stem out of the water. If the stem is not intact, use a slotted spoon. Shock blanched leaves in an ice bath and reserve. Skip this step if you are using canned leaves—they have already been blanched. Just give them a quick rinse to separate and rinse off some of the acidity from preserving.

In a large saucepan, sauté the diced onions over a medium flame with a sprinkle of salt, the cumin, and a drizzle of olive oil. When the onions begin to brown, add the honey and continue cooking for another 3 minutes on medium-low heat until the onions lightly caramelize. Add the rice and sauté for another 3 minutes, stirring frequently. Add 4 cups (16 cups) of the vegetable broth and ½ cup (2 cups) of the lemon juice. Cook the rice uncovered on medium-low heat for 12 to 15 minutes or until the rice is par-cooked, but still a bit al dente. It's important not to stir the rice while cooking.

In a thick-bottomed fry pan on medium heat, toast the pine nuts, stirring every 10 seconds with a wooden spoon, watching carefully so they don't burn. Once the nuts have a few toasty light-brown markings on them, remove them from the pan into a large mixing bowl. De-leaf the lemon thyme and finely chop the parsley into the large bowl with the pine nuts. Drizzle with olive oil, sprinkle with the remaining salt, and stir until all the nuts are coated.

Add the rice to the bowl with the herbs and pine nuts and stir the whole mixture together until thoroughly combined. Allow to cool slightly. Preheat the oven to 350°F.

On a flat cutting board, lay out a grape leaf with the stem side facing toward you. Remove the stem and put a spoonful of rice into the center. Fold the two outer corners of the leaf into the center. Starting from the stem end, roll the leaf into a tight roll, keeping the two edges tucked in around the rice. Stack the dolmas in a single layer in a baking pan or hotel pans at least 2 inches deep.

To steam-bake, pour the remaining vegetable stock and lemon juice over the dolmas in the baking pan. The liquid should just come up the sides of the dolmas, but shouldn't cover them completely. Drizzle with the remaining olive oil. Cook in the oven covered with a fitted cover or a sheet of tinfoil for 20 to 30 minutes. Serve hot or chill for serving cold later.

Quinoa Confetti Salad

The garden at Food for Thought, the Sonoma County AIDS Food Bank, was one of OAEC's first "Daughter Gardens," and continues to receive plant material and support from the Mother Garden. In addition to growing healthy vegetables, fruits, and herbs that go directly into clients' grocery bags (not to mention flowers—clients love getting sweet pea or zinnia bouquets!), the garden serves as the inspiration for cooking and nutrition classes and is a site for both formal and informal gatherings. Clients come to volunteer, to harvest produce for themselves, or just to sit and relax and visit the monarch butterflies and other critters that also frequent the garden.

This cold quinoa salad, contributed by Rachel Gardner, is a dish that nutritionists at Food for Thought teach HIV-positive clients how to prepare. Speckled with a cheerful confetti of summer veggies, this dish is nourishing, simple to make, and keeps well in the refrigerator—a perfect dish for those who may not feel well enough to cook for themselves very often.

Serves 4–6
1 cup quinoa
4 cups water, for cooking*
Pinch of salt

DRESSING

¼ cup lemon juice or half lemon juice/half
    rice vinegar
½ cup extra-virgin olive oil
¼ cup thinly sliced scallions
A few sprigs finely chopped basil or parsley
Salt and pepper to taste

GARNISH

½ pint diced mixed-color tomatoes or
    halved cherry tomatoes

Put the quinoa in a strainer and rinse well under running water; drain. Transfer the quinoa to a 2-quart (10-quart) pot. Add the water and a pinch of salt. Bring to a gentle boil, then reduce the heat and simmer covered for 12 to 15 minutes. Cook until just tender and transparent "halos" have formed around the grains. Drain and add cold water to the pot to cool the quinoa and stop it from cooking any further. When cool enough to handle, drain all the water and transfer the quinoa to a large bowl. This should yield around 2 cups (14 cups) of cooked quinoa.

Toss the veggies with the quinoa. Mix in the lemon juice and/or rice vinegar and olive oil, chopped scallions, and basil. Add salt and pepper to taste. Garnish with tomatoes and serve.

Serves 30–40
8 cups quinoa
8 quarts water, for cooking*
Pinch of salt

DRESSING

1½ cups lemon juice or half lemon juice/
    half rice vinegar
2½ cups extra-virgin olive oil
1 bunch thinly sliced scallions
1 bunch chopped basil or parsley
Salt and pepper to taste

GARNISH

4–6 pints diced mixed-color tomatoes or
    halved cherry tomatoes

VEGGIE CONFETTI

Serves 4–6
any combination of the following to total approximately 3 cups:
¾ cup diced red, orange, and/ or yellow sweet peppers
½ cup diced fennel
½ cup diced cucumber
1 ear of corn, grilled or blanched, kernels cut off the cob
½ cup green beans, sliced crosswise and blanched

Serves 30–40
any combination of the following to total approximately 3 quarts:
6 cups diced red, orange, and/ or yellow sweet peppers
3 cups diced fennel
4 cups diced cucumber
8–12 ears of corn, grilled or blanched, kernels cut off the cob
4 cups green beans, sliced crosswise and blanched

* When serving quinoa hot, use 1⅓ cups of water for each cup of grain. For a cold salad, though, the
  quinoa cooks with more control and doesn't stick together in clumps when cooked in extra water,
  rinsed, and drained.

Summer Risotto: Lemon Verbena and Roasted Cherry Tomato

Serves 4–6

3 cups Roasted Cherry Tomatoes with
    Lemon Verbena and juices (page 160)

6 cups vegetable stock (page 92)

4 sprigs lemon verbena

¼ cup butter or oil

2 cloves garlic, crushed

1½ cups arborio rice

¾ cup dry sherry

Zest of 1 Meyer lemon

½ cup grated hard cheese,
    Parmesan or Romano

Salt and pepper to taste

¼ cup chiffonaded fresh basil

Serves 30–40

3 quarts Roasted Cherry Tomatoes with
    Lemon Verbena and juices (page 160)

6 quarts vegetable stock (page 92)

2 bunches lemon verbena

½ cup (1 stick) butter or oil

6 cloves garlic, crushed

8 cups arborio rice

1 bottle dry sherry

Zest of 4 Meyer lemons

2 cups grated hard cheese,
    Parmesan or Romano

1 tablespoon salt

1 teaspoon pepper

1 cup chiffonaded fresh basil

Prepare the Roasted Cherry Tomatoes with Lemon Verbena and the summer vegetable stock—these steps can be both done ahead of time. Strain the stock and return it to the stockpot. If you're using premade stock, heat it to a low simmer. Add the lemon verbena to infuse in the stock. Keep the stock warm on the back burner.

Make the risotto base: Heat a Dutch oven or a heavy-bottomed saucepan with the butter or oil on medium heat. Add the garlic, arborio rice, and a pinch of salt and stir to coat. Sauté, stirring constantly, until the green smell of the garlic has been released and about 15 percent of the rice grains have turned from translucent to bright white—about 3 minutes. Add the sherry and let everything deglaze in the pan for a few minutes. Add 1 cup of warm stock and stir with a wooden spoon. Turn the heat to medium-low so that it stays at a very low simmer, uncovered. When the cup of stock is almost all absorbed, stir in another cup of stock and repeat the process until all the stock is absorbed and the rice is a creamy fluid texture. This will take about 30 minutes.

After the last addition of stock, gently stir in half of the roasted tomatoes and all of the juice. Add the lemon zest. Stir together and let this mixture cook for a few minutes. Turn off the heat. Mix in the grated hard cheese. Taste and adjust the salt and pepper. Serve the risotto with the remaining roasted tomatoes mounded on top and a sprinkling of freshly chiffonaded basil.

Lemon Verbena Steamed Rice

It's too cold here to grow fresh lemongrass outside the greenhouse, so in many soups and dishes that might call for it, we substitute our garden darling, lemon verbena. We think it's even better!

Serves 4-6

2½ cups water

4 sprigs fresh lemon verbena or 1 cup dried

1 tablespoon coconut oil

2 cloves minced garlic

2 cups jasmine rice

Generous sprinkle of salt (about ½ teaspoon)

Serves 30–40

15 cups water

24 large sprigs fresh lemon verbena or
      8 cups dried

⅓ cup coconut oil

6 cloves minced garlic

12 cups jasmine rice

Generous sprinkle of salt (about 1 tablespoon)

Bring the water to a boil. Turn off the heat, add half the fresh lemon verbena (or all if you're using dried), cover, and let steep for 20 minutes. Remove and discard the spent leaves.

In another medium-sized pot, melt the coconut oil on medium heat. Add the garlic and rice, sprinkle with salt, and cook, stirring frequently, until the rice gets a little toasted but not brown. Nestle the remaining fresh lemon verbena sprigs, if using, among the rice, pour in the lemon verbena tea, and cover. Let the liquid come up to a boil again, then reduce the heat and simmer on low for 10 minutes. Turn off the heat and let the rice steam, covered (no peeking!), for 10 more minutes.

Serve hot with stir-fried veggies (page 172) or Orach Paneer (page 164).

VARIATIONS

Add fresh or thawed peas during the last 10 minutes of steaming.

Add 1 teaspoon (2 tablespoons) dark mustard seeds to the coconut oil along with the garlic and rice.

Tepary Beans with Oregano and Seared Padrón Peppers

Padrón and Shishito (a similar Japanese variety) peppers are all the rage right now in trendy tapas restaurants in San Francisco. Served as a finger food, simply seared and garnished with crunchy salt and lemon, these little hipsters liven up a cocktail party like none other with their secret game. Also known as "roulette peppers," every 1 in 10 is a hottie. But a savvy home gardener knows that there is no need to bust your budget on a pint basket of these at the market—the plants are prolific, popping out dozens of peppers every week, as long as you stay on top of the harvesting. Once they get larger than about an inch and a half, they are guaranteed to be hot and can be put to use as a spicy chile like a jalapeño or Serrano. This recipe utilizes both the mild smalls and a few of the larger hot ones in a bright-green oregano sauce.

Born of this soil, the tepary bean is an ancient North American native variety developed by the Hopi that is miraculously drought-tolerant and high in protein. In our increasingly water-scarce reality, western gardeners have much to learn by befriending the well-adjusted tepary.

Serves 4–6

1¼ cups dry tepary beans or other white bean

Juice of 2 lemons or limes

1 bunch fresh oregano

2 larger, spicy Shishito or Padrón peppers, or
    1 jalapeño or Serrano

Salt to taste

¼ cup olive oil

2 teaspoons ground cumin

1 teaspoon ground coriander

2 cloves garlic, crushed

Oil or fat, for frying

1 pint small, mild Shishito or Padrón peppers

Garnish: lemon wedges

Serves 30–40

8 cups dry tepary beans or other white bean

1 cup juice from about 8–10 lemons or limes

4 bunches fresh oregano

4–6 larger, spicy Shishito or Padrón peppers,
    or 2–4 jalapeño or Serrano

Salt to taste

1 cup olive oil

⅓ cup ground cumin

¼ cup ground coriander

6 cloves garlic, crushed

Oil or fat, for frying

8 pints Shishito or Padrón peppers

Garnish: lemon wedges

Because tepary beans are dry-farmed in the desert, they take extra time to rehydrate. Always soak tepary beans overnight—the quick-soak method is not as effective. Drain and rinse. In a medium stockpot, cover the beans with water by 2 inches. Bring to a boil and skim off any scum that rises to the surface. Reduce the heat and simmer until the beans are completely soft, but not mushy. Despite the tepary beans' small size, they are quite dense and may take as long as 2 hours to cook.

Sort through the Shishito or Padrón peppers—separate out any that are longer than 2 inches. Reserve the smaller, mild peppers for frying.

In a high-powered blender with a tamping baton or in a glass jar with an immersion blender, combine the lemon juice and fresh oregano, pushing down to combine. Add some of the larger, spicy peppers and blend to form a smooth sauce. Add salt, taste, and adjust. The spiciness of the peppers can vary greatly—add more of the spicy peppers if you would like a hotter sauce.

In a small skillet on medium heat, add the olive oil, cumin, coriander, and crushed garlic. Cook briefly, stirring constantly with a wooden spoon, until a nicely toasted spice paste is formed. Add this mixture to the blender and puree until smooth.

When the beans are completely done, drain most of the water off the cooked beans, but reserve about a quarter to a third of the cooking water. Stir the blended sauce into the beans and reserved cooking water—the beans should be loose and swimming but not drowning in sauce. Cover and stew together on low heat, stirring occasionally, for another 20 minutes or more to allow the flavors to marry. Taste and add more salt, if needed.

Heat the fry oil or fat in a skillet or on a flat-top griddle on medium high. Sear the peppers, tossing until blistered on all sides. Sprinkle with salt and a squeeze of lemon.

On a large platter, mound the beans high in the center and encircle with a ring of seared peppers. Serve immediately.

PHOTO BY TALI AIONA.

Nana's Chiles Rellenos

This is a fourth-generation recipe handed down to Ryan Silva, our facilities manager, by his great-grandmother Inez, who was from central Mexico and owned a successful Mexican restaurant in San Luis Obispo called Nana's. *¡Que rico!* While there are peppers being sold now in America under the variety name "chile relleno," *chile relleno* just means "stuffed pepper"—the original variety is most likely Ancho or Poblano.

Serves 4–6

8 large mildly spicy stuffing peppers such as Poblanos or Anchos

4 ounces (about 2 tablespoons stuffing per pepper, or 1 cup total) shredded cheese—Oaxacan cheese is best if you can get it, but a combination of good melting cheeses such as Jack, mozzarella, and Parmesan also works

5 eggs

½ teaspoon paprika

¼ teaspoon chipotle

Cayenne to taste

2 tablespoons cornmeal

Oil, for frying

Salt to taste

Serves 30–40

60 large mildly spicy stuffing peppers such as Poblanos or Anchos

2¼ pounds (about 2 tablespoons stuffing per pepper, or 9 cups total) shredded cheese—Oaxacan cheese is best if you can get it, but a combination of good melting cheeses such as Jack, mozzarella, and Parmesan also works

40 eggs

1½ tablespoons paprika

2 teaspoons chipotle

Cayenne to taste

1¼ cups cornmeal

Oil, for frying

Salt to taste

For the large batch, preheat the broiler to high. Lay the peppers on a cookie sheet and broil on the top shelf until the skins become charred, but the flesh does not become too mushy. For the smaller batch, it is faster and more energy-efficient to char the peppers directly on the stovetop—see the directions on page 98 for quick fire-roasted veggies. Transfer to a pot with a tight-fitting lid and let the peppers steam and sweat for about 20 minutes. (While the peppers are roasting or sweating, you can shred the cheese and separate the eggs.) When they're cool enough to handle, rub off most of the charred skin with your hands. Don't worry if there is a little skin still left on.

Open the skinned pepper and remove the seeds. To do this, cut halfway around the top by inserting a knife at an angle around the stem—but leave the top attached on one side. Gently open the top, being careful not to detach it, and pull out the seed core. Cut off the lump of seeds attached to the top and gently shake out the seeds. Again, don't worry if a few seeds remain. Stuff each pepper with about 2 tablespoons of cheese or other stuffing and replace the top.

To prepare the batter, separate the whites from the yolks of the eggs into two separate bowls. Mix the spices with the yolks. If your peppers are on the spicy side, go easy on the cayenne. With a whisk or electric mixer, beat the egg whites in a separate bowl until stiff. Fold the cornmeal and yolk-spice mixture into the whites. The texture of the batter should be fluffy but pourable. *Large-batch tip:* Depending on the size of your mixer and your frying speed, you may want to make the batter in smaller batches. Otherwise the whites get so fluffy, they may expand beyond the capacity of your mixer. (For an 8-quart mixer, divide the whites in half.) Also, as the batter sits, it separates and loses volume, so only make as much batter as you can use within half an hour or so.

Heat ½ inch of fry oil in a skillet. When the oil is good and hot (a drop of batter sputters in it), ladle in about ¼ cup of batter to create a "bed" about twice the width of the pepper. Lay the pepper on one side of the bed. Fry until the batter starts getting crispy. Then with a spatula, gently turn the pepper over onto the other side of the bed so that it is enfolded in a blanket of batter. If necessary, ladle in a touch more batter to cover. Fry for a few seconds more, rolling the pepper over again if necessary, so that it becomes fully encased and sealed. Remove with a slotted spatula and drain on paper towels. Lightly sprinkle the peppers with salt as soon as they come out of the oil, though you can skip the salt altogether if the cheese is salty.

Chiles rellenos are, of course, delicious when served hot out of the skillet, but they also hold exceptionally well. For a crowd or a dinner party, we recommend making these ahead of time, sparing your guests the greasy mess without sacrificing flavor or freshness in the slightest. Allow the chiles to cool completely as they drain on the paper towels and refrigerate them for up to 24 hours. Reheat in the oven at 375°F until they're crispy and hot. Serve with crema and your favorite salsa.

VARIATIONS

Plain cheese is the traditional stuffing that allows the flavor of the pepper itself to shine through, but you can also replace some or all of the cheese with cooked corn, drained and rinsed black beans, cooked quinoa, or any other plain, unspiced leftovers that will not outcompete the flavor of the pepper. Soft cheeses such as chèvre don't work well as they tend to ooze out the top.

PHOTO BY TALI AIONA.

OAEC Basic Beans

Good bean recipes are key to winning over dubious carnivores to a more plant-centric diet. Proper soaking and the use of epazote herb or kombu seaweed makes them more digestible, especially for those who aren't accustomed to eating beans regularly.

Serves 4–6

1 cup dry beans (about ¼ cup per person)
A few leaves epazote or small strip kombu
1 bay leaf

OPTIONAL SEASONINGS

1 onion, diced
1 clove garlic, minced
A bit of oil
1 teaspoon other spices such as chipotle
    powder, cumin, dried or fresh oregano,
    to taste
Salt* and pepper to taste

Serves 30–40

8 cups dry beans (about ¼ cup per person)
1 sprig epazote or large strip kombu
4 or 5 bay leaves

OPTIONAL SEASONINGS

4 onions, diced
4 cloves garlic, minced
A bit of oil
1 tablespoon other spices such as chipotle
    powder, cumin, dried or fresh oregano,
    to taste
Salt* and pepper to taste

Always sort dry beans to make sure there are no rocks or debris. This is especially important when using bulk beans. Do this by spreading them on a clean baking tray and scanning them like a typewriter with your eyes and fingers. Also, do not be tempted to cook mixed varieties of beans together, as cooking times vary considerably.

Beans will more than double in volume depending on the bean, so as a general rule of thumb, soak beans with a 4-to-1 water-to-bean ratio. Mung beans, split peas, and lentils do not need to be soaked. *Quick soak method:* In a large stockpot, bring beans and water to a boil on high heat. Turn off the heat and let the beans sit for an hour. Drain and rinse with cold water. *Long soak method:* In a large stockpot, leave the beans to soak for 6 to 8 hours or overnight. Drain and rinse. This method is preferred from a nutritional standpoint as it starts the sprouting process and turns some of the indigestible starches into usable proteins. If you're cooking some of the harder dried beans (favas, scarlet runner beans, chickpeas, tepary beans) or beans that are more than a year old, save fuel by employing *both* soaking methods. Soak the beans overnight. Drain and rinse. Then bring them to a boil with fresh water, turn off the heat, and let them soak again for an hour before draining again and finally cooking.

We cook our beans on the stovetop mostly because we don't have a lot of room in our small kitchen to store extra appliances like pressure cookers and Crock-Pots, though these are wonderful tools that save time and energy, if you have them.

Add the soaked beans, epazote or kombu, bay leaves, and water to cover by about 2 inches into a large stockpot and bring to a boil on high heat. After a few minutes of boiling, skim off any scum that has risen to the surface. Reduce the heat to low and simmer. It is nearly impossible to give exact cooking times for beans as they vary greatly depending on the size, variety, moisture content, and freshness of the beans. It may take as little as half an hour for mung or up to 2 hours for large scarlet runner beans or chickpeas. Keep a close eye on them and check frequently as the beans can go from perfectly creamy to mushy in the blink of an eye. Taste more than one bean for doneness—often beans from the same batch cook unevenly.

PHOTO BY TALI AIONA.

* Do not to add salt until after the beans are cooked—salt prevents the skins from softening.

If you'll be using the beans whole without their juices, strain and rinse when the beans are cooked through, but not falling apart. To prevent the beans from becoming mushy, you can halt the cooking process by plunging the beans into a cold-water bath, if necessary. Remove the bay leaves and whatever is left of the epazote or kombu, though most of it may have dissolved.

If you want to serve them in their cooking juices, known by bean aficionados as "pot liquor," cease the cooking process when the beans are still a tad al dente. Strain off some of the liquid if there is excess—at this point, water should just cover the surface of the beans. Then season the beans as directed in your recipe and continue cooking until completely tender.

Here is our favorite basic preparation for a simple side dish: Sauté the optional onions and garlic in a little oil along with your dried spices, if using, until the onions are translucent. Stir this flavor base into the nearly cooked beans. At this time, you may finally add salt.* Continue cooking uncovered until the beans are soft but not mushy and the flavors have married. For a thicker gravy, remove a small amount of the beans and liquid, blend in a blender, and stir back in.

Some beans, especially the big starchy ones like scarlet runners, benefit from sitting overnight in their finished, seasoned juices to really plump up with flavor and moisture.

THE THREE (OR FOUR) SISTERS

The Three Sisters is an ancient Mesoamerican companion planting method where all three partners—corn, beans, and squash—benefit one another. Corn provides a pole for the beans to climb, beans fix nitrogen to feed the soil, and squash provides a "living mulch" with wide, shade-producing leaves to retain moisture and prevent weeds. The little known fourth sister—Rocky Mountain Bee Plant, *Cleome serrulata*, an edible leafy green with showy purple flowers—attracts bees for pollination and fills in the final piece of the ecological and nutritional puzzle.

At OAEC, we often use the Three (or Four) Sisters as a framework for designing a nutritionally balanced vegetarian menu. Corn, beans, squash,

and greens cover all the bases—carbs, protein, vitamins, minerals, and even fats from the oil-rich pumpkin seeds.

Here is a sample four sisters menu:

FOUR SISTERS MENU

Copper Kettle Mother Hubbard beans cooked over an open fire and seasoned with rosemary and Meyer lemon zest

Arugula wilted in a whole roasted pumpkin, sprinkled with chipotle candied pepitas

Hopi Blue and Oaxacan Green Cornbread with butter and honey

Ali's Copper Kettle Beans

Chef Alison Ghiorse, former OAEC garden intern and accomplished caterer, made this for a friend's 70th birthday party; the beans cooked all afternoon, slowly infusing with smoky flavor, as a whole pig was roasted on a spit in the same fire pit. A heartier heirloom bean— such as Good Mother Stallard, Indian Woman, or Rio Zappe—does well with the high temperature. If you don't have a copper kettle treated for cooking, a cast-iron Dutch oven can also be used for this recipe.

Serves 4–6
2 cups heirloom beans
2 bay leaves
5 sprigs rosemary
2 Meyer lemons
½ cup (1 stick) butter
Olive oil to taste
Sea salt to taste

Serves 30–40
8–10 cups heirloom beans
8 bay leaves
10 sprigs rosemary
6 Meyer lemons
2 cups (4 sticks) butter
Olive oil to taste
Sea salt to taste

Soak the beans overnight. Strain off the soaking water and place the beans in a copper pot or cast-iron Dutch oven either with a tripod for hanging or feet for placing over the coals. Cover the beans by about 1 inch with cold water, then set aside while you build a hot fire. When the coals are nice and hot, place the pot on top of the fire and bring the water to a simmer. Once the beans are simmering, add the bay leaves. At this point, keep the fire at a medium to low flame and watch closely.

When cooking beans over an open fire, the temperature can get quite hot and turn your beans to mush quickly. Adjust the height of the pot by lowering or raising the tripod or by putting bricks underneath the feet, depending on your setup. Cover the beans with the lid to preserve moisture if they start to dry out. You may need to remove the pot from the coals periodically while you stoke the fire.

While the beans are simmering, coarsely chop the rosemary and remove the zest from the Meyer lemons with a paring knife and coarsely chop. When the beans begin to soften, add the butter and olive oil; just before the beans reach their perfect texture, add the chopped rosemary and Meyer lemon zest. Once the beans are soft, remove them from fire and season to taste with sea salt, a touch more butter, and, if need be, more rosemary and zest.

VARIATION

Add lovage and garlic: Once the beans begin to simmer, add a sprig of lovage along with the bay leaves. While the beans are simmering, coarsely chop and sauté a few cloves of garlic in a separate pan with the butter and oil. When the beans begin to soften, add the garlic with the butter and oil it was cooked in. Add another sprinkle of coarsely chopped lovage leaves and continue cooking until the beans are done.

Note: Though not as romantic, if you run short on time, you may par-cook the beans on the stovetop and transfer them to the fire for the final stages of cooking to impart the smoky flavor.

PHOTO BY TALI AIONA.

Hot-Pink Fall Risotto with Chèvre

Offset this visually bold dish with a bright-green soup, a salad, and a dry white wine.

Serves 4–6

2 small beets (about 1 cup when chopped)

2½ cups vegetable or chicken broth

1 tablespoon butter

1 medium onion, diced

1 cup arborio rice

½ cup dry white wine

¼ teaspoon sea salt

4 ounces chèvre

Black pepper to taste

2 tablespoons chopped fresh parsley

Serves 30-40

12 small beets (about 6 cups when chopped)

15 cups vegetable or chicken broth

¼ cup (½ stick) butter

4 medium onions, diced

6 cups arborio rice

2 cups dry white wine

1½ teaspoons sea salt

24 ounces chèvre

Black pepper to taste

¾ cup chopped fresh parsley

Trim the tops off the beets and boil in a pot of water for 15 minutes. Strain and submerge in cold water. When they're cool enough to handle, slip the skins off and rinse. Chop the beets into small ½-inch cubes and reserve.

Meanwhile, start the risotto. Warm the broth in a small, covered pot until it's just barely simmering. Keeping the broth warm throughout the process will allow it to absorb faster and keep the total cooking time to about 20 minutes.

Heat the butter in a separate heavy-bottomed saucepan until melted. Add the onions and sauté until tender. Add the rice and toast for 2 to 3 minutes, stirring constantly, until the edges of the rice start to become translucent. Add the white wine and cook until the liquid is almost absorbed, stirring continually.

Add the diced beets, salt, and ½ cup warm broth, and bring to a boil. Reduce the heat to a simmer and cover. Every 4 minutes or so, check the rice to see if the liquid has nearly absorbed. If so, add ½ cup more broth and stir the risotto. Then cover the pot again and check in another 4 minutes. Repeat this process for about 20 minutes or until all the liquid is absorbed.

Remove from heat and stir in chèvre and black pepper until the risotto is thick and creamy. Adjust the salt if needed. The rice should be al dente and firm to the tooth without being crunchy. Top with parsley and serve.

Note: For a less high-maintenance risotto, add all the broth at once when you add the beets and salt. Bring to a boil, then reduce the heat and simmer covered for 20 minutes, stirring occasionally. The rice may be slightly less al dente, but the risotto won't demand your full attention during the cooking process and the outcome will still be delicious.

Fig-Leaf-Infused Basmati Pilaf

Fig leaves are one of our favorite ingredients to experiment with. They can be used as a bed to serve cheeses, crudités, or antipasti, or they can be wrapped around fish, lamb, or goat cheeses and then grilled or baked. They lend a warm, coconut flavor when infused into rice or cream. This is a very attractive simple rice dish that will wow a crowd.

Serves 4–6

2 cups basmati rice

1 teaspoon sunflower oil

1 clove garlic, crushed

5 fresh fig leaves

3 cups water

Serves 30–40

10 cups basmati rice

2 tablespoons sunflower oil

2 cloves garlic, crushed

8–10 fig leaves

15 cups water

Rinse the rice very well. In a good heavy-bottomed rice pot, heat the oil and sauté the crushed garlic just until it is fragrant. Take the pot off the heat and add the fig leaves to the bottom in a nice arrangement. Add the rice and the water. Cook over a low flame for about 20 minutes.

To serve, flip the whole pot upside down on a serving platter. The fig leaves should come right out, stuck to the rice and imparting a subtle coconut flavor.

Art in Community: Revival of the Old-Time Chautauqua

By James Pelican, Chautauqua creative director since 2003

Once upon a time, there existed a way of coming together as a community that combined the entertainment of vaudeville, the inspired education of Lyceum lectures, the sociability of a county fair, and the homegrown feeling that could only be found in rural environments. Hardly a fairy tale, these community-produced gatherings were known as Chautauquas. In the late 19th century on into the 1920s, this wildly popular phenomenon was found throughout the United States.

Held in a great round tent, the first Chautauqua happened in 1879 in Lake Chautauqua, New York. It was initially a summer school program for Sunday school teachers. It quickly took on secular aspects and eventually, entertainment and populist lectures became part of the multiday program. Within a few years, nearby communities were putting together their own gatherings, borrowing program components from one another. As the turn of the century approached, Chautauquas had spread throughout the greater northeastern United States; by 1910, summer encampments could be found as far away as Ashland, Oregon. As the phenomenon took off and spread, the range of content grew proportionately: lectures, vaudeville, music, drama, and even opera.

With the onset of the Great Depression, the introduction of radio, and the escalating costs introduced by commercialization, the Chautauquas faded away. But beginning in the 1970s, there has been a revival of the spirit of the Chautauqua. While nowhere near as ambitious as the multiday encampments that would bring hundreds of people together, these modern descendants nonetheless aim to awaken a sense of what is most positive about American rural culture.

As unique as the stage on which it manifests, the Chautauqua Revue is a show of surprises, laughter, poignancy, and finger-snapping fun like no other. The sold-out run of the 10th annual edition of the revue in September 2013 was a thunderous, energetic romp through a roster of musicians, poets, storytellers, circus performers, and clowns, concluding with a rousing all-in sing-along of "Ain't Gonna Study War No More." PHOTOS BY JIM COLEMAN.

On the night of the inaugural "Chautauqua" variety show performance in a newly constructed enchanting open-air theater in 2003, I walked through the large wooden gate of the center's North Garden. The sun was just setting, backlighting beds of plants grown from OAEC's enormous seed collection—mashua, chard, heirloom tomatoes, feathery amaranth, towering mullein. In the middle of the garden, tiny lights graced the branches of an ancient spreading oak, and candles lined the walk to the theater. Waiting for the program to begin, mothers nursed their infants while the elderly were helped to their seats. Under the great oaks, young interns crowded in next to local landowners on long wooden benches. The program encompassed the very local—the history of the region, the story of a local midwife, the trials of a lawyer who works with death-row prisoners—as well as the global—a ritualized Indian dance, the David-and-Goliath story of a Canadian farmer, Percy Schmiezer, who single-handedly took on Monsanto. It included the ridiculous—vaudevillian clowns—as well as the sublime—the story of the evolution of the earth, music from baroque cantatas to bluegrass ballads.

Sitting under the spreading branches with such a diverse and heartfelt group, I felt transported back to the origins of literature and theater, a moment of wholeness where performers and audience were bound to place, to each other, to something beyond. It was a balm to the spirit, a momentary break from the fragmentation of the world outside. At a time when the world is in such turmoil and what people say is so removed from what they actually do, I am kept from despair by the

knowledge that places like OAEC exist. It gives me faith in the fundamental goodness of human beings and in their ability to work together for a greater whole.

—DAIDIE DONNELLEY,
friend, neighbor, and supporter of OAEC

CHAUTAUQUA BRUNCH MENU

Shipova Coffee Cake

Baked eggs with cherry tomatoes,
New Zealand spinach, and homemade ricotta

Assorted yogurts, granolas, toasts, and jams

Chojuro Asian pear fresh fruit salad
with cinnamon basil

Fresh-pressed Gravenstein apple juice

Soft Pumpkin Polenta

Comfort food for breakfast, lunch, or dinner. Serve mounded with savory stews such as Blackened Tomato and Scarlet Runner Bean Stew (page 103) or sprinkled with herbs and a tab of butter. Or take it in a sweet direction with a little maple syrup or a Rich Autumn Fruit Compote (page 351).

Serves 4–6

4 cups water or stock

Plenty of salt—at least 1½ teaspoons

1 cup polenta

1 cup pumpkin puree (page 180)

¼ teaspoon nutmeg

3 tablespoons butter or olive oil

Serves 30-40

8 quarts water or stock

Plenty of salt—at least 3 tablespoons

8 cups polenta

3–5 cups pumpkin puree (page 180)

1½ teaspoons nutmeg

½ cup butter or olive oil

In a large pot, bring the water or stock and salt to a boil. Keep an additional teakettle boiling with more water nearby. Sprinkle in the polenta slowly by hand while whisking constantly to avoid the formation of lumps. Reduce the heat to low and simmer, whisking often, until fully thickened (when little volcanoes erupt on the surface periodically and the polenta comes away from the pot a little when stirred). This can take as little as 15 minutes for quick polenta or up to an hour for traditional stone-ground polenta.* If the polenta becomes too thick or is still a bit crunchy, whisk in ¼ cup of boiling water and continue cooking, adding more a little at a time if needed.

While the polenta is hot and soft, stir in the pumpkin puree, nutmeg, and as much butter or olive oil as your conscience will allow (2 to 4 tablespoons for a small batch, 1 to 2 sticks for a large one). Keep soft polenta warm in a double boiler to prevent it from solidifying, and serve hot.

VARIATIONS

Creamy Polenta Custard: Omit the nutmeg and pumpkin. The simple addition of eggs (2 eggs for a small batch, 8 to 10 for a large one) whisked vigorously into the polenta during the last few minutes of cooking time turns mundane polenta into a velvety custard and is a great way to sneak a little more protein into a vegetarian meal. For real creamy decadence, replace some or all of the water with milk.

Fresh Sweet Corn Polenta: Omit the nutmeg and pumpkin. Cut fresh sweet corn off the cob (2 cobs for a small batch, 8 cobs for a large one). Pulse half of it in a food processor. Add whole and processed corn to the hot, thickening polenta after the lumps have been whisked out, but while there is still some cooking time left to allow the raw corn to cook. Serve with cilantro butter. Biodiversity option: Use red, blue, or green fresh corn for added color!

* For slow-cooking stone-ground polenta, use a double boiler as this relieves some of the pressure to stir continuously.

Polenta Moons with Roasted Red Peppers, Collard Ribbons, and Feta

You can cut polenta with any shape cookie cutter you like, but the moon method leaves the least amount of wasted polenta around the edges.

Serves 4–6

4 cups water or stock

1½ teaspoons salt

1 cup polenta

3 tablespoons butter or olive oil, for greasing the pan

2 teaspoons whole cumin seeds

2 teaspoons sweet paprika

Olive oil

1 bunch collards or kale

2 cloves crushed garlic

1 cup thinly sliced roasted red peppers, from a jar or from scratch (page 98)

1 tablespoon finely chopped marjoram

1 cup crumbled feta

Pepper to taste

Serves 30–40

4 quarts water or stock

2 tablespoons salt

4 cups polenta

Butter or olive oil, for greasing the pan

2 tablespoons whole cumin seeds

2 tablespoons sweet paprika

Olive oil

6 bunches collards or kale

8 cloves crushed garlic

4 cups thinly sliced roasted red peppers, from a jar or from scratch (page 98)

¼ cup finely chopped marjoram

4 cups crumbled feta

Pepper to taste

In a large pot, bring the water or stock and salt to a boil. Keep an additional teakettle boiling with more water nearby. Sprinkle in the polenta slowly by hand while whisking constantly to avoid the formation of lumps. Reduce the heat to low and simmer, whisking often, until fully thickened (when little volcanoes erupt on the surface periodically and the polenta comes away from the pot a little when stirred). This can take as little as 15 minutes for quick polenta or up to an hour for traditional stone-ground polenta.* If the polenta becomes too thick or is still a bit crunchy, whisk in ¼ cup of boiling water and continue cooking, adding more a little at a time if needed.

Grease a 13 x 18-inch sheet baking tray (two trays for the large batch—the polenta layer for the large batch will be thicker) with the butter or olive oil. When it's completely cooked, remove the polenta from the heat and pour it out onto the greased baking tray to form an even layer. Set aside on a baking rack for about an hour. Polenta will set and firm up as it cools.

Preheat the oven to 375°F. Take a small 1-inch round cookie cutter and cut out a round in the upper left-hand corner. Working across in rows like a typewriter, make overlapping cuts that result in little moons. The first moon of each row will make a "full moon," but the rest will be uniform crescents. Gather the moons in a mixing bowl and toss gently with cumin, paprika, and a little oil to keep them from sticking together and falling apart. Brush any excess polenta crumbs off the baking tray, drizzle with a generous coating of more oil, and lay the moons back out on the tray in a single layer. Bake for 15 minutes, until they are heated through and begin to crisp up on the edges.

Strip the leaves off of the collards. To chiffonade, stack five or six leaves at a time, roll together like a newspaper, and slice into very thin ribbons. Heat some oil in a skillet (use a flat-top griddle for the large batch), add the garlic, and then put the greens on top. Allow to sit for a moment, so that the garlic has a chance to cook and the greens begin to wilt, then toss periodically until all of the greens are wilted. Sprinkle with salt.

Toss the roasted red peppers and marjoram with the hot polenta moons. Try not to stir them too much or they will start to fall apart. Season to taste with salt, pepper, or more fresh herbs. If needed, you can hold the seasoned mixture in a low oven (just the residual heat left in the oven after turning it off is probably enough) for up to 20 minutes until you're ready to serve. Lay the greens out on the serving platter in a large ring around the edges and mound the polenta mélange into the center. Top with the crumbled cheese; toasted pine nuts also make a nice addition.

---

* For slow-cooking stone-ground polenta, use a double boiler as this relieves some of the pressure to stir continuously.

PROCESSING ACORNS

A weekend convergence at OAEC sponsored by the Cultural Conservancy called Decolonizing Our Bodies, Nourishing Our Spirits: Native Foods Think Tank, brought together cultural leaders, scholars, activists, and chefs representing 15 US and Canadian tribes to explore the importance of the restoration of Native foods to community health. Miwok cultural representative Julia Parker demonstrated both traditional and modern acorn preparation methods that we continue to practice whenever we get the chance.

Gather acorns when you notice they are dropping, usually from September to December. Collect only large, dense acorns, passing up those that have obvious weevil holes or that are unusually light. Immediately when you get home, dump them into a large bucket of water—discard (compost or burn in your fireplace) the ones that float, keeping the ones that sink. For maximum yield, you can put them all in the freezer—this will kill any remaining weevils. If you do not have time to immediately proceed to the cracking and leaching step, dry them to prevent molding and sprouting. Spread the good acorns on a flat surface in the sun to dry, or put them on a cookie sheet and place in a very low oven for a few hours (even just the pilot light should be sufficient). Store in a basket with plenty of airflow until you're ready to proceed. According to California Native traditions, acorns are stored with boughs of California bay leaves, a natural antimicrobial, to prevent molding.

Crack the acorns. If you don't have a traditional grinding stone or mortar and pestle, you can improvise by cracking the acorns briskly between a heavy object and a hard surface—say, a piece of firewood or cast-iron skillet against a butcher block. Pick out the nutmeats, discarding any that are moldy.

Acorns *must* be leached. Eating excessive amounts of tannins contained in raw, unleached acorns can be poisonous for humans.

There are many traditional and modern options for leaching, depending upon your setup and how you wish to use them. Julia Parker explained the construction of a traditional sand filter that leaches the acorn meal in a sandbar within a clean running stream—a rarity given modern-day pollution; hence, she offered a garden hose alternative. Below is an adapted version we've used in the kitchen.

Grind the dry nutmeats finely by hand in a mortar and pestle or with a grain grinder. Or process in a food processor or high-powered blender with plenty of water (1 part acorn to 6 parts water, give or take) until a thin slurry forms. Strain this into some kind of permeable cloth sack—a fine cheesecloth bag, the toe of a clean pair of tights, or the sleeve of an old shirt with the end knotted off. Proceed with leaching.

Attach the cloth bag directly to the faucet of your sink and turn the water on very low. Allow the water to wash slowly over the acorn meal for several hours. In more water-scarce regions, pour cold water into a large basin and submerge the cloth sack containing the acorn meal. Massage the sack initially with your hands and let it sit. Drain and repeat every half hour (or whenever you get around to it) for many hours until the water runs completely clean. Finally, you can start tasting the mush. If there is even the slightest hint of bitterness, keep leaching until *all* the bitter flavor is gone. This could take as few as 4 or 5 changes (15 minutes under the faucet), as with black oak, or up to 20 or 30 changes (4 or more hours under the faucet) if using tan oak. Use the acorn mush immediately, or store it in the fridge for up to a week.

To dry the mush into flour, spread it out in a thin layer on cooking sheets and let it dry in the hot sun, in a food dehydrator, or in a low oven (200°F) for a few hours, stirring once in a while for even drying. Once the flour is completely dry, break up the clumps with your fingers or run it through a coffee or grain grinder again if you want to grind the bigger chunks of acorn into a fine flour—though if you'll be reconstituting into mush, the larger chunks are actually kind of nice. Store in an airtight container for up to 3 months.

If all else fails, you can find finely ground acorn starch in Korean markets.

PHOTO BY BROCK DOLMAN.

Savory Tan Oak Acorn Mush

The tan oak, though botanically speaking not a true oak, has nonetheless been particularly devastated by sudden oak death, so we relish it as an endangered food crop. Named for their high content of tannins, tan oaks were used for centuries in the tanning of leather. Removal of these tannins from the acorn makes for a long leaching process, yet one well worth the effort: Tan oak acorns are prized for their superior flavor.

Serves 4–6
2 cups water or rich stock
1¼ cups acorn flour, any variety
Salt to taste

Serves 30–40
12 cups water or rich stock
7½ cups acorn flour, any variety
Salt to taste

Bring the water or stock to a boil and whisk in the acorn flour. Reduce the heat and simmer for 20 minutes, stirring frequently, until the mixture is completely reconstituted and creamy with the consistency of soft polenta. Salt to taste.

Acorn mush can be served as a sweet breakfast porridge with all the usual oatmeal fixin's, but it is most often served as a complement to a meaty stew or roast. Either reconstitute with plain water as directed in the instructions, or for a particularly tasty porridge, try reconstituting the mush with the *jus* of the stew itself, similar in style to polenta served with osso bucco or the Brazilian cassava-based pirão served with Muqueca de Peixe. A rich mushroom soup or stock would also work.

If you're using *jus* from a stew or roast, while it is still hot, remove enough broth or *jus* to reconstitute based on the proportions above, with a ladle (it's okay if a few solid bits slip in) and add it to a saucepot. Bring it to a boil and add more water if needed to make the proportions work. Whisk in the acorn flour. Reduce the heat and simmer for 20 minutes, stirring frequently, until thick. Taste and add more salt or pepper to your liking. Serve in a shallow bowl with the stew on one side and the acorn mush on the other.

Tan oak acorn. PHOTO BY BROCK DOLMAN.

KEYSTONE OAK

Our area is considered "Ground Zero" for the expanding crisis termed sudden oak death in which vast areas of oak forest are dying at unprecedented rates. The primary cause of the disease appears to be a species of fungus-like brown algae, *Phytophthora ramorum*. The epidemic invokes the disconcerting potential that oaks could follow in the direction of elms with Dutch elm disease or American chestnuts with the chestnut blight.

This crisis raises many troubling questions. What impacts has the modern suppression of fire, historically used by Native peoples as a regenerative tool in oak woodlands, had on the health and immune capacity of our oaks? What capacity for resiliency to disease can we expect of our oaks? Like a human body with a weakened immune system being more prone to illness, oaks are indeed compromised by the impacts of deforestation, fragmentation,

lack of fire, and agricultural and development practices that affect ecological and hydrological system integrity. The vision of a much-reduced or oak-less Californian or North American landscape is tragic indeed.

Unlike some other threatened wildcrafted ingredients, the problem is not overharvesting—one could actually argue that it is a lack of harvesting, insofar as it is a lack of human awareness and respect for the value of oaks as a keystone species and a bountiful food source worth caring for and protecting with wise land-use decisions. If the way to people's hearts is through their stomachs, we feel that promoting awareness, knowledge, and enthusiasm for eating acorns will also raise consciousness around the care and protection of oak woodlands and the important lineage of ecological and cultural knowledge associated with this cherished food crop.

PHOTO BY JIM COLEMAN.

Baked Eggs with Seasonal Vegetables

We serve these baked eggs for breakfast at least once during every course because of their cute presentation and ability to incorporate just about any garden vegetable imaginable. From greens and potatoes in the winter to tomatoes and zucchini in the summer, feel free to be creative with it. If the breakfast cook is feeling especially warm and fuzzy in the morning, baked eggs are served with little heart-shaped biscuits.

Serves 4–6

1 medium potato (about 1 cup cubed)
2 teaspoons oil or butter for cooking the
    potatoes, plus 2 teaspoons oil to grease
    the tins, if not using muffin cups
1 small fennel bulb (about ⅔ cup diced)
1 onion (about ⅔ cup diced)
1 small bunch chard or beet greens
6–12 eggs (2 per person)
Salt and pepper to taste

Serves 30–40

7 cups cubed potatoes
¼ cup oil or butter for cooking the potatoes,
    plus ¼ cup oil or butter to grease the
    tins, if not using muffin cups
4 large fennel bulbs (save fronds)
4 large onions
4 bunches chard or beet greens
60 eggs
Salt and pepper to taste

Preheat the oven to 350°F. Cut potatoes into smallish cubes, about ½ inch. Sauté in oil or butter on medium heat until slightly browned, covering halfway and stirring occasionally. While the potatoes are cooking, dice the fennel bulb and save the fronds for garnish. Peel and dice the onions. Remove the stems from the chard or beet greens and chop into half-moons. Chop the greens into thin strips and reserve. When the potatoes are golden brown on all sides and cooked through, remove from the pan and reserve. Add the fennel, onions, and chard stems and lower the heat slightly. Cover halfway and cook until the onions are translucent, stirring occasionally. Toss the greens with the hot mixture and sauté uncovered briefly until the greens wilt and most of the moisture has evaporated. Add the greens mixture to the potatoes, excluding any excess juice. (If you're incorporating leftovers instead of making the vegetable mixture from scratch, simply preheat the leftovers before assembling in the muffin tins.)

Line muffin tins with paper muffin cups, or brush the tins with a few additional teaspoons of oil. Put about 1 tablespoon of the vegetable mixture into each tin, enough to cover the bottom. Break one egg into each tin on top of the veggies, sprinkle with salt and pepper, and top with a small piece of the fennel frond. Bake at 350°F for 15 to 20 minutes, until the eggs are set (the whites become opaque) but the yolks are still a bit jiggly (you can cook until the yolk is set if desired). Remove from the oven and let cool for a few minutes. Use a spoon to cut around the edge and bottom of each egg and remove from the tin onto a serving plate. Decorate the plate with the remaining fennel fronds.

VARIATIONS

You can replace the potato-fennel mixture with delicious leftovers from last night, or follow the suggestions below. Into each muffin tin cup along with the egg, drop:

Summer: A tablespoon of sautéed zucchini, 1 whole fresh basil leaf, 3 raw cherry tomatoes, and a sprinkle of Parmesan cheese on top.
Winter: A few cubes of pre-roasted winter squash, thin ribbons of kale sautéed with garlic, a tiny pinch each of nutmeg and cayenne, and a tablespoon of cream.
Spring: Spears of cooked asparagus, a teaspoon of chèvre, and a teaspoon of nettle or chickweed pesto.

PHOTO BY TALI AIONA.

Shakshuka

Our kibbutz-raised facilities intern used to make a version of baked eggs in a spicy tomato sauce on his cook night using our homemade canned garden tomatoes. Classic food for a marching band; it's easy to make in large batches and the sauce can be made ahead of time.

Serves 4–6

1 medium onion, diced

¼ cup oil

1 red bell pepper, diced (optional)

1 tablespoon ground cumin

1 tablespoon ground or
    fresh-grated turmeric

1 teaspoon ground allspice

1 tablespoon smoked sweet paprika

3 cloves garlic, finely minced

1 tablespoon minced fresh hot pepper,
    or ¼ teaspoon red chili flakes

1 bay leaf

1 quart homemade canned tomatoes, diced
    or sauced

2 tablespoons minced Preserved Meyer
    Lemons (page 293), or juice and zest of
    1 lemon plus 1 teaspoon salt

1–2 eggs per person*

Salt and pepper to taste

Serves 30–40

6 medium onions, diced

1 cup oil

6 red bell peppers, diced (optional)

⅓ cup ground cumin

⅓ cup ground or fresh-grated turmeric

2 tablespoons ground allspice

⅓ cup smoked sweet paprika

16 cloves garlic, finely minced

¼ cup minced fresh hot peppers,
    or 1 teaspoon red chili flakes

4 bay leaves

4 quarts (1 10-pound can) homemade
    canned tomatoes, diced or sauced

½ cup minced Preserved Meyer Lemons
    (page 293), or juice and zest of 6
    lemons plus 2 tablespoons salt

1–2 eggs per person*

Salt and pepper to taste

In a 10-inch ovenproof skillet or shallow Dutch oven* on medium heat, sauté the onions in the oil with a sprinkle of salt, uncovered, until translucent. Add the red peppers and continue cooking until the peppers soften. Add the cumin, turmeric, allspice, and paprika; sauté for a few minutes until the spices become infused in the oil and start smelling really good. Then add the garlic and hot peppers and sauté for a minute more. Finally, make it saucy—add the bay leaves, tomatoes, and preserved lemons. Let this sauce simmer on low for 20 to 30 minutes so the flavors marry.

You can make the sauce ahead of time and store it in the fridge in a Mason jar for finishing later (it also makes a great base for chickpeas or a lamb meatball stew). Or you can proceed directly to making the Shakshuka: Reheat the sauce to a simmer and preheat the broiler. Working one egg at a time, make a little depression in the surface of the hot sauce with the back of a spoon and crack the egg in gently so that it lands in the hole. Try to space the eggs out so that the whites aren't running into each other. Top each egg with salt and pepper or a pinch of red chili flakes.

Broil for 5 minutes or less under the broiler until the eggs cook to your desired doneness. Enjoy with a slice of hot crusty garlic bread, or spooned over polenta, couscous, or Millet with Toasted Cumin Seeds (page 232). Top with feta cheese and fresh-chopped garden herbs such as marjoram, mint, parsley, or basil.

For a quick weeknight dinner, do everything on the stovetop instead of broiling: After the sauce has cooked, reduce the heat to low, add the eggs, cover the pan with a tight-fitting lid, and let the eggs poach in the sauce for 5 minutes or so.

VARIATIONS

Shakshuka, or some version of it, seems to be a common theme across cultures—the need to use up leftovers is universal! Honestly, you can poach eggs swimming in a pool of just about any saucy substance. In the tomato department, try a straight marinara or Bolognese topped with Parmesan or a southwestern chipotle chili with a sprinkle of Jack cheese. Another classic variation uses creamed spinach as the base.

* The amount of sauce in the basic recipe should be enough for four to six people each eating one generously sauced egg. If your four to six people want more than one egg each, divide the sauce into two 9 x 9-inch ovenproof baking dishes or 10-inch skillets so that you have more surface area to fit more eggs—there is enough sauce here to stretch. To accommodate the large crowd recipe, make the sauce in a large heavy-bottomed pot and transfer it into four large 12 x 20-inch baking dishes or entrée pans for broiling.

Millet with Toasted Cumin Seeds

Millet is a group of cereal grains widely grown in the semi-arid tropics of Asia and Africa and could provide a grain alternative here at home if desertification and drought conditions persist in California. This is a reliable method for fluffy millet, every time.

Serves 4–6

2 tablespoons cooking oil or ghee

1 tablespoon whole cumin seeds

1½ cups millet

2 cups water

1 teaspoon salt

¼ cup butter or olive oil, for serving

Serves 30–40

½ cup cooking oil or ghee

⅓ cup whole cumin seeds

8 cups millet

11 cups water

1 tablespoon salt

1 cup (2 sticks) butter or olive oil, for serving

In a medium pot with a tight-fitting lid, heat the cooking oil or ghee on medium heat. Add the cumin seeds and cook for a minute until they begin to give off a toasted aroma. Then add the dry millet. Stir frequently for a few minutes so that the oil and cumin are incorporated and the millet gets toasted a bit. Add the water and salt, cover, and bring to a boil. Reduce the heat and simmer for 5 more minutes. When most of the water has been absorbed (the surface of the millet appears to be dry)—about 10 minutes or a little longer for the large batch—turn off the heat and leave the pot covered (don't peek!) for 15 more minutes while the millet finishes steaming.

To serve, fluff with a fork and toss with the butter or olive oil. Adjust the salt to taste. Top with fresh herbs or a sprinkling of paprika for garnish. For a fabulous presentation, serve this cornucopia-style in a steamed winter squash half (see Wilted Arugula in a Whole Roasted Pumpkin, page 174). Encourage guests to take a scoop of soft squash along with their portion of millet.

Yellow Split Pea Puree with Caramelized Onion and Black Olives

Peas were one of the earliest pulse crops. The Greeks and Romans were cultivating peas in 500–400 BC and serving something very similar to this recipe—a nutty-flavored, protein-rich staple side dish.

Serves 4–6

2 cups yellow split peas

6 cups water

1 tablespoon butter

1 large red onion, sliced in thin half rounds

2 teaspoons balsamic vinegar

1 tablespoon olive oil

1 tablespoon salt, to taste

½ teaspoon black pepper

1 teaspoon apple cider vinegar

½ cup chopped cured black olives

Garnish: parsley

Serves 30–40

10 cups yellow split peas

8 quarts water

¼ cup butter

4 large red onions, sliced in thin half rounds

2 tablespoons balsamic vinegar

½ cup olive oil

3 tablespoons salt, to taste

2 teaspoons black pepper

1½ teaspoons apple cider vinegar

2 cups chopped cured black olives

Garnish: parsley

In a medium-sized pot, start cooking the split peas in the water on medium-high heat.

When they come to a boil, turn down the heat to just a simmer. Cook for about 45 to 50 minutes, just until they get soft. It is very important to catch them just before they get too cooked and fall apart; otherwise they become impossible to strain and the end result is too watery.

While the split peas are cooking, make the caramelized onions. Heat a skillet with the butter on medium-high heat. Add the onion and a pinch of salt. Cook for 10 minutes, stirring a few times. Turn the heat down to low and put a lid over the skillet. Cook another 10 to 15 minutes. Add the balsamic vinegar at the end to deglaze the pan.

When the peas are finished, strain through a fine sieve, discard the cooking water, and put the peas back into the pot. Add the olive oil, salt, and pepper to the peas, and puree using an immersion blender. Stir in the apple cider vinegar to brighten the flavors. If the mixture is too thick, add a bit of hot water to get the consistency of mashed potatoes.

Arrange the peas on a serving platter and top with caramelized onions, black olives, and parsley. Finish with a generous drizzle of your finest olive oil.

Bernie's Pierogi

This recipe is from Bernard Jungle, former facilities manager, inventor of whimsical musical instruments, song-writer, and rock guitar legend. It is a Slovak-Polish combination from both of Bernie's grandmothers and became an intergenerational ritual in the OAEC kitchen—resident kids loved to help Bernie with the rolling and could practically make pierogi by heart by the time they were six. Scale this recipe up if you need to, although make sure you have plenty of help with the rolling if you plan to feed a marching band! We served these for Bernie's going-away party (which we fondly called "Bernie Man") as an appetizer instead of a main course.

Pierogi are an awesome way to use up leftovers. You can pretty much use anything: mashed winter squash, sautéed greens with the water squeezed out, tapenades, sautéed chanterelle mushrooms, roasted garlic, or just about any leftover you find in your fridge. Experiment and have fun with whatever you have, but the standard fillings described in this recipe are mashed potatoes and cheese, and sauerkraut and onion.

Serves 4-6

MAKES ROUGHLY 28 PIEROGI, ENOUGH FOR A MAIN COURSE

2 cups unbleached flour
Pinch of salt, about ¼ teaspoon
2 egg yolks
¾ cup warm water (can vary, so keep water and flour handy when mixing)
2 teaspoons sour cream
Polka music

Serves 30-40

MAKES ROUGHLY 56 PIEROGI, ENOUGH FOR AN APPETIZER

4 cups unbleached flour
½ teaspoon salt
4 egg yolks
1¼ cups warm water (can vary, so keep water and flour handy when mixing)
1½ tablespoons sour cream
Several hours of polka music

In a mixing bowl, sift together the flour and salt. Make a depression in the middle.

In another bowl, whisk together the egg yolks, water, and sour cream. Pour this into the flour and mix until the dough comes together and peels away from the sides of the bowl. Put it out on a floured cutting board and shape the dough into a ball. Add a little more flour as needed to achieve a soft and springy consistency that doesn't stick to your hands, but do not overmix or knead the dough—this makes it tough and too elastic to roll out. Using plenty of flour on the board and rolling pin, roll it out as thin as possible—¹⁄₁₆ to ⅛ inch is great. Set the dough aside to rest and dry out a little, about 10 minutes or so—this makes the pierogi easier to form.

FILLING—ABOUT 1 TEASPOON PER PIEROGI

Serves 4-6
¼ cup cold leftover mashed potatoes, made from *your* grandma's recipe
¼ cup grated cheese—cheddar is standard
or
⅓ cup sauerkraut with the juice squeezed out
2 tablespoons chopped onion, sautéed in a little butter or oil

Serves 30-40
½ cup cold leftover mashed potatoes, made from *your* grandma's recipe
½ cup grated cheese—cheddar is standard
or
⅔ cup sauerkraut with the juice squeezed out
3 tablespoons chopped onion, sautéed in a little butter or oil

Whatever fillings you decide to use, make sure they are cold. Warm fillings heat up the dough and make it hard to form the pierogi properly. Also, make sure your fillings are a dry as possible—drain and squeeze out any excess liquid.

To make the mashed potato filling, just mix the grated cheese into the cold mashed potatoes. For the sauerkraut filling, squeeze the juice out of the sauerkraut and chop finely (Bernie's grandma used to save this juice and add it to a soup). Sauté the chopped onion in a little butter or oil and then stir in the dry, chopped sauerkraut and sauté together for a moment. Allow the filling to completely cool in the fridge before rolling the perogi.

There is a tool that cuts and crimps pierogi, but you can also use a pint-sized drinking glass or cookie cutter and a fork to do the same thing. Cut out as many circles as you can from the dough. Bunch up what's left and re-roll, cut, et cetera.

The amount of filling to use in each pierogi depends on the size of the glass or circular item you use to cut them out. A standard pint glass cuts a shape that can be filled with a level teaspoon. Put a dollop of filling in the middle of each circle, fold over, and crimp the edges together with a fork, forming a semicircular dumpling. Usually, the dough is sticky enough by itself, but if not, brush a little egg white around the edges before folding it over.

Get a giant pot of water boiling. Add between 6 and 10 pierogi at a time, gently lowering them into the boiling water so that they don't fall apart or splash. Boil for just a few minutes, until they float to the surface. Remove with a slotted spoon and let drain in a colander. Some people eat them like this—simply pour them into a serving bowl with some melted butter and serve.

You can also drain them and then fry in a skillet with some olive oil and butter until brown and then serve immediately. If you have a little extra filling left over, you can heat it up and serve it tossed in with the pierogi.

Pierogi freeze really well. After folding and crimping them, set them on a floured cookie sheet, making sure they are not touching, and freeze the whole tray overnight. Once frozen, bag them up and they will keep frozen for 6 months. When you want to cook them, put frozen ones directly into boiling water, but use fewer at a time and do more batches.

PHOTO BY JIM COLEMAN.

PHOTO BY JIM COLEMAN.

Winter Wild Mushroom Barley Risotto

Serves 4–6

8 cups winter vegetable stock (page 93)

2 tablespoons dried mushrooms (porcinis or shiitakes are fabulous)

½ pound mixed wild mushrooms: chanterelles, hedgehogs, oysters, morels, etc.

½ pound button or cremini mushrooms

3 tablespoons olive oil

2 cloves garlic, minced

1 cup dry white wine, divided

2 cups pearled barley

2 tablespoons finely chopped garden thyme

1 teaspoon lemon zest

½ cup grated hard cheese like Gruyère, Asiago, or Parmesan

Salt and pepper to taste

Garnish: fresh-chopped parsley

Serves 30–40

8 quarts winter vegetable stock (page 93)

½ cup dried mushrooms (porcinis or shiitakes are fabulous)

3 pounds mixed wild mushrooms: chanterelles, hedgehogs, oysters, morels, etc.

3 pounds button or cremini mushrooms

½ cup olive oil

4 cloves garlic, minced

5¼ cups dry white wine, divided

8 cups pearled barley

½ cup finely chopped garden thyme

2 tablespoons lemon zest

2 cups grated hard cheese like Gruyère, Asiago, or Parmesan

Salt and pepper to taste

Garnish: fresh-chopped parsley

If you're making stock from scratch, trim the ends off the mushrooms and use for the stock. If you're using premade stock, heat in a large saucepan to a simmer. Keep the stock warm on the back burner. Meanwhile, hydrate the dried mushrooms in a bowl with a little bit of the hot stock or water to cover. When they have fully softened, pour the mushroom water back into the larger pot of stock for added flavor. Squeeze the mushrooms dry and chop finely.

Leave smaller fresh mushrooms whole, especially if you're working with exotically shaped wild varieties, and slice or break up larger mushrooms into bite-sized pieces.

In a large Dutch oven or a heavy-bottomed saucepan on medium heat, add the oil, fresh mushrooms, and a sprinkle of salt. Sauté uncovered, stirring occasionally, for about 15 minutes. The mushrooms will release a lot of water—keep sautéing until *all* of this water evaporates. Add a little more oil if needed to keep mushrooms from sticking to the pan. Then add the garlic, chopped dried mushrooms, and ¼ cup (1¼ cups) of the white wine. Sauté about 3 to 5 minutes, until the wine evaporates and the mushrooms go dry again.

Add the barley to the mushrooms and stir to coat. Cook for 1 minute or so, stirring constantly. Add the remaining white wine and let everything deglaze in the pan for a minute, until most of the wine is absorbed. Add 1 cup (1 quart) warm stock and stir with a wooden spoon. Turn the heat to medium-low so that the mixture stays at a very low simmer, uncovered. When the stock is almost all absorbed, then add another cup (quart) and repeat the process until all the stock is absorbed and the barley is a creamy fluid texture. This will take about 45 minutes.

At the last addition of stock, stir in the reserved mushrooms, thyme, and lemon zest. Let this mixture cook together for a few minutes. Turn off the heat and adjust the seasoning with a little pepper. Mix in the grated hard cheese. The cheese will add quite a bit of salt, but taste and add more if needed. Garnish with a sprinkle of fresh-chopped parsley.

VARIATION

For a dairy-free version, omit the Parmesan cheese. Add a touch of tamari to make up the difference in salty richness.

SALAD DRESSINGS

Recipe List

PHOTO BY TALI AIONA.

OAEC Green Goddess Salad Dressing

Our version uses avocado as the base and whatever fresh herbs are abundant in the Mother Garden. In place of the classic anchovy, we substitute nori flakes for a little taste of the sea.

Serves 4–6

MAKES 1 CUP

1 cup parsley, loosely packed (about 12 sprigs)

¼ cup chervil, dill, basil, or cilantro, or fennel fronds

2 tablespoons chopped scallions, society garlic, or chives

¼ cup water or more

¼ cup lemon juice, vinegar, or a combination

½ avocado

1 tablespoon nori flakes or about ½ nori sheet, crumbled

½ cup olive oil

Salt to taste

Serves 30–40

MAKES 4 CUPS

1 generous bunch parsley

1 small bunch chervil, dill, basil, or cilantro, or fennel fronds

⅓ cup chopped scallions, society garlic, or chives

⅔ cup water or more

⅔ cup lemon juice, vinegar, or a combination

1 avocado

⅓ cup nori flakes or 3 nori sheets, crumbled

2 cups olive oil

Salt to taste

Blitz the herbs with the water and lemon juice in a high-powered blender or in a glass jar with an immersion blender until very finely pureed. Add the avocado, nori flakes, and oil and pulse again to combine. Add more water or lemon juice to thin if desired. Add salt to taste.

The iconic Venus of Willendorf sculpture in the North Garden gathering circle where the Grandmother Oak once stood. PHOTO BY JIM COLEMAN.

Roasted Fennel and Black Olive Salad Dressing

Serves 4-6

MAKES 1 CUP

1 quarter piece roasted fennel bulb
(page 148)

3 tablespoons cured black olives
(kalamata or Niçoise)

3 tablespoons white wine vinegar

1 teaspoon chopped fennel fronds

Pinch of fennel seeds

Pinch of lemon zest

¼ cup olive oil

Serves 30-40

MAKES 4 CUPS

1 large roasted fennel bulb (page 148)

¾ cup cured black olives
(kalamata or Niçoise)

¾ cup white wine vinegar

1 tablespoon chopped fennel fronds

½ teaspoon fennel seeds

1 teaspoon lemon zest

1 cup olive oil

Chop the roasted fennel and black olives very fine. In a blender or a glass jar with a lid, place the vinegar, fennel fronds, fennel seeds, lemon zest, and olive oil. Blend or shake vigorously until emulsified. Whisk in the finely chopped roasted fennel and olives. Taste for salt, though you shouldn't need any. The olives are quite salty.

Strawberry Balsamic Vinaigrette

Serves 4-6

MAKES 1 CUP

¼ cup balsamic vinegar

½ cup olive oil

1 cup fresh strawberries

½ teaspoon finely chopped tarragon
(optional)

Serves 30-40

MAKES 4 CUPS

1 cup balsamic vinegar

2 cups olive oil

1 pint basket fresh strawberries

2 teaspoons finely chopped tarragon
(optional)

In a glass jar with a lid, combine the balsamic and oil. Close the lid and shake vigorously until emulsified. (For a larger volume, use a blender to emulsify.) Wash and lightly crush the berries into chunky bits with a fork. Mix in the berries and tarragon.

VARIATION

In summer, use raspberries, blackberries, or mulberries.

Loquat Ginger Dressing

Loquats, known in Latin America as *nispero*, are native to Japan and are used culinarily and medicinally worldwide. Like a juicy tropical-tasting apricot, they are lovely in jams, syrups, fruit salads, and, in this case, a sweet-and-sour salad dressing. The trees are the first to bear fruit in early May, announcing the beginning of the orchard season at OAEC.

Serves 4–6

MAKES 1 CUP

⅔ cup loquats, quartered and de-seeded, or substitute fresh apricot plus 3 tablespoons water

Zest of 1 lemon

Juice of 1 lemon

1 teaspoon honey

1 teaspoon peeled and grated fresh ginger

½ cup sunflower oil

Salt to taste

Serves 30–40

MAKES 4 CUPS

2½ cups loquats, quartered and de-seeded, or substitute fresh apricot plus ⅔ cup water

Zest of 4 lemons

Juice of 4 lemons

1½ tablespoons honey

2 tablespoons peeled and grated fresh ginger

1⅔ cups sunflower oil

Salt to taste

Place the loquats, lemon zest and juice, honey, and ginger in a blender and whiz until finely pureed. Add the oil and pulse to emulsify. Salt to taste.

Golden Tomato Cumin Salad Dressing

Farallons Orange Beefsteak is a favorite slicing tomato at OAEC, and we love it for this recipe. This orange beauty volunteered and matured in a Mother Garden compost pile in 1982 and its seeds have been saved nearly every year since. Any orange or yellow tomato variety will work, however.

Serves 4-6

MAKES 1 CUP

1 cup chopped golden tomatoes

¼ cup sherry vinegar, or 1 tablespoon sherry
    plus 3 tablespoons apple cider vinegar

1 teaspoon ground cumin

½ clove garlic, to taste

Pinch of sea salt, to taste

¼ cup olive oil

Serves 30-40

MAKES 4 CUPS

3 cups chopped golden tomatoes

1 cup sherry vinegar, or ¼ cup sherry plus
    ¾ cup apple cider vinegar

1 tablespoon ground cumin

2 cloves garlic, to taste

Sea salt, to taste

1 cup olive oil

Place the chopped tomatoes in the blender with the sherry vinegar (or sherry and apple cider vinegar), cumin, half of the garlic, and salt. Blend until smooth. Add the olive oil and pulse to incorporate. Taste for garlic and salt and add more if desired, but be careful not to overpower the mild fruitiness of the golden tomatoes.

PHOTO BY DOUG GOSLING.

Plum Anise Hyssop Salad Dressing

Serves 4-6

MAKES 1 CUP

1 medium-large plum, quartered with the
    pit removed

3 tablespoons red wine vinegar

2 tablespoons flowering tops of anise hyssop

¼ cup olive oil

Pinch of sea salt (optional)

Serves 30–40

MAKES 4 CUPS

5 medium-large plums (3 cups), quartered
    with the pits removed

¾ cup red wine vinegar

½ cup flowering tops of anise hyssop

1 cup olive oil

2 teaspoons sea salt (optional)

Add the plum quarters to a blender with the red wine vinegar and flowering hyssop tops. Blend until smooth. Add the olive oil and pulse; do not overblend. Whisk in the salt, if desired.

Gravenstein Apple Lemon Basil Vinaigrette

The Gravenstein apple ripens early while basil is still coming in from the summer garden.

Serves 4–6

MAKES 1 CUP

½ cup lemon basil, lightly packed

1 Gravenstein apple, quartered and cored

¼ cup champagne or apple cider vinegar

3 tablespoons olive oil

3 tablespoons sunflower oil

Salt to taste

Serves 30–40

MAKES 4 CUPS

2½ cups lemon basil, lightly packed

4 Gravenstein apples, quartered and cored
   (2½ cups)

1 cup champagne or apple cider vinegar

⅔ cup olive oil

⅔ cup sunflower oil

Salt to taste

Place the lemon basil, apples, and vinegar into a blender. Blend until smooth, then pour in the oils in a fast steady stream. Don't overmix with the oil or it will emulsify and get really thick. Taste for salt, stirring it in by hand.

Blue Cheese Dressing for Escarole

We tend to shy away from heavy dressings, but escarole has a punchy bitterness that holds up to other strong flavors like garlic and blue cheese. Store what's left over in a glass container in the fridge for dipping vegetables or spreading on sandwiches.

Serves 4–6, with some left over

MAKES 1¼ CUPS

2 ounces blue cheese, crumbled

1 cup sour cream

2 tablespoons mayo

1 small clove garlic, crushed

1 tablespoon white wine vinegar

½ teaspoon or more fresh-cracked black pepper

Salt to taste

Serves 30–40, with some left over

MAKES 2½ CUPS

¼ pound blue cheese, crumbled

1 pint sour cream

¼ cup mayo

2 cloves garlic, crushed

¼ cup white wine vinegar

1 teaspoon or more fresh-cracked black pepper

Salt to taste

Combine the dressing ingredients in a blender and whiz to combine. For an Escarole Blue Cheese Salad (our favorite way to serve this dressing), toss chopped escarole with just enough of this dressing to coat. Add more if desired or reserve the rest for later use. Top with chopped parsley, more crumbled blue cheese, and croutons or toasted walnuts.

VARIATIONS

Blue Cheese Dip: For a thicker result, stir the ingredients together in a bowl with a spoon rather than in a blender. Serve as a dip or a dollop for beet soup.

Horseradish Dip: Omit the blue cheese and add 1 tablespoon (¼ cup for the large batch) prepared horseradish or 2 teaspoons (2 tablespoons) fresh-grated horseradish and 1 teaspoon (1 tablespoon) apple cider vinegar. Again, if you'd like to make a dip variation, stir the ingredients in a bowl with a spoon rather than in a blender. Serve with Double Roasted Beets with Balsamic Glaze (page 175).

Wild Rose Hip Salad Dressing

Serves 4–6

MAKES 1 CUP

½ cup rose hips

¼ cup water

2 tablespoons red wine vinegar

1 teaspoon orange zest

2 tablespoons orange juice

Pinch of sea salt, to taste

½ cup olive oil

Serves 30–40

MAKES 4 CUPS

2 cups rose hips

1 cup water

½ cup red wine vinegar

Zest and juice of 2 oranges

2 teaspoons sea salt

2 cups olive oil

Clean up the rose hips by removing any stems or leaves. Cook the rose hips and water in a very small saucepan over medium heat for about 10 minutes. (For the small batch, you will need to add a few tablespoons more water to prevent boiling dry, but you should end up with ¼ cup water in the end to blend with the dressing.) When hips are cooked, add them to a blender with the cooking water and red wine vinegar. Blend until smooth—there will be seeds. Pass the blended mix through a sieve and discard the seeds and skin. Pour the blended mixture back into the blender and add the zest, juice, salt, and olive oil. Blend just to incorporate.

Tree Tomato Vinaigrette

Tree tomato or tamarillo, *Cyphomandra betacea*, is another one of our favorite Andean crops that we have grown on-site since the early Farallons days. Tree tomatoes—not true tomatoes—ripen in early winter here, providing red egg-shaped fruit with a flavor uniquely their own: a tropical tartness suggestive of melons and an aftertaste reminiscent of their distant relative the tomato. We have found that they can be used in both savory and sweet recipes, as an ingredient in a winter green salad or salsa, or sliced fresh on the top of a cheesecake.

This sweet fragrant dressing pairs particularly well with hearty greens like endives, radicchios, and mustards. A welcome burst of the tropics in the dead of winter.

Serves 4–6

MAKES 1¼ CUPS

3 whole tamarillos

¼ cup champagne vinegar

1 teaspoon balsamic vinegar

Fresh-squeezed tangerine juice,
    about 2 tablespoons

¾ cup olive oil

Zest from 1 tangerine

1 clove garlic, minced or pressed

Sea salt to taste

Serves 30–40

MAKES 4 CUPS

12 whole tamarillos

1 cup champagne vinegar

1½ tablespoons balsamic vinegar

½ cup fresh-squeezed tangerine juice

3 cups olive oil

Zest from 4 tangerines

2 cloves garlic, minced or pressed

Sea salt to taste

Scoop out the flesh of the fruit into a small bowl (the skin is quite bitter). Add the champagne vinegar and quickly puree with a handheld immersion blender to separate the seeds. Strain the seeds out with a sieve. Add the balsamic vinegar and tangerine juice, and then whisk in the remaining ingredients with the olive oil.

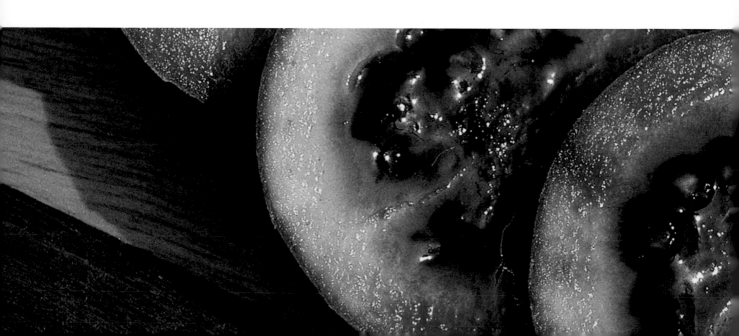

Mixed Citrus Salad Dressing with Lemon Balm

Serves 4–6

MAKES 1 CUP

¼ cup cilantro, washed and de-stemmed

3 tablespoons grapefruit juice

3 tablespoons lemon juice

3 tablespoons orange juice (total juice
should equal about ½ cup)

¼ teaspoon orange zest

½ teaspoon lemon zest

½ cup olive oil

2 tablespoons chiffonaded lemon balm leaves

Sea salt to taste

Serves 30–40

MAKES 4 CUPS

1 bunch cilantro, washed and de-stemmed
(2 cups)

Juice of 1 grapefruit

Juice of 3 lemons

Juice of 1 orange (total juice should equal
1¾ cups)

1 teaspoon orange zest

1½ teaspoons lemon zest

1½ cups olive oil

¼ cup chiffonaded lemon balm leaves

Sea salt to taste

In a blender, place the cilantro, citrus juices, and zests. Blend until smooth. Add the olive oil and salt and blend briefly. Stir in the lemon balm and salt to taste. Use as is or add some small diced chunks of citrus fruit, if a textured dressing is preferred.

PHOTO BY DOUG GOSLING.

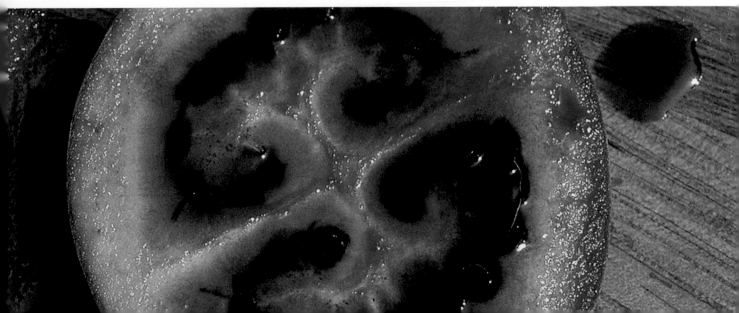

Preserved Lemon Brine Salad Dressing

Serves 4-6

MAKES 1 CUP

2 tablespoons–⅓ cup preserved lemon brine*

2 tablespoons fresh lemon juice, or more
    to taste

⅔ cup oil

2 tablespoons fresh-chopped parsley

1 small clove garlic, crushed

Cayenne pepper or a dash of hot sauce to taste

Serves 30-40

MAKES 4 CUPS

½–1 cup preserved lemon brine*

½ cup fresh lemon juice, or more to taste

3 cups oil

½ cup fresh-chopped parsley

2 cloves garlic, crushed

Cayenne pepper or a dash of hot sauce to taste

Put all the ingredients, starting with the smallest amount of preserved lemon brine, into a lidded jar and shake vigorously. For the larger version, use a blender. Taste and add more brine and/or fresh lemon juice until the lemony flavor pops forward from the olive oil.

  * If you're buying preserved lemons from a store or using a recipe other than the one listed in this book, be aware that the amount of salt can vary considerably. Start with a little, then, after the dressing comes together, taste for saltiness and add more if needed.

Roasted Onion, Sesame Seed, and Tamari Salad Dressing

This is an earthy winter dressing that is lovely to make while you've got something else, like a winter squash or casserole, roasting in the oven and an open rack available for this little side project. It's wonderful tossed warm with baby kale or spinach greens for a barely wilted salad, or served as a dipping sauce for wontons.

Serves 4-6

MAKES 1 CUP

1 medium onion, quartered

Drizzle of sesame oil

Pinch of sea salt

2 tablespoons sesame seeds

2 tablespoons brown rice vinegar

2 tablespoons tamari

¼ cup toasted sesame oil

¼ cup sesame oil

Serves 30-40

MAKES 4 CUPS

4 medium onions, quartered

Drizzle of sesame oil

Pinch of sea salt

⅓ cup sesame seeds

½ cup brown rice vinegar

½ cup tamari

1 cup toasted sesame oil

1 cup sesame oil

Preheat the oven 400°F. Place the peeled and quartered onions in a cast-iron pan with a drizzle of sesame oil and sprinkle of salt. Transfer to the oven and roast for about 40 minutes. Oven space permitting, toast the sesame seeds in the oven at the same time on a small sheet pan for about 8 minutes.

    In a blender place the roasted onions, brown rice vinegar, and tamari. Blend until smooth. Add the oils and blend again briefly. Stir in the sesame seeds.

Recipe List

Tonic Spring Pesto with "Gardener's Choice" Mixed Weeds

Pestos are both a delicious way to take your medicine and a great use for all those spring weeds popping up in the garden. Harvest herbs while they're young and tender before flowering. Make sure you know how to identify these plants with a reliable guide, as there can be a few non-edible look-alikes in the garden. *Weeds of the West* by Larry C. Burrill and Steven A. Dewey is the one we use. The weeds listed in this recipe are somewhat neutral in flavor, but depending on the mix of herbs and the time of year, you may need to be flexible with this recipe and adjust the lemon, salt, and oil according to taste. *Important:* Do not use dandelion or other bitter greens in this recipe as the bitter flavor can be quite strong—for a recipe specific to dandelion, see Dandelion Spread (page 257).

Serves 4–6, with some left over

MAKES 2½ CUPS

3½ cups packed neutral spring herbs: plantain, mallow, or cleavers

⅔ cup aromatic spring herbs: parsley, chervil, cilantro, or basil

1 garlic scape, or 1 very small clove garlic

¼–½ cup lemon juice, to taste

Salt to taste

⅓ cup sunflower seeds

⅓ cup olive oil

Serves 30–40

MAKES 6–8 CUPS

10 cups packed neutral spring herbs: plantain, mallow, or cleavers

3 cups aromatic spring herbs: parsley, chervil, cilantro, or basil

5 garlic scapes, or 3 cloves garlic

¾–1 cup lemon juice, to taste

1½ teaspoons salt, to taste

1 cup sunflower seeds

1 cup olive oil

Blend the herbs, garlic, and lemon juice in a high-powered blender, pushing down with the fitted baton to incorporate. Add the salt, sunflower seeds, and olive oil and blend until smooth. Taste and adjust the salt and acid to your liking. Pour into a serving dish. Top with another drizzle of olive oil and serve.

HERBAL PESTOS

We serve some variation on "pesto" almost every day, year-round, either traditional pesto or its lighter, brighter cousin, pistou—a thinner green sauce without the nuts or cheese. Here are our tricks for incorporating this easy sauce into your repertoire: First, blend the herb with the acid *before* adding oil—it locks in the bright-green color. Second, don't overblend once the olive oil has been added or it will turn bitter. Third, a Vitamix-style blender with a fitted tamping baton is the best tool for this, especially for tougher garden herbs such as cleavers or rosemary. If you don't have one, a handheld immersion wand blender inside a glass jar will also work for pushing the herbs down into the acid to fully incorporate.

Kami's Chickweed Pesto

When Kami McBride, author of *The Herbal Kitchen*, was a garden intern at OAEC, she was told to clear a bed of "weeds" in preparation to plant vegetables. As a trained herbalist, Kami did not see a single weed in the bed. What she saw instead was a bed of medicine. If the garden gives you chickweed, make chickweed pesto!

Serves 4–6

MAKES 2 CUPS

1½ cups fresh chickweed, packed tightly

1½ cups arugula, packed tightly

¾ cup olive oil

2 cloves garlic

¼ cup sunflower seeds

¼ cup Romano cheese (optional)

Salt and pepper to taste

Serves 30–40

MAKES 6–8 CUPS

9 cups fresh chickweed, packed tightly

9 cups arugula, packed tightly

4½ cup olive oil

4 cloves garlic

1½ cups sunflower seeds

1½ cups Romano cheese (optional)

Salt and pepper to taste

Put the olive oil, garlic, sunflower seeds, Romano cheese, salt, and pepper in a food processor and pulse until everything is mixed together well. Add the chickweed and arugula and blend until smooth.

Lemony Chickweed Pistou

In this pistou without cheese or nuts, the zingy minerals in the chickweed really come forward.

Serves 4–6

MAKES ABOUT 1 CUP

1 cup tightly packed chickweed

A few sprigs parsley or chervil

Juice of 1 lemon

¼ cup olive oil

Salt to taste

Serves 30–40

MAKES ABOUT 6 CUPS

12–16 tightly packed cups chickweed

1 bunch parsley or chervil

Juice of 16 lemons (about 1¼ cups)

3 cups olive oil

Salt to taste, about 1½ teaspoons

Pre-chop the herbs, stem and all, and put them into the blender along with lemon juice. Blend, pushing down with the baton, if needed, until all the herbs are completely pulverized and creamy. Add the olive oil and pulse to incorporate. Salt to taste.

Serve as a vibrant green swirl in a soup, a dip for delicate rice crackers, or as a sauce atop simple steamed vegetables.

VARIATION

Substitute blanched nettles (page 198) in addition to, or instead of, the chickweed.

Dandelion Spread

During the sluggish cold months when we are eating lots of heavy, fatty food, dandelion is an important medicinal herb that helps the liver metabolize fat. Coincidentally, the bitter flavor also provides a crisp palate-cleansing contrast to these rich foods. Serve this condiment with lamb, a hearty roast, or as part of a charcuterie and cheese platter.

Serves 4–6

MAKES 2½ CUPS

1½ cups packed dandelion leaves

½ cup packed fresh marjoram leaves

2 tablespoons fresh finely chopped rosemary

½ cup lemon juice

2 small cloves garlic (optional)

½ cup capers

½ teaspoon salt or to taste

¾ cup toasted almonds

⅔ cup olive oil

Serves 30–40

MAKES 6 CUPS

6 cups packed dandelion leaves

2 cups packed fresh marjoram leaves

½ cup fresh finely chopped rosemary

1½ cups lemon juice

6 small cloves garlic (optional)

2 cups capers

1½ teaspoons salt or to taste

2 cups toasted almonds

2½ cups olive oil

Blend the dandelions, herbs, lemon juice, garlic, and capers in a food processor, high-powered blender, or immersion wand in a glass jar, pushing down to incorporate. Add the salt, almonds, and olive oil and blend again until smooth. Taste and adjust for salt and lemon. Because the bitterness of the dandelion can vary widely depending on the season, location, and variety, you may also need to dilute the intensity with more almonds and olive oil to suit your taste. Pour into a serving dish. Top with a drizzle of olive oil and serve.

Chervil Aioli

There is no higher purpose for a freshly laid golden OAEC egg than a batch of homemade mayo. Olive oil is fantastic in this recipe, but only if you whisk it by hand, in a stand-up mixer, or with a handheld eggbeater. If you prefer to blend with an immersion wand or blender, choose sunflower or some other oil—cutting olive oil with metal blades turns it a little bitter.

Serves 4-6

MAKES A LITTLE OVER 1 CUP

1 farm-fresh egg yolk from clean, healthy chickens (don't use factory-farmed eggs for this—or any—recipe)—room temperature

1 very small clove garlic, less than a teaspoon crushed (optional)

1 cup oil

Salt

Squeeze of lemon

1 tablespoon finely chopped fresh chervil, or substitute a combination of tarragon and parsley

Serves 30–40

MAKES 4 CUPS

4 farm-fresh egg yolks from clean, healthy chickens (don't use factory-farmed eggs for this—or any—recipe)—room temperature

2 small cloves garlic, 1 teaspoon crushed (optional)

4 cups oil

Salt

Squeeze of lemon

1/3 cup finely chopped fresh chervil, or substitute a combination of tarragon and parsley

Let your egg sit out on the counter until it comes up to room temperature. Separate the egg and reserve the white for another use. If you're using garlic, crush it with a garlic press or mortar and pestle into a smooth paste and stir it into the egg yolk. Add about a quarter of the oil and whisk until a very well-incorporated mixture forms. Drizzle in the rest of the oil in a thin stream while whisking all the while. Add salt and lemon to taste. Stir or blend in the chopped chervil. Use right away.

The Cardoon

Cardoons, a close relative of the globe artichoke, are a drought-hardy perennial vegetable grown for the midrib of the showy, silver leaves instead of the thistle flower or choke. We love them because they produce way more usable "meat" per plant than artichoke hearts, which are too precious to make from scratch for a large group. Looks like celery. Tastes like artichoke. Yum! Unlike artichokes, however, the flowers and chokes of cardoons are much too spiny to eat. A strong tea made from the flowers can be used as a natural rennet for making goat cheese.

Like olives or acorns, cardoons must be leached to remove bitter tannins. They are less bitter and hence require less leaching when harvested in the cool early spring when the leaves are young and still growing in a low rosette before bolting begins.

To prepare, first strip and discard the leaflets, leaving the celery-like center stalk. Pull off the long fibrous outer strings with the aid of a paring knife. Chop crosswise, according to your recipe, though we usually cut them into 4-inch lengths. In a stockpot filled with plenty of water (at least 10 times as much water as vegetable), add the cardoons, a few tablespoons of salt, and a generous splash of lemon juice. Bring to a boil, reduce the heat, and simmer for 15 minutes. Strain and discard the water. Refill with fresh water, add more salt and lemon juice, and boil again. Repeat this process two or three times until the cardoons are fully cooked and soft. Cut off a small piece of cardoon and taste it—if it's still unpalatably bitter, keep leaching with more changes of brine until it suits your taste. However, do not overleach as it is possible to leach all the good flavors and nutrition out as well. When it tastes like a mellow artichoke with just a pleasant touch of bitter, you are ready for the next step. Rinse and allow to cool. Cardoons may be leached in advance and stored in the fridge for a day or so until you are ready to incorporate the prepared cardoons into a recipe.

PHOTO BY JIM COLEMAN.

PHOTO BY DOUG GOSLING.

Cardoon Tapenade

Use this versatile condiment anywhere you would normally use artichoke hearts. Stir into pasta, mix with spreadable goat cheese, top a pizza, or layer and bake into lasagnas or gratins.

Serves 4–6

MAKES 2 CUPS

4 large cardoon stalks, fully leached and cooked (about 2 cups finely chopped)

¼ cup oil

2 cloves garlic, crushed

2 tablespoons fresh-chopped parsley or fresh herb of your choice

Black pepper to taste

¼ cup grated Parmesan cheese (optional)

Serves 30–40

MAKES 7 CUPS

20 large cardoon stalks, fully leached and cooked (about 15 cups finely chopped)

1½ cups oil

8 cloves garlic, crushed

½ cup fresh-chopped parsley or fresh herb of your choice

Black pepper to taste

2 cups grated Parmesan cheese (optional)

Chop the leached cardoons (see the sidebar, page 261) into ¼-inch pieces—the strings can be fibrous, so cut against the grain. Squeeze any excess water out of the chopped cardoons. In a saucepan, add the oil, chopped cardoons, and garlic. Sauté on medium-low heat until the garlic is cooked but not burned and the oil gets mostly absorbed. Remove from the heat. Toss in the parsley or desired herb and optional grated Parmesan cheese. Taste and add more fresh herbs if needed. Since the leached cardoons were cooked in salt, you probably won't need to add any, but do add pepper to taste. Store in a glass container in the fridge for up to a week.

VARIATIONS

Cardoon Dip: Like artichoke dip, only better! Mix the tapenade with 2 teaspoons more finely chopped parsley, 1 teaspoon lemon zest, 1 cup sour cream, and 2 tablespoons mayo (¼ cup parsley, 2 tablespoons lemon zest, 2 pints sour cream, and ½ cup mayo for the large batch).

Open-Faced Cardoon Melt: Mound a scoop of Cardoon Dip on top of a piece of thinly sliced rye bread and a few leaves of cress or arugula. Top with a sprinkle of Parmesan. Melt in the hot oven and enjoy!

Spring Tonic Vinegar

This spring tonic vinegar was developed by former kitchen manager Bridget Grusecki, who went on to become a naturopathic doctor after leaving OAEC. Along with her lively sense of humor, she brought a unique knowledge of herbs and nutrition into the kitchen and always found ways to sneak medicine into our food! Keep this mineral-infused vinegar on hand and use it in salad dressings, add a splash to bone broths, or sprinkle on stir-fries or sushi rice.

Serves 4–6

MAKES 1 CUP

2 ounces burdock root (about 6 inches of fresh root)

1 ounce fresh cleavers

½ ounce fresh nettle leaf

¼ ounce dried wakame or other edible seaweed

Raw apple cider vinegar or rice vinegar to cover, about 1 cup

Serves 30–40

MAKES 2 PINTS

8 ounces burdock root (about 24 inches of fresh root)

4 ounces fresh cleavers

2 ounces fresh nettle leaf

1 ounce dried wakame or other edible seaweed

Raw apple cider vinegar or rice vinegar to cover, about 2 pints

Wash and pat dry the fresh herbs. Scrub the burdock root. Chop and loosely pack the herbs in a clean and/or sterilized glass jar. Cover with your vinegar of choice. Always ensure that the herbs are completely covered by the vinegar. Cover with a noncorrosive lid, such as plastic, glass, or parchment paper covered by a metal lid. Periodically, shake or stir the contents of the jar, always double-checking that the herbs are submerged in vinegar. After a minimum of 2 weeks, strain the herbs using a mesh strainer or cheesecloth. Filter the vinegar into a clean and/or sterilized bottle. For an extra touch, add a couple of sprigs of cleavers to the bottle. Store in a cool, dark place. For best quality, use within 2 to 3 months from cool storage or 6 to 8 months from the refrigerator.

Summer Superfood Pesto

Magenta lamb's-quarters or Magenta Spreen, *Chenopodium giganteum,* is a Eurasian native that volunteers in every summer bed of the North Garden. Noteworthy for the magenta-colored water-storing hairs that cover the undersides of its leaves, this chenopod is a reliable ingredient for warm-season salads and a delicious sauté green for stir-fries, omelets, and lasagnas. Amaranth is also a fortifying super-green and, like lamb's-quarter, is packed with calcium, protein, and a rich earthy flavor. This pesto is great with roasted root vegetables.

Serves 4–6

MAKES 2 CUPS

1 large bunch amaranth greens and/or lamb's-
    quarters (about 3 cups tightly packed)
Juice of 1 lemon
A few sprigs parsley
1 very small clove garlic
⅓ cup pumpkin seeds
⅓ cup olive oil or flax oil
Salt to taste

Serves 30–40

MAKES 6 CUPS

2 pounds amaranth greens and/or lamb's-
    quarters (about 6 quarts tightly packed)
½ cup lemon juice
1 bunch parsley
3 cloves garlic
1¼ cups pumpkin seeds
1¼ cups olive oil or flax oil
Salt to taste

Put the greens, parsley, and lemon juice into a high-powered blender with tamping baton, or a glass jar with an immersion blender. Blend, pushing down to incorporate. Add the garlic, seeds, and olive oil and continue blending until smooth and creamy. Salt to taste.

VARIATION

Use wild amaranth greens, also known as pigweed.

PHOTO BY DOUG GOSLING.

A Celebration of Pollination

According to the Xerces Society for Invertebrate Conservation (www.xerces.org), it is estimated that two-thirds of the world's food crops, including the majority of fruits, vegetables, seeds, and nuts, rely on insect pollinators. Wild, native insects such as butterflies as well as domesticated honeybees provide an essential ecological service that not only yields food for humans, but also sustains the very foundation of the food chain for all creatures in the ecosystem. The massive decline in pollinator populations largely due to widespread pesticide use, loss of habitat, and decreased diversity of forage plants is a troubling threat to the food supply.

Mason bee hive. PHOTO BY TALI AIONA.

Mason bee hives are installed on the sides of buildings throughout the OAEC grounds to attract native pollinators into the Mother Garden. Having evolved in the California landscape, native orchard mason bees are hardy to disease and drought conditions. While they don't produce honey, their life cycle is perfectly timed with the rhythm of the orchard for optimum pollination—they hatch and forage in sync with the early-summer blossoming of fruit trees and remain dormant, conserving their energy, for the rest of the year in the tiny hollows of these hives.

One of the most rewarding things we can do to reverse the decline of insect pollinators is to grow flowers. Organic perennial borders in the Mother Garden contain a variety of ornamental and edible flowering plants selected to bloom in sequence and provide a year-round forage source for beneficial insects. In turn, they pollinate our heirloom seed crops and help with integrated pest management.

The Mother Garden is a haven for bug life. As a resident entomologist and photographer, I could walk around with my camera and notepad all day in the backcountry looking for insects and come across just a handful of species, but when I step into the garden, particularly near the perennial flower borders, I hit the jackpot. We think that pretty flower gardens are just for our human enjoyment, but their value for biodiversity enhancement for insects is immense; bugs are attracted to the colorful display and sweet smells of the garden as much as we are. —JIM COLEMAN

CELEBRATION OF SUMMER FLOWERS MENU

Local cheese plate with OAEC honeycomb

Trio of flower petal pestos—nasturtium, sunflower, basil flower—on cucumber slices

Roasted Fennel Soup sprinkled with bee pollen

Pepita-Encrusted Squash Blossoms Stuffed with Goat Cheese and Herbs

Angelhair pasta with blossom butter on a bed of sautéed flowering broccoli shoots

OAEC Biodiversity Salad Mix with bee-balm-infused vinegar and olive oil

Vanilla cake liberally decorated with edible garden and orchard flowers

Butterfly on chive flower. PHOTO BY JIM COLEMAN.

Nasturtium Pistou

Edible flowers, such as sunflower and nasturtium, volunteer in legions in our temperate garden, but for most, these brightly colored sauces in smaller quantities are most efficiently used as a garnish or drizzle. Spoon delicately over crustini or slices of cucumber, or drizzle, Jackson Pollock–style, in the white space around a beautifully plated dish. For best control, pour into a squeeze bottle and doodle away.

Serves 4-6

MAKES ½ CUP

1½ cups nasturtium flowers, tightly packed

1 tablespoon lemon juice

½ cup sunflower or other neutral oil (olive oil overpowers the delicate nasturtium taste)

Salt to taste

Serves 30-40

MAKES 2 CUPS

6 cups nasturtium flowers, tightly packed

¼ cup lemon juice

2 cups sunflower or other neutral oil (olive oil overpowers the delicate nasturtium taste)

Salt to taste

Combine everything in a blender and whiz until smooth. Taste and adjust the salt and lemon. The floral honey cayenne taste of the nasturtium kicks in at the end. Add a little more oil if a thinner consistency is desired.

VARIATION

For a brilliant purple or pink variation, try using stock flowers.

Basil Flower Pistou

Most readers are probably used to buying basil in the grocery store in bunches with long stems, but this method of harvesting actually kills the plant in one fell swoop. Basil lasts longer and yields more when the lead shoots are pinched back throughout the season to encourage branching and to discourage flowering. The flowers and tender stems are completely edible—when blended up in a sauce, no one will notice!

Serves 4-6

MAKES 1¼ CUPS

1 bunch basil (1 cup packed leaves, shoots, and flowers)

Zest and juice of ½–1 lemon, to taste

½ teaspoon salt, to taste

1 cup olive oil

Serves 30-40

MAKES 7½ CUPS

6 large bunches basil (about 12 cups packed leaves, shoots, and flowers)

1 tablespoon lemon zest

¾–1 cup lemon juice, to taste

1 tablespoon salt

6 cups olive oil

Remove any tough or woody stems from your fresh herbs. Place the cuttings—including the leaves, tender shoots, and flowers—the lemon zest, juice, and a pinch of salt into your Vitamix fitted with a tamping baton (or use an immersion blender in a glass jar). Push down and blend until completely smooth. You may need to add a touch more lemon juice to get the blades moving. When the herbs are fully blended into the lemon juice, add the olive oil all at once and blend again, ever so briefly, until just emulsified. Taste and adjust the salt. Add more olive oil for a thinner sauce, if desired. Store in the refrigerator until ready to serve.

VARIATIONS

This technique can also be applied to many flowering herbs such as cilantro.

Sunflower Petal Pesto

Pluck sunflower petals and leave the stalk to dry in the field—you can either harvest seeds once they've dried down a bit, leave them for the birds, or allow them to shower down into the garden beds to seed next year's volunteers. If you don't live near a field of sunflowers, just make the small batch and drizzle as a garnish.

Serves 4-6

MAKES ½ CUP

¼ cup toasted sunflower seeds

Pinch of salt or to taste

2 teaspoons lemon juice

½ teaspoon lemon zest

2 cups sunflower petals (30 flowers)

¼ cup olive oil

Serves 30-40

MAKES 2 CUPS

1 cup toasted sunflower seeds

1 teaspoon salt or to taste

3 tablespoons lemon juice

2 teaspoons lemon zest

8 cups sunflower petals (120 flowers)

1 cup olive oil

Combine the sunflower seeds and salt in a mortar and pestle or food processor and mash into a fine paste. Add the lemon juice, lemon zest, and sunflower petals until fully crushed and incorporated. Finally, add the oil and process until smooth. Taste and adjust the salt and lemon to taste.

Summer Herb Flower Vinegar

Olivia's mom, Lola, is famous for her potato salad that seems so simple, but has a certain *je ne sais quoi*—the secret ingredient: chive-flower-infused vinegar. She recalls, "As a child I was enchanted by the apothecary bottles lined up on our kitchen shelves, stuffed with purple pompoms—I just knew there was magic happening inside."

Serves 4-6

MAKES ABOUT 1½ CUPS

1½ cups packed chive flowers, society garlic
    flowers, sage flowers, rosemary flowers,
    basil flowers, monarda (bee balm)
    blossoms, dill flowers, or fennel flowers

Good-quality white wine or champagne
    vinegar to cover, about 1½ cups

Serves 30-40

MAKES ABOUT 3 CUPS

3 cups packed chive flowers, society garlic
    flowers, sage flowers, rosemary flowers,
    basil flowers, monarda (bee balm)
    blossoms, dill flowers, or fennel flowers

Good-quality white wine or champagne
    vinegar to cover, about 3 cups

Pack the herb flowers into the bottom of a clean, small-mouthed pint (or quart) -sized Mason jar or other glass container. Pour in the vinegar to cover by an inch. Vinegar will corrode metal, so use a plastic lid—if you don't have one, create a barrier by putting a piece of plastic wrap or waxed paper over the mouth and screw on the metal lid over it. Keep in a cool dark place for 3 weeks. Strain the infused vinegar, compost the spent flowers, and funnel the vinegar back into the original bottle or another decorative glass vessel. Makes a great gift.

PHOTO BY TALI AIONA.

EDIBLE FLOWERS AT OAEC

Spring

Abutilon or flowering
    maple flowers
Apple, plum, and
    peach blossoms
Arugula flowers
Calendula petals
Chervil flowers
Chickweed flowers
English daisy petals
Lilac flowers
Mache flowers
Johnny jump-ups
Pineapple guava flowers
Primrose flowers
Tulip flowers
Violet flowers
White and blue borage flowers

Summer/Autumn

Anchusa flowers
Anise hyssop flowers
Bachelor's button petals
Basil flowers
Bergamot (monarda) flowers
Bronze fennel flowers
Calendula flowers
Carnation petals/other
    dianthus petals
Chive flowers
Cilantro flowers
Citrus flowers
Dahlia petals
Daylily buds and flowers
Dill flowers
Fuchsia flowers

Hollyhock flowers
Hyssop flowers
Kennikura flowers
Lavender flowers
Lemon verbena flowers
Marigold petals
Mashua flowers
Nasturtium buds and flowers
Garlic chive flowers
Oregano/marjoram flowers
Pansy/viola flowers
Parsley flowers
Passion fruit flowers
Garden pea flowers
Red clover flowers
Rose petals
Rose geranium flowers
Runner bean flowers
Salvia flowers
Shungiku flowers
Snapdragon flowers
Society garlic flowers
Squash blossoms
Stock flowers
Sunflower petals
Thyme flowers
White and blue borage flowers

Winter

Austrian field pea flowers
Brassica flowers
Calendula petals
Fava bean flowers
Pineapple sage flowers
Wild radish flowers
White and blue borage flowers

Basic Garden Herb Butter

Compound butters bring an elegant garden touch to any meal. Serve at the table with fresh bread, melt on top of other vegetables such as steamed carrots or mashed potatoes, or whisk into sauces or soups.

To serve as a condiment for 30 to 40 people, double the recipe, though no matter how many you are cooking for, it's worth making an extra batch just to keep a log or two on hand in the freezer.

MAKES A LITTLE OVER 1 CUP

1 cup (2 sticks) unsalted butter, softened

½ cup finely chopped, fresh tender mild herb such as parsley, dill, chervil, tarragon, basil, mint, shiso, or mitsuba

1 teaspoon lemon zest, or substitute Meyer lemon or other citrus zest

Salt to taste

Garnish: neutral edible flowers—borage, bachelor's button, or calendula petals (optional)

Let the butter sit out until it comes to room temperature. Whip the butter in a mixing bowl with a wooden spoon or with an electric mixer until smooth and fluffy. Add the herbs, zest, and a pinch of salt; whip to combine. Taste and adjust the salt and seasonings to your liking, adding more herbs if you prefer, keeping in mind that the flavor will infuse into the butter with time. Line a bamboo sushi mat with waxed paper and roll the butter into a log. Unwrap it halfway, sprinkle evenly with a few borage, bachelor's button, or calendula petals, and press again to make them stick. Refrigerate until hardened and then slice into serving-sized rounds. If you don't have a bamboo sushi mat, just pack the soft compound butter into a small serving dish or ramekin and press an edible flower into the middle.

VARIATIONS

There are endless ways to incorporate the diversity of the garden into this simple condiment. Substitute whatever herbs you have available in your garden, though if you're using more potent herbs such as rosemary, thyme, or oregano, cut back to ¼ cup and be sure they are very finely chopped.

For a garden herb cheese spread for bagels, omelets, or crustini, substitute 1 cup chèvre or cream cheese for the butter.

Blossom Butter

Bee balm (monarda) petals have the distinct flavor of oregano. Combined with the demure blue flowers of rosemary and society garlic, this combination is a whimsical version of an Italian seasoning blend. Delicious served with angelhair pasta or with raw cucumber slices or radishes.

MAKES A LITTLE OVER 1 CUP

1 cup (2 sticks) unsalted butter, softened

¼ cup bee balm petals

¼ cup rosemary flowers

¼ cup society garlic flowers

½ teaspoon lemon zest

Salt and fresh black pepper to taste

Let the butter sit out until it comes to room temperature. Whip the butter in a mixing bowl with a wooden spoon or with an electric mixer until smooth and fluffy. Add the flower petals, zest, and a pinch of salt and pepper and whip to combine. Taste and adjust. To serve, pack the compound butter into a ramekin or serving dish and press a whole society garlic flower into the middle. Or if you have a bamboo sushi mat, line it with wax paper and roll the butter into a log, finishing with a sprinkle of additional flower petals. Refrigerate until hardened.

VARIATIONS

Experiment with the flavors of other edible flowers—whole petals of gently torn nasturtium (peppery), calendula petals (mildly spicy), borage flowers, bachelor's buttons (neutral), shungiku flowers, pineapple sage (pineapple flavored).

Blossom butter can also be taken in a sweet direction. Omit the pepper. Substitute finely chopped rose petals for the savory flowers and add 2 tablespoons Cecile Brunner Rose Sugar (page 331). Spread on toasted brioche.

Gaby's Baba Ganoush

Serves 4–6

MAKES ABOUT 2 CUPS

3 medium-large eggplants

½ cup tahini

¼ cup olive oil

2 cloves garlic, crushed

2 tablespoons lemon juice

1¼ teaspoons salt

Serves 30–40

MAKES ABOUT 8 CUPS

12 medium-large eggplants

1½ cups tahini

1½ cups olive oil

5 cloves garlic, crushed

½–¾ cup lemon juice

1 tablespoon salt or to taste

Char, sweat, and peel the eggplants as directed in the sidebar for quick fire-roasted veggies (page 98). Cut the eggplants open lengthwise, and with your hands, pull out the seed pockets. A few seeds are okay, but try to get most of them out. If your eggplants are small and tender, this step is not necessary—just peel them whole. Rough-chop the eggplants and put in a food processor with the remaining ingredients. Process to a smooth consistency. If the consistency is too thick, add more oil and/or a little bit of the juice from the sweating process. Garnish with a drizzle of olive oil and a sprinkle of fresh herbs on top and serve.

Roasted Tomatillo Salsa

Tomatillos are self-seeders that can become quite weedy in our climate. Here's a traditional tomatillo salsa to make in bulk if your tomatillo crop gets away from you. Great for freezing.

Serves 4–6

MAKES 1½ CUPS

1 pint tomatillos, husks removed

1–3 hot green chiles, such as jalapeño or Serrano

4 whole cloves garlic, peeled

½ cup chopped cilantro

2 tablespoons white wine vinegar

2 tablespoons olive oil

Salt to taste

Serves 30–40

MAKES 7 CUPS

4 pints tomatillos, husks removed

2–6 hot green chiles, such as jalapeño or Serrano

8 whole cloves garlic, peeled

1 large bunch chopped cilantro

½ cup white wine vinegar

½ cup olive oil

Salt to taste

Preheat the broiler to high. On a baking tray, place the tomatillos, whole chiles, and garlic cloves. Broil for 5 to 10 minutes or so until the garlic begins to soften. Remove the garlic cloves first so that they don't become burned and bitter. Then continue to roast the chiles and tomatillos for another 10 minutes or so until they're browned and beginning to get crispy—a little char gives the salsa a rich, authentic flavor. Remove from the broiler and allow to cool slightly. If you have a large stone mortar and pestle, use that to pound everything into a rustic puree and toss with the cilantro, vinegar, and oil in a serving bowl. Otherwise, place everything in a food processor and pulse into a course texture. Add salt to taste. Chill until ready to serve.

Llajua—Bolivian Picante Sauce

Permaculture-program graduate Leah Quiroga makes this hot sauce based on quilquiña—a uniquely assertive herb that has brought tears of homesickness to the eyes of Bolivian guests visiting the Mother Garden. It has also brought tears to the eyes of those adverse to the herb—like cilantro, you either love it or you hate it. This sauce features an authentically Andean flavor combination—the tropical fruit notes of the manzano peppers (also known as locoto or rocoto peppers) and the intensity of the quilquiña give the sauce a unique depth.

Serves 4–6

MAKES ABOUT 1 CUP

2–3 red manzano peppers, cut in half, seeds removed

2–3 small tomatoes, cut in half, seeds removed*

Handful rough-chopped quilquiña or fresh cilantro (about ¼ cup)

1 teaspoon vinegar (red wine vinegar, apple cider vinegar, or lemon or lime juice can be used)

2 tablespoons olive oil

Salt to taste

Serves 30–40

MAKES ABOUT 6 CUPS

12 red manzano peppers, cut in half, seeds removed

12 small tomatoes, cut in half, seeds removed*

Several handfuls rough-chopped quilquiña or fresh cilantro (about 1 cup)

2 tablespoons vinegar (red wine vinegar, apple cider vinegar, or lemon or lime juice can be used)

½ cup olive oil

Salt to taste

Place all the ingredients into a blender and puree until almost smooth. Serve with just about anything!

PHOTO BY TALI AIONA.

* Manzano peppers just start to ripen near the end of tomato season in West Sonoma County, but really get going in fall and winter. Freeze whole tomatoes to have on hand for just this purpose. No fuss required—just pop the tomatoes whole into freezer bags in the summer and thaw out the frozen red orbs a few at a time to make fresh batches of llajua as needed throughout the year. The skins easily slip off as they defrost.

Aji de Huacatay

Huacatay is a drought- and heat-hearty marigold relative from the Andes. Its bright-green bushy foliage reaches 6 to 8 feet, and its unmistakable minty-lime fragrance fills the late-summer garden. It is traditionally used similarly to cilantro in sauces and marinades for meat, chicken, and guinea pig. Whereas cilantro is best enjoyed fresh and turns lackluster when cooked or dried, the opposite is true for huacatay—its emphatic pungency mellows, giving slow-cooked stews a buoyant lift in a way that cilantro cannot match. This recipe is an Andean dipping sauce that is often served with potatoes and chicken, aka papas y pollo. Some versions call for evaporated milk, crushed soda crackers, or queso fresco, but we prefer this simple mayo-based version. Serve as an alternative to the huancaina sauce in Papas a la Huancaina (page 140).

Serves 4–6

MAKES 1½ CUPS

1 Aji Amarillo, Aji Cristal, or other hot yellow chile, such as yellow cayenne

2 tablespoons dried huacatay leaves or ¼ cup fresh; or substitute half parsley, half cilantro and a pinch of lime zest

¾ cup good-quality mayonnaise with no added sweetener

½ head green romaine or butter lettuce (about 3 packed cups)

2 cloves garlic

Salt to taste

Serves 30–40

MAKES 6 CUPS

4 Aji Amarillo, Aji Cristal, or other hot yellow chiles, such as yellow cayenne

½ cup dried huacatay leaves or 1 cup fresh; or substitute half parsley, half cilantro and a ½ teaspoon lime zest

1¾ cups good-quality mayonnaise with no added sweetener

2 large heads green romaine or butter lettuce

6 cloves garlic

1½ teaspoons salt, to taste

Put all the ingredients in a blender and puree until very smooth. If you like it spicier, add more chiles.

PHOTO BY TALI AIONA.

Pasilla Pumpkin Seed Pesto

Serve with Roasted Eggplant Soup (page 100) or as a sauce with barbecued veggies or meat.

Serves 4–6

MAKES ¾ CUP

1 dried pasilla chile

½ cup boiling water

2 whole roasted red peppers (jarred is fine, or see page 98)

⅓ cup toasted pumpkin seeds

A few sprigs fresh cilantro (about 2 tablespoons chopped)

3 tablespoons olive oil

1 very small clove garlic (½ teaspoon)

1 teaspoon apple cider vinegar

Pinch of salt

Serves 30–40

MAKES 5 CUPS

4 dried pasilla chiles

2 cups boiling water

6 whole roasted red peppers (jarred is fine, or see page 98)

1½ cups toasted pumpkin seeds

1 large bunch fresh cilantro (about 2 cups chopped)

¾ cup olive oil

2 cloves garlic

1 tablespoon apple cider vinegar

1 teaspoon salt

Rehydrate the dried chiles with boiling water in a bowl to cover. Let steep for 10 to 15 minutes. Place all the ingredients in the bowl of a food processor and blend coarsely.

Garden Ranch Dip for Kids

Grazing is the new snacking! Rainbows of instant gratification flourish in the school garden: Sweet cherry tomatoes, spicy peppers, and cool crunchy cucumbers feed a young learner's belly and brain. A far cry from Hot Cheetos!

Kids have a remarkable enthusiasm for eating vegetables that they help to grow, harvest, and prepare. But if, by chance, they still need a little help getting the veggies to go down, this recipe has just six real food ingredients that even a second grader can pronounce. They can even help snip the herbs with scissors. Please pass the ranch!

Serves 4–6

MAKES ABOUT 1½ CUPS

1 cup sour cream
½ cup buttermilk
1 tablespoon finely snipped fresh parsley
2 teaspoons finely snipped society garlic
    or chives
2 teaspoons finely snipped fresh dill or
    tarragon (optional)
Salt and pepper to taste

Serves 30–40

MAKES ABOUT 6½ C

4 cups sour cream
1½ cups buttermilk
¾ cup finely snipped fresh parsley
¼ cup finely snipped society garlic or chives
3 tablespoons finely snipped fresh dill or
    tarragon (optional)
Salt and pepper to taste

Mix all ingredients gently in a bowl. Do not overblend or the dip will be too liquidy. Start with a pinch of salt and pepper, taste with a clean spoon, and add a little more if it needs it.

VARIATION

Ranch Salad Dressing: Reduce the sour cream to ¼ cup (1 cup). Add ½ cup (1¼ cups) sunflower oil and ⅓ cup (1 cup) red wine vinegar and blend everything in a blender.

MAKING SUN-DRIED TOMATOES

The Punta Banda tomato is a variety we obtained through our colleagues at Native Seeds/SEARCH, a Tucson-based organization with a similar mission of preserving food crop diversity through the ancient art of seed saving. This variety was collected from the arid Punta Banda Peninsula in Baja California. It is a prolific, early-season producer that can withstand drought and poor soil. Smaller than a slicer, larger than a cherry, it is believed to have been developed specifically for sun-drying.

There are many great solar ovens and dehydrator designs out there—we've trialed more than a few handmade and prefab ones over the years, with varying results. Actually, dehydrating fruits, berries, and tomatoes in a hot car parked in the sun with the windows rolled up yields excellent results!

Use Punta Banda tomatoes, or another low-moisture tomato such as another Mother Garden favorite bred specifically for drying, the Principe Borghese. Slice tomatoes in half and place faceup, skin down on a large window screen or wire cooling rack. Place the screen in direct sun in a well-ventilated location, but protected from bugs—if you don't have a legit dehydrator setup, you can fashion a tent of cheesecloth for this purpose. Leave out in the sun during the day and bring inside and store in a dry place overnight, rotating the fruit if needed for even drying. In arid regions of inland California and the Southwest, these tomatoes will dry in one day (really!), though here on the coast, we must repeat the process for several days. If a cold, foggy, or rainy spell suddenly hits, finish them off in a 200°F oven until dry. More humid parts of the country may have better luck with the oven-drying method that follows.

The ideal dryness is when the texture is pliable and chewy, but not tacky to the touch. Store them in the refrigerator in a glass container with a little oil to cover until you're ready to use them or freeze for long-term storage. Packing them in oil unrefrigerated is not considered a safe storage option.

If you would like to dry-store the tomatoes, it is necessary to desiccate them completely to prevent molding. Hard, crispy tomatoes like this

Rainbow Solar Oven. Farallons, circa 1976. PHOTO COURTESY OF ALISON DYKSTRA.

aren't so tasty whole, but can be rehydrated with a little hot water and blended as an alternative to tomato paste. They are also great for grinding into flakes for use as a seasoning or as a handy trick for backpacking.

Drying in an Oven

For meatier results and quicker drying times, choose small, low-moisture Roma or paste tomatoes. Save the big juicy slicers such as Brandywines for eating raw.

Line a baking sheet with parchment paper and turn the oven to 250°F. If you're lucky enough to have a brick or earthen pizza oven, seize the moment after your pizza party and dry your tomatoes as the oven is cooling overnight.

Slice the tomatoes in half and arrange faceup, skin down in a single, compact layer. Drizzle with olive oil and sprinkle with a little salt. Roast for 2 to 3 hours, until the tomatoes shrivel and loose 75 percent of their moisture, but are still a little soft in the middle. Transfer to a glass container, cover with more oil, and refrigerate. You can also freeze them.

Resident Jacob Kowalick-Allen captures free energy from the sun to dry Gravenstein apple slices. PHOTO BY BROCK DOLMAN.

Bolted Arugula Spread, aka Green Mustard

When pulling out a bed of bolted arugula, it always seems a shame to put all that food in the compost. Pesto is a perfect use for greens and flowers that are cosmetically challenged, flea-beetle-bitten, or past their prime and a little too spicy to eat raw. This spread is more akin in flavor to mustard than pesto—arugula is from the mustard family, after all. Delicious on pastrami sandwiches, in grilled cheese, or with hard-boiled eggs.

Serves 4–6, with a little left over

MAKES 2 CUPS

1 cup sunflower seeds, toasted

6 tightly packed cups arugula leaves, coarse stems removed

½ cup apple cider vinegar

2 cloves garlic, crushed

½ cup olive oil

Salt and black pepper to taste

Serves 30–40

MAKES 9 CUPS

4 cups sunflower seeds, toasted

6 tightly packed quarts of arugula leaves, coarse stems removed

2 cups apple cider vinegar

4 cloves garlic, crushed

4 cups olive oil

Salt and black pepper to taste

In a food processor or with an immersion wand in a large quart jar, pulse the seeds until they're finely ground but not creamy. Remove and set aside in a mixing bowl. Next blend the arugula and vinegar, pushing more arugula down as it becomes incorporated. Blend until fully smooth and not stringy. Add the garlic and olive oil and continue blending until incorporated. Stir the arugula mixture into the ground seeds in the mixing bowl. Add salt and pepper to taste. A little goes a long way, so feel free to divide the batch in two and freeze half for later.

Walnut Sauce

This protein-rich sauce can be taken in a multitude of directions—serve as a dip for crusty whole grain bread or to accompany roasted root vegetables or chickpea dishes. We especially like it tossed with soba noodles. Simply toasted walnuts can be substituted.

Serves 4–6

2 cups soaked, toasted walnuts (page 301)

¾ cup hot water

1 clove garlic

2 teaspoons apple cider vinegar

Salt to taste, about ¾ teaspoon

⅓ cup olive oil or more

Serves 30–40

8 cups soaked, toasted walnuts (page 301)

3 cups hot water

3 cloves garlic

¼ cup apple cider vinegar

Salt to taste, about 1 tablespoon

1½ cups olive oil or more

Process the walnuts in the food processor with the hot water to form a smooth paste. Add the garlic, vinegar, salt, and oil. Taste and adjust the salt and acid to your liking. Thin the sauce with more oil to the desired consistency if it will be stirred into another dish or leave it thick for a sturdier dip. You may also stir in chopped fresh herbs, if desired.

Olive Walnut Tapenade

Serves 4–6, with a little left over

MAKES 3 CUPS

1 cup walnut pieces

2 cups pitted kalamata olives

4 sprigs fresh herb, 2 tablespoons of it finely chopped—marjoram, thyme, or rosemary

Zest of 2 lemons

¼ cup olive oil

1 clove garlic, minced

Serves 30–40

MAKES 12 CUPS

4 cups walnut pieces

8 cups pitted kalamata olives

1 large bunch fresh herb, ¼ cup of it finely chopped—marjoram, thyme, or rosemary

Zest of 6 lemons

1 cup olive oil

3 cloves garlic, minced

Preheat the oven or toaster oven to 275°F. Lightly toast the walnuts on a sheet pan for about 10 to 15 minutes, until they just start to give off a nutty aroma. Let cool. Pulse the walnuts in a food processor until they are coarsely chopped, but not ground. Dump into a mixing bowl.

Drain and rinse the olives. Finely chop them and add to the walnuts. Add the finely chopped herbs and the lemon zest. In a small skillet, heat the olive oil and the garlic on medium until the garlic just begins to bubble. This takes the sharp, green edge out of the garlic so that it melds more gently with the earthiness of the walnuts. Stir into the olive-walnut mixture.*

Serve with fresh baked bread or crackers, stir into pasta, or use as a filling for savory baked goods.

VARIATION

Olive Tapenade Stuffed Fingerlings—a hot or cold appetizer: Parboil fingerling potatoes (we recently used the Princess LaRette variety) until they're tender but not falling apart; cool completely. Slice in half lengthwise and scoop out no more than a teaspoon of the flesh from each half, creating two little boats for stuffing. Reserve the potato innards for another use. Fill each potato half with a teaspoon of the tapenade. Serve cold with a summer luncheon. For the hot version, heat a skillet or griddle with a generous coating of oil or ghee on medium-high heat. Invert the stuffed potatoes and press down firmly. Cook to form a crusty top—be patient and let the tapenade really crisp up well before peeking, otherwise the tapenade will fall away from the potato and make a big mess. In one smooth motion, use a thin, sharp metal spatula to transfer from the griddle to the serving plate.

* Don't be tempted to mix the ingredients all together in the food processor—you will end up with a uniform glob of nut butter. Chopping everything separately and mixing it together by hand yields a more colorful and texturally interesting spread.

Mother Garden Veggie Kraut

Sauerkraut making is taught in several of our workshops, so we often have a continuous supply fermenting in our kitchen—a batch is made, it ferments, and it's ready for the next class to taste. The recipe is fairly unstructured, passed down by oral tradition depending on the teacher, and based on whatever we happen to have growing in the garden at the time, so no two Mother Garden krauts are ever the same. There have been some pretty wild and eclectic combinations made over the years, but the best krauts are usually the simplest: just carrot with ginger; plain green cabbage with a pinch of caraway; red cabbage and beets with peppercorns; napa cabbage speckled with local seaweed; or a simply spicy bok choi kimchi—to name a few. As long as you more or less follow the universal 3 tablespoons of salt per 5 pounds of veggies ratio, the rest is open for improvisation. For musings on the history, science, health benefits, and metaphysical virtues of sauerkraut, read the definitive tome *The Art of Fermentation* by fellow communitarian Sandor Katz.

Small batch

**FOR A 1-GALLON CROCK OR
4 GLASS QUART JARS**

5 pounds fresh veggies—cabbage is the
    classic because it's nice and juicy,
    but any vegetable can be used: leeks,
    peppers, carrots, radishes, even beets
    (which will stain everything pink!)
Your choice of spices to taste—garlic,
    ginger, peppercorns, chili flakes,
    seaweed, etc. (optional)
3 tablespoons salt
1 tablespoon whey or juice from your last
    batch of naturally fermented veggies
    (optional)

Large batch

**FOR A 5-GALLON BUCKET OR CROCK
OR FIVE 1-GALLON-SIZED GLASS JARS**

25 pounds fresh veggies—cabbage is
    the classic because it's nice and juicy,
    but any vegetable can be used: leeks,
    peppers, carrots, radishes, even beets
    (which will stain everything pink!)
Your choice of spices to taste—garlic,
    ginger, peppercorns, chili flakes,
    seaweed, etc. (optional)
15 tablespoons salt (1 tablespoon shy
    of a cup)
⅓ cup whey or juice from your last batch of
    naturally fermented veggies (optional)

Chop the veggies to small slices, thin julienne matchsticks, or shreds. Add thinly sliced or grated ginger, minced garlic, or other whole spices to taste. Then add salt. With very clean hands, massage the vegetables or pound them with a heavy object until the natural juices are released. Taste it and adjust the spices to your liking—it will taste a little too salty at first, but this will mellow as it ferments. For a foolproof kraut, inoculate with a tablespoon of whey or juice from your last batch—this will kick-start fermentation with lots of good probiotic organisms, though this is not necessary.

Pour the veggies and juice into a clean widemouthed jar, noncorrosive bucket, or traditional ceramic fermentation crock. If you're using cabbage or bok choi, you should have plenty of natural juice to fully cover the veggies, but with drier root veggies, you may need to top it up with some "seawater" (1½ tablespoons salt dissolved into 4 cups very clean water) until the veggies are just barely covered with brine.

The veggies now need to be weighted down so that they stay submerged under the brine during fermentation, otherwise a film of mold will grow on the surface. Traditional crocks have a fitted ceramic weight, but you can improvise by filling up a ziplock bag with water—lay it over the top so that the veggies are weighted below the surface of the brine and air can get out but not back in. Place the whole setup in a larger dish so that any brine that bubbles out during fermentation doesn't end up all over your counter.

Leave out for 5 to 10 days (the length of time will vary depending on how warm your kitchen is: warmer = faster, cooler = slower). Taste periodically and when the kraut is ripe and tangy, put a lid on it and store it in the fridge to halt fermentation. Enjoy a tablespoon or two on your plate with every meal, for its delicious umami flavor as well as its nutritional benefits.

PHOTO BY TALI AIONA.

Cistocera Relish

The cold-water tide pools of our rocky Sonoma coast are one of the most abundant edible seaweed habitats in the world and are heavily populated with varieties practically identical to those found in Japan including nori, dulce, wakame, sea palm, cistocera, fucus, bladderwrack, and kombu. Seaweed is harvested during the low "king" tide of the summer solstice; then it is dried and ready to use in fall.

Cistocera is our favorite local seaweed variety for its form and texture—it has little air bladders like miniature clusters of grapes that really hold on to flavors when pickled. In fact, our friends at the California School of Herbal Studies in Forestville advocate marinating a handful of dried cistocera in a jar of pickle brine after eating all the pickles! The familiar taste makes eating seaweed approachable for the uninitiated.

Serve this Japanese-style relish as a condiment with rice, soups, or sushi, or stir it into simply stir-fried vegetables.

Serves 4–6

MAKES 1 CUP

2 ounces (about 1 cup) crumbled cistocera, arame, or hijiki

1 cup hot water

¼ cup mirin or dry rice wine

⅓ cup rice vinegar

3 tablespoons tamari or soy sauce to taste

2 teaspoons sugar

1 teaspoon fresh grated ginger

Pinch of red chili flakes

3 scallions sliced into very thin rounds

Serves 30–40

MAKES 4 CUPS

8 ounces (about 4 cups) crumbled cistocera, arame, or hijiki

4 cups hot water

1 cup mirin or dry rice wine

1⅓ cups rice vinegar

½ cup tamari or soy sauce to taste

3 tablespoons sugar

1 tablespoon fresh grated ginger

Pinch of red chili flakes

1 small bunch scallions sliced into very thin rounds

Hydrate the seaweed by placing it in a bowl and pouring the hot water over it. As the seaweed softens, stir it around and push it down so that it all becomes submerged and the liquid gets absorbed. When fully plumped up after 20 minutes or so, drain it and squeeze it dry. Save the juice for a nice miso soup later. Add the rice wine, vinegar, soy sauce, sugar, ginger, and red chili flakes. Allow to marinate for 20 minutes or more in the fridge. Seaweed can vary considerably in its saltiness and flavor, depending on the variety and where and when it was harvested. Taste and adjust the seasonings—add more tamari, chili flakes, vinegar, or sugar to suit your taste. Stir in the scallions.

20th-Century Asian Pear Vinegar

For some reason, OAEC interns love fermentation projects. During the fall harvest season, every spare shelf and corner of the pantry becomes occupied by briny crocks and bubbling jugs. From brewing beer from the Cascade hops growing outside the kitchen, to sauerkrauts and fermented hot sauces, the garden's bounty never goes to waste. Culture begets culture, in the largest and smallest senses of the word. The seconds from our Asian pear harvest are put to good use, thanks to Matt Phillips, office intern 2012, in this delightfully bright and fruity vinegar.

You will need two essential, yet inexpensive, items from a brew shop: an air lock and rubber stopper that fits into the mouth of the jar, and a 2-toot length of flexible plastic tubing for siphoning. You will also need a 1-quart (or 1-gallon, for the large batch) empty apple cider jug or glass carboy with narrow neck, a small 3 x 3-inch piece of cheesecloth, and a rubber band.

Makes 1 quart
1 quart fresh-pressed Asian pear juice from
    about 5 pounds of Asian pears, give
    or take
½ teaspoon champagne yeast (about 2g)

Makes 1 gallon
1 gallon fresh-pressed Asian pear juice from
    about 15–20 pounds of Asian pears,
    give or take
1 packet champagne yeast (about 5g)

To convert fresh pear cider into vinegar, the cider will go through two steps. In the first stage, yeast will convert the sugar in the cider into alcohol and carbon dioxide, producing a dry, uncarbonated hard cider. Next, acetic acid bacteria present in the air convert the alcohol into vinegar.

Asian pears are much juicier than apples and produce more juice per pound. Pour your Asian pear juice into a clean* jug until the jar is nearly full, leaving about 3 inches of headroom at the top. Add champagne yeast to the jar, put on the cider jar lid, and shake/invert the jar briefly to mix the yeast, air, and cider. Remove the lid and put the clean air lock unit into the jar. It should become very bubbly within 1 day or so (if you haven't left enough headroom in your jar, it may bubble over—in that case, pour out a little cider, then rinse out and replace the air lock). Let the jar sit and ferment for 2 weeks at room temperature and you'll have hard cider. If hard cider is what you're after, stop here and consult a brewing book for bottling a carbonated beverage. OAEC's 20th-century variety of Asian pears makes the best homebrewed cider ever!

Without disturbing the cloudy yeast residue at the bottom of the jar, siphon out the clear cider into another container—save the yeast residue for fermenting your next batch of beer, wine, vinegar, or soda pop (it should last at least a month in the fridge). Rinse out the jar and put the cider back into the glass jar (or a larger vessel where there is a lot of surface area exposed to the air.) Cover the jar mouth with cheesecloth and use the rubber band to hold it in place. Acetic acid bacteria from the air will fall into the jar and begin converting the hard cider into vinegar. It can take from 3 to 9 months to fully convert the cider to vinegar using the wild acetic acid bacteria.

One method to help quicken the process is to add some (approximately 1 to 2 cups) raw, unfiltered apple cider vinegar to the jar just before putting on the cheesecloth. This introduces an active vinegar culture, called the vinegar "mother," into the hard cider, so it can begin working immediately. After the vinegar is complete, you can keep using your own raw vinegar to add to your next batch and keep the cycle going.

It may take a while before you have really good vinegar, but the beauty is in the simplicity: fresh cider, yeast, and time. Just keep tasting the brew every couple of months and you'll know when it's ready by its acidic vinegar taste and aroma.

* Instead of using harsh chemicals for sanitation, just use boiling water to rinse your equipment and jar right before using.

Marjoram Pistou

Serve with Blanched Romanesco on a Bed of Ornamental Kale (page 137) or as a winter pizza sauce (page 307).

Serves 4–6

MAKES 1¼ CUP

2 cups packed arugula leaves

½ cup packed marjoram leaves

1 clove garlic

½ teaspoon salt

2 tablespoons lemon juice

1 teaspoon lemon zest

½ cup olive oil

Serves 30–40

MAKES 5 CUPS

8 cups packed arugula leaves

1½ cups packed marjoram leaves

3 cloves garlic

1 teaspoon salt

½ cup lemon juice

1 tablespoon lemon zest

1½ cups olive oil

Place all the ingredients, except the oil, into a blender and mix on high. Add the oil in a thin stream and continue blending. Taste and adjust for salt and lemon. Add more oil if a thinner sauce is desired.

French Sorrel Sauce

Low-maintenance perennial French sorrel grows all year round in the North Garden. Somewhere between an herb and a sauté green, it is classically paired with potatoes, leeks, or fish, and has a bright tanginess that can be a nice alternative to lemon. This easy "sauce" could almost be considered "creamed greens" and is wonderful with poached eggs, salmon, or fettuccine. If you have weedy sheep sorrel growing in a nearby field, feel free to substitute.

Serves 4–6

MAKES 2 CUPS

½ cup (1 stick) butter

2 large bunches (8 packed cups) French or sheep sorrel leaves, de-stemmed and chopped

1½ cups half-and-half

Salt and pepper to taste

Serves 30–40

MAKES 8 CUPS

2 cups (4 sticks) butter

6–8 bunches (8 packed quarts) French or sheep sorrel leaves, de-stemmed and chopped

6 cups half-and-half

Salt and pepper to taste

Melt the butter in a stainless steel skillet or saucier on the lowest possible heat. Add the sorrel, toss with the melted butter, and let it cook down a little. Add the half-and-half and bring to a simmer, uncovered, for a few minutes until the sorrel leaves become fully cooked and silky and the sauce thickens. Season to taste. Keep warm until ready to serve.

Quick Roasted Garlic and Infused Garlic Oil

Even if you aren't planning to turn on the oven for a slow-roasted dinner, you can roast garlic quickly on the stovetop. Crush roasted garlic into a paste with a pinch of dried spices in a mortar and pestle and use as a flavor base for stews and sauces, mash into potatoes, or simply spread the softened mellow cloves on bread.

Serves 4–6
1 whole head garlic
1 cup oil or cooking fat

Serves 30–40
5 whole heads garlic
4 cups oil or cooking fat

Cut the top and bottom of the head of garlic so that the cloves are exposed. Place in a small cast-iron skillet with high sides, add the oil, and cover. Heat on *very low* heat, letting the garlic roast for 15 to 20 minutes, until the garlic has softened and mellowed but not burned. The oil will be infused with rich garlic flavor—reserve it for incorporating into other sauces and dressings.

PHOTO BY DOUG GOSLING.

Basic Béchamel Sauce

Here is a béchamel sauce that can be used to make simple vegetable gratins or to top the winter pizza on page 306.

Serves 4–6
MAKES 1¼ CUPS
1½ cups whole milk
2 tablespoons unsalted butter
3 tablespoons all-purpose flour
⅛ teaspoon fresh-grated nutmeg
2 teaspoons fresh-chopped thyme
Salt and black pepper to taste

Serves 30–40
MAKES 7 CUPS
6 cups whole milk
½ cup (1 stick) unsalted butter
¾ cup all-purpose flour
½ teaspoon fresh-grated nutmeg
2 tablespoons fresh-chopped thyme
Salt and black pepper to taste

Heat the milk in a small saucepan just until it steams—don't bring it to a boil—and remove from the heat. In another larger heavy-bottomed saucepan, melt the butter on medium heat. When the butter is all melted, add the flour all at once and stir vigorously with a wooden spoon or heat-resistant spatula for about 4 to 6 minutes. Cook until it is a soft golden color and has a nutty aroma. Pour the milk in all at once and switch to a whisk. Whisk until the lumps smooth out. Cook about 10 minutes, stirring constantly, until it reaches the desired consistency (on the thin side for a pizza sauce). Remove from the heat and add the nutmeg, thyme, salt, and pepper.

Winter Squash Dip with Dukkah

Serve with toasted pita and bowls of extra-virgin olive oil and Dukkah, a classic Middle Eastern spice mix (see the following recipe), for dipping.

Serves 4–6

MAKES ABOUT 3 CUPS

2 cups winter squash or pumpkin puree

1 tablespoon tahini

1 clove garlic, crushed

¼ cup fresh lemon juice

2 teaspoons paprika

2 teaspoons cumin

½ cup olive oil

Salt to taste

Serves 30–40

MAKES ABOUT 12 CUPS

8–10 cups winter squash or pumpkin puree

⅓ cup tahini

4 cloves garlic, crushed

1 cup fresh lemon juice

2 tablespoons paprika

2 tablespoons cumin

1½ cups olive oil

Salt to taste

Blend all the ingredients in a food processor. Spoon into a serving bowl, smooth out the surface, and top with a drizzle of olive oil and a sprinkle of paprika.

PHOTO BY TALI AIONA.

Dukkah Spice Mix

This is one of a million versions of the Middle Eastern seed-and-spice mix, sometimes called Zaatar, that is used as an all-purpose crunchy garnish, most commonly for dipping flat bread with olive oil and hummus. Sometimes it contains other nuts such as almonds, hazelnuts, or a multitude of other top-secret spices. Our version uses the seeds left over from winter squash and nigella seeds—aka Persian Pepper or Black Cumin—a culinary species of nigella related to "love in a mist" that we sometimes grow in the Mother Garden. We also grow a wild oregano variety native to the Middle East gathered especially for zaatar, but any oregano will do. It adds a spicy crunch when sprinkled atop roasted vegetables, rice, or sautéed chickpeas, too.

Serves 4–6

MAKES ¾ CUP

¼ cup seeds from the pumpkin or winter
   squash, rinsed and patted dry*

¼ cup sesame seeds

2 tablespoons nigella seeds or 2 teaspoons
   whole cumin seeds

2 teaspoons dried thyme

2 teaspoons dried zaatar oregano

¼ teaspoon fresh-cracked black pepper

½ teaspoon salt

Serves 30–40

MAKES 2¼ CUPS

1 cup seeds from the pumpkin or winter
   squash, rinsed and patted dry*

1 cup sesame seeds

¼ cup nigella seeds or 2 tablespoons
   cumin seeds

1 tablespoon dried thyme

1 tablespoon dried zaatar oregano

1 teaspoon fresh-cracked black pepper

2 teaspoons salt

Using a dry cast-iron skillet on medium-high heat, toast the pumpkin seeds until they are fully toasted and begin to pop. Taste one to make sure they're not too fibrous.* Pulse the seeds in a food processor until the outer shells of the pumpkin seeds are fully broken down. Add to a bowl. Now toast the sesame seeds and whole nigella seeds or cumin seeds for a minute or two in the skillet until they begin to pop. Toss the remaining ingredients together with the seeds. Serve with pita, winter squash dip, and a nice olive oil.

* Not all pumpkins and winter squash make seeds that are especially tasty. Some varieties, such as styrian squash—also called oilseed pumpkins—are bred especially for their seeds, but have mediocre flesh at best. Other sweet-fleshed varieties, like most pie pumpkins, have tough fibrous seeds. Delicatas and butternuts are nice all-purpose varieties to use for this recipe. Taste your seeds after toasting. If they are too fibrous for your liking, replace with store-bought pumpkin seeds or any seed or nut of your choice such as hazelnuts, almonds, or sunflower seeds.

Mixed Winter Citrus Salsa with Yacon and Pineapple Sage

This is a standard pico de gallo recipe, subbing in a diversity of winter citrus for tomatoes and skipping the garlic and onions. Note that the sweet–tart balance has a *huge* range, even among citrus fruits of the same variety, so taste frequently and adjust the level of added lime or lemon juice and salt accordingly. Serve with a Winter Adapted Taco Bar (page 176).

Serves 4–6

MAKES 4 CUPS

3 medium cara-cara or navel oranges

4 small blood oranges

4 satsumas, clementines, mandarins, or
   tangerines

2 cups yacon or jicama, peeled and cubed

¼ cup chopped cilantro

1 teaspoon fresh finely minced manzano
   pepper, or small pinch of cayenne

Salt to taste

⅓ cup olive oil

3 tablespoons Bearss lime juice or ¼ cup
   fresh Meyer lemon juice

Pineapple sage flowers

Serves 30–40

MAKES 10–12 QUARTS

18 medium to large cara-cara or navel
   oranges (about 7 pounds)

24 blood oranges, about 7 pounds

24 satsumas, clementines, mandarins, or
   tangerines (about 7 pounds)

12 cups (about 7 pounds) yacon or jicama,
   peeled and cubed

1 cup chopped cilantro

2 teaspoons fresh finely minced manzano
   pepper, or small pinch of cayenne

Salt to taste

1⅓ cups olive oil

¾ cup Bearss lime juice or 1 cup fresh
   Meyer lemon juice

Pineapple sage flowers

Make citrus "supremes." First, cut off the outer rind and pith with a knife. Then slice the fruit in lengthwise wedges along either side of the segment membranes. Follow this pattern around the fruit, and when just the membranes remain, squeeze out the rest of the juice into the mixing bowl. Chop the supremes into smaller pieces suitable for balancing on a chip.

Peel and cube the yacon slightly smaller than the citrus pieces, chop the cilantro, mince the pepper, and toss everything with the citrus. Add lime or lemon juice, salt, and olive oil. Taste and adjust for salt and tartness until it suits your liking. Sprinkle the top with festive pineapple sage flowers.

PHOTO BY TALI AIONA.

Preserved Meyer Lemons

It is generally too cold to grow regular Eureka lemons here on the coast, but we get a bumper crop of cool-tolerant Meyer lemons every year. A cross between a lemon and a mandarin orange with a soft thin rind, they are juicy, sweet, and floral—quintessential California flavor. Meyers are our favorite, but any lemon variety you can get your hands on will work (we've even experimented with other citrus like kumquats and clementines).

When good lemons are in season and go on sale in the wintertime, stock up and preserve them—they keep unrefrigerated for up to a year, and refrigerated for even longer. The finely minced preserved rind adds a tangy bite to stews, dips, sauces, even risotto. Substitute a few drops of the golden brine wherever you would use fresh lemon and salt together. Once you've gotten used to having this versatile condiment on hand, you'll wonder how you ever lived without it. The small quart-sized batch is enough for a small family to use up in a year. A little goes a long way (note there is up to a whole cup of salt per quart), so feel free to divide the recipe into smaller jars and give away as presents.

Makes 1 quart jar

8–10 lemons

1 cup salt

8 or so whole cardamom pods (optional)

8 black whole peppercorns (optional)

1 bay leaf (optional)

More *fresh* lemon juice, if needed

Makes 5 quart jars

10 pounds (½ produce case) lemons

5 cups salt

2 tablespoons whole cardamom pods (optional)

2 tablespoons whole peppercorns (optional)

5 bay leaves (optional)

More *fresh* lemon juice, if needed

Wash the lemons and pour boiling water over them in a colander in the sink. This both kills bacteria and helps to soften the skins. Pour boiling water over a clean Mason jar, inside and out, and its lid; let dry on a clean rack to sterilize.

Sprinkle 3 tablespoons of salt into the bottom of each jar. Using a sharp knife, cut four lengthwise slits into the lemons but leave them intact at the top and bottom. Pour a tablespoon of salt into each fruit by squeezing open the slits. Then arrange them snugly into the jars, distributing the optional whole spices evenly as you go. Add a little more salt on top of it all and mash everything down with a clean spoon so that as much of the juice comes up to cover the lemons as possible. If the juice isn't covering the tops of the lemons, add a little more fresh lemon juice to top it up. Cover with a plastic lid—salt tends to corrode the metal ones after a while. If you don't have a plastic lid for your Mason jar, fashion a barrier out of plastic wrap or parchment paper and screw the lid over it. Leave for a month in a cool, dark place to cure.

VARIATION

Preserved Lemon Mayo: Stir 1 tablespoon finely minced preserved lemon rind into 1 cup homemade or store-bought mayo. Delicious on fish or asparagus.

SAVORY BAKED GOODS
AND SNACKS

RECIPE LIST

PHOTO BY TALI AIONA.

Kale Chips for Kids

Kale chips earned Janell, OAEC's former kitchen manager, the highest praise she had ever received for her cooking. Resident Ezra, who was six at the time, tried a chip fresh out of the oven and ran to his mother, shouting, "Mom! Mom! These kale chips are better than chocolate cake!" Needless to say, this is a kid-friendly recipe that is sure to please the parents, too. Serve as a snack by themselves or as a crunchy garnish.

Serves 4–6
1 bunch green kale (frizzy kale is best, but any variety will work)
2 tablespoons olive oil
¼ teaspoon sea salt

Serves 30–40
6 bunches green kale (frizzy kale is best, but any variety will work)
⅔ cup olive oil
1½ teaspoons sea salt

Turn on the broiler or preheat the oven to 500°F. Remove the stems from the kale. Tear the leaves into bite-sized pieces (approx. 2 to 3 inches each). If the kale is still wet from washing, spin it in a salad spinner to dry or pat dry with a towel (wet leaves won't crisp as well). Toss the kale with the oil and salt. Use your hands to coat the kale thoroughly, making sure the oil gets into all the crevices.

Spread the kale out in a single layer on a large sheet pan. Bake or broil for 3 minutes, or until the kale starts to brown and crisp. Remove the pan from the oven and, using a large spatula or pancake flipper, turn the kale over. This ensures that it will cook evenly and prevents sogginess. Return the pan to the oven and bake or broil another 2 to 5 minutes. Watch the kale closely, as it only takes a minute to go from perfectly toasted to burned-to-a-crisp!

VARIATION

For a more dramatic presentation, toast the kale leaves whole with their stems. Serve in a vase as a snack or appetizer or as a theatrical garnish to another dish.

Seaweed "Bacon Bits"

This crispy, salty treat is almost as satisfying as the real thing. Amazing in a BLT or on salads, or you can crumble the fried seaweed and use like Japanese furikake—a crispy seaweed sprinkle to accompany rice, fish, or fried eggs.

Serves 4–6
1 cup dried wild nori or 5 nori sheets (the kind for sushi)
Cooking oil or ghee
Salt to taste

Serves 30–40
5 cups dried wild nori or 25 nori sheets (the kind for sushi)
Cooking oil or ghee
Salt to taste

If you're using nori sheets, stack and cut them into 1½-inch bacon-sized strips. If you're using wild nori, use as is in their naturally mismatched pieces. Prepare a plate with paper towels or a reused brown paper bag* for draining. Heat 2 tablespoons of oil on high; when it shimmers, drop in the strips of nori one at a time. If the oil is nice and hot, the seaweed will shrivel up and sizzle immediately—all it really has to do is touch the hot oil for a few seconds and it's done. Remove with tongs and drain. The seaweed will soak up the oil fast, so add a few more tablespoons of oil to the pan as you go and let it heat up before adding more seaweed. Serve whole or crumble as a garnish.

* Remember, grease-soaked paper towels and paper bags can go in the compost, green waste bins, or to feed the worms.

Crispy Fried Beans

Serve these crunchy garnishes as a textural foil like croutons or bacon bits. Sprinkle atop salads, roasted vegetables and gratins, noodles, and more.

Serves 4–6
2 cups small dry beans such as mung,
    adzuki, or split peas
Cooking oil or fat, for frying
Salt to taste

Serves 30–40
8 cups small dry beans such as mung,
    adzuki, or split peas
Cooking oil or fat, for frying
Salt to taste

Soak the beans overnight up to 18 hours. Rinse the beans well, drain, and pat completely dry with towels. Spread the beans out on a towel and let them dry out before frying. Even the smallest amount of moisture will cause the oil to sputter.

Use caution while deep-frying. Heat ½ inch of oil suited for high heat in a frying pan until it shimmers and ripples, about 375°F. Drop in a bean as a tester first. It should pop and sizzle immediately in the oil. If it doesn't—the oil isn't hot enough. When the oil is good and hot, gently add a portion of the beans so that they are completely covered and floating in the oil—in other words, don't overload the pan with too many beans. Let them fry in the oil for about 4 to 7 minutes until they crisp up. Scoop out with a slotted spoon or wire-mesh ladle and lay out on paper towels to drain. Immediately season generously with salt or your favorite spice mix. Work in batches. Remove any floating bits between rounds and start over with fresh oil if it gets cruddy.

VARIATION

Larger beans, such as black-eyed peas, pintos, or chickpeas, can be delicious prepared this way, but need to be par-cooked first and must be perfectly al dente—fully cooked beans will not work, nor will most canned beans, as they fall apart, get mushy, and absorb too much oil. Soak and cook according to directions on page 218 but halt the cooking process when still slightly firm. Rinse well and dry completely. Proceed with deep-frying as directed above.

SERVING IDEAS

- A winter composed salad of mung beans fried in coconut oil atop a salad of frisée, avocado, grapefruit, and watermelon radishes (page 137).
- Black-eyed peas seasoned with Old Bay to top a gumbo.
- Navy beans with crispy garlic and rosemary over sautéed savoy cabbage. Before frying the beans, fry a few rosemary sprigs and slices of garlic in the same oil.
- Adzuki beans fried in high-heat sesame oil on top of noodles, wilted shungiku, and black sesame seeds.
- Chickpeas tossed with crunchy salt, smoked paprika, and a tiny squeeze of lemon juice as a snack or side all by themselves.
- Black beans with crispy sage (fry the sage first in the same oil) on top of roasted winter squash and wilted escarole.
- Yellow split peas tossed in curry powder atop rice with vegetable masala.

PHOTO BY TALI AIONA.

Heirloom Tomato Mozzarella Pie

This tart is chef Gabriel Tiradani's famously decadent and addictive crowd pleaser. Make multiple tarts (about six to eight) for a group of 30 to 40, as tart pans don't come in extra-large.

Serves 4–6

MAKES ONE 10-INCH TART

BASIC FLAKY BUTTER CRUST

1¼ cups all-purpose flour, plus a little
  for dusting
2 teaspoons sugar
½ teaspoon salt
½ cup (1 stick) cold butter
¼ cup ice-cold water

FILLING

1 cup Basil Flower Pistou (page 268)
4 large heirloom tomatoes
4 ounces fresh mozzarella, in small rounds
2 cups grated mozzarella cheese
Salt and pepper to taste

Preheat the oven to 375°F. Measure the flour, sugar, and salt into the bowl of a food processor and pulse to incorporate. Cut the cold butter into small squares and add a little at a time. Pulse the dough until the butter is mostly cut small and worked in but there are still a few larger pea-sized chunks. Add the water in a steady stream while the motor is running. Be sure not to overmix—the water should incorporate in 30 seconds or less. Turn the dough out onto a floured surface and press it together. It should be a bit shaggy and come together as you press. Moisture content can vary in different weather conditions and in different places of the world. If the dough still feels really dry and crumbly, add a few more sprinklings of water.

Roll the dough into a log. Turn the log on end and flatten it out so that you have a round disk about 5 inches in diameter. Wrap in plastic. Chill for at least 1 hour before rolling out to bake. This dough can be frozen for up to 2 months.

To par-bake the crust: Prepare a 10-inch tart pan by lightly brushing it with olive oil. Roll out the prepared flaky crust bigger than your tart pan, about 16 inches in diameter. Transfer the dough into the pan and press into the crease. Trim the excess dough and dock the bottom of the crust with fork marks. Place in the refrigerator for 20 to 30 minutes. This can be done ahead of time.

After the dough has chilled, line the shell with aluminum foil or parchment paper and fill with about 2 cups of dry beans on top to weight it down while it par-bakes. Bake for 15 minutes, then remove the foil and bean weights, and bake for another 10 to 15 minutes until light golden in color.

While the tart is blind baking, make the basil sauce. Also, wash and slice the tomatoes ½ inch thick and reserve. Cut small rounds of mozzarella in half.

When the crust is done par-baking, smooth the basil sauce on the bottom; layer on the grated mozzarella, then the slices of tomato in a circular pattern. Fill in the gaps with the fresh mozzarella. Sprinkle with salt and freshly ground pepper. Bake for 20 to 25 minutes. After you remove the pie from the oven, let it cool slightly, about 10 minutes. Serve warm. The prepared tart can be refrigerated for up to 2 days.

Tricolor Corn Bread

According to Michael Pollan in his book *In Defense of Food*,[11] 99 percent of Americans get a third of their calories from one crop: corn. Not the hundreds of artisan varieties of corn originally bred by farmers in Mexico, one single variety of genetically modified corn patented and owned by one multinational corporation. As a wind-pollinated crop whose pollen can travel for miles, corn is a very tricky crop to save seed on, so heirloom corn varieties are becoming increasingly rare.

This bread is as good as the cornmeal. Freshly grown and ground heirloom cornmeals such as Bloody Butcher, Hickory King, Oaxacan Green, or Hopi Blue are what make this bread deliciously different. A coarse grind gives the bread a nice texture. Chef Ali Ghiorse makes one batch of each color of cornmeal and serves the assorted kinds stacked like a checkerboard.

Serves 4–6

**MAKES ONE 9 X 13-INCH BAKING PAN
OR ONE 12-INCH CAST-IRON SKILLET**

2 cups cornmeal—preferably an heirloom
    corn, freshly grown and ground into a
    coarse meal

2 cups flour

2 teaspoons baking powder

1½ teaspoons sea salt

½ cup maple syrup

½ cup safflower oil

2 cups water

Melted butter

Coarse sea salt

Serves 30–40

**MAKES ONE 21 X 13-INCH HOTEL PAN
OR TWO 16-INCH CAST-IRON SKILLETS**

8 cups cornmeal—preferably an heirloom
    corn, freshly grown and ground into a
    coarse meal

8 cups flour

2 tablespoons baking powder

2 tablespoons sea salt

2 cups maple syrup

2 cups safflower oil

8 cups water

Melted butter

Coarse sea salt

Preheat the oven to 350°F. Lightly grease a baking pan or cast-iron pan. Sift the dry ingredients into a bowl. In a separate bowl, mix the wet ingredients. Combine the wet and dry and mix thoroughly. Spread the batter into the baking pan. Bake until golden brown, about 30 minutes. Just before removing baked bread from the oven, brush the top with melted butter and dust with coarse sea salt.

Pictured is a variety of rare red sweet corn called Red Stalker. Reminiscent of pomegranate seeds, the fresh kernels are wonderful on top of salads, in salsa, or stirred into fresh corn polenta. The deep-scarlet husks are incredible for wrapping tamales. PHOTO BY DOUG GOSLING.

Chickpea Flat Bread

We rely heavily on this healthy, quick, and easy standby. Sometimes called farinata or socca, it is a nutty-flavored, high-protein pancake that takes well to a wide variety of dips and spreads, such as any of our seasonal pestos, Olive Walnut Tapenade (page 281), Gaby's Baba Ganoush (page 272), or Pasilla Pumpkin Seed Pesto (page 276).

Serves 4–6
MAKES ONE 12-INCH SKILLET
1–1½ cups garbanzo flour
2 cups water
3 tablespoons olive oil, plus a dash more
     for the pan
½ teaspoon salt
¼ teaspoon black pepper
Choose one or two optional spices:
     ½ teaspoon whole toasted cumin seeds,
     ¼ teaspoon chili flakes, 4–5 fried sage
     leaves, ½ teaspoon minced rosemary,
     ½ teaspoon smoked paprika

Serves 30–40
MAKES TWO FULL-SIZED
18 X 26-INCH SHEET PANS*
12–16 cups garbanzo flour
20 cups water
2 cups olive oil, plus a dash more for the pan
2 tablespoons salt
1 tablespoon black pepper
Choose one or two optional spices: ¼ cup
     whole toasted cumin seeds, 2 teaspoons
     chili flakes, 12–20 fried sage leaves, ¼ cup
     minced rosemary, ¼ cup smoked paprika

In a medium mixing bowl, sift the garbanzo flour. Whisk in the water, oil, salt, and pepper together to form a thin, clump-free batter. Garbanzo flour can vary, so start with 1 cup (12 cups) and add a little more, up to 1½ cups (16 cups), until you get the consistency of heavy cream. Cover with a towel and let sit for at least 30 minutes to an hour. It should thicken a bit more as it sits.

Preheat the oven to 450°F. Pour a generous dash of olive oil into your cast-iron skillet or sheet tray and place in the oven to preheat for 10 minutes. Preheating the pan and oil makes the pancake really crispy on the edges. Remove the hot skillet or sheet pan and gently pour in just enough batter to form a ¼-inch-thick layer. Sprinkle with optional spices. Bake for 15 to 20 minutes until the edges become golden and crispy. Let cool slightly, cut into wedges, and serve.

VARIATION

Crepe/Dosa: Drizzle spoonfuls of batter onto a very hot griddle or wide cast-iron skillet on the stovetop on high heat to form thin, saucer-sized crepes. When cooked on one side, flip and crisp the other side. Serve topped with goat cheese, pesto, greens, et cetera. Or for an Indian-style crepe similar to a dosa (dosas technically use a lentil flour batter, though the flavor is similar), top with curried vegetables or Indian pickles and a dollop of chutney or raita. An elegant and nutritious crepe for any meal of the day.

* Using a skillet makes a much crisper flat bread, but this isn't practical for a large group. The best substitute is a large sheet pan on top of a preheated pizza stone.

Soaked and Toasted Walnuts

Soaking nuts catalyzes the sprouting process and converts some of the starch into protein. Aside from the health benefits, this process has the added taste perk of removing the astringency and smoothing out the tannic edge of the papery skins.

Serves 4–6
1 cup raw walnuts
4 cups water
½ teaspoon salt

Serves 30–40
6 cups walnuts
6 quarts water
1 tablespoon salt

Soak the walnuts in salted water overnight, 6 to 10 hours. Rinse the walnuts, pat them dry, and spread in a single layer on a cookie sheet. Toast in a 200°F oven for about 1½ hours or until the walnuts crisp up.

Roasted Luther Burbank Chestnuts

Luther Burbank (1849–1926), West Sonoma County resident and world-renowned horticulturalist, was famous for his pioneering work in plant breeding. His groundbreaking development of some 800 new varieties of food crops at his experimental farm in nearby Sebastopol include a thornless blackberry, the predecessor of the Idaho russet potato, winter rhubarb, and many California nuts and stone fruits in production today, including our beloved Santa Rosa plum and an avocado that thrives even in chilly coastal Northern California. His experimentation in cross-pollinating for disease hardiness resulted in a chestnut hybrid of European and Chinese varieties that boasts resistance to the devastating chestnut blight that wiped the North American continent of its native chestnuts in the last century. There are still a few giant Luther Burbank chestnut trees planted on old homesteading properties throughout West Sonoma County today.[12]

Serves 4–6
2 cups chestnuts, husked

Serves 30–40
8–12 cups chestnuts, husked

With leather work gloves, remove the nut from the barbed outer husk. Score the thin skin of each nut with sharp knife in a crosshatch. Roast on a cookie sheet in a 450°F oven for 30 minutes or on top of a wood-burning stove for a few hours, shaking the pan periodically for even cooking. As soon as the chestnuts are cool enough to handle, peel immediately—otherwise the skins harden and they become difficult to peel once completely cooled.

Toasted Hazelnuts with Thyme

Serves 4–6
1 cup raw hazelnuts
1 tablespoon oil
1 sprig fresh thyme
Generous sprinkle of salt

Serves 30–40
6 cups raw hazelnuts
¼ cup oil
3–6 sprigs fresh thyme
Generous sprinkle of salt

Preheat the oven to 325°F. Spread the hazelnuts on a cookie sheet and toast for 25 minutes or so until they begin to darken slightly. Keep a close eye on them, as they can go from perfect to burned in a heartbeat. Remove from the oven and allow to cool slightly.

To winnow, pour the nuts out onto a clean kitchen towel and fold the towel over to cover them. With your hands, rub the nuts back and forth until their papery skins loosen and flake off in the towel. Open up the towel and let the skins settle to the bottom. Roll the peeled nuts off into a bowl and discard the skins (shake the towel outside). There may be a few that didn't release their skins or others that could benefit from another round of towel rubbing. Repeat the process if desired, but it isn't necessary to remove every scrap of skin. Toss with oil, thyme, and salt.

Pan-Fried Almonds with Rosemary

Serves 4–6
1 cup almonds
¼ cup oil
1 sprig fresh rosemary
Generous sprinkle of salt

Serves 30–40
6 cups almonds
1 cup oil
3–6 sprigs fresh rosemary
Generous sprinkle of salt

Warm up a cast-iron skillet on medium-high heat. Add all the ingredients and fry, stirring frequently with a wooden spoon, until the almonds begin to darken in color and the rosemary gets crispy, about 7 minutes. Taste and add more salt if needed.

Popped Amaranth

Loved for its beauty as an ornamental as well as its versatility as both a green and a grain, we promote amaranth seeds widely at our seed exchanges. Generous, resilient, and grown on almost every continent, amaranth is one of the world's most nutritious and protein-rich plants. Its seeds are used whole, ground into flour, or popped like miniature popcorn. Popped amaranth seed makes a fun snack, cold breakfast cereal (think mini Rice Krispies), or textural addition to muffins, cookies, and caramel corn.

1 tablespoon amaranth seed =
⅓ cup popped

Put 1 or 2 tablespoons of amaranth seeds into the bottom of a dry, high-sided pot with a lid. Don't be tempted to put more than 2 tablespoons in at a time as the little puffs burn quickly. Cover, turn the heat onto high, and shake continuously, like popcorn, until the tiny seeds have mostly popped. Dump the popped seeds out into a bowl as soon as the popping has slowed down, otherwise the residual heat in the pot will burn them. Unfortunately, popped amaranth isn't great for making in huge amounts (air poppers have holes that the tiny seeds fall down into).

To harvest amaranth for grain or seed, shake the seed head over a large paper bag every few days throughout the late-fall dry season while the plant is still in the ground and the stalk dries down. Before the winter rains come, cut the seed heads off and store in a paper bag. When completely dry and ready to process, crush the dried seed heads with your hands so that the tiny seeds are loosened. Shake through a fine screen into a bowl and winnow off the chaff.

PHOTO BY DOUG GOSLING.

WEEKNIGHT COMMUNITY DINNER

We hire cooks from our OAEC team to prepare food for large workshops, but most nights of the year, especially during the winter slow season, the residential community of around 20 people shares dinner together by taking turns with the cooking. Like most American households with full-time jobs and busy schedules, each of us individually does not have time to make a healthy dinner from scratch every night, as seen in many of the meals featured in this book. But with rotating kitchen duties, we each only have to cook dinner once every two or three weeks, if that. So when your night rolls around, it's like throwing a dinner party! We have time to plan ahead and take great pride in preparing something delicious and wholesome for everyone, each one trying to outdo the other with an over-the-top creation that we could never otherwise pull off on a daily basis.

Preparing a community dinner at OAEC usually starts with the question "What do I feel like eating?" Chances are, that's what everyone else wants, too. Is it time for a BBQ or a cozy dinner by the woodstove? Then comes a stroll through the garden to harvest the requisite salad plus whatever else is abundant and looking vibrant. What's in the "up for grabs" section of the walk-in cooler that needs using up? Check the chalkboard for a head count—who has signed out for dinner or is anyone expecting extra guests? Once all the variables are accounted for and a plan is made, it's time to dig in. Start to finish, most people take around three hours to pull it together, from harvest to dinner bell, plus another couple of hours for the cleanup—sounds like a lot, but the payoff is that for the rest of the month, it's simply a matter of showing up to the feast!

WEEKNIGHT COMMUNITY DINNER MENU

Winter Sourdough Pizza Duo: one with winter pesto, celery root, olives, and almonds, the other with béchamel, winter squash, radicchio, parsley, and lemon

Easy roasted cauliflower

Wintry Oven-Crisped Tree Collards

Winter Biodiversity Salad Mix with Preserved Lemon Brine Salad Dressing

Jacob's Lavender Crème Brûlée

PHOTO BY JIM COLEMAN.

Winter Sourdough Pizza Duo

Resident chef Gabriel Tiradani created these pizzas in the heart of wintertime, long after the last ripe garden tomato came through the kitchen, and wanted to highlight the garden offerings of winter in these two pizzas paired together: one with winter pesto, celery root, olives, and almonds; the other with béchamel, winter squash, radicchio, parsley, and lemon. As always, you are welcome to improvise additional toppings, such as fresh ricotta or chèvre instead of or in addition to mozzarella, or add any fresh herbs that might be ready in your garden.

PIZZA DOUGH

Serves 6

**MAKES FOUR 12-INCH PIZZAS
(1000G DOUGH)**

3 cups bread flour

1½ cups water

1 teaspoon sea salt

¾ cup sourdough starter (page 309)

Serves 30–40

**MAKES SIXTEEN 12-INCH PIZZAS
(4000G DOUGH)**

13 cups bread flour

6 cups water (70°F)

2 tablespoons plus 1 teaspoon sea salt

3½ cups sour dough starter (page 309)

To make the small batch: Place all the ingredients in the bowl of a stand mixer. Mix on low with the dough hook for 2 minutes. Increase the speed to medium and mix for 4 minutes to develop the gluten. The dough should be elastic and smooth.

To make the large batch: Place all ingredients into a clean bus tub or a 12-quart cambro. Mix by hand using a squeezing motion with your hands. Have a plastic dough scraper nearby to scrape the sides of the tub down and scrape the dough from your hands. The hand method takes a lot of upper-arm strength; it helps to have the tub you are mixing in about waist-high so that you can lean into it. Once it is all mostly incorporated, you can start folding the dough over and onto itself to create strength and develop the gluten. Dough should be semi-smooth. Don't worry if it still looks shaggy; it will smooth out as it ferments and is folded.

Place the dough into an oiled bowl or cambro and cover with a dish towel. Put in a warm place (70°F) to let rise for 2 hours total. One hour into the rise, fold the dough: Grab one side of the dough, lift up, and let it stretch then fall over the top. Do this to the four sides of the dough and let rise the final hour.

After the dough has risen for 2 hours, turn it out onto a floured counter. With a dough knife, divide the dough into four 250-gram portions (16 portions for the large batch). Shape the dough portions into tight boules or rounds by cupping the dough in your hand and rolling it against the table in a circular motion. Place the dough balls on a heavily floured sheet pan about 3 inches apart. Wrap well and refrigerate overnight or a minimum of 5 hours.

Preheat the oven to 450°F (if you're using a baking stone, make sure it is in the oven getting hot while you're preheating). Remove the dough from the refrigerator. Take each ball of dough and work it open by rotating it in your hand, letting gravity stretch the dough into a bigger circle. Place onto a well-floured or cornmealed cutting board or pizza peel. Arrange the toppings. Slide off the peel onto the pizza stone. Bake until the underside is golden and the crust is dark. Time will vary depending on your oven. Remove, cut, and serve hot!

---

* For a proper pizza party, plan on about one 12-inch pizza (250 grams of dough) for every two people. The proportions listed in this recipe assume that you will make both variations of pizza. In other words, they are designed to be paired together, so if you want only one kind of pizza, then double the amount of dough and toppings. Ready to improvise? Just make the basic dough recipe at the top and eyeball the toppings—about ¾ cup of sauce, ¼ pound of shredded cheese, and 2 cups of assorted toppings per 12-inch pizza.

SOURDOUGH PIZZA WITH WINTER PESTO, CELERY ROOT, OLIVES, AND ALMONDS

Serves 4–6 when paired with the other variation*
500g sourdough pizza dough, divided into two 12-inch pizzas
1½ cups marjoram pistou (page 286)
½ pound grated mozzarella
2 cups slivered celery root, tossed with olive oil and salt and
    roasted at 350°F for 25 minutes
½ cup cured olives, chopped
½ cup almonds, chopped
1 cup grated Parmesan

Serves 30–40 when paired with the other variation*
2000g sourdough pizza dough, divided into eight 12-inch pizzas
5 cups marjoram pistou (page 286)
1½ pounds grated mozzarella
16 cups slivered celery root, tossed with olive oil and salt and
    roasted at 350°F for 25 minutes
2 cups cured olives, chopped
2 cups almonds, chopped
2½ cups grated Parmesan

Stretch out your pizza dough on a cutting board sprinkled with lots of cornmeal to prevent sticking. Layer on the toppings by starting with a thin layer of winter pesto, then mozzarella, then a layer of roasted celery root, olives, and almonds. Top with Parmesan last. See the baking instructions opposite.

SOURDOUGH PIZZA WITH BÉCHAMEL, WINTER SQUASH, RADICCHIO, PARSLEY, AND LEMON

Serves 4–6 when paired with the other variation*
500g sourdough pizza dough, divided into two 12-inch pizzas
1¾ cups Basic Béchamel Sauce (page 287)
½ pound grated mozzarella
4 cups cubed winter squash, tossed with olive oil, crushed garlic,
    and salt, and roasted at 350°F for 30 minutes
1 large head radicchio, sliced thin
½ cup finely chopped parsley
Zest of 1 lemon
1 cup grated Parmesan

Serves 30–40 when paired with the other variation*
1000g sourdough pizza dough, divided into eight 12-inch pizzas
7 cups Basic Béchamel Sauce (page 287)
1½ pounds grated mozzarella
10 cups cubed winter squash, tossed with olive oil, crushed garlic,
    and salt, and roasted at 350° for 30 minutes
4 large heads radicchio, sliced thin
2 cups finely chopped parsley
Zest of 3 lemons
2½ cups grated Parmesan

Stretch out your pizza dough on a cutting board sprinkled with lots of cornmeal to prevent sticking. Layer on the toppings by starting with a thin layer of béchamel, then a layer of mozzarella. Next, a handful of roasted winter squash, sliced radicchio, a smattering of chopped parsley and lemon zest. Finish with the Parmesan last. See the baking instructions opposite.

STARTING A SOURDOUGH CULTURE: TAMING THE WILD YEAST

by OAEC chef Gabriel Tiradani

We are so lucky to be in an area of the world where there is an abundance of wild yeast in the air. To make a sourdough starter, also known as levain, you have to make an inviting environment for a combination of yeast (*Saccharomyces exiguous*) and bacteria (*Lactobacillus*) to live, grow, and give rise to your bread. This mixture is a paste of flour and water, from the freshest wheat berries possible and filtered water. It is then set out in your kitchen and allowed to breathe the air you breathe. The starter is freshened or fed every day until you start to see a regular pattern of expansion and contraction from enzyme activity. Once the sourdough starter rises and falls predictably, it is then stable and can be used every day or fed every day for future use. You will see that taking care of your sourdough starter will be like having an addition to your family. I started one 12 years ago on rye and wheat that I grew on my farm, and it has continued to live and feed many. I have traveled with my starter across the country twice and shared it with family, friends, and even strangers. This ancient act of tending yeast is so simple and yet so profound: to make leavening happen from two tangible ingredients and a third immeasurable ingredient-spirit.

PHOTO BY TALI AIONA.

Day 1

Have ready a clean quart-sized container, either a jar or a plastic container with a lid. In the container, mix ½ cup filtered water with ¼ cup rye flour and ¼ cup white bread flour. Mix well with a spoon and scrape the sides and flatten the paste. Leave this starter out, covered, for 24 hours in a warmish room.

Day 2

Hopefully you can see some activity on day 2—a few bubbles here and there, and perhaps a rise in the dough mix from the day before. If you see no growth or bubbles, then leave it for another 12 hours.

Discard all but ⅓ cup of the starter paste and feed it with ⅓ cup water, 2 tablespoons rye flour, and ⅓ cup white bread flour.

Day 3 and On

Feed as you did before: ⅓ cup starter, ⅓ cup water, ⅓ cup white bread flour, and 2 tablespoons rye. Continue doing this every 12 hours. By day 4, the starter will be very active and will fall into a predictable rhythm of rising and falling. At this point, you can feed the starter all white flour; by days 5 through 7, you should have a natural levain sourdough starter! If you want to grow your starter to a larger volume, just use the equal proportions (for the miche recipe here, you will want to grow the starter—1 cup starter, 1 cup water, 1 cup flour).

If you will not be using your starter every day and don't have time to feed it, you can put it to rest in the refrigerator. Make sure it is in a sealed container and take it out to feed every 1 to 2 weeks. Discard any dark water that collects on the top and feed as above, with equal parts starter, water, and flour.

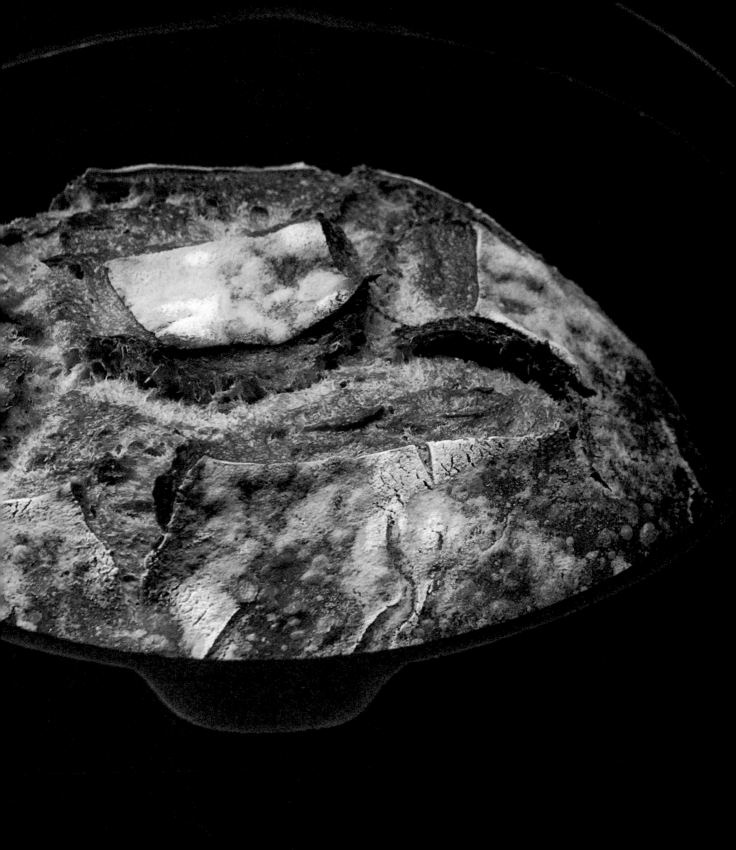

PHOTO BY TALI AIONA.

Hand-Mixed Miche Bread

Miche is the ultimate community bread: large enough to feed at least 20 and crusty with a distinctive fermented flavor of sourdough. A miche loaf begs to be the bread you serve alongside a hearty soup for supper, or the bread you wake up to with jam and butter. It is the all-around everyday bread. When miche comes out of the oven at OAEC, word spreads like wildfire. People stream into the kitchen for a slice of steamy hot bread to commune together for a moment before going back to their day.

Historically, French villages had communal ovens where the people would bring their dough to be baked, and the miches weighed from 4 to as much as 12 pounds. The large loaves would feed a family for days or weeks, until the next baking day. Today you can often buy miche by the quarter or half loaf. But why not make your own communal loaf and share it with friends and family? Take a moment and break bread together.

Miche is, by design, a large communal loaf—enough for 15 to 20 people to share in a single meal, or a week's worth of bread for a family of four to six people. For gatherings of 30 to 40 people, double the recipe, or—depending on the heaviness of the other dishes in the meal you are serving it with—triple it to be on the safe side. This is a hand-kneaded, artisanal bread, so unless you have a giant industrial mixer (we don't), it's best to measure and mix the dough in sequential batches and bake three loaves of this size.

MAKES ONE 2-KILO LOAF
IN A 4- TO 6-QUART DUTCH OVEN

5¼ cups bread flour
1 cup whole wheat flour
⅓ cup rye flour
1 tablespoon plus ½ teaspoon salt
3 cups water (68°–70°F)
2 cups liquid levain (sourdough starter)
Dash of olive oil for the bowl

Place all the ingredients into a very large bowl or a plastic bin. Since you will be mixing by hand, you want enough room to push the dough around. Mix all the ingredients with your hands, squeezing the dough to get a thorough mix for about 5 minutes or until it comes together. Your dough might look a bit shaggy, but don't worry: The strength for this dough comes from many folds in the fermenting process.

Grease a medium bowl with a little olive oil. Place the dough into the oiled bowl and set in a warm place. The dough will need to ferment for 3 hours with three folds spread out in the fermenting time. Make sure to note the time you finish mixing and the end of the fermenting time. I like to do this on a piece of masking tape with the time the dough was finished and the three folding times.

To fold the dough, lift one end, pull up, let it fold over the mound of dough in the middle, then repeat on all four sides. After you have pulled and folded on all sides, flip the dough over so the smooth underside is up: This is one fold. Repeat this three times in the three hours. The folds increase the strength of the dough and release any build up of fermentation gas.

After the 3 hours, the dough is ready to be shaped. Turn it out onto a floured surface, stretching the sides out and over, folding up the mound of dough into a ball one more time. Flip the dough so that the smooth side is up. Cup your hands around the dough, pinkie fingers resting on the table surface and thumbs up. Start pulling and pushing the dough in a round circular motion to tighten the gluten. This shape is called a *boule*.

Have ready another bowl with a clean tightly woven kitchen towel lying in it. Coat it with plenty of flour—whole wheat flour is good to use for the towel. Place the tight boule top-side down and bottom-seam-side up. Be sure you have a good amount of flour down to prevent the dough from sticking. Fold the towel over to cover the dough. Place in the refrigerator overnight—12 to 15 hours.

When you're ready to bake, preheat the oven to 450°F. Have ready a 4- or 6-quart Dutch oven. When the oven is hot, put the Dutch oven (with the lid) in for 20 minutes to get it completely hot. Pull out the dough from the refrigerator and let it get the chill off. When the pan is hot, take it out of the oven (carefully!), unmold your bread from the towel, and place it seam-side down in the hot Dutch oven. Score the top with a very sharp knife or a lamm (bread baker's razor) in any pattern you like. The scoring gives the bread a place to expand from; otherwise it will just tear. I often score a simple diamond with the cuts overlapping.

Place in the oven with the lid on. Turn the oven down to 400°F. Remove the lid after 25 minutes and continue baking for another 35 to 40 minutes until the crust is golden to dark brown. Remove from the hot pan immediately and cool on a wire rack for at least 1 hour.

PHOTO BY TALI AIONA.

PHOTO BY TALI AIONA.

RECIPE LIST

Good Morning Tea

One of the beauties of having a backyard garden, or even a container garden on your porch, is being able to step outside and pick some fresh herbs for tea. As your mood and the seasons change, so does the brew. Mixing and matching, picking what is calling, and brewing a tea is an easy way to engage the garden on a daily basis.

In the Mother Garden, our herbs are interspersed throughout. Some are beloved volunteers that show up where they will, and if that's in a convenient spot, they get to stay. Some grace our perennial border beds, some are in the herb circle, and some can be found at the edges of the garden, along pathways, and wherever they may pop up.

On this foggy morning, as we travel the garden picking our many-ingredient salad mix, it is easy to reach over and collect herbs for tea as well: borage, a volunteer in the bed next to the cut-and-come-again salad mix; chamomile from a whole bed that has volunteered where last year's planting was; lavender from the border bed; lemon balm from the path to the kitchen; a handful of rose petals. This morning ritual, a favorite of former OAEC gardner and kitchen manager Kalanete Baruch, eases stress and is sure to set the day right.

The small batch makes enough to share, or you can fill a quart-sized Mason jar for yourself to carry with you all day.

Serves 4 people

MAKES 1 QUART

A handful (1 loosely packed cup) fresh
   garden herbs—chamomile, lavender,
   borage, lemon verbena, thyme, yerba
   buena, mint . . .
1 quart hot water

Serves 30–40

**MAKES 1 GALLON (ENOUGH FOR TWO
9-CUP-CAPACITY HOT PUMP POTS)**

4–6 packed cups fresh garden herbs—
   chamomile, lavender, borage, lemon
   verbena, thyme, yerba buena, mint . . .
1 gallon hot water

Take a walk in the garden and pick a good handful (or basketful) of herbs. Boil the water. Turn off the heat, and add the herbs, cover, and let steep for 5 to 10 minutes. Strain and enjoy with breakfast or throughout the day.

PHOTO BY DOUG GOSLING.

Ridgetop to Rivermouth: Foods from Our Watershed

Right now, you and this book are in a watershed, a natural drainage basin extending from the ridgetops to where the river mouth empties into the ocean. Not just static geology, this watershed is a complex super-organism that includes the landforms that define its boundaries as well as you and all other life in it. Dependence on the health of this common water system binds us together with our neighbors and with other species in a relationship that calls for collaborative awareness and stewardship.

Our Dutch Bill Creek watershed begins as rain falls on the tops of the rolling hills around Occidental, studded with Douglas fir and open oak savannas. The water trickles its way down through pastures and vineyards, then meanders through the redwood-tree-lined canyons of Camp Meeker, and eventually joins the Russian River about 6 miles north of OAEC. As one of the final small tributaries to feed into the wide and mighty Russian River, Dutch Bill Creek merges with one of the largest drainage basins in Northern California, which encompasses much of Sonoma and inland Mendocino Counties. The fertile floodplain and estuary along the final miles of the Russian, where fresh meets salt water, is occupied by a rare mix of animal life—herons, white egrets, river and sea otters, and an abundance of fresh- and saltwater fish. Tumbling

amid the roiling surf of river current that plunges into the salty waves, a colony of harbor seals hunts for eels and salmon while great white sharks hunt for them!

While our tiny watershed territory is sparsely populated with little heavy industry, the potential for erosion and pollution into the creek from real estate development, overgrazing, and industrial viticulture must be kept in check to protect this delicate bionetwork downstream.

Producing and enjoying premium food and wine comes with the responsibility to maintain clean water and pristine ecosystems. As locavores ponder the definition of *local food*, an awareness of and concern for the health of one's own regional watershed is an excellent place to start. What relationships define your watershed?

PHOTO BY TALI AIONA.

Drinking Water with Seasonal Garnishes

So often taken for granted, clean drinking water is the highest purpose of H_2O. With herbs and flowers from the garden to spruce up ordinary pitchers or coolers of water, even a weekday lunch becomes a reminder and celebration of its importance. May all have clean water to drink.

We serve a large crystal punch bowl or glass beverage dispenser of cold-infused herb water bedazzled with a multicolored flotilla of sweet edible flowers at our plant sales and garden parties. The amounts listed here are for longer events—figure that each person will (or at least should!) drink between 1 pint and 1 quart of water over the course of 3 or 4 hours, especially when it's hot out or if alcoholic beverages will be served.

Serves 4–6
1 gallon cold water
A few sprigs melissa, lemon balm,
    rose geranium, or basil
A few sprigs peppermint and/or spearmint
Sweet edible flowers

Serves 30–40
6–8 gallons cold water
1 bunch melissa, lemon balm,
    rose geranium, or basil
1 bunch peppermint and/or spearmint
Sweet edible flowers

Simply wash the herbs and allow then to steep overnight in the cold water to capture their ephemeral flavor. Serve with a sprinkling of sweet edible flower petals.

VARIATIONS

Forgot to infuse the herbs ahead of time? No worries, just garnish each gallon of fresh water with: 6–8 slices of fruit, 5 sprigs of herbs, 2 tablespoons of edible flowers. Serve within a few hours, as the fruit won't keep. Here are some ideas:

Spring: Mint + Johnny jump-ups; orange slices + fennel fronds + borage; lovage + apple, peach, or plum blossoms; loquats + pineapple sage; lemon + chamomile flowers
Summer: Strawberry + rose geranium + rose petals; cucumber + basil + borage flowers; wild plums + anise hyssop + carnation petals; blood peaches + holy basil + sunflower petals; melon + purple shiso
Fall: Apple + rosemary flowers; persimmon + calendula petals; pear + lemon thyme
Winter: Meyer lemon + rose petals; mandarin + rosemary; sweet pepino + mint

Ridgetop Fir-Tip Tisane

Douglas fir is found growing all over North America and Europe. The young, tender tips make a zingy vitamin-C-infused herbal tea.

For 1 cup of tea
1 Douglas fir tip
1 cup water

Pick the bright green Douglas fir tips from this spring's growth, as opposed to the older needles that are dark green and waxy. Place one tip in each cup and pour in hot boiling water. Steep and enjoy as a closure to a meal.

PHOTO BY TALI AIONA.

Mother Garden Bitters

Medicine is everywhere. It's in the weeds pushing up in the sidewalk, the cultivated plants growing in the front yard, and the native shrubs and trees growing wild in a park. The Mother Garden at OAEC—where all the plants in this recipe can be found—balances the wild and cultivated.

Bitter foods and herbs are the people's medicine and have long been used in liqueurs in the form of aperitifs and digestifs to support digestion. They promote the secretion of digestive juices, which break down foods and provide essential nutrients for life. Historically, bitter herbs and greens like dandelion, chicory, endive, and escarole were considered an essential part of meals, but modern tastes tend to avoid this important flavor. Bitters consist of herbs that taste bitter (dandelion root, artichoke leaf, and motherwort) in addition to other aromatic and spicy herbs (fennel seed and orange peel) that add flavor and warmth. Bitters connect the wild medicine of herbs with the food at our table, activating our senses and supporting our body.

Approximately 10 to 15 minutes before each meal, herbalist and former garden intern Bryan Bowen recommends following the ancient tradition of waking up your digestion with this infused liqueur. Enjoy a tablespoon or two added to mixed drinks, to soda water, or to a little water. Dry herbs are best for this recipe.

Makes 1½ cups

FOR 1 PINT JAR

2 tablespoons angelica root
2 tablespoons dandelion root
2 tablespoons artichoke leaf
2 tablespoons fennel seed
2 teaspoons motherwort leaf
2 teaspoons orange peel
Vodka, brandy, or other liquor to cover,
  about 1½ cups

Makes 3 cups

FOR 1 QUART JAR

½ cup angelica root
½ cup dandelion root
½ cup artichoke leaf
½ cup fennel seed
¼ cup motherwort leaf
¼ cup orange peel
Vodka, brandy, or other liquor to cover,
  about 3 cups

Add the herbs to a Mason or other jar. Pour the vodka (or brandy or other liquor, though vodka has a neutral taste that allows the flavor of the herbs to flourish) to cover the herbs by at least 1 inch. Let soak for 3 weeks, strain, and bottle.

Michelle's Blueberry Melissa "Wine"

Michelle Vesser serves this nonalcoholic drink with dinners in the garden during her Healing with Food, Herbs, Gardening and Ceremony course. It has the dry and subtle flavor complexities of wine and is enjoyable sipped with conversation or paired with food. Sure to lighten the spirits without the spirits!

Serves 4–6
3 quarts water
A few sprigs of melissa
A few sprigs of spearmint
1 fresh stevia leaf, 1 teaspoon dried
    stevia leaf, or ⅛ teaspoon liquid stevia
    concentrate (optional)
1 (8-ounce) jar unsweetened blueberry juice

Serves 30–40
4 gallons water
1 bunch melissa
1 bunch spearmint
5 fresh stevia leaves, 1½ tablespoons
    dried stevia leaf, or ½ teaspoon liquid
    concentrate (optional)
2 (16-ounce) jars unsweetened blueberry juice

Bring the water to a boil then turn off the heat and add the melissa, spearmint, and sweetener. Allow the herbs to steep until the liquid cools to room temperature. Then strain out the herbs, add the juice, and refrigerate until chilled. Serve in wineglasses.

Mallow Hibiscus Cooler

Mallow is a benevolent summer herb found volunteering in summer gardens almost everywhere in America. The root is deeply hydrating on a hot summer day, as is vitamin-C-packed hibiscus flower. You can find hibiscus flowers or "Jamaica" in Mexican grocery stores.

Serves 4–6
2 quarts water
¼ cup dried or ⅔ cup fresh, scrubbed
    mallow root
⅓ cup dried hibiscus flowers
Sweetener to taste

Serves 30–40
2 gallons water
⅔ cup dried or 1¼ cups fresh, scrubbed
    mallow root
1¼ cups dried hibiscus flowers
Sweetener to taste

To cold-infuse the herbs, add the mallow and hibiscus to the water and cover. (If you're using whole, dried stevia leaves as a sweetener, add them here as well.) Allow to steep overnight into a strong concentrate. Strain and compost the spent herbs. Add honey, sugar, or prepared stevia concentrate, if using, to taste. If a cold beverage is desired, chill in the refrigerator until you're ready to serve, or pour over ice.

Rose Geranium Sparkler with Raspberries

Serve this in champagne flutes—the raspberries are so cute when they bounce up and down on the bubbles.

Small batch: for each 6-ounce flute

1 tablespoon Rose Geranium Honey Syrup
(below)

1 tablespoon fresh-squeezed lemon juice

½ cup sparkling water or club soda

Garnish: a few fresh red raspberries,
¼ cup total

For a party of 30–40 guests

3 cups Rose Geranium Honey Syrup (below)

3 cups fresh-squeezed lemon juice

8–10 liters sparkling water or club soda

Garnish: a few fresh red raspberries,
about 1 cup

For a party, combine the infused syrup and the lemon ahead of time in a pitcher or bottle to keep on hand in the fridge or cooler until go time. Pour the mixture into the bottom of the flutes, then add sparkling water with minimal splashing to preserve the bubbles. Drop in the berries. Cheers!

VARIATIONS

Winter Feijoa Sparkler: Replace the Rose Geranium Honey Syrup with half the amount of infused feijoa simple syrup left over from the Candied Feijoa Peels on page 362. Garnish with slices of fresh feijoa or a lemon twist.

Herbal-Infused Honey Syrups

Honey, especially if it has crystallized, can be tricky to dilute when sweetening cold or even room-temperature drinks. Thin down your honey with a hot herbal infusion of rose geranium, lavender, or other garden herbs for a fresh addition to party drinks or lemonade, or for stirring into sun tea.

Makes 1 cup, enough to flavor
6–8 beverages

½ cup water

½ cup honey

2 sprigs rose geranium, lavender, or other
garden herb such as sage, thyme, basil,
shiso, lemon verbena, mitzuba, or mint

Makes 4 cups, enough to flavor
30–40 beverages

2 cups water

2 cups honey

6 small sprigs rose geranium, lavender, or
other garden herb such as sage, thyme,
basil, shiso, lemon verbena, mitzuba,
or mint

Boil the water in a small saucepan, then remove it from the heat and let it cool a few degrees. Stir in the honey until it dissolves. Add the herbs, cover, and allow to steep until the infusion cools to room temperature. Remove the herbs.

Store the infused syrup in a glass bottle in the refrigerator or freeze into ice cubes.

Pear Cider with Thyme-Infused Tea

Fresh-pressed cider and other fruit juices can be way too sweet to drink straight. Diluting with herbal tea cuts the cloying sweetness and makes for a refreshing afternoon beverage.

Serves 4–6

MAKES AROUND 2 QUARTS

½–1½ quarts water, to taste

4–6 large sprigs thyme or other fresh
    garden herb such as lavender, lemon
    balm, lemon verbena, basil, mint, shiso,
    or even rose petals

1 quart fresh-pressed pear (or apple) cider,
    or 1 cup frozen concentrate*

Serves 30–40

MAKES AROUND 2 GALLONS

½–1½ gallons water, to taste

4–6 large sprigs thyme or other fresh
    garden herb such as lavender, lemon
    balm, lemon verbena, basil, mint, shiso,
    or even rose petals.

1 gallon fresh-pressed pear (or apple) cider,
    or 1 quart frozen concentrate*

Bring the water to a boil, turn off the heat, and add the herbs. Cover and steep for 30 minutes. Strain and allow to cool. This can be done ahead. In your serving pitcher or dispenser, add the fresh juice or concentrate. Stir in the tea 1 quart at time. Dilute to taste. Chill or serve at room temperature as desired. If you plan to add ice, leave it a little stronger and save the extra tea for another time. Garnish with a sprig of fresh herb.

Making fresh cider in old-fashioned hand-cranked presses is a harvest ritual that still brings people together in small communities all over the United States. Resident Kelsey Henson Dunnigan presses epergne pears. PHOTO BY JIM COLEMAN.

* To make room in your freezer, you can make your own concentrate from fresh apple or pear cider: Freeze the fresh-pressed juice in large plastic 1-gallon jugs. Defrost halfway, leaving a core of ice down the center, and pour off the liquid concentrate—the natural sugars and flavor compounds melt first and diffuse out into the sides. Discard the ice. Pour the concentrate into a smaller container and refreeze. Commercial frozen juice concentrate may need higher dilution.

Prickly Pear Sunrise—aka *Tuna Rita*

A classic OAEC holiday party cocktail. For a party of 30 to 40, mix up four pitchers.

Serves 1

MAKES A 12-OUNCE GLASS

3 ounces cactus pear juice

2 ounces tequila

1 ounce triple sec

½ ounce lime or lemon juice

Ice

Salt mixed with a pinch of cayenne for the
    rim (optional)

Serves 8

MAKES A 60-OUNCE PITCHER

3 cups cactus pear juice

2 cups tequila

1 cup triple sec

2 cups lime or lemon juice

Ice

Salt mixed with a pinch of cayenne for the
    rim (optional)

For a blended Prickly Pear Sunrise, put your strained juice (see the sidebar) back in the blender with the rest of the ingredients, including ice, and blend well. As the drink sits (that is, if you don't slurp it down immediately), it will naturally separate into a beautiful red sunrise.

For a straight *Tuna Rita*, shake the strained juice along with the rest of the liquids in a cocktail shaker and serve over ice with a cayenne-salted rim.

PHOTO BY DOUG GOSLING.

PRICKLY PEARS—AKA TUNAS

The rich, syrupy fruit of the prickly pear—*tuna* in Spanish—has a deep orange-red hue (though there are also other varieties that are purple, yellow, or green when ripe) and a watermelon-like flavor. We've heard that you can make jams and other sweets with prickly pear, but we never seem to get that far since the juice is so fabulous for cocktails!

Harvest *tunas* in winter when they are bright red and beginning to drop to the ground. Most people will want to wear gloves for this, as they're quite prickly. The easiest way to de-spine the pears is to use an open flame to burn them off. The other method is to wear thick work gloves and scoop out the seedy middles. Once the fruit has been scooped out, put it in a food mill to squeeze out the seeds and form a pulp. Or put the peeled fruit, seeds and all, into a blender, then pour the liquid through cheesecloth draped over a colander to drain.

Dave's Fruit-Infused Liqueurs

Pictured in the photo is a sampling from Dave Henson's extensive library of fruit-infused cordials that he has been experimenting with ever since moving here in 1994. With infinite choices of rare fruits, herbs, and flowers from the Mother Garden to mix and match, there is endless fun to be had by an adventurous alchemist-bartender; we can always find an excuse to throw a cocktail party.

Neutral-flavored alcohols, such as vodka or white rum, work best for bringing out the inherent flavors of fruit, though some fruits pair well with more assertively flavored alcohols (strawberries in silver tequila, peaches in light bourbon, prune plums in gin, pears in brandy, and so on). The value of a simple single-fruit infusion cannot be overstated, though once you get a feel for it, you can branch out and incorporate herbs and edible flowers into the mix.

To make 1 pint of infused liquor
3 cups chopped fruit or berries
About 2 cups spirits, to cover

To make 2 quarts of infused liquor
12 cups chopped fruit or berries
About 2 quarts spirits, to cover

Fill a Mason quart jar three-quarters full, loosely packed, with your choice of fruit. For the large batch, divide the fruit among four quart jars. Cover the fruit with a high-proof alcohol to cover by an inch or two. Close with a noncorrosive lid and store in a cool dark place for 1 to 3 months. Decant and strain, pressing as much liquid and juice out of the fruit as possible through a fine-mesh strainer or cheesecloth. Discard the spent fruit, or reserve it to make into jam or chutney. Allow the sediment to settle for an hour and then pour off the clear infused liquid into a decorative bottle, leaving behind any sediment. Store finished cordials in a cool dark place for longevity.

PHOTO BY TALI AIONA.

PHOTO BY TALI AIONA.

RECIPE LIST

Spring

Dougo's Cecile Brunner Rose Sugar
Sensuous Sweet Spring Tart

Summer

Summer Fruit Fools
Cardamom-Rose-Plum Preserves
Cardamom-Rose-Plum Bars
Blood Peach Torta
Pink Pearl and Pippin Applesauce with Lemon Thyme
Baked Gravenstein Apples

Fall

Epargne Pear Frangipane Tart
Simply Roasted Cape Gooseberries
Poached Russian Quince
Quince Bars
Quince Membrillo
Amaranth Breakfast Porridge
Rich Autumn Fruit Compote
Bay-Infused Cheesecake with Bay Nut Crust
Buckwheat Buzz-Nut Skillet Bread
Shipova Coffee Cake
Fig-Leaf-Infused Goat's-Milk Panna Cotta

Winter

Dark Roast Winter Squash Tart with Hazelnut Crust
Farallons Gingerbread
Dorothy's Carrot Cake
Candied Feijoa Peels and Infused Simple Syrup
Jacob's Lavender Crème Brûlée
Best Lemon Tart
Freeke's Lemon Angel Delight
Stevia Lemon Curd
Persimmon Pudding
American Persimmon Brandy Sauce
Medlar Cream Cake
Saint Lucy's Tutu

PHOTO BY DOUG GOSLING.

Dougo's Cecile Brunner Rose Sugar

Our Cecile Brunner rose was one of the first rose varieties planted on the land some 40 years ago and is one of the most distinctive heirloom roses ever: an exuberant shrub that can vine 30 feet up a redwood tree in a matter of a few years and explode in the spring with thousands of tiny pale-pink blossoms. These perfect, highly fragrant buds and flowers have earned her the nickname "Sweetheart Rose."

This is truly one of the most cosmic concoctions you will ever learn to make—it will elevate even the most common dessert to celestial new heights. It has a much fresher living floral essence than even the finest rose oil used in baking. Use it to flavor whipping cream, custard, ice cream, cake batter, or cocktails. Dougo's absolute favorite use is to fold it into whipping cream and serve it on freshly picked garden-ripened strawberries, a combination that is nothing less than ecstatic. The serving sizes given for this preserve are approximately enough for a small family (or large community) to use all year. Make the big batch to give away as presents.

Makes 1 quart
2¾ cups Cecile Brunner rosebuds and
    slightly open flowers, tightly packed
2 cups sugar, or more to cover

Makes 1 gallon
2¾ quarts Cecile Brunner rosebuds and
    slightly open flowers, tightly packed
2 quarts sugar, or more to cover

Pack as many flowers as you possibly can into a glass quart jar (four jars for the large batch) up to the 2¾-cup line—this will be several hundred flowers. If you don't have quite enough, downsize to a smaller jar. Dump the flowers out into a bowl and reserve. Cover the bottom of the jar with ¼ inch of sugar and then put down an even layer of flowers, closely nestling them next to one another. Put down another layer of sugar until you have just covered them, and then pack in another layer of flowers. Continue alternating in this way until your jar is filled.

Lid the jar and put it in the refrigerator. The sugar will extract the perfume from the flowers in scarcely 2 weeks, and will continue desiccating the flowers until the sugar melts into a syrup. It will keep in the refrigerator for literally years. Always strain out the preserved flowers with a small sieve before using.

Sensuous Sweet Spring Tart

Spring flavors that make you crazy! For a large-scale batch, make three 10-inch circular tarts or one 15½ x 20-inch rectangular one (see the sidebar on page 333).

Makes one 10-inch tart,
about 10–12 servings

DOUGH

1½ cups all-purpose flour

2 tablespoons sugar

¼ teaspoon salt

Zest of 1 lemon

½ cup (1 stick) cold butter, cut into
    ¼-inch pieces

2 tablespoons water

1 tablespoon vanilla extract

FILLING

1 tablespoon sugar

2 cups chopped rhubarb (about 5 stalks)

½ vanilla bean pod, split open, seeds
    removed into rhubarb

2 tablespoons marmalade

1¾ cups strawberries, raspberries,
    or mulberries

⅓ cup sugar

2 farm-fresh eggs

½ cup cream

1 tablespoon vanilla extract

Combine the flour, sugar, salt, and lemon zest in the bowl of a food processor; pulse to combine. Add the cold cut-up butter and pulse until it is broken up small and looks sandy. Add in the water and vanilla extract; mix just until these are incorporated. Turn the dough out onto a lightly floured surface and bring it together into a disk; if it's really crumbly and dry (which happens, depending on the weather), sprinkle on a little bit of water until it sticks together. Wrap the dough and chill for at least an hour.

Preheat the oven to 375°F. When the tart dough is good and chilled, roll it out to fit in your tart pan by rolling from the center outward, making quarter turns until you reach the right circumference. Transfer the dough by rolling up the circle on your rolling pin, then unrolling it over the pan. Push the dough into the corners and let the excess hang over the edge. Cut the excess dough off flush with a knife. Dock the bottom of the dough using a fork and line it with foil and pie weights (we often use beans). Blind-bake for 15 minutes, then remove the pie weights and foil and bake for another 10 minutes.

While the tart is blind-baking, mix the chopped rhubarb, sugar, and vanilla seeds in a small saucepan. Heat on low, stirring often. Cook this down for about 15 minutes, until the fruit just starts to break down. Remove the pan from the heat and stir in the marmalade. In a mixing bowl, toss the berries with the sugar and set aside. Mix up the custard by whisking together the eggs, cream, and vanilla extract in a bowl.

When the tart shell starts to get golden, after about 25 minutes, take it out and fill right away. First, scatter the cooked rhubarb-marmalade mixture, then evenly disperse the berries; lastly, pour in the custard. Transfer carefully back to the oven and bake for 30 minutes. Let cool completely before serving.

MAKING TARTS AT LARGE SCALE

Tarts are much prettier when made in their traditional, home-scale 10-inch pans with the removable fluted edge. If you're scaling up to feed 30 to 40 people, we recommend tripling the recipe and separating the dough and filling evenly into three separate 10-inch tart pans, making sure to cut the maximum 12 slices per tart for a total of 36 servings. If your numbers are closer to 40 or there will be some kind of cake cutting ceremony, make four tarts to be on the safe side.

That said, we have made tarts in industrial-scale metal sheet pans for really big gatherings. A double batch can be rolled out to fit nicely in a "half" 13 x 17½-inch sheet pan, a triple batch in a "three-quarter" 15½ x 20-inch sheet pan (and technically, a quadruple batch will fit in a "full" 17½ x 20-inch sheet pan, but we don't recommend it—cutting makes them more like bars than tarts.) Keep an eye on the tarts toward the end of baking—depending on your oven, you may need to increase the final baking time slightly to account for the increased mass.

To cut a rectangular tart into uniform pieces, don't eyeball it—it really helps to use a ruler. Start by laying the sheet pan horizontally on the counter. Cut and remove about ½ to ¾ inch of crust from the short, vertical edges, leaving the long edges of crust intact. Make a long horizontal cut lengthwise across the middle of the tart to form two halves. Now make vertical cuts, one every inch, to form long slices, each with a short piece of crust on one end. Use a long rectangular spatula for serving instead of a traditional wedge-shaped pie server.

Summer Fruit Fools

Forget the fruit salad of our canned, high-fructose childhoods. A touch of natural honey and lemon is all that is needed to make the sunshiny sweetness of fresh fruit pop. Fruit salads can be made simply for a light breakfast side or extravagantly enough to stand alone as a dessert for a fancy dinner. Here are a few of our more over-the-top "fools"—fruits paired with fresh garden herbs, infused whipped creams, and edible flower petal garnishes.

Pink Pearl Apples with Mulberries, Rosemary-Infused Whipped Cream, Pine Nuts, and Rose Petals

Crisp, tart Pink Pearl apples ripen earlier than other apples. Their cheerful pink color deserves a summery treatment, especially when paired with the crimson-hued mulberries that ripen at the same time in the August garden.

Serves 4–6

1 tablespoon lemon juice, plus more to taste

2 teaspoons honey, plus more to taste

4 Pink Pearl or Pink Lady apples cut into bite-sized pieces (about 3½ cups), or substitute any pink apple variety

2 cups Rosemary-Infused Whipped Cream

½ pint mulberries

¼ cup pine nuts

2 tablespoons multicolored rose petals

Serves 30–40

¾ cup lemon juice, plus more to taste

⅓ cup honey, plus more to taste

30 Pink Pearl or Pink Lady apples cut into bite-sized pieces (about 12 to 15 cups), or substitute any pink apple variety

6 cups Rosemary-Infused Whipped Cream

2 pints mulberries

1 cup pine nuts

½ cup multicolored rose petals

Combine the honey and lemon juice. Peel, core, and slice the apples into paper-thin wedges (an apple-corer-peeler-slicer tool works really well for this). As you go, toss with the lemon honey mixture to prevent browning. Taste and add more honey or lemon juice if needed for balance.

Make the Rosemary-Infused Whipped Cream. When you're ready to serve, make a base of the marinated apples, top with whipped cream, and sprinkle with mulberries, pine nuts, and rose petals.

ROSEMARY-INFUSED WHIPPED CREAM

Serves 4–6

Two 4-inch sprigs rosemary, thyme, lemon thyme, lemon verbena, or anise hyssop

1 cup heavy cream

1 tablespoon honey or maple syrup

Serves 30–40

Eight 4-inch sprigs rosemary, thyme, lemon thyme, lemon verbena, or anise hyssop

2 pints heavy cream

¼ cup honey or maple syrup

Any fresh or dried herb can be infused into whipping cream to create interesting variations.

Cold-infuse the cream ahead of time by adding the sprigs of herbs to the container of cream. Steep overnight in the refrigerator. For best results, chill the bowl of a stand-up mixer (or a ceramic bowl if you're using a handheld mixer) for 20 minutes before starting. Strain the herbs from the cream into the chilled bowl. Add the sweetener. Beat for 5 to 10 minutes on medium speed, keeping a close eye not to over whip. Serve immediately.

VARIATIONS

Infuse the cream with any herb: mint, basil, tarragon, rose geranium, culinary bay leaves (these impart a creamy vanilla flavor), lavender flowers, vanilla bean, grated ginger, dried crushed fig leaves (imparts a warm coconutty flavor), or fresh peach leaves (imparts an amaretto flavor.)

Elephant Heart Plums, Dapple Dandy Pluots, and Blueberries with Shiso, Cardamom Whipped Cream, and Carnation Petals

Plums and pluots do very well in our temperate orchard and, in the cool June fog, pair nicely with slightly warming shiso, cardamom, and carnation petals. Carnations, or "pinks," have a hint of clove flavor—a divine garnish for any sweet dessert. Use only fresh-picked, organic carnations—store-bought ornamental carnations are often treated with pesticides and toxic preservatives and are not meant for eating.

Serves 4–6

4 Elephant Heart plums and Dapple Dandy pluots, washed, de-seeded, and cut into bite-sized pieces (about 3½ cups), or substitute any juicy plum and pluot varieties

1 tablespoon lemon juice, plus more to taste

2 teaspoons honey, plus more to taste

1 tablespoon very finely chiffonaded purple shiso, cinnamon basil, or purple ruffles basil

2 cups Yogurt Cardamom Whipped Cream

1 cup blueberries

½ cup crushed, toasted hazelnuts (page 303)

2 tablespoons pink carnation petals or other sweet or neutral-flavored edible flowers, such as bachelor's buttons

Serves 30–40

6 pounds Elephant Heart plums and Dapple Dandy pluots, washed, de-seeded, and cut into bite-sized pieces (about 12 to 15 cups), or substitute any juicy plum or pluot varieties

¾ cup lemon juice, plus more to taste

¼ cup honey, plus more to taste

¼ cup very finely chiffonaded purple shiso, cinnamon basil, or purple ruffles basil

6 cups Yogurt Cardamom Whipped Cream

2 pints blueberries

1½ cups crushed, toasted hazelnuts (page 303)

½ cup pink carnation petals or other sweet or neutral-flavored edible flowers, such as bachelor's buttons

Place the plums and pluots in a large mixing bowl. Combine the lemon juice and honey in a glass jar with a lid, shaking until it dissolves into a syrup. Add the honey-lemon mixture to the fruit, a little at a time, tasting and stirring as you go. Add more honey or lemon juice if needed. Toss in the herbs. Chill until you're ready to serve.

Prepare the cardamom-infused whipped cream. When you're ready to serve, make a base of the marinated plums, top with whipped cream, and sprinkle with blueberries, crushed hazelnuts, and flower petals.

YOGURT CARDAMOM WHIPPED CREAM

Serves 4–6

1 cup heavy cream

½ cup whole vanilla yogurt

½ teaspoon cardamom, to taste

Maple syrup to taste (optional)

Serves 30–40

2 pints heavy cream

2 cups whole vanilla yogurt

2 teaspoons cardamom, to taste

Maple syrup to taste (optional)

This whipped cream is quickly spiced up at the last minute and cut with yogurt for a less cloying mouthfeel.

For best results, chill the bowl of a stand-up mixer (or a ceramic bowl if you're using a handheld mixer) for 20 minutes before starting, as cold cream is easiest to whip. Pour the cold heavy cream into the chilled bowl and fit your mixer with the whisk attachment. Beat for 5 to 10 minutes on medium speed, keeping a close eye. Once the cream reaches your desired texture, stop the beaters immediately to prevent it from turning into butter. Fold in the yogurt and cardamom. Most vanilla yogurt is presweetened, so you shouldn't need to add sweetener, though feel free to fold in a little maple syrup if you think it needs it.

VARIATIONS

Flavor the whipped cream with any of these additions instead of the cardamom: ¼ teaspoon (1 teaspoon) nutmeg, 1 teaspoon (1 tablespoon) vanilla or other extract, 2 teaspoons (2 tablespoons) rose flower water or orange blossom water, 1 teaspoon (1 tablespoon) lemon or orange zest, 2 teaspoons (2 tablespoons) rum or flavored liqueur (page 327).

PHOTO BY DOUG GOSLING.

Cardamom-Rose-Plum Preserves

In the summer when all the wild plums are falling off the trees, we scramble to keep up with the bounty. Making a large pot of jam, wine, or juice from the little wild plums really pays off for these otherwise labor-intensive fruits. This sauce is perfect for the marble-sized plums that are not as convenient or tasty as the larger table varieties. The recipe makes enough to use in the Cardamom-Rose-Plum Bars that follow, plus a few pints extra to can or keep in the fridge for eating on their own. Add to morning yogurt with granola, spread on toast, or drizzle over a fabulous fruit "fool."

Serves 4–6

MAKES 4–6 CUPS

2½ pounds small native plums

2 cups sugar

Juice and zest of 1 lemon

2 teaspoons cardamom powder

1 tablespoon rosewater

Serves 30-40

MAKES 12–14 CUPS

8½ pounds small native plums

8½ cups sugar

Juice and zest of 4 lemons

2 tablespoons cardamom powder

¼ cup rosewater

Place the plums in a heavy-bottomed stockpot. Heat on medium-high heat, smashing and stirring often. Keep stirring to prevent the plums from burning. Use a potato masher to speed the breakdown process if they are not juicing in the first few minutes. Once there is enough juice, turn the heat down and let the fruit simmer until it is broken down and falling away from the pit, about 15 minutes. Take off the heat and let cool for 15 minutes.

Have ready a colander with quarter-inch holes, set over a bowl. Pour the contents into the colander and swirl around with a metal spoon. The juice and some pulp will go through, and you will be left with just the pits and skin in the colander to discard.

Clean out your heavy-bottomed stockpot. Place the plum juice and pulp, sugar, lemon juice, and lemon zest into the pot and cook on high heat for about 20 to 30 minutes. Stir often and turn the heat down a notch if you smell any burning. After 20 minutes of continuous boiling, the jam is probably ready. You can test for set by dropping a teaspoon of jam onto a cold plate (that has been refrigerated) and see how it sets up. If it runs across the plate, then it needs to cook longer; if it gels, it's done. Take it off the heat, add the cardamom powder, and mix well. Let the jam cool a little so it is not piping hot, then add the rosewater.

At this stage, it is ready to be used in the Cardamom-Rose-Plum Bars, refrigerated for future use, or canned in jars for the winter months.

Cardamom-Rose-Plum Bars

Serves 4–6, with some leftover

MAKES ABOUT TEN 2 X 2-INCH SQUARES USING ONE 9 X 13-INCH SHEET PAN

2½ cups flour

⅔ cup granulated sugar

½ teaspoon salt

1 cup plus 2 tablespoons (2¼ sticks) butter, room temperature, divided

¼ cup brown sugar

½ cup rolled oats

½ cup toasted pecans, chopped

2 cups Cardamom-Rose-Plum Preserves (above)

Serves 30–40, with some left over

MAKES FORTY-EIGHT 2 X 2-INCH SQUARES USING ONE 13 X 17½-INCH BAKING TRAY ("HALF"-SIZED INDUSTRIAL SHEET PAN)

7½ cups flour

2 cups granulated sugar

1½ teaspoons salt

3¼ cups (6½ sticks) butter, room temperature, divided

¾ cup brown sugar

1½ cups rolled oats

1½ cups toasted pecans, chopped

6 cups Cardamom-Rose-Plum Preserves (above)

Preheat the oven to 375°F. Line a 9 x 13-inch (18 x 24-inch) sheet pan with parchment paper. Mix the flour, granulated sugar, and salt in the bowl of a stand-up mixer. Add 2 sticks (6 sticks) of the butter, a quarter at a time, and mix until the dough has the consistency of sand. Measure out 1¼ cups (3¾ cups) of the dough into a bowl and set aside. Press the rest of the dough into the bottom of the pan. To make an even flat surface, use the back of a dry measuring cup to press it in firmly. Bake 14 to 18 minutes until the crust is slightly golden.

To make the streusel topping, take the remaining dough and add the brown sugar, rolled oats, pecans, and remaining 2 tablespoons (½ stick) of butter; mix well. Spread the jam evenly over the hot crust right when it comes out of the oven, and sprinkle the streusel over the jam. Bake for another 20 to 25 minutes, until the top darkens to golden and the jam bubbles, possibly longer for the large batch, depending on your oven. When it is finished baking, let cool 30 minutes. Run a knife around the outsides and cut into 2¼-inch squares. If needed, cut the outer crusts off for neat, slightly smaller bars.

Blood Peach Torta

Leesa Jackson, our breakfast angel, has been cooking here on and off since the Farallons days and welcomes guests into the kitchen in the morning with a gentle smile and a spread of thoughtfully prepared, seasonal creations such as this fruit torta. Blood Peaches melt into a custardy yet fluffy sponge, staining it with fuchsia streaks. Blood Peaches and other canning peaches are thick-skinned and fuzzy. We recommend peeling off the skin by briefly blanching first.

Serves 4–6, with some left over

MAKES ONE 9-INCH CAKE

2 eggs

¼ cup milk

1 cup sugar

Pinch of salt

1½ cups all-purpose flour

2 pounds Blood Peaches or other assorted
    seasonal fruit, peeled, cored/pitted, and
    sliced into bite-sized chunks

Serves 30–40, with some left over

**MAKES FOUR 9-INCH ROUND
CAKE PANS***

8 eggs

1 cup milk

4 cups sugar

1½ teaspoons salt

6 cups all-purpose flour

8 pounds Blood Peaches or other assorted
    seasonal fruit, peeled, cored/pitted, and
    sliced into bite-sized chunks

Preheat the oven to 400°F. Butter and flour your 9-inch cake pans and place a circle of parchment paper in the bottom. In a large mixing bowl, whisk the eggs and milk together until foamy and add the sugar and salt. Beat well, then mix in the flour. The batter should be similar to pancake batter, but a bit more sticky and thick. Fold the diced fruit into the batter—there will be a lot of fruit, with the batter holding it together. Scrape into the cake pans and bake for 45 minutes to 1 hour, until the top is browned and a pick stuck into the center of the cake comes out clean. Cool on a rack for about 5 minutes. Run a knife around the edge and turn the cake out onto a plate, then turn it right-side up onto another plate and serve. The cake will be on the soft side due to the fruit-to-batter ratio. It's meant to be sort of custardy, so don't worry, it's not undercooked. Good as a breakfast cake or dinner dessert and keeps well for a couple days.

VARIATIONS

This versatile torta will exalt any summer fruit. Fresh apricot is a particularly divine choice, but a mix of peaches, plums, pluots, cherries, and/or berries is also delicious. In the fall, try apples, pears, Asian pears, shipova, or Cape gooseberries.

* For a group of 30 to 40, it is preferable to make four round cakes of this size—when this recipe is made as a large sheet, the center doesn't set up as uniformly and it is tricky to decant as an upside-down cake. Quadruple the recipe as indicated, then divide the batter evenly into four 9-inch round cake pans. More mass in the oven means the cakes will take a little longer to cook through.

THE BLOOD PEACH

This heirloom late-season peach, with dramatic crimson flesh and juice, can be found growing wild in the southern United States, and is known by many names: Wine Peach, Georgia Black, Cherokee Peach, Indian Blood Peach, and Sanguinole Peach.

According to the Thomas Jefferson Center for Historic Plants,[13] "Spaniards introduced this novel peach to Mexico in the sixteenth century. By the next century, European explorers in southeastern North America were astonished to find this Old World fruit being grown by native tribes. This was possible because, unlike most fruit varieties that are maintained solely by complex methods of budding or grafting, the 'Indian Blood' can be grown easily from seed. Nomadic tribes and traders must have carried it north from Mexico."

Our beloved Blood Peach is one of the only peach varieties that we can successfully grow in our coastal, fungus-prone orchard due to its remarkable resistance to peach leaf curl—a testament to the built-in resilience of open-pollinated genetics, reproduced from true seed.

Pink Pearl and Pippin Applesauce with Lemon Thyme

The Pink Pearl apple is an early-ripening favorite in the OAEC orchard with striking rose-colored flesh and a sweet-tart flavor. Lemon thyme adds a subtle complexity to this pink sauce, which lends itself to either savory or sweet pairings.

Serves 4–6
5 Pink Pearl apples
5 Pippin apples
¼ cup water
5 sprigs lemon thyme
Honey to taste

Serves 30–40
35 Pink Pearl apples
35 Pippin apples
1 cup water
2 bunches lemon thyme
Honey to taste

Wash, core, and chop the apples into chunks. Whether or not you decide to peel the apples is up to your personal preference. In a medium pot, simmer the apples with the water and lemon thyme. When the apples begin to break down but still retain a few chunks of texture, turn off the heat and add honey to taste. The Pink Pearl and Pippin apples are tart in flavor and firm in texture. The honey is meant to bring out the sweetness of the apples, but go light so you do not lose the tart complexity of the fruit. Leave the lemon thyme sprigs in the applesauce as they will continue to infuse the apples with flavor.

Baked Gravenstein Apples

The Gravenstein is particularly fragrant when baked. This recipe from longtime Sowing Circle member Martha Kowalick makes cute little cups of soft, spiced apple with a crunchy almond topping. She says, "In a place where we are blessed with so much abundance, especially during apple season, I love to share the wealth with my neighbors." She goes out to the thrift store and picks up an inexpensive basket, fills it to the brim with fruit, and tucks this recipe into a card.

Serves 4–6
¾ cup toasted almonds, crushed into pieces
¼ cup brown sugar
½ teaspoon ground cinnamon
¼ cup (½ stick) soft butter
6 medium Gravenstein apples, or any sweet
    sauce apple
Crème fraîche, yogurt, or ice cream, for serving

Serves 30–40
7½ cups toasted almonds, crushed into pieces
3 cups brown sugar
2 tablespoons ground cinnamon
2 cups (4 sticks) soft butter
36 medium Gravenstein apples, or any
    sweet sauce apple
Crème fraîche, yogurt, or ice cream, for serving

Preheat the oven to 350°F and line a baking tray with parchment paper. Toss the almonds, sugar, cinnamon, and butter in a small bowl until well combined. With an apple coring tool, core the apples in one swift downward push. Pull out the cylindrical core; cut off the very bottom ½ inch of the core and replace it in the bottom of the hole so that the filling won't escape when baked. (If you don't have an apple corer, scoop out the core with a melon baller or other small sharp spoon. Try to keep the bottom of the cup intact, but if it gets accidentally poked open, wedge a sliver of apple in the bottom.) Form a neat cup that will stand facing up on the baking tray—if your apple is topsy-turvy, whittle off some of the bottom to even it out so that it will stay right-side up, and cuddle it tightly together with its neighbors for support. Fill each cup with a heaping spoonful of the almond mixture.

Bake on the middle rack of the oven for 25 minutes or until the apples are just soft and the almond crust is slightly toasted. Serve with a dollop of crème fraîche, yogurt, or ice cream.

THE GRAVENSTEIN APPLE

If you wish to make an apple pie from scratch, you must first invent the universe.

—CARL SAGAN

Our beloved Gravenstein, after which Sebastopol's main street is named, was brought to the area by Russian fur traders in the early 1800s as an early-ripening processing apple for cider, vinegar, and sauce. The immense, hardy trees (some local specimens are now over 150 years old) are well suited to our local soil and climate, digging their roots deep into the well-drained sandy loam to pull up water even after six months of summer drought and no irrigation. At one time, Sebastopol was known for apples, but the Gravenstein fell out of favor due to its short shelf life and large tree size, both impractical for industrial production. In the last 40 years as the price of apples dropped and land prices in Sonoma County jumped, apple country has given way to encroaching wine country.

Ironically, though Sonoma County is blessed with one of the most idyllic Mediterranean climates for growing food, it seems the only way to make real money in agriculture here is to grow intoxicants—at one time it was apples for cider, then came the wine industry, and increasingly these days it's marijuana! Wouldn't it be great to have land-use policies and functional economic models in place that provide real livelihoods for farmers who are producing real food for real people?

In the 1800s, the United States had literally thousands of apple varieties—practically every town in America could boast of its own locally adapted favorite. Industrialization, however, has whittled this incredible diversity down to the scant handful found in grocery stores today. Thanks to Slow Food's campaign to raise awareness about endangered heritage food crops—and to being named as a heritage variety on the Ark of Taste—the Gravenstein was saved from extinction and is enjoying a renaissance as a source of local agricultural pride. What's your local apple?

PHOTOS BY TALI AIONA.

Epargne Pear Frangipane Tart

While pears are typically considered a fall fruit, this tart is especially spectacular when we use the small July-ripening dessert pears from our most prized matriarch fruit tree on the land flanking the OAEC kitchen, the stately Epargne pear planted by Italian homesteaders at least 100 years ago. It can be made with any other sweet, later-ripening baking pears, however, and is especially beautiful with buttery Bosc pears.

While somewhat labor-intensive, this recipe works for a crowd because most of the work is done in advance—you make the dough and poach the pears the day before, chill overnight, and then assemble and bake off the tarts the next day. For a gathering of 30 to 40 people, make four individual tarts. See the sidebar on page 333.

Serves up to 12

MAKES ONE 10-INCH TART

DOUG'S RICH TART DOUGH

1½ cups all-purpose flour

2 tablespoons unrefined sugar

Pinch of salt

½ cup (1 stick) cold unsalted butter, cut into pieces

3 tablespoons cold heavy cream

POACHED PEARS

8 pears (roughly 2 pounds), peeled, sliced in half, and cored

2 tablespoons fresh-squeezed lemon juice

3 cups water

¾ cup honey

1 fresh vanilla bean, split lengthwise

Garnish: ¼ cup toasted hazelnuts, peeled and chopped coarsely

FRANGIPANE

½ cup (1 stick) unsalted butter

¼ cup brown sugar

2 whole eggs

¾ cup toasted hazelnuts, peeled and ground fine in a food processor

2 tablespoons dark rum

The day before, make the dough. In a large bowl, sift together the flour, sugar, and salt. Quickly cut the butter into the dry mixture with your fingertips or mix in a stand-up mixer with a paddle attachment until it resembles a coarse cornmeal. Sprinkle the cream into the dry ingredients and mix until it seizes up into a dough. Remove the dough and gather into a ball or disk. Wrap and refrigerate for at least an hour, and up to overnight, before baking.

Also in advance, poach the pears. Toss the pear halves with the lemon juice in a large bowl. Set aside. Combine the water, honey, and vanilla bean in a medium saucepan. Stir over medium heat until the honey dissolves. Add the pears. Reduce the heat to medium-low and simmer until the pears are just tender when pierced, about 15 minutes. Using a slotted spoon, transfer the pears to a large bowl. Boil the poaching liquid until it's reduced to ¾ cup. Cool the syrup. Remove the vanilla bean, scrape the remaining seeds out of the pod, and pour the syrup over the pears. Cover and refrigerate for at least 8 hours or ideally overnight along with the dough.

When you're ready to bake, press the chilled dough into a 10-inch tart pan and bake at 350°F until golden brown. Cool. To make the frangipane, cream the butter and sugar in a mixer. Add the eggs and mix in well. Add the ground hazelnuts and rum and whip to a creamy consistency. Keep the frangipane at room temperature. Spread a layer of frangipane about ¼ inch thick in the cooled tart shell. At this time, take the pear mixture out of the fridge and drain the pears of their poaching liquid, reserving the liquid. Reduce the poaching syrup to about 2 tablespoons in a small saucepan over low heat.

Thinly slice each pear half lengthwise, into ⅛-inch slices, leaving the slices attached at the stem end. Using a metal spatula, transfer the pears to a plate and gently press to fan them out slightly. With the spatula, carefully place the fanned pear halves onto the frangipane layer, including an arrangement of slices in the middle of the tart.

Bake the assembled tart at 350°F for 45 minutes, or until the frangipane is golden brown and set. Using a pastry brush, paint the pears with the thickened poaching syrup. Garnish the tart with toasted hazelnuts and/or fresh berries.

VARIATION

Instead of the pears, use Cape gooseberries! Follow the instructions for making the prebaked tart shell, and spread about ¼ inch of frangipane on the cooled shell. Toss a full pint basket of Cape gooseberries in a tablespoon of melted butter and a tablespoon of sugar. Put down a layer of the berries, shoulder-to-shoulder, on the frangipane layer. Garnish the outer edges with coarsely chopped toasted almonds. Bake for 45 minutes or until the frangipane is nicely set and golden brown.

Simply Roasted Cape Gooseberries

A close relative of the ground cherry or cossack pineapple, the Cape gooseberry is not a true gooseberry but a member of the nightshade family. It comes packaged in a papery husk, much like a tomatillo. They burst with an addictive tropical sweetness that sends garden grazers searching under the soft leaves for more. Cape gooseberries can be enjoyed with the husk peeled back to act as a dainty handle for dipping into melted chocolate. This Peruvian perennial fruit is also wonderful cooked into jams, tarts, or cakes such as Leesa's fruit torta (page 341).

The birds always decimate our one cherry tree every year, but lucky for us, no one seems to like eating Cape gooseberries except for us humans. Turns out, simply roasted Cape gooseberries bear an uncanny likeness to cherries and can be used as the base for any number of sweet or savory dishes where cooked cherries might be used. The recipe sizes given here refer to this as a stand-alone dessert with whipped cream; it will serve more if the berries are added to other recipes.

Serves 4–6

MAKES ABOUT 2 CUPS

2 pints of Cape gooseberries, husks removed
1 tablespoon melted butter
Light dusting of coarse sugar (optional)

Serves 30–40

MAKES ABOUT 12 CUPS

12 pints of Cape gooseberries, husks removed
¾ cup (1½ sticks) melted butter
Light dusting of coarse sugar (optional)

Toss the Cape gooseberries in the melted butter and use whatever is left over to grease a 9 x 13-inch baking pan. If you're using the berries in a sweet application, toss with a light dusting of sugar. Spread the Cape gooseberries out on the baking sheet in a single layer and bake at 300°F for about 15 minutes, until shriveled and very slightly browned, but not bursting. Serve with whipped cream and shortcake, or puree into a fruit curd. For a savory twist, omit the sugar and mash them into a simple vinaigrette or serve with pork.

PHOTO BY DOUG GOSLING.

Poached Russian Quince

Serves 4–6

3 cups water

½ cup white wine

½ cup orange juice

¼ cup honey

½ cup sugar

½ vanilla bean split lengthwise or
    1 tablespoon vanilla extract

Optional spices: 1 small cinnamon stick,
    5 cardamom pods, 2 tablespoon fresh
    thinly sliced ginger

3–4 medium quince

Serves 30–40

12 cups water

2 cups white wine

2 cups orange juice

1 cup honey

2 cups sugar

1 vanilla bean split lengthwise or ¼ cup
    vanilla extract

Optional spices: 1 cinnamon stick,
    3 tablespoons cardamom pods,
    ½ cup fresh thinly sliced ginger

20 medium quince

Combine all the poaching ingredients into a large nonreactive pot on medium heat. While the liquid is heating, peel and core the quince and cut into quarters. Place the fruit pieces into the pot as you go to keep them from discoloring. Once all the fruit is in, cut out a round parchment "lid" for the pot with a quarter-sized hole in the middle and place directly on the surface of the water. Bring the liquid to a low simmer, making sure the pot never boils. Quince can take anywhere from 20 minutes to 2 hours, depending on the variety. Our Russian quinces, a softer variety, take about an hour for the large batch. Check for doneness after 20 minutes by piercing one with the tip of a knife; continue poaching if needed. Remove the quince and whole spices with a spider ladle and reduce the syrup by half, over low heat. Serve warm, with the reduced syrup, over ice cream, cake, waffles, or whipped cream. Freeze the fruit and poaching liquid and blend in a Vitamix for an amazing frozen sorbet.

QUINCE

Quince is a heretofore underappreciated fruit in the United States, though it's wildly popular in much of Europe and Latin America. Raw, they are practically inedible, pithy and astringent, but cooked down, they become rosy-hued, floral ambrosia of the gods! The sweet Russian Aromatnaya quince, pictured here, is a particularly aromatic variety that does very well in our garden and graces many of OAEC's late-fall and winter desserts. If you're using other quince varieties, you may need to extend cooking times slightly.

PHOTO BY JIM COLEMAN.

Quince Bars

Serves 4–6, plus a few extras

**ABOUT EIGHT 2¼ X 2¼-INCH BARS
IN ONE 9 X 9-INCH BAKING PAN**

½ cup confectioners' sugar

1½ cups all-purpose flour

¼ teaspoon ginger

½ teaspoon cinnamon

¼ teaspoon cardamom

Pinch of cloves

½ teaspoon salt

1 cup (2 sticks) butter, room temperature,
    for the crust

3–4 quince, poached according to previous
    recipe, then strained from poaching
    liquid (reserve liquid for another use)

4 large egg yolks

2 large whole eggs

½ cup sugar

1 tablespoon lemon zest

2 tablespoons lemon juice

3 tablespoons butter, for the curd

Serves 30–40, plus a few extras

**ABOUT FORTY-EIGHT 2 X 2-INCH
BARS IN ONE 13 X 17½-INCH
BAKING PAN ("HALF"-SIZED
INDUSTRIAL SHEET PAN)**

3 cups confectioners' sugar

4½ cups all-purpose flour

¾ teaspoon ginger

1½ teaspoons cinnamon

¾ teaspoon cardamom

½ teaspoon cloves

1½ teaspoons salt

3 cups (6 sticks) butter, room temperature,
    for the crust

12 medium quince, poached according to
    previous recipe, then strained from
    poaching liquid (reserve liquid and extra
    quince for another use)

12 large egg yolks

6 large whole eggs

1½ cups sugar

¼ cup lemon zest

⅓ cup lemon juice

¾ cup butter (1½ sticks), for the curd

Preheat the oven to 350°F. Grease the baking pan. Sift the confectioners' sugar, flour, spices, and salt into the bowl of a stand mixer fitted with a paddle attachment. Process the dry mixture for a minute to incorporate. Add the softened butter and mix on low speed until a smooth dough forms. Press the dough evenly into the baking pan. Bake for 20 to 25 minutes, until the crust is an even golden brown.

Puree the poached quince in a blender and reserve. Start heating a few inches of water in the bottom chamber of a double boiler. (Or fashion one from a stainless steel bowl nested on top of a saucepot. Make sure the bowl you choose is not touching the water.) Bring the water up to a simmer—not a boil. Whisk the egg yolks, eggs, sugar, lemon zest and juice, and butter all in the top bowl. While it heats up, continue to whisk; you are looking for the curd to thicken and cook. Keep whisking as you see the edges start to firm up. This process will take 15 to 20 minutes. When the curd is good and thick, pull it off the heat and fold in the pureed quince.

Pour the curd-quince mixture into the pan with the crust. Reduce the oven temperature to 325°F and bake for another 20 minutes, a little longer for the large batch. Cool completely before cutting into squares. Dust with confectioners' sugar to finish. If needed, cut ¼ inch of crust away from the edges of the pan for neat, slightly smaller squares.

Quince Membrillo

Membrillo is a deep rose-colored jelly made from quince puree that is cooked down and dehydrated to a thick fruit-leather-type consistency. It is enjoyed all over the Spanish- and Portuguese-speaking world as a simple teatime treat or dessert and is usually sliced and served with a mild farmer's cheese and crackers. Like other preserves featured in this book, the batches are not intended to be eaten in one sitting, but rather shared and consumed over a longer period of time. Membrillo is an energy-intensive thing to make. Might as well go big.

Small batch

MAKES ONE 9 X 9-INCH BAKING PAN

3–4 pounds ripe quince fruit, peeled
(about 4–6 quince)

½ vanilla bean

⅓ cup dry sherry or white wine

⅓ cup water

Zest and juice of 1 small blood orange or
any orange

1 small cinnamon stick

1 teaspoon sunflower oil

3–4 pounds sugar

Large batch

**MAKES ONE 20 X 15 ½-INCH
BAKING PAN (THREE-QUARTER-
SIZED INDUSTRIAL SHEET PAN)**

10 pounds ripe quince fruit, peeled
(about 12–15 quince)

1 vanilla bean

1 cup dry sherry or white wine

1 cup water

Zest and juice of 1 large blood orange

1 cinnamon stick

1 tablespoon sunflower oil

10 pounds sugar

Quarter the peeled quince with pip intact and place into a large heavy-bottomed stainless steel pot. Split the vanilla bean lengthwise and, with the tip of a knife, scrape its seeds into the pot along with the shell of the bean. Add the sherry, water, zest and juice of the blood orange, and cinnamon stick. Cook over high heat until tender, about 20 minutes. Meanwhile, grease a baking pan with a thin coat of sunflower oil.

Take the quince off the heat and let rest 5 minutes. Prepare a food mill or a sieve over a clean bowl. Process the fruit through the food mill, straining out the pips and seeds. Weigh the resulting puree and place it back into the pot. Add an equal amount of sugar to the fruit puree, 1:1 ratio. If you reduce the sugar, you will end up with a nice jam, but not sliceable membrillo.

Cook over medium-low heat, stirring constantly to keep the mixture from sticking to the bottom of the pan. The mixture will turn color from a light pink to a burnt orange and become very thick over the course of 45 minutes to 1 hour. Be very careful—this mixture will bubble and spit as it cooks and gets hotter. Wear a long oven mitt on the hand you stir with to protect it from burning. You will know the mixture is done when it turns a deep-orange color and is so thick it is hard to stir.

Pour the cooked quince into the baking sheet. Smooth out the top of any lumps and let the pan set up and cool overnight. Once the membrillo is cool, leave it in an oven with just the pilot light's warmth to dry and cure it for a few days. You will feel the surface go from sticky to dry to the touch. Once it's done, cut it up into pieces of any size and store in an airtight container for up to a month. If you want to preserve it even longer, you can store it in the fridge, but it will get the surface-moist again.

Amaranth Breakfast Porridge

Kiwicha (*Amaranthus caudatus*), pictured here, is one of the many amaranth varieties being grown at OAEC. It carries with it a many-thousand-year history dating back to pre-Columbian civilizations and was a central player in the evolution of the culture and spirit of the Maya, Aztec, and Inca. Once a staple grain throughout the Americas, this particular amaranth is now little known outside the high Andes. Amaranth is high in protein and has an interesting texture, similar to caviar. Like any hot breakfast cereal, it can be served sweet or savory, depending on your mood.

Serves 4–6
1 cup whole amaranth grain
3 cups water or milk of choice
Pinch of salt

Serves 30–40
4 cups whole amaranth grain
12 cups water or milk of choice
1 teaspoon salt

In a saucepot, add the amaranth grain, liquid, and salt. Heat on high, covered, until the liquid comes to a boil. Reduce the heat to a low simmer and cook for 15 to 20 minutes.

VARIATIONS

Sweet: Serve with butter and honey or top with fall fruit compote (see following recipe).
Savory: Serve as a bed for eggs over-easy topped with sautéed greens or with any meal as an alternative to quinoa or millet.

PHOTO BY DOUG GOSLING.

Rich Autumn Fruit Compote

Serves 4–6

5 cups fruit juice (white grape or orange)

½ cup dry white wine

2 tablespoons honey

1 whole star anise

3 whole cloves

1 cinnamon stick

5 cups fresh fall fruit, cubed (pears, apples, quince)

½ cup dried mission figs

⅔ cup dried apricots

3 tablespoons golden raisins

Peel from ½ orange, removed with a vegetable peeler in strips

Peel from ½ lemon, removed with a vegetable peeler in strips

Serves 30–40

20 cups fruit juice (white grape or orange)

2 cups dry white wine

½ cup honey

12 whole star anise

12 whole cloves

1 cinnamon stick

20 cups fresh fall fruit, cubed (pears, apples, quince)

2 cups dried mission figs

2 cups dried apricots

¾ cup golden raisins

Peel from 2 oranges, removed with a vegetable peeler in strips

Peel from 2 lemons, removed with a vegetable peeler in strips

Bring the fruit juice to a boil in a heavy sauce pan. Reduce the heat to low and let the juice simmer uncovered for about 45 minutes until it reduces by half—longer for the large batch, shorter for the small. Add the rest of the ingredients and let simmer on low for about another hour, until the fruit is soft. Transfer the compote to a bowl and let it cool to room temperature. Use immediately or store in the refrigerator for up to 4 days.

PHOTO BY BROCK DOLMAN.

CALIFORNIA BAY LAUREL

The California bay laurel tree, *Umbellularia californica*, sometimes called pepperwood or Oregon myrtle, is prolific up and down the Pacific Coast and can be identified by its leathery camphor-scented evergreen leaves, similar to its Mediterranean cousin, the more familiar culinary bay, *Laurus nobilis*.

California bay leaves can supposedly be used in minute proportions as a replacement for culinary bay, although we don't recommend it—many an eager forager's meal has been ruined by its turpentine redolence. In fact, the scent of the volatile oil is so potent it can be used as a natural preservative and insect repellent and causes headaches in some people.

The chocolaty "peppernuts," on the other hand, are a delicacy. The brown inner nut, after being roasted in the oven or over an open fire, has a rich caramel-coffee flavor and contains a caffeine-like stimulant. It is traditionally eaten whole or ground with salt or seaweed and wrapped in a clover leaf. More modern recipes bake the toasted nuts into sweet cakes or infuse them to make a coffee-like beverage with actual kick. Cultivation of bay nuts as a local, sustainable coffee substitute has real commercial promise—a comforting thought for West Coast coffee lovers staring peak-oil in the wigged-out, caffeine-driven face.

Warning: Don't eat too many of these at a time! Bay nuts are a stimulant, the equivalent of eating straight espresso beans—that's why some of us call them buzz nuts! While they are irresistible, especially in the form of a sweet treat, be careful—more than a few nuts can really spin you up. Similar to coffee, don't serve bay nuts too late at night or they will keep your guests awake.

The fresh bay fruit resembles a miniature avocado, a related species, that ripens and falls to the ground for gathering in the fall. Husk them by peeling off the outer layer of green flesh to expose the pit. Dry and store the nuts indoors in a warm room in a well-ventilated basket for at least a few days. Once dry, they will keep in their shells almost indefinitely.

When you're ready to use them, roast the whole, dry nuts in their shells. There are many methods to do this. You can toast them over open coals in a basket or on the stovetop in a dry cast-iron skillet over low heat, stirring and shaking the pan frequently until darkened in color. The most controlled result can be achieved by roasting in a hot 450°F oven for 15 to 20 minutes, rotating the pan at least once. If you heat your home with a woodstove, just put a cookie tray of bay nuts on top and keep an eye on them for a few hours. Easy.

Once the nuts are darkened in color, but not burned, remove them from the heat and let them cool. Then crack the shells with a nutcracker or whack them open with a heavy object, like a cast-iron skillet against a cutting board. Toss into baked goods like chocolate chip cookies or savory dishes like wild rice pilaf. For a coffee substitute, grind and steep just like coffee.

Bay-Infused Cheesecake with Bay Nut Crust

A family reunion of European bay, *Laurel nobilis,* and New World California bay. The culinary bay leaves imbue a warm vanilla flavor into the cream. This is a good dessert to serve after a dinner party where the guests might want a little waker-upper for the drive home. For a gathering of 30 to 40 guests, make three cheesecakes.

Serves up to 12

MAKES ONE 9-INCH SPRINGFORM PAN

CHEESECAKE

1 cup cream
10 fresh culinary bay laurel leaves (not California bay)
½ cup plus 2 tablespoons sugar, divided
16 ounces cream cheese, room temperature
5 eggs, room temperature
¼ teaspoon salt
1 teaspoon vanilla extract

CRUST

1⅔ cups roasted California bay nuts
1⅔ cups raw pecans, or a total of about 3¼ cups nuts
½ cup sugar
½ cup butter, cut into smallish cubes
Generous pinch of salt

For cheesecake, it is important that all ingredients be at the same temperature when mixing to ensure a creamy, unified texture. Set the ingredients out ahead of time to let them come to room temperature, and allow the infused cream to fully cool before mixing.

Heat the cream, bay leaves, and 2 tablespoons of the sugar on the stovetop on medium-high heat until the cream barely begins to simmer. Reduce the heat and simmer for 20 minutes until the cream reduces by half for a total of ½ cup infused cream. Turn off the heat and cover. Leave the mixture to infuse until the liquid cools back down to room temperature. Remove and discard the bay leaves.

Preheat the oven to 325°F. Toast the bay nuts and remove their shells as directed in the sidebar on page 352. In a food processor, pulse the bay nuts and pecans together two or three times, leaving a fair number of pea-sized pieces. Add the rest of the crust ingredients and pulse a few more times until the mixture comes together and the butter is mostly evenly distributed. Press the mixture firmly into the bottom and sides of the springform pan, up to ½ inch below the rim. Put the springform pan in the refrigerator for 20 minutes while mixing the filling

Beat the room-temperature cream cheese until creamy and smooth, totally free of lumps. Then add the remaining sugar and the salt until incorporated. Scrape down the sides of the bowl and beat in the eggs one at a time, scraping the bowl between additions. Add the vanilla and cooled infused cream and beat until fully smooth. The batter will be a little runny, but it should set up during baking.

Place the springform pan on a sheet tray. Bake at 325°F until golden brown on top and mostly set except for a silver-dollar-sized giggle in the middle. This should take from around an hour up to an hour and a half. Allow to completely cool so that the cake can really firm up. Remove from the springform pan when you're ready to serve.

PHOTO BY TALI AIONA.

Buckwheat Buzz-Nut Skillet Bread

The earthiness of buckwheat complements native bay nuts in this rustic pick-me-up breakfast cake.

Serves 4–6

MAKES ONE 8-INCH
CAST-IRON SKILLET

⅔ cup butter (2 tablespoons for topping,
    about ½ cup for cake)

¼ cup pecans

2 tablespoons brown sugar

Pinch of salt

Pinch of nutmeg

⅔ cup buttermilk

2 whole eggs

½ cups maple syrup

1 teaspoon vanilla extract

1¼ cups buckwheat

¼ teaspoon baking soda

⅛ teaspoon baking powder

½ teaspoon salt

¼ teaspoon cardamom

⅔ cup bay nuts, toasted and hulled

Serves 30–40

MAKES TWO 16-INCH
CAST-IRON SKILLETS

2½ cups butter (¾ cup for topping,
    1¾ cup for cake)

1¼ cups pecans

⅔ cup brown sugar

1 teaspoon salt

½ teaspoon nutmeg

3½ cups buttermilk

12 whole eggs

2 cups maple syrup

1 tablespoon vanilla extract

7 cups buckwheat

1 tablespoon baking soda

1½ teaspoons baking powder

2 teaspoons salt

1 tablespoon cardamom

4 cups bay nuts, toasted and hulled

Preheat the oven to 350°F. In an 8-inch cast-iron skillet (two 16-inchers), melt the butter by putting it in the oven while it's preheating. Meanwhile, in a food processor, grind the pecans into a coarse meal, but do not overprocess. Empty into a small bowl. Add the brown sugar, salt, and nutmeg; combine. Remove the preheated skillet from the oven, measure out the melted butter for the topping, and pour it into the pecan mixture. Fluff with a fork to create a crumbly texture. Stir in the bay nuts. Set aside.

Swirl the rest of the melted butter around to thoroughly grease up the sides of the skillet and pour the rest into a medium mixing bowl. Add the buttermilk, eggs, maple syrup, and vanilla and stir to combine. Separately sift together the buckwheat, baking soda, baking powder, salt, and cardamom in another bowl. Combine the dry and wet ingredients and stir everything together until smooth. Pour the batter into the buttered skillet(s). Top with the bay nut crumble topping. Bake on the middle rack for 20 minutes or so (longer for the large batch) until a knife inserted comes out clean. Remove the cake immediately from the skillet with a large spatula and set it onto a serving plate or board (or else it will continue cooking and become too dry). Best served warm.

PHOTO BY JIM COLEMAN.

Shipova Coffee Cake

The shipova, originally imported from the Balkans, is a hardy, disease-resistant cross between a European pear and a mountain ash that requires very little maintenance or pruning. Similar in flavor and texture to an Asian pear, the small teardrop-shaped shipovas are sweet and crunchy as a hand fruit and wonderfully buttery when baked.

CAKE

Serves up to 12

MAKES ONE 9-INCH ROUND CAKE PAN

1½ cups all-purpose flour

1 teaspoon baking powder

1 teaspoon baking soda

½ teaspoon salt

6 tablespoons (¾ stick) butter, room temperature

1¼ cups sugar

1 tablespoon vanilla extract

3 eggs

1 cup sour cream

FILLING

1 tablespoon brown sugar

1½ tablespoons cocoa

½ teaspoon cinnamon

3 cups, peeled, cored, and diced shipovas or Asian pears

Serves 30–40

MAKES THREE 9-INCH ROUND CAKE PANS

6 cups all-purpose flour

4 teaspoons baking powder

4 teaspoons baking soda

2 teaspoons salt

2 cups (4 sticks) butter, room temperature

5 cups sugar

3 tablespoons vanilla extract

12 eggs

4 cups sour cream

FILLING

¼ cup brown sugar

6 tablespoons cocoa

1½ teaspoons cinnamon

12 cups peeled, cored, and diced shipovas or Asian pears

Preheat the oven to 325°F. Butter the sides of the cake pan and line the bottoms with a parchment circle.

To make the filling: Mix the brown sugar, cocoa, and cinnamon into a small bowl and set aside. Set the diced fruit aside separately.

To make the cake: Mix the flour, baking powder, baking soda, and salt in a small bowl and whisk to incorporate. Set aside. Paddle the butter in a stand mixer until it's very soft and fluffy, about 3 minutes, continually scraping down the sides of the bowl. Add the sugar and vanilla and mix for 2 to 4 minutes; scrape the bowl. Add the eggs one at a time, mixing just until they are integrated. Stop the mixer and scrape the bowl down, making sure all is thoroughly mixed. Add the flour mix alternating with the sour cream in three stages, ending with the flour. Stop and scrape the bowl down to the bottom. Mix to incorporate any last bits that were stuck to the sides.

Pour half of the batter into your prepared pan (or for the large batch, divide half the batter evenly among three pans). Smooth out the top and sprinkle on the dry filling mix in one layer. On top of the filling mix distribute the cut fruit. Add the rest of the batter on top of the fillings and smooth the top. Sprinkle on the almond streusel in one thick layer. Bake for 1 hour to 1½ hours, until a toothpick inserted into the center comes out clean.

ALMOND STREUSEL

Serves up to 12

⅔ cup fresh-ground almonds

½ cup all-purpose flour

⅓ cup sugar

⅛ teaspoon salt

6 tablespoons butter

Serves 30–40

2 cups fresh-ground almonds

1½ cups all-purpose flour

1 cup sugar

½ teaspoon salt

1 cup (2 sticks) butter, room temperature

To make the almond streusel: Place the whole raw almonds in the bowl of a food processor and grind up to a pea size. Pulse the flour, sugar, and salt in with the almonds. Add the soft butter and pulse to combine. You are looking for a sandy texture with some chunks of butter.

Fig-Leaf-Infused Goat's-Milk Panna Cotta

Panache or Jaspée Limone, pictured below, is a tiger-striped fig that barely ripens before the beginning of the cool fall weather in coastal Sonoma County. Also valued as an ornamental variety, each fig is relished for its blood-red interior that has the sweetness and flavor of strawberry jam. Though we don't get many figs, we love cooking with the leaves for the gentle vanilla flavor they infuse into savory dishes like rice (page 221) or this sweet panna cotta.

Serves 4–6

**MAKES SIX 6-OUNCE RAMEKINS
OR TEACUPS**

1 cup goat's milk

2 cups heavy cream

½ vanilla pod, sliced and de-seeded

¾ cup fine sugar

6 fig leaves, dried and crushed into powder

2½ teaspoons gelatin (usually 1 packet)

Serves 30–40

**MAKES THIRTY-SIX 6-OUNCE
RAMEKINS OR TEACUPS**

6 cups goat's milk

12 cups heavy cream

2 large vanilla pods, sliced and de-seeded

4½ cups fine sugar

36 fig leaves, dried and crushed into powder

⅓ cup gelatin (usually 6 packets)

Heat the goat's milk, cream, vanilla, and sugar in a saucepan. Bring the mixture to a boil then remove it from the heat and add the fig leaf powder. Let infuse for 15 minutes.

In a mixing bowl, cover the gelatin with just enough cold water to dissolve it; let this sit for 10 minutes. Pour the warm cream mixture over the gelatin and stir until it completely dissolves. Pass the mixture through a fine sieve and divide among ramekins, molds, or any container you are drawn to. Since panna cotta is not baked, the custard can go into wineglasses, jars, teacups, what have you. Let it cool to room temperature then chill for 3 to 4 hours or overnight in the refrigerator. Serve with ripe figs or fig compote.

Dark Roast Winter Squash Tart with Hazelnut Crust

This is a spicy, rich, harvest-season tart that can be made with any orange sweet winter squash such as red kuri, sugar pumpkin, or sweetmeat. The addition of Doug's secret ingredient—a small amount of finely ground coffee—gives the filling an unidentifiable depth of flavor. For gatherings of 30 to 40, make 3 tarts.

Serves up to 12

MAKES ONE 10-INCH TART

CRUST

1¼ cups unbleached all-purpose flour
2 cups (¼ pound) finely ground toasted
    hazelnuts (page 303)
¼ cup brown sugar
½ teaspoon freshly ground cinnamon
Pinch of nutmeg
½ cup (1 stick) butter, softened
1 large egg
1 teaspoon vanilla extract
Zest of 1 lemon

FILLING

3 cups winter squash puree (page 180)
¾ cup maple syrup
2 tablespoons molasses
¼ teaspoon ground cloves
1 tablespoon freshly ground cinnamon stick
    (a coffee grinder works well for this)
1 teaspoon salt
1 tablespoon vanilla extract
1 tablespoon finely ground dark roast coffee
4 eggs, slightly beaten
1 cup heavy cream

Preheat the oven to 450°F.

To make the crust: Mix the dry ingredients together first. Then mix in the butter with a fork until the mixture has the consistency of cornmeal. Stir in the egg and vanilla until the pastry just sticks together. Form into a ball and let rest in the refrigerator for 20 to 30 minutes. Press into a 10-inch tart pan.

To make the filling: Mix the filling ingredients in the order given. Pour into the hazelnut tart shell and bake for 10 minutes. Reduce the heat to 350°F and bake for 40 more minutes until set. Let cool completely before serving.

Farallons Gingerbread

When we contacted Peter Zweig, former resident and now neighbor, for his legendary gingerbread recipe that he used to make here back in the 1980s, he replied saying that he adapted it from *The New Laurel's Kitchen*.[14] Laurel had actually taught a baking class here during his tenure as beekeeper; hence, he always added more honey to the original recipe. Sure enough, when we took our tattered copy off the shelf, half a lifetime later, the binding was broken to that page and the recipe was splattered with batter, oily fingerprints and Peter's scrawled notes—the sign of a great recipe! Thumbing through our old cookbooks, one can feel the history of this place and the benevolent "spirits of meals past" lingering in our pots and pans, passing on sweet blessings of deliciousness to future generations.

Serves 4–6

MAKES ONE 9 X 9-INCH PAN

⅓ cup oil

½ cup molasses

⅔ cup honey

1 egg

1 cup buttermilk

2½ cups whole wheat flour

1 teaspoon baking soda

1 teaspoon cinnamon

2 teaspoons powdered ginger

½ teaspoon salt

Serves 30–40

MAKES TWO 12 X 20-INCH HOTEL PANS

1⅓ cups oil

2 cups molasses

2⅔ cups honey

4 eggs

4 cups buttermilk

10 cups whole wheat flour

4 teaspoons baking soda

4 teaspoons cinnamon

2 tablespoons powdered ginger

2 teaspoons salt

Preheat the oven to 350°F. Mix together the wet ingredients; sift the dry ingredients together separately. Then mix everything together and pour into a greased baking pan. Bake for 40 minutes until a toothpick comes out clean.

Farallons kitchen, 1978. THE FARALLONS ARCHIVE.

Dorothy's Carrot Cake

No hippie commune cookbook would be complete without a carrot cake recipe! This Sowing Circle family heirloom is passed down by Dorothy, Adam Wolpert's mother, who made it every year for him when he was growing up. Adam's wife, Katy, has since added her own twist and now makes it for their daughter Sabine. She says, "As a parent interested in garden-healthy eating for my kid, I've found it hard to find good recipes for sweet things without too much sugar. Healthy-ish cake and frosting recipes like this feel hard to come by."

CAKE

Serves 4–6

MAKES ONE 9 X 9-INCH CAKE PAN

1 cup sugar

1 cup sunflower oil

4 eggs

2 teaspoons vanilla extract

2 cups flour

Pinch of cloves

½ teaspoon cardamom

½ teaspoon nutmeg

1 tablespoon cinnamon

2 teaspoons baking powder

2 teaspoons baking soda

½ teaspoon salt

3 cups tightly packed grated carrots

1 cup chopped walnuts (optional)

½ cup golden raisins (optional)

Serves 30–40

MAKES ONE 20 X 12-INCH HOTEL PAN

4 cups sugar

4 cups sunflower oil

16 eggs

3 tablespoons vanilla extract

8 cups flour

1 teaspoon cloves

2 teaspoons cardamom

2 teaspoons nutmeg

4 tablespoons cinnamon

2 tablespoons baking powder

2 teaspoons salt

2 tablespoons baking soda

12 cups tightly packed grated carrots

4 cups chopped walnuts (optional)

2 cups golden raisins (optional)

To make the cake: Preheat the oven to 350°F. Cream the sugar and oil in a stand-up mixer with a paddle attachment or by hand. Add the whole eggs one at a time and beat well until very smooth. Mix in the vanilla. Sift the dry ingredients in a separate bowl. Add the dry ingredients to the wet ingredients little by little and stir to incorporate. Fold in the grated carrots, nuts, and raisins by hand. Bake in a greased cake pan for 50 to 60 minutes or until a toothpick inserted in the center comes out clean. Allow to cool completely (at least an hour) before frosting.

FROSTING

Serves 4–6

1 pint heavy cream

1 (8-ounce) package cream cheese, softened to room temperature, or mascarpone cheese

¼ cup confectioners' sugar or maple syrup, to taste

1 teaspoon vanilla extract

Serves 30–40

4 pints heavy cream

4 (8-ounce) packages cream cheese, softened to room temperature, or 32 ounces mascarpone cheese

1 cup confectioners' sugar or maple syrup, to taste

2 tablespoons vanilla extract

To make the frosting: Whip the heavy cream for about 3 to 5 minutes to form a stiff whipped cream. Set aside. Next, whip the softened cream cheese or mascarpone with a paddle attachment until very soft and fluffy, scraping down the sides several times. Add the sweetener and vanilla and continue whipping to blend. Gently fold the whipped cream into the cream cheese mixture until incorporated and not lumpy. Chill in the refrigerator while the cake bakes and cools completely. This is a light and fluffy frosting that will easily melt. For best results, chill the frosting in the refrigerator until the last minute and frost the cake right before serving.

Candied Feijoa Peels and Infused Simple Syrup

Feijoas, also known as pineapple guavas, are one of our favorite edible landscaping plants. The hardy 12-foot-tall bushes require little pruning and can be shaped into a visual screen with attractive, dense green foliage. Though not a true botanical guava, these fruits have incredible tropical flavor given their hardiness at our latitude.

Most of us at OAEC like to eat the feijoa whole, peel and all, but a few are overwhelmed by the powerful flavor of the dark green skin. If you are making a delicate fruit salad or feeding kids with just the tender middles, save the skins and transform them into little candies! Added bonus: You are left with an infused simple syrup that can be used later in desserts and drinks, like the Feijoa Sparkler variation(page 324).

MAKES 1 CUP OF CANDY AND
1 ¼ CUP INFUSED SYRUP

2 cups feijoa peels
1 cup water
2 cups granulated sugar
Superfine sugar, for dusting

Preheat the oven to 200°F. With a sharp paring knife, peel the zest from the fruit in long strips, avoiding as much of the bitter white pith as possible. Bring the water to a boil and add the granulated sugar. Stir until dissolved, then reduce the heat so that the liquid just bubbles on a very low simmer. Gently drop in the feijoa peels. Let the peels cook until they're soft and limp but not falling apart. Fish out the cooked pieces with a slotted spoon and transfer them individually to a baking tray covered with parchment paper. Separate and arrange each piece into a nice shape for drying. Dry in the oven for 1 to 2 hours, flipping thick pieces once midway through. Or use a food dehydrator, if you have one, according to the directions. Dry until the material is hard, dust with superfine sugar, and store in an airtight container. Reserve the infused syrup in a glass bottle or jar with a tight-fitting lid. Keep in the refrigerator.

VARIATION

Use this basic technique to candy citrus peels (Meyer lemon is delish!), rhubarb slices, ginger, edible flowers such as violets or rose petals, or even small sprigs of herbs like rosemary!

Jacob's Lavender Crème Brûlée

Jacob was born and raised here on the OAEC land and, from a young age, showed a precocious propensity for experimenting in the kitchen, particularly with baking. In elementary school while his peers were making cupcakes from a box, Jake and his sister Alex were making crème puffs, tiered chiffon cakes, and heirloom fruit turnovers. Doug showed Jake how to infuse cream with garden herbs, and after a little rifling through the wood-shop for a blowtorch, this creation was born.

Serves 4–6

MAKES SIX 6-OUNCE RAMEKINS

1 quart heavy cream

10 fresh sprigs of lavender, or 2 tablespoons dried crumbled flowers

1 cup sugar, divided in half

6 large egg yolks

Hot water

Serves 30–40

MAKES FORTY 4-OUNCE RAMEKINS

5 quarts heavy cream

50 fresh sprigs of lavender, or 1¼ cups dried crumbled flowers

5 cups sugar, divided in half

30 large egg yolks

Hot water

Preheat the oven to 325°F. Place the cream into a medium saucepan set over medium-high heat and bring to a boil. Meanwhile, crumble the lavender flowers off the stem and reserve. Remove the cream from the heat, cover, and allow to sit for 15 minutes. Add the lavender to the cream and let sit for 1 hour.

To make the custard: Put the cream through a strainer to remove the lavender sprigs. In a medium bowl, whisk together half the sugar and the egg yolks until the mixture is well blended and just starts to lighten in color. Add the cream a little at a time, stirring continuously. Pour the liquid evenly into the ramekins, not quite to the top. In our kitchen, we don't have ramekins, so we substitute ceramic teacups.

Place the ramekins into a large cake pan or roasting pan. Pour enough hot water into the pan to come halfway up the sides of the ramekins, being careful not to splash any water into the cups. Bake just until the Crème Brûlée is set, but still trembling in the center, approximately 40 to 45 minutes.

Remove the ramekins from the roasting pan and refrigerate for at least 2 hours and up to 3 days. Remove the Crème Brûlée from the refrigerator for at least 30 minutes prior to browning the sugar on top. Divide the remaining sugar equally among the dishes and spread evenly on top. Using a torch, melt the sugar to form a crispy top. Allow the Crème Brûlée to sit for at least 5 minutes before serving.

Best Lemon Tart

This is a reliable, easy lemon tart. Because it uses whole eggs and does not have an excessive amount of sugar, the custard isn't too eggy, but allows the citrus to sing through clearly and brightly. It works best with a tart lemon variety like Eureka and is not recommended for the sweeter Meyer lemons.

Serves 4–6

MAKES ONE 10-INCH TART PAN

RICH TART DOUGH

1½ cups all-purpose flour

2 tablespoons unrefined sugar

Pinch of salt

½ cup (1 stick) cold unsalted butter, cut into pieces

3 tablespoons cold heavy cream

LEMON CUSTARD

⅓ cup fresh lemon juice (from about 2 Eureka lemons)

1 teaspoon vanilla extract

⅔ cup unrefined sugar

6 large eggs

1 tablespoon freshly grated lemon zest (from about 2 lemons)

10 tablespoons (1¼ sticks) cold unsalted butter, cut into pieces

To make the dough: Into a large bowl, sift together the flour, sugar, and salt. Quickly cut the butter into the dry mixture with your fingertips or mix in a stand-up mixer with a paddle attachment until it resembles a coarse cornmeal. Sprinkle the cream into the dry ingredients and mix until it seizes up into a dough. Remove the dough and gather into a ball. Wrap in plastic and refrigerate for at least an hour before baking.

Cut the refrigerated tart dough into ½-inch slices. Working quickly, press the slices with your fingertips into a 10-inch tart pan with a removable fluted rim, ultimately to a thickness of about ⅛ inch. Chill the shell for at least 15 minutes before baking.

Preheat the oven to 350°F. Bake the shell in the middle of the oven for about 25 minutes, until it turns a nice golden brown and is baked all the way through. Cool to room temperature.

To make the lemon custard: In the top of a double boiler or in a heavy noncorroding saucepan, whisk together the lemon juice, vanilla, and sugar, warming on low heat just to the point that the sugar dissolves. Remove from the heat. In a bowl, whisk together the eggs so that the yolks and whites are thoroughly mixed. Stir the eggs slowly into the warming sugar mixture back on the stove. At this point, add the zest and butter pieces. Cook this mixture on low to medium heat, whisking constantly, melting the butter thoroughly; continue until the custard is thick and smooth, about 10 minutes or so. Do not let it boil. Pour the custard through a fine sieve into a clean bowl to strain out any cooked egg pieces and the zest, pressing it through with a rubber spatula if necessary. This step makes for a velvety-smooth custard.

Pour the custard into the cooled shell and bake until just set, about 30 minutes. Watch closely—if you overbake, the custard can bubble up and collapse or dry out. Remove the tart from the oven and cool on a rack before serving. Garnish with candied lemon slices or peel, and serve with whipped cream.

PHOTO BY DOUG GOSLING.

VOLUNTEER DAY

Part of what makes the Mother Garden so magical is that countless hands have come together to work the soil, infusing it with hand-tilled goodness. Almost every Wednesday without fail for the past 30 years, eager garden enthusiasts have shown up, rain or shine, to lend a hand—they have donated a total of over 12,780 volunteer hours to date! Pictured here, garden volunteers massage the soil, preparing or rather *pampering* the bed for planting. Thank you, garden volunteers!

After a morning of serious hard work in the garden made easier by plenty of lighthearted humor, garden volunteer Michael Hathaway recounts: "Around noon, a gong sounds, and we walk over to the dining area, where we've each left the food we've brought for the day's—*very* high-quality—potluck. We form a circle around the serving table and the gardeners thank everyone for coming to volunteer. Simplicity then, deep quiet, happiness, and gratitude. Even *serenity* in some—yet ornamented by the small sounds of suppressed cresting wavelets of chuckles and titters in others . . . While I delighted proudly in my own dessert contribution (Shawnee blackberries on fleshy-sweet orange pieces, with candied ginger bits sprinkled over brandied whipped cream), it turned out that another extravagant, boisterous volunteer had produced a giant, astonishing full-blown trifle, with absolutely beautiful layerings of peaches, sherried cake bits, custard, blueberries, and whipped cream! As we each tell the group about our dishes, one of the volunteers gasps, "*Sweet Baby Jesus*," in a faux-ecstasy falsetto. It makes me very happy . . . *So much* generosity of spirit, so much enjoyable learning, *such* fine wit and humor. We're so fortunate in the garden and in each other."

PHOTO BY TALI AIONA.

VOLUNTEER DAY LUNCH MENU BOARD

Open-faced cardoon melts
Buttery Thumbelinas on a
Bed of Baby Amaranth Greens
OAEC salad with OAEC Green Goddess Salad Dressing
Drinking water garnished
with fennel fronds and orange slices
Freeke's Lemon Angel Delight

Freeke's Lemon Angel Delight

Jerry and Freeke Kohl were dear and faithful garden volunteers for years until they finally retired from service in their 80s. Back when volunteer day lunch was a potluck, Freeke frequently graced our table with this "retro" dessert that naturally separates into a fluffy angel food cake on top and a creamy lemon curd on the bottom.

Serves 6 to 8

MAKES ONE 9 X 9-INCH BAKING PAN

3 egg whites

1 cup sugar, divided

½ cup flour

¼ teaspoon salt

3 egg yolks, beaten

Juice of 2 large lemons

2 tablespoons melted butter

1½ cups milk

Serves 30–40

MAKES THREE 9 X 13-INCH CASSEROLES

12 egg whites

4 cups sugar, divided

2 cups flour

1 teaspoon salt

12 egg yolks, beaten

Juice of 8 large lemons

½ cup (1 stick) melted butter

6 cups milk

Preheat the oven to 375°F. You will need two baking dishes or casseroles, one 9 x 9-inch and one slightly bigger, that can be nested together for a hot-water bath. (For the large batch, use three 9 x 13-inch baking dishes and 20 x 12-inch hotel pans for the bath.) Grease the smaller pans with butter. Start a teakettle of water to boil on the stove. Beat the egg whites until stiff and then beat in ¼ cup (1 cup) of the sugar. Set aside.

In a separate bowl, mix the remaining ingredients in the order given with an electric mixer or eggbeater to achieve a thin batter with a smooth consistency. Fold in the egg-white mixture. Pour into the greased glass or ceramic baking dishes.

Nest the baking dishes one inside the other and fill the outer dishes with 1 inch of hot water, being careful not to spill any into the batter. Bake for 30 to 40 minutes (longer for the big batch) on the middle rack in the oven until set—the top will just begin to become golden. Allow to cool. Serve with whipped cream.

Stevia Lemon Curd

Gently flecked with real stevia, this is a naturally sugar-free version of an old classic. Serve as part of a light-as-air trifle: In a tall decorative glass, layer Stevia Lemon Curd with a plain, rich whipped cream, sweet berries, and nuts and top with a few sweet edible flower petals.

Serves 4–6

MAKES ABOUT 1 CUP

3 eggs

2 teaspoons dried stevia leaves or ⅛ teaspoon store-bought liquid stevia concentrate

Juice and zest of roughly 3 medium lemons (about ⅓ cup lemon juice and 1 tablespoon zest)

2 tablespoons unsalted butter

Serves 30–40

MAKES ABOUT 4 CUPS

12 eggs

2½ tablespoons dried stevia leaves or ½ teaspoon store-bought liquid stevia concentrate

Juice and zest of roughly 12 medium lemons (about 1⅓ cups lemon juice and ¼ cup zest)

½ cup (1 stick) unsalted butter

In the top chamber of a double boiler, whisk everything (except the butter) together until very smooth. Cook on very low heat, stirring constantly, until the mixture comes to 160°F. This should take about 10 minutes. If it cooks too fast or too hot, you get scrambled eggs. Remove from the heat. Push the mixture through a fine-mesh strainer with a rubber spatula. This step will sift out most, but not all, of the stevia leaves and zest and will smooth out any lumps of egg white, ensuring a velvety texture. Whisk in the butter while the mixture is still hot. Keep stirring until it's smooth and incorporated. Pour into a glass container and refrigerate. As it cools, it will firm up to the thickness of pudding.

STEVIA

Stevia is a tropical plant that we grow in our greenhouse and garden—a godsend for diabetics or anyone trying to kick a sugar habit. While the barely perceptible anise aftertaste doesn't always work well as a straight sugar substitute in some recipes, citrus dishes, fruity desserts, and herbal teas can be made to sing with stevia!

Harvest stevia in the late summer to early fall well before the first frost, when the plant is at its fullest. Dry the leaves indoors on a mesh screen, in a shallow basket, or hung on a clothesline. There are several ways to use raw, garden-grown stevia:

- Brew fresh or dried stevia leaves as a strong tea. Store the liquid in the fridge and use it to sweeten lemonade, tisanes, and other drinks.
- Dry the loose leaves and infuse them in the liquid portion of recipes, as in the following recipe for Stevia Lemon Curd.
- Dry the leaves and crush them into a fine powder with a mortar and pestle or clean herb grinder. Stevia is 30 times sweeter than sugar, so a little goes a long way—1 tablespoon of this dried leaf powder is roughly equal to 1 cup of sugar.

Persimmon Pudding

Some of us plan our holiday parties around a few special recipes, and this is definitely one of them. This tried-and-true recipe is now at least three generations old and is contributed by friend and La Tierra community member Laurel Brody. Her favorite memory of this persimmon pudding is arriving with a panful at the annual solstice party at La Tierra a few years ago. As she entered the room, pudding in hand, the infamous Brock Dolman and a couple of other salivating guests descended and proceeded to eat their lion's-share portion right out of the pan! Make a lot . . . it goes fast!

Serves up to 12

MAKES ONE 9 X 13-INCH BAKING PAN

2 cups Haichya persimmon puree
    (about 4–6 persimmons)
½ cup (1 stick) melted unsalted butter
1 tablespoon honey
3 eggs
1½ cups buttermilk
⅓ cup cream or half-and-half
1 teaspoon vanilla extract
1 tablespoon dark rum
1½ cups flour
⅔ cup sugar
1 teaspoon baking soda
1 teaspoon baking powder
½ teaspoon cinnamon
Pinch of salt
Raisins and/or chopped nutmeats (optional)

Serves 30- 40

MAKES ONE 13 X 20-INCH HOTEL PAN

7 cups Haichya persimmon puree
    (about 14–20 persimmons)
1¾ cups (3½ sticks) melted unsalted butter
¼ cup honey
11 eggs
5¼ cups buttermilk
1¼ cups cream or half-and-half
1 tablespoon vanilla extract
3 tablespoons dark rum
5¼ cups flour
2 cups sugar
1 tablespoon baking soda
1 tablespoon baking powder
2 teaspoons cinnamon
½ teaspoon salt
Raisins and/or chopped nutmeats, optional

Use dead-ripe Haichya persimmons that are completely squishy. Peel and blend the persimmons, then measure out the puree and reserve. Preheat the oven to 325°F. Pour the melted butter in the bottom of the baking pan and set aside. Mix together the wet ingredients, making sure your eggs are well beaten. Sift together the dry ingredients and add to wet ones. Mix well. Pour into a buttered pan and bake for 2 hours or until a toothpick comes out clean. The larger batch will take a little more time. For a crispier, more cake-like result, bake for 1 hour at 350°F. Serve with bay-leaf-infused whipped cream (page 334).

VARIATIONS

This recipe is very forgiving and can accommodate many alterations. All-purpose wheat baking flour can be traded for gluten-free flour. Dairy can be traded for nondairy of your choice. Sugar can be reduced or traded for any sweetener of your choice—if you add raisins, it will be naturally sweeter.

An edible wreath made of bay leaves and acerola berries. PHOTO BY TALI AIONA.

American Persimmon Brandy Sauce

American persimmons, *Diospyros virginiana*, are found growing wild in forests in the southeastern United States and are perfectly at home as cultivars in most parts of the country. They produce small cherry-tomato-sized fruits that must be bletted like miniature haichya persimmons. We have a delicious American persimmon tree at the bottom of the North Garden that produces just a few lucky handfuls of fruit each winter. As they sit on the tree to blet in the cold weather, their densely sweet, slightly fermented flavor suggests brandy. While we don't get a huge crop of these to make a big dessert for everyone, there are just enough for this simple sauce that goes wonderfully atop some holiday eggnog ice cream!

Serves 4–6

MAKES A LITTLE OVER 1 CUP

1 packed cup bletted American persimmons, de-seeded, or 1 medium Haichya persimmon

Small pinch of ground cloves

2 tablespoons rich brandy, bourbon, or dark rum

Serves 30–40

MAKES A LITTLE OVER 4 CUPS

4 cups bletted American persimmons, de-seeded, or 2 Haichya persimmons

½ teaspoon ground cloves

1 cup rich brandy, bourbon, or dark rum

Place the persimmons and cloves in a blender and puree until smooth. Stir in the brandy and pour over ice cream.

PHOTO BY TALI AIONA.

MEDLAR

The fruit of the medlar tree, *Mespilus germanica*, tastes like lightly spiced apple butter scooped soft right out of the russeted skin. OAEC has a small but significant collection of these rare trees, which have been cultivated for over 3,000 years in Central and Northern Europe. They are one of the few fruits that ripen in cold winter conditions—a welcome treat for seasonal eaters during an otherwise fruit-scarce time.

Medlars, like Haichya persimmons, serviceberries, and some pears, must be bletted, meaning they must be chilled and overripened to render their otherwise astringent fruit soft and palatable. The first frost triggers or accelerates the bletting process by breaking down cell walls to release sugars and begin a mild fermentation. In modern times, pears and other fruits requiring bletting often have it done artificially for better control through refrigeration.

PHOTO BY JIM COLEMAN.

Medlar Cream Cake

This cake is so simple and yet so good—a crunchy crust forms while the medlar pastry cream filling bakes into the center of the cake. Don't worry if you have never seen or heard of a medlar! They are extremely rare and never sold at markets, but you might just have a neighbor that grows this long-forgotten fruit. You can make this cake without the medlar and still will have your guests oohing and aahing. For a gathering of 30 to 40, make two 12-inch cakes.

Serves 16

MAKES ONE 12-INCH ROUND CAKE

MEDLAR PASTRY CREAM

1¾ cups whole milk

⅓ cup sugar, divided

3 large egg yolks

2 tablespoons plus 2 teaspoons cornstarch

2 tablespoons butter

¾ cup medlar fruit, de-seeded through a
    sieve, or substitute dark apple or
    pear butter

CAKE

2 cups (4 sticks) unsalted butter, softened at
    room temperature

2 cups sugar

4 large eggs, room temperature

2 teaspoons vanilla extract

2¼ cups all-purpose flour

2 teaspoons baking powder

1 teaspoon salt

1 cup medlar pastry cream or regular
    pastry cream

To prepare the medlar: Gather about a quart of bletted fruit. Medlar fruit is ripe when completely soft and squishy. We let the medlar blet or ripen on the tree, but you can harvest while firm and ripen in a cool room or fridge. The consistency is like pudding with a cluster of seeds. To get just the flesh with no seeds, push all the interior contents through a medium-sized sieve until you have ¾ cup.

Place the milk in a heavy-bottomed saucepan with half of the sugar. Heat on medium just until it starts steaming. While the milk is heating, whisk the egg yolks in a metal bowl with the other half of the sugar and the cornstarch. When the milk is hot, remove from the heat and whisk a little at a time into the yolk mixture, until you have added all the milk. Pour back into the saucepan. Turn the heat back to low and stir constantly with a spatula. Watch for the pastry cream to thicken to the point that your stirring spatula will leave an opening to the bottom of the pot and the mixture is thick like a pudding—this will happen fast! Remove from the heat immediately. Stir in the butter until smooth. If you are using the medlar fruit, then add this now by folding into the pastry cream. Set aside in the refrigerator. This can be made up to 2 days in advance, stored in the fridge.

To make the cake: Preheat the oven to 350°F. Before beginning, it is very important to be sure that all your ingredients are soft and warm. Ideally, even the temperature in your kitchen should be warm to ensure a soft batter! Prepare a 12-inch cake pan with a parchment circle for the bottom and a thin layer of butter for the sides.

Cream the soft butter with the sugar in a stand mixer with a paddle attachment for a few minutes until the mixture is free of lumps and soft and creamy. Add the eggs, one at a time, scraping the bowl down after all the eggs have been added. Add the vanilla extract and mix to incorporate. Sift the flour, baking powder, and salt together into a separate bowl with a sieve. Gradually add the flour mixture to the butter-egg mixture without overmixing.

Spoon the cake batter into a large tipless pastry bag. Pipe half of the batter in a tight spiral into the bottom of the pan. Pipe an extra ring around the inside edge of the pan, building up the sides slightly to create a well in the center that will prevent the filling from seeping out to the edge. Spread the medlar pastry cream evenly in this well using a small spatula or knife. Pipe the remaining cake batter in a spiral on top, sandwiching the pastry cream in the center. Use your spatula to move the cake batter over the top, covering the filling as much as possible. It's okay if a bit of the filling shows through; when it heats in the oven it will spread out more.

Bake for 1 to 1½ hours. Check the cake at 1 hour; if it needs more time, let it continue baking for up to another half hour. It should spring back lightly in the center when it is done. Remove from the oven and let cool for 15 minutes before unmolding. Dust the top with powdered sugar, then slice and enjoy.

Saint Lucy's Tutu

Saint Lucy's Tutu has become a winter tradition in and of itself as the apropos dessert of OAEC's patron saint. A riff on the New Zealand classic Pavlova, named after the great Russian ballerina Ana Pavlova whose snow-white skin and fluffy tutu resemble this billowy wreath of meringue filled with goodies. OAEC's peak winter fruits are the crown jewels—kiwi, feijoa, and mandarins.

The large batch will serve 30 to 40, but don't be tempted to scale it up beyond that as the center doesn't set up properly in the middle. Olivia tried making a huge one for our blowout "end of the world" party in 2012 for 80 people, and it was literally a bit of a flop. It does scale down nicely, however—make individual meringues in small 4-inch rounds, but reduce the cooking time to 1 hour.

Serves 4–6

MERINGUE

6 large egg whites (¾ cup), room temperature (save yolks for lemon curd)

¼ teaspoon cream of tartar

⅔ cup sugar

CURD

6 egg yolks

⅔ cup sugar

8–10 Meyer lemons, to make ¼ cup zest and ⅔ cup juice

¼ teaspoon salt

¼ cup (½ stick) butter, cut into tablespoon-sized pieces

FRUIT

6 cups peeled and sliced seasonal or tropical fruits—at OAEC, our homegrown favorites at winter solstice include kiwi, feijoa, and mandarins

WHIPPED CREAM

2 cups heavy cream

1 teaspoon orange blossom water or ½ teaspoon vanilla extract

GARNISHES

Chiffonaded seasonal sweet fresh herbs such as mint, anise hyssop, or basil

Chopped nuts—macadamia is classic in New Zealand, but we prefer California nuts such as almonds, hazelnuts, or pistachios

¼ cup candied fruit—feijoa peel, ginger, or lemon zest (page 362) (optional)

Edible flowers

To make the meringue: Preheat the oven to 350°F. Cover a large baking sheet with parchment paper. With an electric mixer, beat the egg whites and cream of tartar until they form peaks. Gradually beat in the sugar a little at a time and continue beating until the meringue achieves a very stiff texture, about 8 minutes. The egg whites will more than quadruple in size. For the large quantity, divide the egg whites and whip in two batches.

Using a spatula, scoop the meringue out onto the parchment paper to form a large circle that reaches to the edges of the baking sheet. Create a ruffled tutu shape by piling it up high and irregular on the outsides and leaving a depression (but not a completely bare spot) in the center.

Put the meringue in the oven, reduce the heat immediately to 200°F, and bake for 2 hours. The outside should become dry and crispy and the middle should remain soft and pillowy. Keep an eye on it—if you notice it browning too much, reduce the heat or simply leave it in the warm oven with the pilot light on to dry all the way down until you're ready to assemble and serve. While the meringue is baking, make the fillings.

To make the curd: In a double boiler, boil a few inches of water in the bottom chamber and reduce heat to low. Nest the upper pot into the lower one, making sure that the upper one does not touch the surface of the water. Keep the water at a low simmer throughout the cooking process to ensure that the eggs don't curdle.

Put all of the ingredients (except the butter) in the top chamber of the double boiler and whisk constantly until the yolks thicken, about 8 minutes or so. Remove from the heat. Whisk in the butter, melting in one piece at a time. For a velvety consistency, use a rubber spatula to push the curd through a mesh sieve. Refrigerate until set while the meringue is baking. Store any leftover curd (you might not use it all for the meringue) refrigerated in a glass jar for up to a week. To make curd from other tart fruits such as rhubarb, wild plums, or berries, puree the fruit and stir it in with the eggs in place of the lemon juice.

To make the whipped cream: Whip the cream with the orange blossom water or extract until it forms soft peaks. Chill until ready to assemble.

To assemble the desserts: Wait until the very last minute before serving to assemble, as the meringue will get soggy if it sits. Fill the center indentation with layers of curd, fruit, and whipped cream. Top haphazardly with herbs, nuts, fruit, and finally the edible flowers. Serve immediately—the photogenic Saint Lucy will sweat and deflate soon after her debut, so enjoy the moment of her ephemeral beauty.

Serves 30–40

MERINGUE

24 egg whites (2⅔ cups), room temperature
  (save yolks for lemon curd)

1 teaspoon cream of tartar

2⅔ cups sugar

CURD

24 egg yolks

2½ cups sugar

40 Meyer lemons, to make ⅔ cup zest and
  3 cups juice

1 teaspoon salt

1 cup (2 sticks) butter, cut into
  tablespoon-sized pieces

FRUIT

6 quarts peeled and sliced seasonal or tropical fruits—at OAEC, our homegrown
  favorites at winter solstice include kiwi,
  feijoa, and mandarins

WHIPPED CREAM

3 pints heavy cream

1½ tablespoons orange blossom water or 2
  teaspoons vanilla extract

GARNISHES

Chiffonaded seasonal sweet fresh herbs
  such as mint, anise hyssop, or basil

Chopped nuts—macadamia is classic in
  New Zealand, but we prefer California
  nuts such as almonds, hazelnuts,
  or pistachios

¼ cup candied fruit—feijoa peel, ginger, or
  lemon zest (page 362) (optional)

Edible flowers

VARIATIONS

Spring: Strawberries, raspberries, loquats, rhubarb curd, mint.

Summer: Blood Peaches, blueberries, mulberries or blackberries, Cardamom-Rose-Plum Preserves (page 338),
  purple basil.

Fall: Muscat grapes, Cape gooseberries, soft Haichya persimmon, quince curd, anise hyssop.

SAINT LUCY'S PARTY

Winter solstice is an important celebration for residents at OAEC. Aside from there being many December birthdays, winter is a time when the community members get to have the place to themselves, when there isn't a constant flow of people here to visit "the human exhibit at the zoo." This much-needed privacy and renewal time allows us to let our hair down.

The tradition of the Feast of Santa Lucia dates back to ancient Europe and is still celebrated among Nordic peoples as a way to bring light to the darkest time of year. A young woman portrays Lucia, "the saint of light," and parades with a crown of greenery and candles in her hair through the villages handing out sweets. However, the Saint Lucy's parties of the late Farallons and early OAEC years took the tradition several steps farther in the San Francisco style of the "Sisters of Perpetual Indulgence." They invited everyone to parade as the Lucia Maid resplendent in white and silver—and fishnets and stilettos! Following the birthday boys dressed in not-so-angelic white, the procession marched through the Mother Garden burning "hags tapers" (dried mullein stalks dipped in wax) in a celebration of sweetness and light and in gratitude for another momentous turning of the yearly cycle.

Photo by Jim Coleman.

Afterword

Through the love and labor of hundreds of individuals who have lived or worked at OAEC over the past 20 years, the daily practice of learning from trial and error in one place—on the land, in the gardens and kitchen, and throughout our efforts to advance social change—has created a rich culture. Ours is a culture of observation, action, evaluation, and adjustment. We hope this book, with the recipes, ingredients, and stories it offers, reflects that culture and has inspired you to continue to develop your own rich culture, in your own place, with your own community.

Most of the concepts here, and throughout this book, emerged from OAEC's culture of co-exploration and cocreation. "*Did I come up with that idea, or did you?*" The answer most of the time is "*We came up with that idea.*" The same is true for the recipes in this cookbook and for the homegrown ingredients that bring life to the recipes. They have been trialed and adjusted repeatedly, benefiting over and over from the feedback of an ever-growing spiral of colleagues and visitors. Here, a fabulous meal prepared from Mother Garden fresh produce is an achievement of both the gardener and cook, and also of the whole community that holds the cultural continuity and wisdom for those individual efforts.

Yet most people in the overdeveloped "Global North" have in recent generations lost connection with the experience of living in a place-based community of extended family, clan, or tribe. Due to the destabilizing effects of colonization, migration, and urbanization, many have lost the knowledge and culture that were held by the intact communities of their ancestors.

Furthermore, so many of us are profoundly estranged from nature, engaging mostly in digitally mediated human-to-human interaction. Most have forgotten their relationship with the natural world, and most lack awareness of the perilous state we have created for the ecological life-support systems upon which we rely for every human requirement. We suffer a mainstream culture and economy that celebrates and rewards self-interested behavior over care for the commons.

OAEC's experience, however, is that despite living in such a self-centered moment in time, people actually crave to come home to the heart of what it is to be human: to live the golden rule; to act today for the seven generations; to respect and steward the earth for all life and for the future. We are evolved to want to tend deep, healthful, and reciprocal relationships with the rest of the natural world. E. O. Wilson called it *biophilia*, meaning "love of life." OAEC's work, in the gardens, kitchen, and beyond, embodies this ethos. This cookbook, then, has been about remembering our way home: about calling memory forward to re-story a culture of caring for all life and to settle in like we plan to stay awhile on this planet.

With 20 years behind us now, what will OAEC do in the next 20 years? What does "right action" look like for our community and our social change project in an era of rapidly changing climate, resource, and social conditions? What is our "20/20 vision"? OAEC's mission is to build the capacity of change makers and whole communities to strengthen their own cultures to lead the necessary transition from ecological crisis to a healthy, just, and sustainable future. OAEC's work forms bridges among spheres that are too often isolated from one another: environmental and social movements; rural and urban populations; creative thought and right action; and self and community.

To continue OAEC's work for the long haul, at our 20th anniversary, we are nearing the completion of a comprehensive plan for restoring and adding key elements to the center's facilities and unifying the capacity of OAEC's facilities to serve an even greater spectrum of change makers for many decades to come. In developing and caring for our center—the wildlands, gardens, buildings, and pathways—we seek to reveal to the visitor a place of beauty and inspiration full of hundreds of examples, small and large, of how anyone and any community can "think it yourself" and live a richer, more economically and ecologically sustainable life.

The good work OAEC has done over the past two decades has earned us the support of thousands of individual donors, and dozens of private foundations and public agencies. We are so very grateful for all their support. We are particularly grateful to three remarkable women—Daidie Donnelley, Susannah Schroll, and Nancy Schaub—each with her own beautiful vision for a better world and each investing with great generosity in OAEC's passionate work to help achieve that better world.

Programmatically, OAEC's work will inevitably evolve over the next 20 years. Certainly, we will continue our main thrust of educating and organizing to build regionally connected, community-scale ecological, economic, and cultural resilience. And we also aspire to develop more effective advocacy projects. By capitalizing on the strength of new alliances and networks, we seek to change the rules of governance and economy to legalize and support those human activities that restore and protect biological and cultural diversity, and to make illegal and disincentivize those human activities that destroy biological and cultural diversity.

This revolution needs all types: gardeners, cooks, writers, builders, farmers, caregivers, healers, artists, orators, strategists, investors, donors, and facilitators. What is your role? What is your 20-year plan to restore your culture and community? With whom will you create your vision and take bold steps forward? It is always good to start any major venture with a meal. Maybe invite some friends over—you'll need lots of them.

Go harvest what is ready from the garden and, while you are there, pause for a moment. Feel the calm power of our earth and the amazing diversity of life it sustains. Relax a bit into the arms of our ancestors—they have our back if we will learn from them. Commit yourself to love of life and finding right action in your place, in your community, in your own life. And if you need some inspiration for what to cook, flip back a few pages!

—DAVE HENSON,
OAEC executive director

Acknowledgments

I extend my deepest heartfelt gratitude to the countless named and unnamed family, friends, and spirits of the land who have supported and inspired me, OAEC, and this project in direct and indirect ways.

Special thanks to:

Doug Gosling for his life's work in the Mother Garden; his passion for trialing unusual food crops and experimenting with them in the kitchen provides the basis for so many of the recipes in this book. Dave Henson for his steadfast encouragement, vision, and leadership. Gabriel Tiradani for sharing the creativity that flows so gracefully through her and into these recipes. Tali Aiona for the exquisite lens through which she sees the world and contributions too multifaceted to name. Michelle Vesser for growing the most nourishing produce on earth and for showing us how to tend to the plants and to our hearts.

The rest of the OAEC core staff, past and present, for the decades of physical and intellectual work that has gone into word-smithing the many chapters of our collective story. Brock Dolman, Jim Coleman, Adam Wolpert, Kate Lundquist, Kendall Dunnigan, Vanessa Carter, Tina Poles, Lisa Preschel, Janell Lundgren, Bridget Grusecki, Kalanete Baruch, Janel Healy, Renata Brillinger, Tynes Viar, Lindsey Elliot, Carson Price, James Pelican, Ryan Silva, Bernard Jungle, Philip Tymon, Jenyng Wu, Samara Seibel, Kate Taylor, Lindsay Dailey, Carol Neukirk, Dusan Pomothy, Kristen Gardner, and many countless other staff, interns, and volunteers.

The OAEC kitchen staff, past and present, not only for the magic in the House Recipes, but especially for the tireless work feeding the masses and then cleaning up after them with a smile. Thank you, early morning breakfast cooks! Thank you, late night dishwashers! Thank you, salt-shaker refillers, napkin launderers, and compost bucket scrubbers, everywhere!

All the recipe contributors and volunteer recipe testers—Lola Rathbone, Sharon Jones, Trish Johnson, Holly Carter, Bridget Grusecki, Janell Lundgren, Angela Ginsberg, Kami McBride, Sarah Shimizu, Coby Leibman, Tali Aiona, Maragret Grace Stewart, Grace Lee, Doug Gosling, Leesa Jackson, Leah Quiroga, Matt Phillips, Martha Kowalick, Jacob Kowalick-Allen, Anna Stufflebeam, Katy Mamen, Dorothy Wolpert, Laurel Brody, Cissy Monroe, Kendra Johnson, Stacy Lippencott, Ali Ghiorse, Kalanete Baruch, Ryan Silva, Michelle Vesser, Bernard Jungle, Peter Zweig, Freeke Kohl, Rachel Gardner, Bryan Bowen, Sara Burghart, and many others.

Sowing Circle members for dreaming up, manifesting, and sustaining this crazy-beautiful collaboration with each other and with the land and for sharing your home so generously—Adam Wolpert, Katy Mamen, Sabine Wolpert, Brock Dolman, Dave Henson, Kendall Dunnigan, Kelsey Henson Dunnigan, Susan McGovern, David Berman, Ezra Berman, Carol Nieukirk, Nick Allen, Martha Kowalick, Alexandra Kowalick-Allen, Jacob Kowalick-Allen, Lisa Bruce, and Doug Gosling.

Thanks to all those who have ever reached their hands into this soil. Thanks to the ancestors and to living Native Pomo and Coast Miwok people for their legacy of land stewardship. Thank you to all our members, donors, and volunteers for believing in us and supporting our work.

Extra special thanks to Alice Waters, Sharon Jones, Daidie Donnelley, Edward Aiona, Ken Dickerson,

Movement Generation Collective, Greg Sarris and the Federated Indians of Graton Rancheria, Michael Hathaway, Alison Dykstra, all the Farallons pioneers, Nancy Schaub, Susannah Schroll, and Kevin Paul.

Thank you!

Olivia Rathbone
December 2014

Recipe Contributors List

Soups

Carrot Chamomile Soup—Olivia Rathbone

OAEC's Basic Veggie Stock—House Recipe

Roasted Vegetable Stock—Gabriel Tiradani

Spring Hot Pot Soup with Shungiku—House Recipe

Roasted Fennel Soup—House Recipe

Crema de Calabacín—Kendra Johnson

Smoky Corn Chowder with Fire-Roasted Poblano Peppers—Olivia Rathbone

Roasted Eggplant Soup with Pasilla Pumpkin Seed Pesto—Gabriel Tiradani

"Shady" Tomato Soup with Mint—House Recipe

Midsummer Fresh Runner Bean Soup—Olivia Rathbone

Blackened Tomato and Scarlet Runner Bean Stew—Gabriel Tiradani

Escarole White Bean Soup with Shaved Celery Root—House Recipe

Spiced Turnip Stew with Chickpeas and Turnip Green Yogurt Sauce—Angela Ginsburg

Borscht with Dollop and Swirl—House Recipe

Creamy Parsnip Soup with Candy Cap Mushrooms—Olivia Rathbone

Rutabaga Soup with Lovage Butter—House Recipe

Cold Vegetable Plates and Salads

Delicate Wild Spring Greens with Mache, Violets, and Champagne—House Recipe

Blanched Asparagus and Garlic Scapes with Preserved Lemon Dip—Olivia Rathbone

Veggie Mandala—House Recipe

Fava Beans in Vinaigrette—House Recipe

Heirloom Tomato Platter—House Recipe

Summer Squash Ribbons with Purple Shiso—Holly Carter

Summer Salad with Giant Yellow Mangel and Pickled Rainbow Chard Stems—Doug Gosling

Hydrating Lemon Cucumber Purslane Salad—House Recipe

School Garden Sprout Wraps—Vanessa Carter

Rainbow Beet and Carrot Salad with Garden Herbs—House Recipe

Cumin-Marinated Runner Beans—House Recipe

Coriander Carrot with Black Olives and Orange Zest—House Recipe

Marinated Shaved Fennel—House Recipe

Raw Kale Salads—Three Variations—House Recipe

Zesty Purple Cabbage Slaw—House Recipe

Blanched Romanesco with Winter Pistou on a Bed of Ornamental Kale—House Recipe

Winter Frisée Salad with Crunchy Fried Mung Beans—Olivia Rathbone

Yacon and Radish Platter with Chili and Lemon—House Recipe

Papas a la Huancaina—Doug Gosling

Hot Vegetable Dishes

Fresh Shelling Peas with Mitsuba Meyer Lemon Butter—House Recipe

Grilled Fava Pods—House Recipe

Garlicky Sautéed Fava Leaves—House Recipe

Roasted Fennel with Chili Flakes—House Recipe

Fennel Frond Fritters—House Recipe

Crispy Garlic Scapes—House Recipe

Sautéed Cabbage, Leeks, and Green Coriander with Roasted Garlic Scapes—Gabriel Tiradani

Roasted Rainbow Carrots with Marinated Favas and Tarragon—Gabriel Tiradani

Buttery Thumbelinas on a Bed of Braised Baby Amaranth Greens—House Recipe

Sautéed Shungiku Shoots with Sesame Seeds and
  Garlic—House Recipe
Simple Sautéed Chard with Onion—House Recipe
Early-Summer Flash-Braised Baby Amaranth
  Greens—House Recipe
Cumin-Roasted Summer Squash—House Recipe
Tromboncino Coins on a Bed of Their Own
  Greens—House Recipe
Pepita-Encrusted Squash Blossoms Stuffed with
  Goat Cheese and Mint—House Recipe
Young Runner Bean Pods with Marjoram Butter
  and Scarlet Flowers—House Recipe
Roasted Cherry Tomatoes with Lemon Verbena—
  Gabriel Tiradani
Biodiversity Beans with Lemon Dill Butter—
  House Recipe
Orach Paneer—Spicy Creamed Mountain Spinach—
  House Recipe
Barbecued Eggplant Stacks with Coyote Mint Sauce
  and Chèvre—Olivia Rathbone
Griddle-Seared Brassica Shoots with Chili Flakes
  and Garlic—House Recipe
New Zealand Spinach Shoots with Parmesan and
  Almonds—House Recipe
Fall Garden "Stir-Fry" with Fresh Herbs—
  House Recipe
Wilted Arugula in a Whole Roasted Pumpkin with
  Candied Pepitas—Gabriel Tiradani
Double-Roasted Beets with Balsamic Glaze—
  House Recipe
Grilled Nopalitos with Herbs and Cotija—
  Olivia Rathbone
Basic Winter Squash Puree—House Recipe
Brussels Sprouts with Alexanders, Leeks, and Dijon
  Beurre Blanc—Olivia Rathbone
Roasted Baby Turnips with Smallage, Lemon, and
  Capers—House Recipe
Perfect Sautéed Mushrooms—Sarah Shimizu
Slow-Roasted Sunchokes with Wild Mushrooms—
  House Recipe
Gently Boiled Variegated Collards with Lemon,
  Garlic, and Olive Oil—Gabriel Tiradani
Wintry Oven-Crisped Tree Collard Ribbons—
  Gabriel Tiradani

Dougo's Melted Leeks—Doug Gosling
Domino Potatoes with Society Garlic and Bay
  Leaves—Gabriel Tiradani
Mashua Mashed Potatoes—Janell Lundgren
Curried Mashua and Potatoes—House Recipe
Roasted Andean Tubers with Ocopa—Doug Gosling

Main Dishes: Using Grains, Beans, Eggs, and Cheese

Green Garlic White Bean Primavera—House Recipe
Spring Risotto: Roasted Asparagus and Nettle with
  Pea Tendrils—Gabriel Tiradani
Spring Carrot Soufflé with Sorrel Sauce—
  Gabriel Tiradani
Lemon Thyme Duck Egg Soufflé—Gabriel Tiradani
Garden Vegetable Frittata—House Recipe
Thai Omelet—Anna Stuffelbeam
Smoky Bitter Greens Over Griddled Potatoes and
  Scrambled Eggs—Olivia Rathbone
Stuffed Tomatoes with Borage, Nettles, and
  Ricotta—Olivia Rathbone
Wine Country Grape Leaf Dolmas—Coby Leibman
Quinoa Confetti Salad—Rachel Gardner
Summer Risotto: Lemon Verbena and Roasted
  Cherry Tomato—Gabriel Tiradani
Lemon Verbena Steamed Rice—Olivia Rathbone
Tepary Beans with Oregano and Seared Padrón
  Peppers—Olivia Rathbone
Nana's Chiles Rellenos—Ryan Silva
OAEC Basic Beans—House Recipe
Ali's Copper Kettle Beans—Alison Ghiorse
Hot-Pink Fall Risotto with Chèvre—Janell Lundgren
Fig-Leaf-Infused Basmati Pilaf—Gabriel Tiradani
Soft Pumpkin Polenta—Olivia Rathbone
Polenta Moons with Roasted Red Peppers, Collard
  Ribbons, and Feta—Olivia Rathbone
Savory Tan Oak Acorn Mush—House Recipe
Baked Eggs with Seasonal Vegetables—Leesa Jackson
Shakshuka—House Recipe
Millet with Toasted Cumin Seeds—House Recipe
Yellow Split Pea Puree with Caramelized Onion and
  Black Olives—Gabriel Tiradani
Bernie's Pierogi—Bernard Jungle
Winter Wild Mushroom Barley Risotto—
  House Recipe

Salad Dressings

OAEC Green Goddess Salad Dressing—House Recipe

Roasted Fennel and Black Olive Salad Dressing—House Recipe

Strawberry Balsamic Vinaigrette—House Recipe

Loquat Ginger Dressing—House Recipe

Golden Tomato Cumin Salad Dressing—House Recipe

Plum Anise Hyssop Salad Dressing—House Recipe

Gravenstein Apple Lemon Basil Vinaigrette—Gabriel Tiradani

Blue Cheese Dressing for Escarole—House Recipe

Wild Rose Hip Salad Dressing—House Recipe

Tree Tomato Vinaigrette—Doug Gosling

Mixed Citrus Salad Dressing with Lemon Balm—House Recipe

Preserved Lemon Brine Salad Dressing—House Recipe

Roasted Onion, Sesame Seed, and Tamari Salad Dressing—House Recipe

Pestos, Sauces, and Condiments

Tonic Spring Pesto with "Gardener's Choice" Mixed Weeds—Michelle Vesser

Kami's Chickweed Pesto—Kami McBride

Lemony Chickweed Pistou—House Recipe

Dandelion Spread—Gabriel Tiradani

Chervil Aioli—House Recipe

Cardoon Tapenade—House Recipe

Spring Tonic Vinegar—Bridget Grusecki

Summer Superfood Pesto—Michelle Vesser

Nasturtium Pistou—Doug Gosling

Basil Flower Pistou—House Recipe

Sunflower Petal Pesto—Gabriel Tiradani

Summer Herb Flower Vinegar—Olivia Rathbone

Basic Garden Herb Butter—House Recipe

Blossom Butter—Olivia Rathbone

Gaby's Baba Ganoush—Gabriel Tiradani

Roasted Tomatillo Salsa—House Recipe

Llajua—Bolivian Picante Sauce—Leah Quiroga

Aji de Huacatay—Olivia Rathbone

Pasilla Pumpkin Seed Pesto—Gabriel Tiradani

Garden Ranch Dip for Kids—House Recipe

Bolted Arugula Spread, aka Green Mustard—Olivia Rathbone

Walnut Sauce—Gabriel Tiradani

Olive Walnut Tapenade—House Recipe

Mother Garden Veggie Kraut—House Recipe

Cistocera Relish—House Recipe

20th-Century Asian Pear Vinegar—Matt Phillips

Marjoram Pistou—House Recipe

French Sorrel Sauce—House Recipe

Quick Roasted Garlic and Infused Garlic Oil—House Recipe

Basic Bechamel Sauce—House Recipe

Winter Squash Dip with Dukkah—House Recipe

Dukkah Spice Mix—House Recipe

Mixed Winter Citrus Salsa with Yacon and Pineapple Sage—House Recipe

Preserved Meyer Lemons—House Recipe

Savory Baked Goods and Snacks

Kale Chips for Kids—Janell Lundgren

Seaweed "Bacon Bits"—House Recipe

Crispy Fried Beans—House Recipe

Heirloom Tomato Mozzarella Pie—Gabriel Tiradani

Tricolor Corn Bread—Alison Ghiorse

Chickpea Flat Bread—House Recipe

Soaked and Toasted Walnuts—House Recipe

Roasted Luther Burbank Chestnuts—House Recipe

Toasted Hazelnuts with Thyme—House Recipe

Pan-Fried Almonds with Rosemary—House Recipe

Popped Amaranth—House Recipe

Winter Sourdough Pizza Duo—Gabriel Tiradani

Hand-Mixed Miche Bread—Gabriel Tiradani

Drinks

Good Morning Tea—Kalanete Baruch

Drinking Water with Seasonal Garnishes—House Recipe

Ridgetop Fir-Tip Tisane—House Recipe

Mother Garden Bitters—Bryan Bowen

Michelle's Blueberry Melissa "Wine"—Michelle Vesser

Mallow Hibiscus Cooler—House Recipe

Rose Geranium Sparkler with Raspberries—House Recipe

Herbal-Infused Honey Syrups—House Recipe

Pear Cider with Thyme-Infused Tea—House Recipe

Prickly Pear Sunrise—aka *Tuna Rita*—House Recipe
Dave's Fruit-Infused Liqueurs—Dave Henson

Desserts and Sweet Stuff

Dougo's Cecile Brunner Rose Sugar—Doug Gosling
Sensuous Sweet Spring Tart—Gabriel Tiradani
Summer Fruit Fools—House Recipe
Caradmom-Rose-Plum Preserves—
    Gabriel Tiradani
Cardamom-Rose-Plum Bars—Gabriel Tiradani
Blood Peach Torta—Leesa Jackson
Pink Pearl and Pippin Applesauce with Lemon
    Thyme—Ali Ghiorse
Baked Gravenstein Apples—Martha Kowalick
Epargne Pear Frangipane Tart—Doug Gosling
Simply Roasted Cape Gooseberries—House Recipe
Poached Russian Quince—Gabriel Tiradani
Quince Bars—Gabriel Tiradani
Quince Membrillo—Gabriel Tiradani
Amaranth Breakfast Porridge—House Recipe
Rich Autumn Fruit Compote—Gabriel Tiradani

Bay-Infused Cheesecake with Bay Nut Crust—
    Gabriel Tiradani and Olivia Rathbone
Buckwheat Buzz-Nut Skillet Bread—Olivia Rathbone
Shipova Coffee Cake—Gabriel Tiradani
Fig-Leaf-Infused Goat's-Milk Panna Cotta—
    Gabriel Tiradani
Dark Roast Winter Squash Tart with
    Hazelnut Crust—Doug Gosling
Farallons Gingerbread—Peter Zweig
Dorothy's Carrot Cake—Dorothy Wolpert and
    Katy Mamen
Candied Feijoa Peels and Infused Simple Syrup—
    House Recipe
Jacob's Lavender Crème Brûlée—Jacob Kowalick-Allen
Best Lemon Tart—Doug Gosling
Freeke's Lemon Angel Delight—Freeke Kohl
Stevia Lemon Curd—Michelle Vesser
Persimmon Pudding—Laurel Brody
American Persimmon Brandy Sauce—House Recipe
Medlar Cream Cake—Gabriel Tiradani
Saint Lucy's Tutu—Olivia Rathbone

Resources

Intentional Communities, Group Facilitation, Democratic Arts

Creating a Life Together: Practical Tools to Grow Ecovillages and Intentional Communities
  Diana Leafe Christian, New Society Publishers, 2003.
The Sharing Solution: How to Save Money, Simplify Your Life and Build Community
  Janelle Orsi and Emily Doskow, Nolo, 2009.
Consensus Oriented Decision Making
  Tim Hartnett, New Society Publishers, 2011.
The Way of Council
  Jack Zimmerman & Virginia Coyle, 1996.

Bio-Intensive Gardening, Herbs and Weeds, Soils and Composting

How to Grow More Vegetables than You Ever Thought Possible on Less Land than You Can Imagine
  John Jevons, Ten Speed Press, 1991.
The New Organic Grower
  Elliot Coleman, Chelsea Green, 1989.
Golden Gate Gardening: The Complete Guide to Year-Round Food Gardening in the San Francisco Bay Area and Coastal California
  Pam Pierce, Sasquatch Books, 1998.
Soil Biology Primer
  Elaine R. Ingham, Andrew R. Moldenke, Clive A. Edwards. United States Department of Agriculture, 1999.
Perennial Vegetables: From Artichoke to 'Zuiki' Taro, a Gardener's Guide to Over 100 Delicious, Easy-to-Grow Edibles
  Eric Toensmeier, Chelsea Green, 2007.
Weeds of the West
  Larry C. Burrill and Steven A. Dewey, University of Wyoming, 1996.

Mycelium Running: How Mushrooms Can Help Save the World
  Paul Stamets, Ten Speed Press, 2005.

Climate Change and Agriculture

CalCAN
  The California Climate and Agriculture Network (CalCAN) is a coalition that advances policies to support California agriculture in the face of climate change (http://calclimateag.org).
Growing Food in a Hotter, Drier Land: Lessons from Desert Farmers on Adapting to Climate Uncertainty
  Gary Nabhan, Chelsea Green, 2013.

Ecological Design

Gaia's Garden: A Guide to Home-Scale Permaculture, 2nd edition.
  Toby Hemenway, Chelsea Green, 2009.
Permaculture: A Designer's Manual
  Bill Mollison, Tagari, 1988.
Urban Homesteading: Heirloom Skills for Sustainable Living
  Rachel Kaplan and K. Ruby Blume, Skyhorse Publishing, 2011.
EcoMind: Changing the Way We Think, to Create the World We Want
  Frances Moore Lappé, Nation Books, 2011.
Creating Rain Gardens: Capturing the Rain for Your Own Water-Efficient Garden
  Cleo Woelfle-Erskine and Apryl Uncapher, Timber Press, 2012.

Seed Saving and Biodiversity

Seed to Seed: Seed Saving and Growing Techniques for the Vegetable Gardner
  Susan Ashworth, Chelsea Green, 2012.

Growing Unusual Vegetables: Weird and Wonderful Vegetables and How to Grow Them
Simon Hickmott. Eco-logic Books, 2006.

Cornucopia: A Source Book of Edible Plants
Stephen Facciola, Kampong Publications, 1990.

The Compleat Squash: A Passionate Grower's Guide
Amy Goldman, Artisan, 2004. In the same series by Amy Goldman—*Melons* and *Tomatoes.*

Lost Crops of the Incas: Little-Known Plants of the Andes with Promise for Worldwide Cultivation
National Resource Council, National Academy Press, 1989.

The Organic Seed Grower
John Navazio, Chelsea Green, 2012.

Wildlands Restoration and Traditional Ecological Knowledge

Farming with the Wild: Enhancing Biodiversity on Farms and Ranches
Dan Imhoff, Watershed Media, 2003.

Gardening with a Wild Heart: Restoring California's Native Landscapes at Home
Judith Larner Lowry, University of California Press, 1999.

Tending the Wild: Native American Knowledge and the Management of California's Natural Resources
M. Kat Anderson, University of California Press, 2005.

Enough for All: Foods of My Dry Creek Pomo and Bodega Miwok People
Kathleen Rose Smith, Heyday Books, 2014.

The Cultural Conservancy
www.nativeland.org. Nonprofit organization whose mission is to protect and restore indigenous cultures, empowering them in the direct application of their traditional knowledge and practices on their ancestral lands.

School Garden Teacher Training

Occidental Arts and Ecology Center School Garden Teacher Training Program
OAEC's School Garden Program has been instrumental in establishing curriculum-based school gardens and ecological literacy programs in over 225 schools, including 170 in the Greater Bay Area (www.oaec.org/school-garden).

The Collective School Garden Network
A great clearinghouse of curricula and grant opportunities (www.csgn.org/steps).

The National Farm to School Network
Resources supporting schools to make healthy food choices (www.farmtoschool.org/resources).

The California Farm to School Network
From school gardens to local food procurement (www.cafarmtoschool.org/resources).

Edible Schoolyard Project
http://edibleschoolyard.org.

Center for Ecoliteracy
www.ecoliteracy.org.

Education Outside: Open the Classroom Door
https://www.educationoutside.org.

Last Child in the Woods: Saving Our Children from Nature-Deficit Disorder
Richard Louv, Algonquin Books, 2005.

How to Grow a School Garden: A Complete Guide for Parents and Teachers
Arden Bucklin-Sporer, Timber Press, 2010.

Asphalt to Ecosystems: Design Ideas for Schoolyard Transformation
Sharon Gamson-Danks, New Village Press, 2010.

Schoolyard-Enhanced Learning: Using the Outdoors as an Instructional Tool, K-8
Herbert W. Broda, Stenhouse Publishers, 2005.

Moving the Classroom Outdoors: Schoolyard-Enhanced Learning in Action
Herbert W. Broda, Stenhouse Publishers, 2011.

Ecological Literacy: Educating Our Children for a Sustainable World (The Bioneers Series)
David Orr (author); Michael Stone and Zenobia Barlow (editors); Fritjof Capra (foreword), Sierra Club Books, 1991.

Place-Based Education: Connecting Classrooms and Communities
David Sobel, The Onion Society, 2004.

Learning Gardens and Sustainability Education: Bringing Life to Schools and Schools to Life
Dilafruz Williams and Jonathan Brown, Routledge, 2011.

Food Fight
A music video with free curriculum supporting students to deconstruct the violence of our corporate food system and take action to make change (http://sosjuice.com /foodfight video & curriculum; embedded YouTube: https://www.youtube.com/watch?v=mu8QthlZ6hY)

Food Politics and Ecological Justice

Movement Generation Justice and Ecology Project
The Movement Generation Justice and Ecology Project provides in-depth analysis and information about the global ecological crisis and facilitates strategic planning for action among leading organizers from urban-based organizations, in the Bay Area and beyond, working for economic and racial justice in communities of color (www.movementgeneration.org).

Center for Food Safety
Center for Food Safety (CFS) is a national nonprofit public interest and environmental advocacy organization working to protect human health and the environment by curbing the use of harmful food production technologies and by promoting organic and other forms of sustainable agriculture (www.centerforfoodsafety.org).

Stolen Harvest: The Hijacking of the Global Food Supply
Vandana Shiva, South End Press, 2000.

Monocultures of the Mind: Perspectives on Biodiversity and Biotechnology
Vandana Shiva, Zed Books, 1993.

Food Fight: The Citizen's Guide to Food and the Farm Bill
Dan Imhoff, Watershed Media, 2007.

Omnivore's Dilemma: A Natural History of Four Meals
Michael Pollan, Penguin Press, 2006.

In Defense of Food: An Eaters Manifesto
Michael Pollan, Penquin Press, 2008.

Regional, Ecological Food Systems and Procurement

Slow Food USA
Slow Food USA is part of the global Slow Food network with over 150,000 members in more than 150 countries. Through a vast volunteer network of local chapters, youth, and food communities, they link the pleasures of the table with a commitment to protect the community, culture, knowledge, and environment that make this pleasure possible (www.slowfoodusa.org).

Ecological Farming Association
The Ecological Farming Association nurtures healthy and just farms, food systems, communities, and environment by bringing people together for education, alliance building, and advocacy (www.eco-farm.org).

Bi-Rite Market's Eat Good Food: A Grocer's Guide to Shopping, Cooking, and Creating Community Through Food
Sam Moganna and Dabney Gough, Ten Speed Press, 2011.

Rebuilding the Local Foodshed
Phillip Ackerman-Leist, Chelsea Green, 2013.

Conservation Hydrology

Basins of Relations: A Citizen's Guide to Protecting and Restoring Our Watersheds
A 20-page WATER Institute booklet for individuals to educate themselves and for those working to educate others about the myriad issues facing our watersheds and the steps we can take to preserve them (2nd edition 2008; http://oaecwater.org/education/bor-publication).

Water Matters: Why We Need to Act Now to Save Our Most Critical Resource
Tara Lohan (editor), AlterNet Books, 2010.

Watersheds: A Practical Handbook for Healthy Water
Clive Dobson and Gregor Gilpin Beck, Firefly Books, 1999.

Water: A Natural History
Alice Outwater, Basic Books, 1997.

Rainwater Harvesting for Drylands, Volume 1: Guiding Principles to Welcome Rain into Your Life and Landscape
Brad Lancaster, Rainsource Press, 2006 (www.harvestingrainwater.com).

Let Water Do the Work: Induced Meandering, and Evolving Method for Restoring Incised Channels
Bill Zeedyk and Van Clothier, Chelsea Green, 2014.

Totem Salmon: Life Lessons from Another Species
Freeman House, Beacon Press, 1999.

Cookbooks

The Herbal Kitchen
Kami McBride, Conari Press, 2010.

The Herb Farm Cookbook
Jerry Traunfeld, Scribner, 2000.

The New Vegetarian Cooking for Everyone, revised edition
Deborah Madison, Ten Speed Press, 2014.

The Savory Way
Deborah Madison, Broadway, 1998.

*Vegetable Literacy: Cooking and Gardening with
Twelve Families from the Edible Plant Kingdom*
    Deborah Madison, Ten Speed Press, 2013.
Stalking the Wild Asparagus and *Stalking the
Healthful Herbs*
    Euell Gibbons, Alan C. Hood, 2005.
Cooking from the Garden
    Roslyn Creasy, Sierra Club Books, 1989.
Chez Panisse Menu Cookbook
    Alice Waters, Random House, 1982.
The Art of Simple Food
    Alice Waters, Clarkson Potter, 2007.

*Uncommon Fruits and Vegetables:
A Commonsense Guide*
    Elizabeth Schneider, William Morrow Cookbooks, 2010.
Plenty
    Yotam Ottolenghi, Ebury Publishing, 2010.
Jerusalem
    Yotam Ottolenghi and Sami Tamimi, Ten Speed
    Press, 2012.
Victory Garden Cookbook
    Marian Morash, Knopf, 2010.
The Sauce Book: 300 World Sauces Made Easy
    Paul Gayler, Kyle Books, 2009.

Notes

1. John Muir, "Hetch Hetchy Valley," in *The Yosemite* (New York: Century, 1912).

2. Steven Erlanger, "After a 2,000-Year Rest, a Seed Sprouts in Jerusalem," *New York Times*, June 12, 2005.

3. Washington State University, "'Superweeds' Linked to Rising Herbicide Use in GM Crops, Study Finds," *ScienceDaily*, www.sciencedaily .com/releases/2012/10/121002092839.htm, accessed August 20, 2014; Charles M. Benbrook, "Impacts of Genetically Engineered Crops on Pesticide Use in the US: The First Sixteen Years," *Environmental Sciences Europe* (2012): 24, doi:10.1186/2190-4715-24-24.

4. E. B. White, "Coon Tree," in *The Points of My Compass: Letters from the East, the West, the North, the South* (New York: Harper & Row, 1962).

5. Wendell Berry, *Citizenship Papers* (Washington, DC: Shoemaker & Hoard, 2003).

6. Norman Myers, Russell Mittermeier, Cristina Mittermeier, Gustavo Fonseca, and Jennifer Kent, "Biodiversity Hotspots for Conservation Priorities," *Nature* 403 (2000): 853–58, doi:10.1038/35002501.

7. Rachel Carson, acceptance speech for the John Burroughs Medal, reprinted in *Atlantic Naturalist* 7, no. 5 (1952).

8. California Environmental Protection Agency Office of Environmental Health Hazard Assessment, "Indicators of Climate Change in California," August 2013, http://oehha.ca .gov/multimedia/epic/2013EnvIndicator Report.html.

9. Hank Shaw, "Foraging for Miner's Lettuce, America's Gift to Salad," *The Atlantic*, March 7, 2011, accessed February, 16, 2015, http:// www.theatlantic.com/health/archive/2011/03 /foraging-for-miners-lettuce-americas-gift-to -salad/72106/.

10. Serena Milano, Rafaella Ponzio, and Piero Sardo, eds., *Biodiversity: What Is It, What Does It Have to Do with Our Daily Food, and What Can We Do to Preserve It?* (Carru, Italy: Slow Food International, 2010).

11. Michael Pollan, *In Defense of Food: An Eater's Manifesto* (New York: Penguin, 2009).

12. "Luther Burbank Biography," Sonoma County Historical Society, last modified 2014, www.wschsgrf.org/articles/biography lutherburbank1849-1926, accessed September 4, 2014.

13. Thomas Jefferson Center for Historic Plants, www.monticello.org/site/house-and-gardens /in-bloom/indian-blood-cling-peach, accessed September 4, 2014.

14. Laurel Robertson et al., *The New Laurel's Kitchen: A Handbook for Vegetarian Cookery and Nutrition* (Berkeley, CA: Ten Speed Press, 1986).

Index